As a bona fide expert on emotions, Greenberger is surely destined to be an enduring cont integrative work incorporates sources ranging Schopenhauer, to Spinoza, attachment research, ... the most cutting-edge emotion-focused empirical work. The number of subtle distinctions that many readers will likely be unaware of will make this book a great source of learning—guiding the reader through emotion-focused therapy in an explicit, step-by-step fashion, with many clear, concrete, and rich transcripts. It is a true gift to the field to have such a seasoned clinician and scholar delve so deeply into two emotions that are so central to the work of depth-oriented psychotherapy.

—**Andre Marquis, PhD,** Associate Professor, Counseling & Human Development, Warner School of Education, University of Rochester, Rochester, NY

This is a treasure trove of a book written by one of the foremost experts on the role of emotion in psychotherapy. Readers will gain a richly detailed understanding of how both anger and shame function, as well as of clients' subjective experience of them. The book presents concrete and practical research-based suggestions for practice. These are illustrated by extensive and useful clinical examples. This is a book for practicing therapists, theorists of psychotherapy, researchers, and students.

—**Arthur C. Bohart, PhD,** Counseling Psychology Department, Santa Clara University, Santa Clara, CA; Professor Emeritus, California State University, Dominguez Hills

Ask therapists about their clients' sadness or anxiety and many of them will tell you, "I got that." The author skillfully describes when and how to help regulate such toxic and pervasive effects of shame and anger. And as in his previous books, Greenberg scores at the theoretical, practical, and empirical levels. This book is another majestic hat trick from a clinical researcher extraordinaire.

—**Louis G. Castonguay, PhD,** Pennsylvania State University, University Park; Former President of the Society for Psychotherapy Research

In this very well-written volume, Leslie Greenberg, who is a world expert on the study of emotion and a pioneer of emotion-focused psychotherapy, brings his sophisticated theoretical and clinical acumen to bear on two central affective states—shame and anger. He elucidates both the obvious and subtle interactions between these emotions—for example, how one can mask the other—thereby easing the clinician's recognition of and ability to work with these emotions. The fascinating and informative cases bring to life the various ways in which such feelings manifest themselves in therapy, and provide an unusually helpful guide for clinicians to enhance any brand of therapy they practice. Highly recommended!

—**Stanley B. Messer, PhD,** Distinguished Professor Emeritus and Former Dean of the Graduate School of Applied and Professional Psychology, Rutgers University, New Brunswick, NJ

Shame and Anger in Psychotherapy

Shame and Anger in Psychotherapy

Leslie S. Greenberg

 AMERICAN PSYCHOLOGICAL ASSOCIATION

Copyright © 2024 by the American Psychological Association. All rights reserved. Except as permitted under the United States Copyright Act of 1976, no part of this publication may be reproduced or distributed in any form or by any means, including, but not limited to, the process of scanning and digitization, or stored in a database or retrieval system, without the prior written permission of the publisher.

The opinions and statements published are the responsibility of the author, and such opinions and statements do not necessarily represent the policies of the American Psychological Association.

Published by
American Psychological Association
750 First Street, NE
Washington, DC 20002
https://www.apa.org

Order Department
https://www.apa.org/pubs/books
order@apa.org

Typeset in Charter and Interstate by Circle Graphics, Inc., Reisterstown, MD

Printer: Sheridan Books, Chelsea, MI
Cover Designer: Gwen J. Grafft, Minneapolis, MN

Library of Congress Cataloging-in-Publication Data

Names: Greenberg, Leslie S., author.
Title: Shame and anger in psychotherapy / Leslie S. Greenberg.
Description: Washington, DC : American Psychological Association, [2024] | Includes bibliographical references and index.
Identifiers: LCCN 2023023523 (print) | LCCN 2023023524 (ebook) | ISBN 9781433838965 (paperback) | ISBN 9781433838972 (ebook)
Subjects: LCSH: Shame. | Anger. | Psychotherapy. | BISAC: PSYCHOLOGY / Clinical Psychology | PSYCHOLOGY / Emotions
Classification: LCC BF575.S45 G74 2024 (print) | LCC BF575.S45 (ebook) | DDC 152.4--dc23/eng/20230802
LC record available at https://lccn.loc.gov/2023023523
LC ebook record available at https://lccn.loc.gov/2023023524

https://doi.org/10.1037/0000393-000

Printed in the United States of America

10 9 8 7 6 5 4 3 2

*To all my clients, students, and trainees from whom
I have learned so much.*

Contents

1. Introduction: The Complementary Emotions of Shame and Anger — 3
2. Emotion: Its Nature and Function — 15
3. Shame in Psychotherapy — 31
4. Helping Clients Arrive at Shame: Relational Validation and Acknowledgment — 57
5. Regulating Shame — 81
6. Transforming Shame — 101
7. Case Examples — 127
8. The Many Shades of Anger — 157
9. Activating Interrupted Anger — 183
10. A Model of the Resolution of Interrupted Anger and Its Validation — 203
11. Working With Nonadaptive Anger — 227
12. Case Example — 245
13. Anger and Shame, For Better or For Worse — 283

References — *287*
Index — *307*
About the Author — *317*

Shame and Anger in Psychotherapy

1

INTRODUCTION

The Complementary Emotions of Shame and Anger

You should never soak anybody in shame. It's the prolonged existence of shame that then flips out into destructive rage.

—Hannah Gadsby

Whatever is begun in anger ends in shame.

—Benjamin Franklin

Shame and anger both appear to play crucial roles in therapeutic change. How to work with them in psychotherapy often presents challenges to therapists and clients alike. In this book, I discuss each emotion, their relationship with one another, and how to work with each of them to produce change.

The importance of shame in psychological disorder has often gone unrecognized by therapists or has been avoided because it produces such pain for the client. Often, therapists shy away from shame because they do not know how to deal with it. On the other hand, anger, which is possibly the most socially undesirable emotion and is often confounded with aggression, is viewed as

---

https://doi.org/10.1037/0000393-001
Shame and Anger in Psychotherapy, by L. S. Greenberg
Copyright © 2024 by the American Psychological Association. All rights reserved.

needing to be controlled. In this book, I discuss how shame and anger need to be approached by both the client and the therapist, and I discuss how intimately they are intertwined. This approach will help therapists work with each emotion separately and together to facilitate therapeutic change.

Finally, it is well known that shame can lead to rage, and a shame–rage cycle has been well documented (Scheff & Retzinger, 1991). It is therefore important when dealing with anger to see it as often protecting against shame. However, shyness and shame often prevent people from being assertive and expressing empowering anger. In this book, I distinguish between different types of shame and anger and discuss how they interact. This understanding will help therapists make process diagnoses of what is occurring at different moments in sessions and thus guide them regarding how to intervene.

WHY DISCUSS SHAME AND ANGER TOGETHER?

Shame and anger are important emotions, each in its own right, and they share a complex relationship in society, in disease, and in therapeutic change. An underlying experience of shame often manifests in overt anger. It is easier for people to feel angry than to feel shame. Like the cry of an infant who is in distress, anger can be a reaction to and distraction from emotional pain—like shame. Anger can be the smoke that distracts attention from the pain. It also can hamper our capacity for connection and intimacy and may even be used to distance. Again, anger can be seen as protection against shame (Kaufman, 1996; Paivio, 1999). On the other hand, people often feel ashamed of or guilty about their anger (Kim et al., 2011; H. B. Lewis, 1971a, 1971b). Because anger is often socially unacceptable, people feel ashamed of being seen as losing control. Shame and anger often then are sequenced, and they interact. When people feel inadequate or defective, they get angry to protect themselves, and they may even later feel ashamed that they got angry. This sequence can develop into a type of shame–rage cycle that can erupt into violence, domestic or otherwise (Retzinger, 1995). But anger that is not expressed or is unacknowledged can lead to lack of assertion, withdrawal, hopelessness, and depression (Bridewell & Chang, 1997; Gross & John, 2003; Gross & Levenson, 1997). Therefore, therapists need to consider what type of shame and what type of anger they are dealing with and how the two emotions interact.

For instance, when people feel primarily ashamed, they often show secondary anger, but they may later feel ashamed of their anger. However, almost paradoxically, primary adaptive anger is generally a resolution to shame. Becoming empowered and expressing assertive anger, and feeling deserving of respect, often help undo shame. People sit up, feel stronger and more worthy, and this transforms shame into confidence. As a result, anger can be a consequence of shame, a cause of shame, or even a cure for shame (Harper & Arias, 2004; Tangney, Miller, et al., 1996). Shame at times can also help people transform anger into harmony and conciliation, or into healing apology or submission. This last relationship is less frequent and a bit more tenuous, but it is a relationship of interest.

Both shame and anger play a crucial role in society in terms of what is viewed as morally correct and the norms that develop about the experience and expression of these emotions (Plaks et al., 2022). This affects how these emotions appear in dysfunction, in therapeutic work, and in different cultural contexts. Anger is the most eschewed emotion in many cultures, and shame is differentially favored (Matsumoto et al., 2010). Some cultures or countries with more individualistic views, such as countries in North America, have more anger–guilt moralities. Anger is more freely expressed, and children are socialized by anger, which leads to guilt. Other more collectivist cultures, such as in Japan, have shame–disdain norms in which anger is avoided and disdain is used to socialize, leading to shame (Flanagan, 2022). The societal norms around shame and anger therefore play a role in how these two emotions give rise to dysfunction.

AN OVERVIEW OF EMOTION AND EMOTION-FOCUSED THERAPY

An emotion-focused therapeutic approach privileges bodily sensing over language and emotion over cognition. To understand how to work therapeutically with shame and anger, it is important to start with a basic understanding of emotion in general. Emotion is a complex state that results in physical and psychological changes that influence thought and behavior. At its core, emotion carries our most essential needs, which have evolved to help us survive and grow. The nature and function of emotion, as well as emotion schemes, are discussed extensively in Chapter 2.

TYPES OF EMOTION

Emotion assessment, which consists of a moment-by-moment assessment of the client's emotional experience as it unfolds in the here and now, is crucial in working with emotion. In this process, therapists attempt to understand the client's subjective experience as it unfolds. This assessment is done by attending to both nonverbal cues, such as vocal quality, facial expression, body gestures, and posture and verbal communication about emotional states. It is crucial for therapists to distinguish between primary, secondary, and instrumental emotion and between primary adaptive and primary maladaptive emotion. No single emotion, such as shame, belongs exclusively to one category, and all can move among being primary, secondary, or instrumental and being adaptive or maladaptive depending on the situation and the specific activation. Therapists, therefore, need to assess the type of emotion being expressed and to intervene appropriately based on which type of emotion is being expressed. These distinctions prove very useful in helping the client deal with shame and anger and their sequencing.

ADAPTIVE OR MALADAPTIVE PRIMARY EMOTIONS

Primary emotions are a person's very first gut feelings in response to internal or external situational cues. People come into the world with an evolutionarily derived adaptive emotion system, and they rely on it throughout life to survive and thrive. Primary emotions are irreducible to any prior emotions or cognitions. They are direct, unmediated reactions to events and communicate intentions to others (Izard, 1990).

Primary emotions can be either adaptive or maladaptive. Adaptive emotions promote adaptation and survival. They orient us to the environment and provide good information. Adaptive emotions fit the activating situation and help a person to cope with it (e.g., sadness at loss that reaches out for comfort; fear at threat that prepares the individual to escape). They organize the individual for adaptive action and help the person get their needs met (Frijda, 1986). These emotions need to be attended to and expressed in therapy to access the adaptive information inherent in them and to experience the action tendencies that guide problem solving. Because they are fundamental, irreducible responses, primary emotions are not explored to unpack their cognitive–affective components but rather are validated. For example, anger at violation is a rapid, irreducible, primary emotional response. It is helpful in therapy to facilitate access to its experience, to be disposed by the adaptive action tendency of anger to protect the self and establish appropriate boundaries.

Primary maladaptive emotions differ from primary adaptive emotions in that they are chronic dysfunctional feelings that originally were adaptive responses to bad situations but are currently no longer adaptive. Primary maladaptive emotions are immediate reactions to external events that are unmediated by cognition or emotion, but they do not guide adaptive behavior. A traumatic history can result in a core sense of self as unworthy or vulnerable or in maladaptive emotional reactions such as fear, shame, and rage to harmless situations. Maladaptive emotions are reactions to the past in the present, often as a result of trauma, neglect, or attachment problems, and they do not help people cope adaptively to the situation or satisfy needs. These emotions are feelings such as shame in response to a boss's voice that is reminiscent of humiliation by one's critical father and disgust at the touch of one's partner due to past sexual abuse. These emotions lead to reactions that are extreme or inappropriate to the situation, and they need to be activated to make them accessible to new experience. It is important to note that accessing these bad feelings in therapy is not making people feel bad. They already feel bad. What they feel is already there inside them. Speaking these feelings doesn't create the feelings or make them feel worse. Furthermore, not speaking them doesn't make them not exist or go away. The difficult feelings are already there, and people can stand to feel what is there because they are already feeling it.

SECONDARY EMOTIONS

Secondary emotions can be reactions to primary emotions or to cognitive processes. Secondary emotions in reaction to primary emotions often protect against primary emotions that are experienced as intolerable. Some classic examples are feeling angry to protect against the vulnerability of shame and feeling scared of one's assertive anger or of one's sadness. Symptoms often involve secondary emotions, such as the hopelessness of depression, which may cover primary maladaptive shame of feeling inadequate, or anger that covers the hurt of rejection. These are secondary responses to primary emotional reactions, and they often obscure or interrupt the primary emotional reactions. They are also often self-protective, and they generally hide primary emotions. For example, a husband who feels shame at not being an adequate provider may blow up at his wife, children, or dog rather than feel his shame. Emotions about emotions, what we can call meta-emotions, such as feeling shame about one's sadness, are also secondary emotions. Emotions can also be secondary to more cognitive processes (e.g., anger in response to conscious thoughts of unfairness but what led to the thoughts could come from more enduring automatic primary processes of feeling inferior). Most symptomatic feelings, such as panic, helplessness, or hopelessness, are generally secondary emotions.

INSTRUMENTAL EMOTIONS

Instrumental emotions are expressed to obtain a desired reaction from others. They are either used consciously or expressed automatically to influence others or to make others behave or feel a certain way. Examples include expressing sadness to evoke caring without having to ask for it and expressing anger to intimidate others. These emotions are used strategically and serve a manipulative function. They are essentially an indirect way of getting what one wants, without having to experience the vulnerability of making direct requests or showing primary feelings. They often backfire, in the long run, and do not result in good relationships.

A QUICK OVERVIEW OF SHAME

Shame is a powerful master emotion. It is one of the most painful and least understood human emotions and probably the most avoided (Dearing & Tangney, 2011). Shame is the feeling that one is not good enough and is about the self's inadequacy and lack of worth. It arises from the sense of being unacceptable or immodest in the eyes of others. When shame is chronic, it can involve the feeling that one is defective and fundamentally flawed. Shame essentially makes people want to hide, close down, and avoid thinking too much because thinking makes them feel bad about themselves. It is typically characterized by an action tendency of withdrawal but may motivate defensive anger.

The evolutionary adaptive function of shame was to promote belonging to one's group by not violating social norms or by showing submission if one did (Izard, 1971, 1977). Shame promoted appeasement rituals such as eye aversion and making one's body smaller, prevented social devaluation and ostracism, as did a sense of anticipated shame and what would produce it All these tendencies promoted survival. Shame could therefore be adaptive or maladaptive, either keeping one belonging to the group or leading to unhealthy withdrawal.

Shame in psychotherapy, however, presents itself as problematic and in need of change. Shame operates everywhere in therapy as clients are constantly concerned about what aspects of their experience to reveal and what aspects to hide. When therapists work with shame, it is like shining a light in the hidden corners of a person's most private experience, which, because it has remained in the dark for so long, has left them feeling very alone.

A QUICK OVERVIEW OF ANGER

Anger, which is often viewed as a socially undesirable emotion, is an innate response to frustration and can be an adaptive feeling when it provides information of danger and an action tendency to protect people from harm

(Izard, 1971, 1977). Anger is an adaptive response to violation, boundary intrusion, or the thwarting of one's goals and can play a positive role in psychotherapy. It is characterized by antagonism toward someone or something whom one feels has deliberately treated one unfairly. Acknowledging previously unacknowledged anger in therapy can be highly therapeutic because it informs the person of unfairness, promotes the expression of negative feelings so they can be dealt with interpersonally, and motivates the person to overcome obstacles or to find solutions to problems. It promotes behaviors designed to remove the object of the anger or to protect boundaries against intrusion (Berkowitz, 1990).

Excessive or misplaced anger, however, can cause problems. Anger can range in intensity from a slight annoyance to destructive rage. It is important to note that while anger is a feeling, not a behavior, it can lead to acting-out behavior through aggressive actions or to blowing up because it was suppressed. As opposed to aggression, however, anger can be dysfunctional and can lead to rejection and rage; it can be destructive when it is acted out (Retzinger, 1995). Anger is not aggressive behavior intended to harm, but it becomes a problem when it is excessive and/or affects everyday functioning and relationships. Anger can be beneficial when, for example, assertive or loving anger sets boundaries. It is destructive when it is payback anger for revenge or is pain-inducing anger when, for example, one kicks the cat.

Much has been written about anger control, but anger suppression also needs to be recognized and discussed as a major therapeutic problem (Gilbert & Gilbert, 2003). Clients can present with problems of either too much or too little anger. A lot of attention in behavior modification approaches has been directed at teaching skills to manage excessive anger. This book attempts to balance this excess by focusing on the underrepresented problems of interrupted anger. Anger that is not expressed is as much a problem as excessive anger, and it needs therapeutic attention (Pascual-Leone et al., 2013). Many disorders, such as depression and anxiety, involve suppressed anger. Although secondary anger can be a symptom of depression, many depressions have primary underlying unexpressed anger (Greenberg & Watson, 2006). Suppressed rage is often at the base of somatization. Anger inhibition, submissive behavior, and poor assertiveness are linked with depression (Akhavan, 2001; Harmon-Jones et al., 2002), and many depressed clients show signs of strong feelings of anger (Brody et al., 1999; Fava et al., 1990). When anger is inhibited and its expression is blocked, it increases stress and contributes to depression (Gilbert, 2006; Gilbert & Gilbert, 2003).

SHAME-ANGER RELATIONSHIPS

Shame and anger, although quite different emotions with anger being an approach emotion and shame a withdrawal emotion, can be highly related in therapy. As outlined earlier in this chapter, there is a definite two-way street between anger and shame that deserves therapeutic attention because each can be the cause or the cure of the other. Therefore, the causal direction can go in both directions. There are four main ways in which shame and anger can interact:

1. One can be assertively angry at having been invalidated or at not having a deserved need met. Primary maladaptive shame is transformed by empowered anger.
2. One can kick the cat or yell at one's partner when one feels inadequate or like a failure. Primary maladaptive shame leads to secondary reactive anger or destructive rage.
3. One can feel embarrassed about being angry. Secondary shame hinders or prevents primary, adaptive, assertive anger.
4. One can be maladaptively angry from a history of trauma and maltreatment initially as protection against harm but now overgeneralized. This hair-trigger anger is a response to a primary perceived threat, such as shame, loss, or danger, that no longer exists. When the threat is accessed, attended to, and symbolized, the focus shifts away from the anger to understanding its origins.

Thus, primary maladaptive shame can lead to secondary anger and rage while primary anger can transform primary maladaptive shame. Alternatively, primary anger can be blocked by secondary shame while understanding the origins of maladaptive anger, which is somewhat primary (see Chapter 8) and can access even more primary shame and threat.

CASE DESCRIPTIONS

The cases in this section exemplify the concepts discussed in this chapter.[1]

Dell is a 39-year-old African American man who expresses a lot of secondary anger to protect against his underlying core shame. This case indicates

---
[1] The clinical material used in this book has been adequately disguised to protect client confidentiality. Client identity has been maintained.

one of the key ways in which shame and anger intersect and how important accurate process diagnosis guides therapists on how to intervene (Goldman & Greenberg, 2015). Not seeing that anger is a protection against shame might lead to anger management interventions, which would provide Dell with only a palliative treatment and would leave unresolved his underlying shame, the determinant of the anger. Dell has been recently released from prison and is on parole. He is struggling to find employment and expresses a lot of anger at societal unfairness. As a result, he approaches potential employers with a chip on his shoulder, which protects him from his shame. His wife refuses to support him, as he has previously let her down so often. He blows up at the frustration of not being able to come home or to see his son. He grew up with an alcoholic abusive father who both modeled shame, as he was a failure and was in and out of prison, and humiliated his son by putting Dell down at every chance he got.

Therapy involved first validating Dell's secondary anger and slowly approaching the shame of feeling so looked down on as an ex-convict. Eventually, with the help of his therapist, he was able to access his core feelings of shame and his unmet needs for validation and security as a child. Feeling that he deserved to have had a childhood free of fear and shame led him to access assertive anger at his father for all the unfairness. This anger empowered him and undid his shame. After accessing his primary adaptive anger, as often happens, he grieved the loss of safety and nurturance as a child. This example illustrates accessing anger to transform shame.

In another example, Susan, a 32-year-old heterosexual White woman, experienced lots of social anxiety and felt ashamed of her lack of wit and conversational skills in groups. She came from a family who wittily put each other down and made jokes at her expense because she was the baby. As the youngest, she was not equipped to retort and instead withdrew even as she yearned for recognition and approval. In therapy, accessing her need for recognition and anger at the unfairness helped her develop a voice and stand up for herself. As she became more confident, she was more able to speak up in social settings. This example shows how accessing suppressed anger helps overcome shame-based anxiety.

An example of how shame can suppress anger features Jamael, a 22-year-old African American man who grew up learning that expressing anger as a Black man was both dangerous and socially disapproved of, making him "just another angry Black man." Consequently, he made sure never to assert or challenge others at work. He had been so forced to internalize systemic racist attitudes that he never expressed anger, and if his anger ever broke through, he felt shame and immediately closed down. This example shows how shame can suppress anger and how anger expression is influenced by societal factors.

In a final example, Paul, a 45-year-old White man, defended himself angrily for having had an affair, which he said was because of his wife's lack of interest in sex. When he grew to express his underlying shame at having betrayed their sacred vows of fidelity, he changed from being angry to disclosing how he felt that, in his own eyes, he had failed to find a better way of dealing with his feelings. He said he felt that he had not lived up to his moral standards. This expression of healthy self-directed shame led his wife to feel more trusting that he wouldn't betray her again. Seeing him suffer his own shame helped her feel a sense of justice for the pain she had suffered (Greenberg & Woldarsky Meneses, 2019; Woldarsky Meneses & Greenberg, 2014). This case exemplifies the acceptance of adaptive shame as it gets beneath defensive anger and helps resolve conflict.

MAP OF THE CHAPTERS

The chapters that follow expand on the content introduced here. Chapter 2 discusses the role of emotion in general and illustrates the basic approach for working with emotion to change emotion. Emotion is contrasted with cognition to understand the primacy of emotion in human function. Furthermore, the role of emotion schemes in producing bodily felt experience is described and contrasted with cognitive schemas that produce beliefs.

Chapters 3 through 7 are dedicated to the topic of shame. They include discussions of different aspects of working with shame and numerous transcript examples. Chapter 3 focuses on the nature and function of shame, highlighting the differences between primary and secondary and adaptive and maladaptive shame. Interventions for working with these varying types of shame are discussed. This chapter also covers different types of in-session shame presentations, such as core shame, self critical shame, and societal shame, all of which require various forms of intervention.

Chapters 4 through 7 cover the three specific ways to treat shame. Chapter 4 includes discussion of relational validation and accessing shame. Three important subprocesses in working with shame are considered: the provision of a safe relationship, the provision of a corrective interpersonal emotional experience, and helping clients to acknowledge and experience shame in the session. Chapter 5 on regulation of shame follows from accessing and facing shame and illustrates how to manage shame when it is overwhelming in order to be better able to cope with it. Interventions that teach explicit emotion regulation skills are presented along with processes that promote the development of automatic, implicit, right-hemispheric affect regulation.

In Chapters 6 and 7, the focus is on how to facilitate the transformation of shame. Chapter 6 describes the novel principle of transformation by synthesis. This chapter presents methods to facilitate access to disclaimed adaptive anger at invalidation and illustrates how to help synthesize this experience with shame. One cannot withdraw in shame while asserting in anger. This chapter demonstrates how these emotions synthesize into a confident standing of one's ground. Chapter 7, the final chapter on shame, presents all these processes in transcripts from examples of cases with both good and poor outcomes. The transcripts[2] provide a view of what actually happens, rather than a reflective account of the process. Therapist actions and intentions are described within the transcript. Analyzing the therapist interventions in this way provides an opportunity to see what the therapist does, moment by moment. This analysis demonstrates that the therapist is a moment-by-moment emotional processing facilitator and every therapist response has an influence on the client's manner of emotional processing in the next moment. Looking at transcripts in this fashion is a way of staying close to the action and is an excellent training tool, as it reveals what therapists actually do that is helpful, not what they, or their theory, says they do.

The focus in the latter half of the book shifts to working with anger and highlighting its relationship to shame. Chapter 8 focuses on the nature and function of anger and its different manifestations, as well as gender-based and cultural and racial aspects of how anger is viewed and managed. Chapters 9 through 11 look at how to work with anger in therapy. These chapters deal with three ways of treating anger, activating interrupted anger, steps in facilitating the resolution of anger, and, finally, working with overcoming nonadaptive anger. Throughout these chapters, the importance of accessing previously unexpressed adaptive anger as an important therapeutic process of change, rather than anger management to down-regulate anger, is highlighted. Noting that anger management is so prevalent, these chapters offer an expansion of this view by discussing the therapeutic importance of accessing interrupted anger to help clients become more empowered.

Specifically, Chapter 9 illustrates ways to help clients overcome blocks to anger, express their interrupted anger, and become more empowered. Clients need to be helped to be able to access and accept their underlying adaptive anger. They have to overcome their myriad ways of blocking their anger. So, the major work is helping clients overcome the fear of anger and

---

[2]All clinical material and transcripts used in this book have been adequately disguised to protect client confidentiality. Client identity has been maintained.

the guilt of expressing it by dealing with the many processes they engage in to deflect and not feel the anger. Chapter 10 presents the process of helping clients resolve interrupted anger, based on a task-analytic study of this process in clients. This chapter also proposes a set of treatment steps to help clients access and resolve their interrupted anger. Chapter 11 focuses on working with nonadaptive anger. This chapter discusses work with secondary protective anger and with primary maladaptive anger. Chapter 11 also looks at how to regulate and to explore these nonadaptive forms of anger. Chapter 12 provides a session-length case example. And finally, the book ends with a short conclusion integrating how to work with shame and anger.

CONCLUSION

In summary, this book discusses the role of shame and anger in psychotherapy and shows therapists how to work with each of these two important emotions separately and together, when appropriate. Understanding the different kinds of shame and anger may help therapists facilitate therapeutic change. The reader may see, for example, how often anger protects against shame and essentially hides it. Conversely, this book also shows how shame can prevent people from asserting their adaptive anger. Seeing these differences may help therapists make process diagnoses of what is occurring at different moments in sessions, and this process diagnosis may guide them on how and when to intervene. The earlier chapters in the book focus on the nature of shame and how to work with this emotion, while the latter chapters focus on anger and how to work with this quite different emotion. Helpful discussions of how and when to work with both together to promote change are dispersed throughout the chapters.

2. EMOTION

Its Nature and Function

One ought to hold on to one's heart; for if one lets it go, one soon loses control of the head too.

—Friedrich Nietzsche

Before delving into shame and anger and how to work with them therapeutically, it is useful to reflect on the nature and function of emotion in general. Emotion produces physical and psychological changes that influence both thought and behavior. Basic emotional responses have been preserved because they serve adaptive functions (Darwin, 1872; Panksepp, 2008; Plutchik, 1962). Emotion puts a basic mode of processing in action (Greenberg, 2002; LeDoux, 1996). Emotions alert us, rapidly, to situations important to our survival and well-being and prepare us to act to meet our needs. They provide an assessment of the degree to which goals or needs have been met in interaction with the environment.

---

https://doi.org/10.1037/0000393-002
Shame and Anger in Psychotherapy, by L. S. Greenberg
Copyright © 2024 by the American Psychological Association. All rights reserved.

EMOTIONS VERSUS COGNITION

In contrast to beliefs, emotions evaluate whether something is good or bad for me, if I like something or do not, whereas beliefs evaluate whether something is true or false. Conscious thought (or intention), although it believes it is the master, is in fact the servant of implicit emotions and needs. Hume (1882) famously said that "reason is, and ought only to be, the slave of the passions and can never pretend to any other office than to serve and obey them" (p. 43). And Schopenhauer (1969) offered that consciousness or intellect is like a lame man who is riding on the shoulders of a blind giant of desire. The lame man can see ahead of him, but it is the giant who determines what he sees and does. Emotions move us while cognition guides.

In life, the more important, personal, and social the decision, the more emotion influences cognition (Forgas, 1995). Although cognition believes it is the master and that emotions are the servant, it really is the other way round. Emotion is the master, and cognition is its messenger (McGilchrist, 2009). Emotion sets problems for reason to solve—for example, it sets the problem: Is this dangerous?—and cognition works, in the service of attaining affective goals, to solve this problem. In this way, emotion defines the problem and provides an orientation to the world in the form of an action disposition. For instance, emotion says this is good for me or bad for me or potentially dangerous and prompts me to approach or withdraw. Conscious cognition enters to help us make sense of what emotion has alerted us to and has oriented us to in a particular way so that we can find good ways to achieve emotion's aim.

Most of what determines people's actions and conscious narratives wells up from automatic processes below the level of consciousness. Not only do we have emotions at an automatic primary level, but humans also had meaning and intentions long before they had language. So do present-day 1-year-olds. Humans' first narratives were nonverbal, narratively structured images of their bodily sensed feeling of what happened to them. It was through the storying of their affective experience that people came to know what had happened to their bodies. As Damasio (1999) offered us, knowing emerges in the feeling of what happened when changes in the body are connected to impacts from the environment. The first human narratives were stories constructed by prelinguistic beings who coded their lived experiences into stories such as "You throw a stone at me and it hits my body it hurts." So, narrative-based meaning was created long before language, and it organized experience into stories that had beginnings, middles, and ends as well as agents, actions, and intentions.

EMOTION AND LANGUAGE

People later used language to shape personal experiences into narratives. They organized their experiences into stories, and these stories allowed them to reflect on and make sense of what had happened to them, to reflect on experience to create new meanings, and to share meaning with other people. Organisms organize—they make sense of their world, others, and themselves. Language helped people organize their experience into conscious narratives, but it did not determine what was felt. Rather, it made sense of deeply felt experience.

Meaning is actively created by people by integrating head and heart, reason and emotion, biology and culture. As people experience new things, they integrate new information with current knowledge. Language also helps them make sense of emotions' messages and to use reason to attain emotion's goals. People also learn to reflect on and create meaning from life experience in ways that fit their cultural environments. The meanings they make are sustained in important interpersonal relationships. Thus, there is an ongoing process of integrating organismically based, bodily felt experience with culturally based meaning to create the narratives that govern our lives.

What, then, is the role of language? We know that naming emotions helps down-regulate amygdala arousal (Kircanski et al., 2012), so mentalizing and symbolizing experience are important aspects of therapeutic change. Spinoza (1677/1967) highlighted how symbolizing emotion in awareness is helpful in that emotion ceases to be a passion (something that controls us) as soon as we form a "clear and distinct idea of it." He suggested that when the mind knows a painful emotion such as shame or anger or sadness, the activity of knowing signals an increase of power, which generates a feeling of joy. Spinoza was suggesting that putting emotions into words makes us agents in our lives and that understanding is inherently joyful. So languaging experience is important but is not exactly the master; rather, it works in the service of meaning creation and emotion management.

Shame is a giant emotion, one that is felt as extremely unpleasant and disposes one to withdraw. Anger is a strong feeling of displeasure or hostility to a perceived provocation, hurt, or threat and disposes one to approach. These emotions are not the consequences of beliefs or evaluations of truth. Remember, beliefs are not felt; they are held, whereas emotions are felt and impel beliefs into action. A belief, such as "I believe something is violating or shaming," is not necessarily accompanied by a feeling of anger or shame. Bodily reactions come first, and only later do we have a label, and that label is learned. The label doesn't cause the feeling. It represents it. When we revisit the bodily feeling, it often is so unpleasantly disorganizing that we don't want to revisit it, and we start putting it aside. We don't want to label it in awareness any longer because even touching the idea of it can trigger the bodily response. But the idea doesn't cause the response; it merely represents it in language. Often, however, naming what we feel provides a sense of mastery and coherence. When we know what we feel, the emotion then ceases to control us. Knowing what one feels provides a sense of agency; one can make sense of emotion and use it for information, orientation, or transformation.

EMOTION AND MOTIVATION

In addition to understanding the primacy of emotions and their influence on cognition and behavior, emotion and motivation are highly intertwined. Tompkins (1963) in his affect theory proposed that affect (i.e., emotion) is the principal innate motivating mechanism and is biologically based. From an emotion-focused view, we understand motivation to be developed and amplified by affect. Emotions evolved to aid and enhance goal attainment (Frijda, 1986, 1988; Plutchik, 1962, 2000). Emotions that aided survival through attaching to others and achieving mastery in the world were handed down generationally. Now human beings seek relational connection and identity-based achievement because they result in desirable feelings. Higher level motives such as attachment and identity/agency thus are constituted and amplified by affective processes. Without feeling anxiety or feeling soothed there would be no attachment motivation; without fear there would be no avoidance motivation; without interest there would be no motivation to be involved; without anger there would be no assertion; without pride people would not strive to achieve; and without joy there would not be pleasure in connection. Without emotions people would not seek out others and would not bond nor feel supported; nor would people pursue goals and achievements. Thus, without emotion there would be no attachment motive, nor would there be an achievement motive. People wouldn't develop the bonds or identities that help sustain them.

EMOTION SCHEMES

Infants come into the world with basic psychoaffective motor programs and inborn activating cues. These inborn affect programs automatically produce the basic affects, including anger, sadness, fear, shame, and joy.

Affective schemes provide action tendencies and primary meaning. They automatically evaluate what is significant for our well-being, thus orienting us, dispositionally, to the world, and they are carriers of personal meanings. With development, however, emotional experience becomes organized into complex affective–cognitive networks, which we term *emotion schemes*. These schemes combine affect and cognition and include cueing situations (Greenberg, 2002; Oatley, 1992). As opposed to cognitive schema, emotion schemes are prelinguistic. The activation of these emotion schemes generates automatic emotion responses. Inborn shame schemes thus develop with experience; what we come to be ashamed of or angry at and how we react to shame or anger are influenced by experience and learning.

A central tenet of emotion-focused theory is that emotion schemes serve a central organizing aspect of human functioning. Sensorimotor stimuli, emotion-schematic memory, and conceptual-level information are all synthesized automatically to provide our experience of ourselves (Greenberg, 2002), but the schematic level of processing is most influential in determining our experience (Greenberg & Safran 1987, 1989; Leventhal, 1979). Emotion schemes are internal mental structures that produce action and experiencing. Emotion schemes produce lived experience, in contrast to cognitive schemas, which are described as core beliefs formulated in language that produces concepts. Outputs of emotion schemes, rather, provide action tendencies that orient us to the environment and affect bodily felt experience, and these are not mediated by thought. Schemes are cue-activated and response-producing internal organizations or neuronal networks.

It is important to note that people are agents in their construction of reality (Neimeyer & Mahoney, 1995). Rather than being passive responders to stimuli, people are active creators of their own environmental niches, which are filled with cues relevant to them. Cues, then, are "reality as construed" uniquely by each individual rather than simply reality stimuli. For example, the tone of the bell, the shape of the bell, or the sight of the bell is a cue constructed from the bell as a result of what is paid attention to, and the cue attended to acts as a future releaser of a scheme. This constructed cue helps activate schemes.

Cues act to boost the activation weight of certain schemes, which are already actively seeking to apply (J. Pascual-Leone & Johnson, 2021). The cocktail-party effect of selectively hearing your name mentioned in a room amidst a whole lot of noisy conversation exemplifies schemes being active seeking to apply. Emotional experience is formed into cue-activated schemes that serve as emotion-schematic memories that code lived-experience aspects of the situations in which they occurred and that were salient to the individual. When a cue constructed by an individual from experience matches a releaser in a scheme, the activation of the scheme, which is seeking to apply, is boosted. Thus, a look on a mother's face might be a cue for fear or for joy, and when this facial configuration or something similar to it appears, the scheme's activation is boosted, and it, in combination with other coactivated schemes, is synthesized into the ultimate complex emotional response of fear or joy.

People are complex, dynamic, self-organizing systems, and emotion schemes coordinate a variety of types of information at different levels in the brain to determine experience. Emotion schemes are activated by cues, often at an automatic level out of awareness, such as the way color or ambience influences, out of awareness, how we feel. These schemes produce the experience of emotions, such as shame, and the higher level self-organizations, such as feeling worthless, which are complex syntheses of a variety of cue-activated schemes. Schemes thus interpret the life-world and embody implicit or explicit expectancies about future outcomes of the scheme's application as well as contain a gist or script of what will happen when applied.

THREE MAIN COMPONENTS OF EMOTION SCHEMES

Emotion schemes comprise three main components (J. Pascual-Leone & Johnson, 2021): a releasing component, an effecting component, and a functional component. The *releasing* component is the set of conditions that activate or release the scheme. These are perceptual–situational elements. The *effecting* component is the set of effects that emanate from the scheme's application. These are the experiential, action tendency, sensorimotor outputs, including immediate sensations, expression of the emotion, and action tendencies plus the experience of the associated desires, needs, and wishes. When the scheme applies, the *functional* component embodies the gist of the goal(s) and implicit expectancies for future outcomes (what the schemes are about and intend). This is the nuclear process of the emotion scheme, which organizes the different components around a particular emotion script or narrative. It may only be crystallized in awareness after reflection on the other elements. Therapists need to focus on the releasing components to activate the scheme and then work to help clients experience the scheme's experiential effects (feelings) and be informed by their aims.

Unlike stimulus–stimulus and stimulus–response associations or reinforcement, schemes are self-propelling to codetermine performance under minimal activation. They also apply together to overdetermine performance. There are always many causes of smoking a cigar! The coactivation of cofunctional schemes informs experience and action.

Schemes, as previously mentioned, carry expectancies about what should happen next based on what has happened before. They are meaning-bearing structures that carry expectancies about what leads to what in the current situation. When expectancies are violated by experience (errors of anticipation), a loss of organismic balance occurs, which produces organismic arousal (affect) and motivates automatic attention to search for and resolve anomalies and rebalance. Schemes do not act singly, but many are coactivated in any situation. Repeatedly coactivated shame-related emotion schemes in response to similar cues combine to form higher level self-organizations such as "I feel worthless or unlovable." Thus, a repeatedly scolded child with a variety of experiences of being scolded, with cues of a contemptuous face, a derisive tone of voice, and rough physical handling, may come to synthesize these experiences into one feeling: "I am bad."

SELF-ORGANIZATIONS

Self-organizations are complex, synthesized experiences of self that combine compatible elements of the constituent schemes that can be articulated in language. Therefore, shame schemes, when coactivated, lead to higher self-organizations that are articulated in therapy as feelings of inferiority or worthlessness. These experiences are not cognitive beliefs but rather symbolization in language of the internal experience of the organismic tendency to drop one's eyes and head, to make oneself small and shrink in an effort to disappear; the sinking sensation in the stomach; the rushing of blood to the face while attending externally and becoming painfully aware of oneself as being gazed at and judged by others. Thus, rather than a belief that one is worthless or a thought that one is inferior, a person has a bodily felt sense of humiliation and an experience of social disdain.

In emotion-focused therapy (EFT), this primary maladaptive shame-based self-organization—of being defective, flawed, and not good enough—needs to be accessed and transformed. To reiterate, these shame responses are not mediated by thinking or self-judgment but arise when emotion-schematic shame memories are evoked automatically by a set of cues that match the scheme releasers. The experience occurs before any conscious judgments or automatic thoughts that occur in language. The beliefs are the articulation in language of the experience of shame, rather than the cause of shame. Thus, a person's face of contempt is sufficient to evoke emotion schemes of shame, which produce a tendency to shrink into the ground, a sinking feeling in the stomach, and a desire to hide.

In addition to the development of self-organizations from the synthesis of a variety of coactivated schemes, the dialectical–constructivist view of human functioning featured in EFT suggests that people are dynamic self-organizing systems, continually making sense of their internal, emotional experiences that arise from the activation and synthesis of a number of schemes (Greenberg & Pascual-Leone, 1995; Greenberg et al., 1993). The emotion system automatically evaluates whether something is good or bad for one and informs the organism of this evaluation through its body. The narrative system, driven to understand the meanings of the experience and action, creates narratives to understand and explain these experiences. Personal meaning, in this view, emerges by the explication of one's experienced emotion-schematic synthesized self-organization and emotional experience in language-based narratives. An ongoing process of attending to bodily felt sense in order to make sense of it, symbolizing bodily felt sensations in awareness and articulating them in language, leads to the construction of experience. Adaptation ultimately involves an integration of reason and emotion, head and heart.

CHANGING EMOTION WITH EMOTION

This book illustrates how to change chronic enduring shame in the personality and how to change anger that is either excessive or blocked. A key principle of change in an emotion-focused approach is that the best way to change emotions is with other emotions. Clients change deep-seated, amygdala-based emotions by having new emotional experience—not by learning skills, not by understanding or insight, and not by reduction due to exposure, but by new procedural learning through new emotional experience in the session. This change process occurs through implicit processes of *transformation by synthesis*, in which newly evoked experience in the session blends with existing elements of experience stored in emotion-schematic memory to form truly novel experiential states of mind (Greenberg, 2021). This process works as a result of the brain making new implicit linkages and laying down new neuronal pathways. In this process, when primary adaptive anger at unfairness—with its approach action tendency—is coactivated to the same stimulus situation with the experience of shame—with its withdrawal action tendency—a truly novel experience is developed: pride, strength, calm, or whatever idiosyncratic state is formed by the person's synthesis of schemes. Emotion is generated psychologically by the emotional brain appraising situations in relation to need. Thus, when a situation is appraised as not meeting a need, the emotional brain automatically generates an emotional response to the blockage of need satisfaction and generates anger to overcome the block or appraises this situation as a loss and feels the sadness of grief.

EFT is a process of facilitating these types of self-reorganization. For example, a man with an abusive father feels unbearable shame because of the way he has been treated, which leaves him feeling socially anxious for fear of being invalidated or mistreated. Therapeutic work involves first accessing his shame. Then, having experienced the pain of the shame with the therapist's help, the man is able to access his need for safety and for his mother's protection. He begins to feel that he deserved to have a childhood free of all his shame and fear. This sense of deservingness leads his emotional brain automatically, without words, to appraise his treatment as unfair, thus generating the experience of empowered anger. In the session, he expresses his anger to his imagined father in an empty chair and by doing so produces a bodily felt mobilization and sense of thrusting forward to establish a boundary that now is integrated at the neuronal level with his evoked withdrawal tendency in shame. This produces a newly synthesized sense of bodily strength and is accompanied by new feelings and a new narrative in which he no longer sees himself as bad but instead sees his father as incapable of being a parent.

Research on the process of memory reconsolidation has shown that the introduction of new emotional experience in the present in response to the same cueing situation can change emotional memories (Lane et al., 2015; Nadel & Bohbot, 2001; Nader et al., 2000). Memory reconsolidation involves the assimilation of new contradictory material from the present into memories of the past (Nadel & Bohbot, 2001). Novel emotional experience in the present, such as anger instead of shame, allows implicit automatic connections that occur at neuronal and schematic levels to sculpt new pathways that generate new ways of feeling and being. Breathing new experience into old painful memories allows clients to rewire their shame with corrective experiences.

The process of changing memory requires that the memory be activated to accept new input. To be changed, emotional memories need to be brought alive in therapy. New experiences in therapy can then be amalgamated into the memory, changing the original memory. Thus, people who are paralyzed by fear because of past trauma need to evoke the memory and experience the fear of the past in the present and then experience new emotions that provide a sense of mastery that helps to overcome the fear. It is important to note that this process does not involve not substituting one emotion with another emotion but, rather, creating a new synthesis between old and new emotions in the memory.

Corrective experience has long been proposed as a core change principle across approaches (Alexander & French, 1946; Bridges, 2006; Castonguay & Hill, 2012). Changing emotion with emotion is a specific form of this principle, highlighting that the best way to change an emotion is with another opposing emotion (Greenberg, 2021). Feelings change in tandem with a bodily felt shift, and only when this experiential process has occurred can change be profitably symbolized in language, or *mentalized*, and formed into a new narrative meaning that consolidates the change experienced at the bodily felt, emotional level. The basic transformation takes place automatically at a neuronal level. The brain automatically lays down new pathways to form new internal mental structures (emotion schemes) that represent the person's new emotional experience. Change takes place because new emotional experience changes old emotional experience (Greenberg, 2021).

Transformation comes from close contact with new experience, not from what we tell ourselves by positive self-talk or by different skills to soothe anxieties. Change occurs not from a therapist's advice and not from therapist-offered new understandings or interpretations. Instead, change involves development as a result of new experience. The therapeutic task is to facilitate new emotional experience. Rather than reason with emotion, psychoeducate, or train new skills, the therapist needs to facilitate new emotional experience in the session to change old emotional experience; new experience is change-producing. Conscious change in beliefs, narratives, insight, and understandings come later in the change process, and only after a bodily felt emotional shift has occurred, which then can be consolidated in conscious awareness.

In this process of transformation by synthesis, people must feel emotions to change emotions. They need first to feel shame to change shame and to feel previously unacknowledged anger to harness its adaptive power. This process goes beyond only accepting emotions. Simply experiencing and expressing emotions, although important in change, is not enough. It is true that a person needs to feel an emotion to heal an emotion and has to arrive at a place before they can leave it. People benefit from experiencing and accepting previously disowned adaptive emotions so as to be informed by them and to be guided by their action tendencies. But those emotions that are painfully maladaptive and that do not provide adaptive information or action tendencies need first to be accepted and then to be transformed. Acceptance often is not enough; one has to leave the painful emotion and move on. To only accept one's shame or one's anger leaves one feeling ashamed or angry. Transformation is needed.

Transformation by synthesis, however, differs from the view that change occurs by exposure to reduce emotion or that emotions can be changed by changing the behavior that the emotion is driving (Barlow, 1988; Izard, 1971; Linehan, 1993). The classical mechanisms of change in exposure based on learning theory are habituation, extinction, and newer suggested mechanisms such as inhibitory learning (Craske et al., 2014) and opposite action (Linehan, 1993). The view of transformation proposed here offers a developmental perspective in which the new experience is mobilized from within rather than coming from the outside. Views that propose new inhibitory learning at a cognitive level have some similarities to changing emotion with emotion, but in transformation by synthesis, change is emotional development, not learning. Transformation by synthesis also differs from exposure in that transformation is not the mere reduction of negative affect but rather promotes activating underlying emotion, accepting, and making sense of it, and it involves the synthesis of primary adaptive and maladaptive emotion. This transformation involves increasing the emotional arousal of primary underlying emotions rather than reducing arousal, often of symptomatic emotions, by extinction or habituation. Transformation by synthesis also involves the creation of new meaning by bringing cognition to emotion to make sense of it and to consolidate change.

Opposite action as proposed by Linehan (1993) also has some similarity to the changing-emotion-with-emotion concept, except it works from the outside, at a behavioral level. This theory proposes that enacting a new behavior prevents the action tendency associated with the old emotional experience and replaces it with a new one. Changing emotion with emotion works from the inside out—the new action tendency in a newly activated emotion changes the old action tendency by synthesizing with it rather than replacing it.

To exemplify, clients who experience underlying primary maladaptive shame of inadequacy and have a tendency to withdraw may present with symptoms of social anxiety. In EFT, therapists don't treat the symptomatic anxiety but instead work to transform the underlying shame. Enduring change to extinguish the anxiety is not achieved by exposure to social situations but by facing the underlying painful emotion and then by the coactivation to the same evoking situation of an incompatible, more adaptive opposing tendency of approach that comes from empowered anger or compassion for the self. Rather than replacing the old emotion, the new emotion *undoes* the old emotion and transforms it into something new. So, shame may become confidence. This process involves more than just attenuating emotions by facing them or accepting symptomatic secondary feelings such as anger or anxiety to diminish them. Rather than modifying anxiety by exposure, therapeutic work on emotion involves gaining access to and staying in contact with the action tendencies of withdrawal in the underlying primary maladaptive shame and then co-activating the transformative-approach action tendencies in anger, sadness, or compassion.

Changing emotion with emotion and memory reconsolidation therefore needs to be distinguished from behavioral extinction. Extinction is assumed to create a new memory that overrides the previously trained response. Thus, an "extinguished" response is not really gone, since it can spontaneously recover over time or be reinstated if the organism is exposed to a relevant cue in a new context. Changing emotion with emotion leads to the creation of novel states, while memory reconsolidation is understood to change actual components of the old memory. Reconsolidation and extinction therefore represent different ways of working with memory reactivation (Lane et al., 2015). Cellular/molecular differences have been found that distinguish the processes from one another; the temporal dynamics of the test procedure and how recently the memory in question was formed and/or reactivated determine if it is reconsolidation or extinction (de la Fuente et al., 2011; Inda et al., 2011; Maren, 2011).

The process of changing emotions and emotional memories requires that the emotion or the memory is activated to accept new input and to be confronted with new, somewhat contradictory experience. Painful maladaptive emotions or emotional memories thus need to be brought alive in therapy in order to be changed. New contradictory experiences in therapy can then be amalgamated into the old emotion or memory modifying the original experience. Thus, people who are paralyzed by shame because of past trauma need to evoke the memory and experience the shame of the past in the present and then experience new emotions that provide a sense of mastery that helps them to overcome the shame. The idea of changing emotion with emotion suggests that new experience at an emotional level, rather than habituation or extinction, is at work. In addition, the process involves not substituting one emotion with another emotion but rather creating a new synthesis between old and new emotions in the memory.

Therapists need to help clients arrive at core maladaptive feelings of shame, symbolize them in awareness, and access more adaptive emotional resources as an antidote to the maladaptive feelings. With shame, anger is often the antidote. A helpful intervention for accessing an adaptive emotional response is to inquire as to what the client's feeling needs to feel better. A central aspect of this change process is feeling deserving of having a previously unmet adaptive need met. Feeling deserving of validation generates a new adaptive anger response, generated automatically by the emotional brain, whose agenda is to get the need for validation or the need safety met to promote survival and well-being (Greenberg, 2002, 2011).

Research studying actual change events in therapy (Greenberg 1984, 2007) suggests that changing emotion with emotion is the most helpful way to understand how emotional change actually takes place (Herrmann et al., 2016; A. Pascual-Leone & Greenberg, 2007). This principle of emotional change was first stated by Spinoza (1967), who said, "An emotion cannot be restrained nor removed unless by an opposed and stronger emotion" (p. 195). Reason is seldom enough to change automatic amygdala-generated emotional responses. Darwin (1872) wrote that when he approached a glassed-in snake, he jumped back automatically from its strike, in spite of his determination not to react. Even though he knew he was safe and had never experienced the danger of a snake's strike in his life, his will and reason were ineffective against the imagined danger of being bitten by a snake.

Repeated coactivation of an adaptive and a maladaptive emotion to the same cueing situation facilitates the synthesis of a new emotional state, thereby transforming the original maladaptive emotion. A variety of processes are involved in the transformation by synthesis of emotion by the coactivation of opposing emotional states. Most fundamentally, the action tendencies in the newly activated adaptive emotion incline the person to engage in an action tendency opposing the action tendency in the old emotion. This leads to a synthesized novel response. A person cannot run away in fear while the action tendency to thrust forward in anger is coactivated. The new emotion therefore *undoes* or *transforms* the old emotion by a process of dialectical synthesis to produce a new experiential state. Just as the color yellow combines with blue to create green, so do approach tendencies combine with withdrawal tendencies to make up a truly novel response, such as assertive boundary setting or soothing calm. This process is not one emotion *replacing* another emotion but rather the construction of a new state.

At the schematic level, the coactivated emotion schemes of shame and anger synthesize to form a new higher level scheme. Hebb's (1949) first law of neuroscience is that neurons that fire together wire together and continue to fire together. When two or more schemes seek to apply to the same stimulus, they synthesize to form a new scheme. A newly synthesized action tendency plus a newly formed scheme lead to a newly felt body experience and a changed action orientation to the environment. This new way of being in the world is now articulated in a new narrative that leads to the construction of new meanings and new views of self, world, and other.

Maladaptive shame, if aroused in a session, can begin to be transformed into a new state, such as feeling confident, by accessing the boundary-setting emotion of adaptive anger or of disgust or by evoking the closeness-seeking behaviors associated with feelings of sadness or compassion. Maladaptive anger can be transformed by the coactivation of adaptive sadness, and coactivation often leads to letting go of the anger, acceptance, and possibly forgiveness. Maladaptive shame, as discussed earlier, can be transformed into self-acceptance by accessing anger at violation. Anger can transform maladaptive shame into pride, self-worth, and self-acceptance, or the pain of the shame can lead to self-comforting compassion. In this way, withdrawal emotions are transformed by approach emotions. Thoughts and narratives change after emotion has changed. Angry thoughts change after anger turns to sadness. When people who were neglected as children no longer feel unworthy, they change their narratives that they were unlovable to ones in which they rather see unloving others as having been incapable of love. Alternatively, people who blamed themselves for their abuse and felt ashamed or guilty about it may change to hold the other accountable for the wrongs done and may come to see that they were not responsible.

Most people intuitively understand that feeling good can change feeling bad, but it is important to note that we are not primarily advocating the replacement of negative feelings with positive ones. Rather, I am talking about a process of undoing one emotion, a maladaptive one, with another emotion, an adaptive one that has an opposing action tendency. For example, having a client imagine his emotionally and physically abusive father in an empty chair in front of him evokes his emotion-schematic shame memories of prior abuse and makes these memories amenable to the new experience that comes from expressing his adaptive anger at violation and standing up against his imagined father. The client then has a corrective emotional experience in which he feels stronger and more able to assert and protect himself, and the memories are reconsolidated to include this stronger sense of self. Clearly, emotions change emotions, and they also change cognition.

ROUTES TO EMOTIONAL CHANGE

Within the process of working with emotion in therapy are two somewhat different routes to emotional change. One path involves arriving at previously disclaimed adaptive emotion, such as unacknowledged assertive anger, and accepting it. The other path involves a primary maladaptive experience of feeling, such as shame-based worthlessness, that is disclaimed and requires transformation as well as acceptance.

The first path is relevant to problems created by disowning an adaptive emotion and not experiencing the adaptive information and action tendencies it offers. This path is simpler to work with therapeutically, and the emotion, once accessed, can be used as a guide to behavior change. This path involves two therapeutic steps—first moving from secondary reactive emotions to primary adaptive emotions, such as from secondary hopelessness to primary adaptive anger. The client is helped to experience the adaptive emotion in the therapy, not just talk about it or have insight. What is transformative is having the experience of feeling empowered at an experiential level in one's body, which leads to asserting the right to not be violated. The client then symbolizes this new experience in words and reflects on it to create new narratives, new meaning, and new actions.

The second path involve problems created by disowning core maladaptive emotions. This therapeutic route involves a three-step sequence. The path begins with bypassing the secondary symptomatic emotions and going to primary maladaptive emotions and then to adaptive emotion (Greenberg, 2015). For example, one might move from secondary worry to underlying primary maladaptive fear and then to a transformation through access to primary adaptive assertive anger (Greenberg & Paivio, 1997). When working on this more complex second path, therapists need first to facilitate clients to arrive at the previously disowned painful, maladaptive emotion. Painful maladaptive states need to be approached, re-owned and accepted. The important first sequence of moving from secondary to primary maladaptive emotion, however, is incomplete without the third step of accessing healthy, adaptive emotions and motivations. This three-step sequence is the most important change process, that of changing emotion with emotion, and it has been shown to predict outcome (Herrmann et al., 2016; A. Pascual-Leone & Greenberg, 2007).

CONCLUSION

This chapter has covered the nature of emotion and the role of emotion schemes in functioning. The importance of bodily sensing over language and emotion over cognition has been emphasized. As useful as language is for exchanging facts and for reasoning, facts and logic are relatively less important in the formation of human relationships and personal identity than is the experience and expression of emotion. Emotions tell us what is good for us and bad for us and speak through our bodies, without saying a word, whereas cognition tells us what is right or wrong and speaks through symbolic language. Emotions are about value—what is good for me or bad for me. Cognition is about truth—what is right or wrong. Language works at the level of conscious awareness, but most of what we do is determined below the surface of consciousness by implicit processes.

The roles of schemes and schematic functioning were described as the best way to understand the generation of emotion and its transformation. Finally, the principle of changing emotion with emotion and the process of memory consolidation were introduced to help understand transformation by synthesis as opposed to change by cognitive or behavior modification or by insight and new understanding. Chapter 3 focuses on the emotion of shame, its characteristics, the different types of shame, and how to work with these different types in therapy.

3 SHAME IN PSYCHOTHERAPY

The only shame is to have none.

–Blaise Pascal

Shame is a soul-eating emotion.

–Carl Gustav Jung

This chapter addresses the nature of shame and its varied forms in psychotherapy. Shame appears in psychotherapy in different forms, as both primary and secondary responses, or as deep shame, or as more superficial embarrassment. It is also often conflated with guilt. Different aspects of shame are discussed in this chapter as a way of highlighting both the complexity of working with shame and the need for guidelines for differential intervention for various types of shame experiences. This chapter also presents the effects of societal, cultural, and gender-based issues related to working with shame.

---

https://doi.org/10.1037/0000393-003
Shame and Anger in Psychotherapy, by L. S. Greenberg
Copyright © 2024 by the American Psychological Association. All rights reserved.

Tompkins (1963) was the first to theorize about shame in detail. He claimed that *shame-humiliation* was probably the most pervasive affect and that it interacted with all the other affects. He defined shame-humiliation as a feeling of desire that was unattained. For Tompkins, shame occurred when positive affect was incompletely reduced. In other words, shame happens when you are feeling good and something gets in the way of your good feeling but doesn't stop you from wanting to continue with that good feeling. It is a sudden reduction in excitement. Helen Block Lewis (1971a, 1971b, 1987) was the first therapist to focus on the importance of shame in treatment and to clarify the difference between shame and guilt in psychoanalytic theory. She viewed shame as about the whole self, whereas guilt was about behavior. When discussing emotion-focused therapy (EFT), Greenberg and Paivio (1997) described shame as "feeling exposed and found lacking in dignity or worth" (p. 229). A person experiencing shame feels that they are not worthy of attention or love and fears that they will be rejected if they are seen as they really are (Tangney & Dearing, 2002). Shame may have emerged from an innate desire to belong and to be perceived as attractive and to maintain hierarchical social position (Gilbert & Andrews, 1998). The fundamental emotional responses of shame have been evolutionarily preserved because they promoted survival and they rise up automatically (Frijda, 1986; Tompkins, 1963).

In a therapeutic context, shame is described as the familiar pain of "who I am is not okay," "I am not acceptable," or "I don't belong." The pain of this feeling pushes people to withdraw. This withdrawal could have had an original function, to help people reflect on themselves and their relationships, but that tendency can become social avoidance or even self-harm. People can feel shame about various aspects of the self. They can feel shame about their bodies, about their needs for affection and recognition, about their sexual desires or their sexual orientation, about their competence or ideas or ambitions. People experience shame when they feel diminished in the eyes of the other and feel small and inferior or when they feel that others see them as undignified (Dearing & Tangney, 2011). Sometimes the most helpful way to overcome shame is for a person to get it out into the open, out of their head, by having a conversation with someone who cares about and accepts them.

People also feel shame when they experience themselves as overexposed, as if appearing naked in public or having lost control of themselves. Shame also can arise when a person is excited and the feeling is not matched, or not mirrored, by others (Tompkins, 1963). People feel shame when they reveal their emotions or show their excitement and these expressions are not seen or not responded to (Nathanson, 1994). For example, children experience shame when their emotional excitement or their efforts at exhibiting their talents or competence are not validated. When a child stands on a diving board about to jump off into a swimming pool and excitedly yells "Mommy! Daddy! Look at me!" they might shrink away in shame if their parents ignore them (Kohut, 1977). This shrinking response to the absence of expected responsiveness from a meaningful other person is shame. When people experience shock because someone ignores or turns away from them in the moment of expression, they feel shame. Shame overwhelms all aspects of self and disrupts the ability to regulate affect. Self-coherence is lost, as is access to a healthy core sense of self and the motivation to survive and thrive, leaving the person defeated and depleted.

A study on shame found it to be more about having an undesired, or unattractive, self than about failing to be an ideal self (Lindsay-Hartz et al., 1995). Participants in this study reported feeling shame when they were being who they did not want to be. Shame involved experiencing themselves as an anti-ideal, rather than simply not being who they wanted to be. The participants said things like "I am ugly," not "I failed to be pretty" or they said "I am bad," not "I am not as good as I want to be." This difference was not simply semantic, as participants stressed that the distinction was meaningful. It is therefore not so much failing to meet standards, but the experience of falling short. This difference brings in the condemning nature of maladaptive shame and the role of self-contempt in shame.

Kaufman (1996), drawing on Tompkins (1963), proposed that contempt is a blend of anger with smelling something foul (*dis-smell*), in which the action tendency is to move one's nose up and away. Disgust, on the other hand, stems from *distaste* (i.e., tasting something foul in the mouth), in which the action tendency is to spit it out—the same action tendency as in disgust. Negatively evaluating oneself and feeling contemptuous of oneself can be thought of as the cognitive and emotional aspects, respectively, of a self-critical process. Feeling contemptuous of the self is also characterized by particular body language, facial expression, and vocal quality (Whelton & Greenberg, 2005). The body language of contempt includes curling the lip, raising the nose as though to move away from a bad smell, lifting oneself to a superior position, and possibly making hand gestures that suggest scolding, dismissal, rejection, or squashing.

THE DIFFERENCE BETWEEN SHAME AND RELATED EMOTIONS

The term *embarrassment* is often used interchangeably with *shame*, but it is useful to distinguish the two concepts. They differ in two aspects. First, shame is morally reprehensible and probably includes self-contempt to some degree, whereas embarrassment is morally neutral. People feel embarrassed when some aspect of themselves that they feel is likely to undermine the image they want to project is witnessed by another, not when they feel defective or worthless. For example, people feel embarrassed when their fly or blouse is open, or when, in modern society, they are witnessed passing gas or picking their noses. A second distinction is that shame is only about the self, whereas people can feel embarrassed about others. For example, people can feel embarrassed for performers when they make blatant mistakes on stage in front of an audience or embarrassed about a spouse's foolish statement or a child's misbehavior. People can feel embarrassed not only by things beneath their own image but also by things not in keeping with it, such as feeling embarrassed in front of others less fortunate or because they have an elite education or wealthy or ostentatious parents. Shame, then, as opposed to embarrassment, is a response to something that is morally wrong or reprehensible. Shame arises from evaluating ourselves against some moral standard and finding ourselves falling short. Embarrassment occurs when the way we wish to be seen is undermined.

Humiliation is another term often used interchangeably with shame, but humiliation differs from shame in that it is something inflicted upon us by others in public. It involves having one's dignity debased and suffering a loss of standing or status. It is the public denigration of one's status rather than a self-condemning personal evaluation. It cuts deep and is viscerally painful when someone asserts power over a person and destroys that person's honor or reputation. For this reason, humiliation has long been used as a form of punishment, for example, being put in the stocks in the public square and being pelted with rotten vegetables or spat on.

Shame and guilt are also often confounded with each other, but a distinction can be made between them (Tangney & Dearing, 2002). Guilt possesses surface similarities to shame but is not the same. The two emotions are often used interchangeably or confused (Kim et al., 2011) but need to be differentiated. An often-described distinguishing feature is that guilt involves a negative evaluation of one's specific action, whereas shame involves a negative evaluation by the self of the whole self—of the person's self, worth, or dignity—and/or perceptions of a negative evaluation of the self by others. This distinction is held academically to be true, but therapeutically and experientially one certainly sees people feeling shame about only parts of the self. For example, some people can feel ashamed of their academic grades but not of their attractiveness. A further, more clear distinction is that guilt has an action tendency to move toward, to repair or atone for hurt caused, whereas shame activates an action tendency to move away from, to hide or to attempt to disappear. Shame can be seen as related to a person's sense of worth, referring often to the whole self, and as making people want to hide. Guilt, in contrast, is about behavior and prompts apology or making amends. A way to separate shame from guilt is to see that shame involves "I'm bad" while guilt involves "I did something bad." Shame is a focus on the self; guilt is a focus on one's actions, not on the self: A parent saying "You're stupid" leads to shame, whereas "You're a good kid, and you made a bad decision" is more guilt oriented. People may also experience a type of guilt–shame process, in which they feel guilty about being hurtful to someone and simultaneously feel shame about being hurtful. They may try to hide their responsibility or get defensively angry.

Shame developed evolutionarily to protect social rank and status and to maintain one's belonging to the group, while guilt evolved from caring, making amends, and maintaining relational connections. Shame prompts people to withdraw, to shut down, and to avoid thinking about what occurred that made them feel bad about themselves. Guilt, on the other hand, propels people to repair. Guilt arises when people have behaved in ways which they regret, whereas shame arises from being the object of another person's gaze or actions. Guilt thus arises when people had agency, whereas shame arises from the experience of feeling powerless, of being the object of another's actions, of feeling denigrated or without dignity. Survivors of assault, interpersonal violence, and sexual abuse often experience shame (Wolfgang, 1998).

Healthy guilt and healthy shame differ in their action tendencies. Adaptive shame helps a person in the current situation to not be seen negatively or not to be overexposed, and adaptive guilt leads to repair. Maladaptive forms of guilt and shame also differ. Maladaptive shame does not help one in the current situation, as it is a response to the past. Freud (1923) saw guilt as a key primary emotion in pathology resulting from a harsh superego, but I see shame as a core primary emotion in pathology that is more fundamental than guilt and that comes from having been shamed and internalizing the shame. Unhealthy guilt, rather than being a primary emotion, often is a secondary emotional reaction to introjected "shoulds" in the personality.

In this discussion of shame and other emotions, we cannot leave out a word or two on pride, which can be considered the opposite of shame. Pride has been viewed as both a vice and a virtue. Pride, one of the seven deadly sins, refers to an inflated sense of self, to vanity, and even to self-idolization. Pride as a virtue, however, is the feeling of having a self-image confirmed, of feeling pleased with one's performance. If pride is love of one's own excellence or worth, shame is clearly the opposite. So, on the one hand, pride has been seen, especially in religious circles, as an unforgivable sin, but on the other hand, especially in psychological circles, pride is a celebration of self-worth, achievement, and of self-esteem and a possible ally in the fight against shame.

ADAPTIVE OR MALADAPTIVE SHAME

As noted previously, shame can be adaptive or maladaptive, keeping one belonging to the group or leading to unhealthy withdrawal. But most often in therapy, shame is the painful feeling that one is not good enough; it is about inadequacy and lack of worth. Shame essentially makes people want to disappear from the gaze of others, and so withdrawal is often a consequence of shame. Cooley (1902) in *The Looking Glass Self* wrote that many ordinary people deny that they care about what others think of them. He said that this is an illusion and that if failure or disgrace arrives, they will discover that they were living in the minds of others without knowing it, just as they walk on the ground without thinking of how it bears them up. People are highly interdependent, and shame, which involves living in the eyes of others, makes them so.

Shame is frequently conceptualized in experimental and developmental psychology as a self-conscious emotion that comes on only after a person has developed a self-concept. The experience of shame is thought to require the capacity to have a representation of a "self" and an awareness or imagining of others' opinions of one's self (M. Lewis, 2008; Tangney & Dearing, 2002). In EFT, however, from a clinical perspective and from the perspective of other basic emotion theorists and therapists (Bradshaw, 1988; Darwin, 1872; Izard, 1977; Nathanson, 1994; Panksepp, 2008; Tompkins, 1963), shame is a basic affect that comes on-line much earlier than the development of a self-concept and is not dependent on it, so a toddler shows shame/shyness long before they have a self-concept (Izard, 1977). Animals such as dogs do not possess the equivalent of a self-concept in any conceptual fashion, but they still express shame when they have violated a rule. They defer, show signs of submission to the alpha owner, and slink away in shame. In therapy, shame often is not a product of cognitive negative self-evaluation but rather is a deep visceral reaction linked to the corporeal, bodily self and free of any form of conscious self-evaluation. Shame is a primitive, automatic physiological response to rejection and threat of being cast out and isolated socially. After the initial affective shame response, cognitive process come into play to cope with the loss of face.

Shame needs to be seen as in-wired, like disgust and fear. Darwin (1872) described shame as turning the body away in an attempt to avoid.

He compared it to disgust, which involves a reciprocal action tendency of pushing away in an attempt to guard the self. Shame and disgust both are believed to have evolved as solutions to different adaptive challenges (Terrizzi & Shook, 2020). The experience of shame can be deeply painful, so many clients access a deep pain as part of or directly in reaction to accessing shame or articulating self-contempt (Greenberg & Bolger, 2001; S. Miller, 2021). Shame in some ways can also be likened to fear. Similar to fear, shame is hard-wired, has a very rapid physiological response, has a withdrawal action tendency, and can be overwhelming at times. Shame, then, is best understood as a basic universal human emotion rather than a cognitively derived one.

COMPONENTS OF SHAME

Shame is a multifaceted experience. It can be thought of as having the following five components, all of which need to be addressed in therapy.

1. **An emotional component:** A bodily felt sinking feeling, shame-anxiety, self-disgust, self-contempt.

2. **An internal self-evaluative component:** I am bad, inadequate, flawed, useless, a failure.

3. **A social component:** Others see me as bad, inadequate, useless, a failure and are contemptuous of me.

4. **A motivational/behavioral component:** Desire and tendency to hide or conceal own behaviors, feelings of rage or thoughts about retaliating against shamer.

5. **A physiological component:** Increased arousal, sympathetic/parasympathetic autonomic nervous system, stress hormone release.

The word *shame* derives from "to cover" and is often expressed by covering the eyes and the brow and by a downward gaze. The action tendency in shame is to hide the self from the gaze of others, to want to become small or disappear or even to cease to exist, and to withdraw from others. Action tendencies can be classified as moving toward, moving away, or moving against; all of these may emanate from shame. The tendency to move away in shame involves trying to disappear, hide, and keep secrets. Shame that involves moving toward shows itself as being overly pleasing to others, especially others of higher status. Moving against involves fighting back and can lead to the rage and aggression that emanates from shame. It involves revenge seeking and a sense of "If you shame me, I will hurt and shame you right back."

As shame often provokes anxiety, physiological manifestation of anxiety may be part of the experience of shame. Shame can be caused not only by the perception of negative evaluation but also by a fear of such negative evaluation. Shame-anxiety is a signal that alerts people to the possibility of imminent shaming or humiliation and mobilizes them to withdraw, hide, or inhibit their behavior. Pain is also an aspect of the experience of shame, which can be an intense and fragmenting experience that leaves the person feeling broken and shattered (S. Miller, 2021). The experience of shame can be deeply painful, so many clients access a deep pain as part of or directly in reaction to accessing shame or articulating self-contempt (S. Miller, 2021). The brain registers the pain of shame in the same way as it registers physical pain. When we feel emotions like shame, we are vulnerable and wounded, but we must arrive at and endure the pain to access the shame so that we can bring new emotional experience to bear on the shame to promote change.

Shame has many nonverbal indicators (Julle-Danière et al., 2020). Blushing and hiding the face are characteristic of the body language of shame. The head drops, eyes are downcast or gaze is averted, shoulders may be slumped and chest collapsed, and contact with others is avoided. Shame is also hidden by going blank, shutting down, refusing to engage, and dissociating. Verbal indicators involve negative self-evaluation and concerns about being negatively evaluated by others. Statements about feeling humiliated or embarrassed and dismissal of their own behavior are all indicators of shame, as are being self-critical or overly apologetic and having perfectionistic standards, feelings of powerlessness, and feeling trapped, isolated, and alone. Many words are used to indicate feeling shame, including (in English) *embarrassed, ashamed, humiliated, shy, bashful, sheepish, mortified, demeaned, self-conscious, foolish, silly,* and *powerless*. Potter-Efron (2011) outlined five "deficiency statements" that clients use to describe their own shame experiences: "(a) "I am not good," (b) "I am not good enough," (c) "I do not belong," (d) "I am unlovable," and (e) "I should not be." Wille (2014) described the most extreme form of shame as the "shame of existing." In this form of shame, people feel they do not deserve to exist—a "merciless and total rejection of the subject's self" (p. 695).

Shame triggers are many, including perceived criticism, real or imagined; the failure to cope; being socially diminished; and anything that undermines one's view of self. Reactions involve automatic responses to hide or escape, not to apologize and repair. The pain is great, and the job of transforming the self from fundamentally flawed to good seems impossibly immense. Shame has also been linked to evading responsibility, blaming the victim, mismanaging anger, and, in the extreme, hostile aggression. When shame is activated in interactions, people shift to automatic threat-focused processing with little reflective thought. Interactions spiral out of control, and protective defenses become more extreme. People can become either more dominant or more submissive. When people feel damaged or feel that they have damaged relationships and do not know how to repair them, they feel shame and dissociate, avoid, minimize, externalize, and ruminate.

VARIETIES OF SHAME

As mentioned previously, shame in psychotherapy is not singular and can arise in several distinct forms. Different types of processes, such as primary and secondary shame and adaptive and maladaptive shame, need to be discriminated to guide differential intervention. *Primary adaptive shame* is the most fundamental, direct, initial, rapid reaction to a situation, accessed for its adaptive information and capacity to organize adaptive action. *Primary maladaptive shame*, often stemming from past maltreatment, earlier trauma, or poor attachment experience, comes from reactions to the past experienced in the present and does not help to adapt to the current situation. Adaptive survival strategies that were developed in reaction to abuse, humiliation, and rejection can be internalized and may become maladaptive feelings of worthlessness and withdrawal. *Secondary shame* is a person's emotional reaction to a primary emotion, such as when one feels ashamed of one's sadness or anger (Dearing & Tangney, 2011). Everyone experiences this type of shame on occasion in response to some specific situation. Secondary shame needs to be explored to discover and process the underlying primary emotion. For example, a depressed client tearfully says, with protest in her voice, "Why do I have to suffer like this? I feel so useless. I'm so ashamed that I'm such a mess." She has a tone of complaint and hopelessness in her voice. This is a secondary shame, accompanied by hopelessness or helplessness, the emotional reaction to an underlying feeling and unmet need. In responding, the therapist first acknowledges the secondary feelings of shame and her hopeless feelings and then guides the client to her underlying primary vulnerable emotion of shame, her sense of worthlessness, and ultimately to her need for validation. This example shows a type of secondary shame covering a core primary maladaptive shame.

Instrumental shame, on the other hand, is an emotionally based behavior pattern that the person has developed over a lifetime; it is used, consciously or unconsciously, to achieve an interpersonal aim. The person has learned to use emotion to influence or manipulate others, such as feigning embarrassment to appear socially appropriate or crying crocodile tears to evoke sympathy. Therapy can help draw attention to clients' use of instrumental shame and help them to become aware of the goal of their shame expressed in this manner. Conveying submission with expressions of shame is often a cultural form of greeting. Instrumental shame, however, can be dysfunctional when it is used rigidly and repeatedly to satisfy unmet needs (Dearing & Tangney, 2011). Instrumental shame does not arise that much as an emotion in therapy sessions except with personality disorder clients. If it is expressed in therapy, the therapist feels an interpersonal pull to have to react in a certain way. For instance, the therapist may feel like they need to laugh at the client's jokes or have to deal with dependency needs after the client hangs on at the end of a session by "door knobbing" (bringing up something important on the way out). Instrumental shame is dysfunctional when it is used repeatedly to satisfy unmet needs and is best dealt with by raising clients' awareness of what they are doing and their aims.

Primary Adaptive Shame

The adaptive function of shame is to keep people connected to the group and not overexposed. Adaptive shame informs people that they have violated important standards or values and their social group's norms or that they are overexposed or in danger of not getting people's support. Shame helps people not become alienated from their group; it keeps them connected and belonging to the group while protecting their privacy. By preventing us from breaking the rules of the social fabric and not erring too much in public, shame prevents us from being ostracized.

Primary adaptive shame, then, is an emotion that is activated when people have contravened their personal standards or values or those of their social group. It is often an automatic evaluation free of any conscious thought. In its adaptive form, shame is a prosocial emotion that guides people to behave in ways that promote cohesion within their social groups. Shame also serves an appeasement function that reduces interpersonal or intragroup violence and reaffirms rank in hierarchical or dominance-oriented contexts.

When it occurs in proportion to the evoking circumstance, adaptive shame is a healthy and necessary emotion for an individual to function well within their social context and for overall social cohesion. People who do not experience shame often frequently offend or violate the rights of others; in fact, psychopathy is characterized by a complete lack of consciously experienced shame (Loader, 1998). In the English language, the adjective *shameless* is a negative evaluation, defined as being "imprudent, brazen" (The Canadian Oxford Dictionary, 1998, p. 1329).

In therapy, adaptive shame is experienced and explored to get its adaptive information and to help organize adaptive action. Anticipation of the shame of rejection guides people to behave in ways that promote belonging to the group. Showing shame also serves to reduce others' aggression and increases the likelihood of reconciliation by evoking the activation of more affiliative responses, such as sympathy and forgiveness from others. In therapy, primary shame is the person's most fundamental, direct, initial, rapid reaction to a situation of diminishment (Dearing & Tangney, 2011). From an evolutionary perspective, shame probably served an important social function, but in general—in modern Westernized urban culture, at least—shame seldom serves a helpful function. It is not very facilitative in individual or larger social interactions.

Primary Maladaptive Shame

Primary maladaptive shame is felt in the present by the activation of a long-standing sense that the self is unworthy, defective, or inherently flawed. That sense comes from earlier experiences of not mattering or being shamed, invalidated, or violated. Core shame is not an episodic reaction, felt in a moment, but is a more enduring part of a person's experience that influences their whole personality and forms the undercurrent of experience without emerging explicitly into awareness. Early experiences of being ignored, invalidated, ridiculed, and rejected, as well as experiences of abuse and neglect, generally lead to the development of a core sense of self as flawed, defective, worthless, not mattering, and unlovable (Dearing & Tangney, 2011). When parents hit their children and offer explanations that their children are bad, the children internalize these explanations; when people are angry with them, they feel that they are bad and that it is their fault. They don't see that the parent might be out of control or bad, and they exclude their own experience of rage and desire to attack the parent back. Their rage has to be disclaimed as too dangerous to the attachment bond (Bowlby, 1982).

Maladaptive shame, because it is a reaction to the past, does not provide useful information to help deal with the present. This shame can show up in many forms, including as feelings of humiliation, powerless, mortification, or shyness. People who chronically react to situations in the present with primary maladaptive shame can be thought of as having *core primary maladaptive shame self-organizations* constructed from emotion-schematic memories of past shame experiences. It is a more trait-like experience—people with core maladaptive shame organizations often have a sense of themselves as inherently defective, as having fatal flaws, or as incompetent and lacking in worth. Shame is their core emotion experience; it is the emotional underbelly of low self-esteem and a negative self-concept (Greenberg & Iwakabe, 2011).

Kaufman (1996), in a seminal work on shame, referred to *internalized shame* as an important form of dysfunctional shame. A person who has internalized shame from the behaviors and opinions of others may experience great deal of shame in the present without the others being there and in response to situations that might elicit only mild embarrassment in other people in that situation (Greenberg & Paivio, 1997). This is an experience of primary maladaptive shame.

There are two different experiences of core shame. One is internalization of humiliation and having been shamed, usually from some form of abusive treatment. The other is shame for being alive. If the self's vitality and essence have never been recognized or nurtured, the person comes to feel insignificant and to feel that any self-expression is shameful. Based on previous experiences in which expressions of emotion or initiatives were not supported, the person comes to feel they have no right to be. Without permission to be, the core self withdraws to a deep buried place within, to protect it from the experience of not being seen and of being left hanging, alone and isolated. Internalized shame comes from the development of primary maladaptive schematic memories, which synthesize into a shame-based self-organization of worthlessness. This type of self-organization often develops in clients who were subjected to emotional, physical, and/or sexual abuse as children and/or in people who were repeatedly humiliated, diminished, or treated with contempt by important attachment figures, such as parents, or by peer groups. If one is treated like garbage, one comes to feel one is garbage. People may also have mini traumatic childhood experiences such as not being selected by peers to play on a team. Experiences of being shunned or not chosen can be internalized and may leave an indelible mark on a person's sense of self.

Another form of core maladaptive shame can be described as the shame of existing—of being a person with vitality, feelings, and needs. This form of shame develops when parents make children feel that their aliveness, feelings, desires, and behaviors are all unwanted. The parents have a total lack of recognition and responsiveness to the child's joy of being alive. Shaming is one of the most common modern child-rearing practices. It has replaced physical punishment, and all people are to some degree damaged by it. Sayings that reflect shaming in its milder form include "Children should be seen but not heard," and in its most intense form, "Don't exist or be a center of initiative." In between is experiencing that any self-expression is not welcome, is ignored, or is scolded. The effect is to have all vitality and any assertion snuffed out at the source. As a result, the self withdraws to where it is unreachable. This produces people who seem to be broadcasting "I'm not here." They have voices with very low energy, no eye contact, and postures of insignificance. The message is "I won't be a bother." These people's vitality has been so extinguished that it is hard to see, and they barely know it exists. But somewhere deep at the bottom of the inner vault it exists, alone and lonely. For these individuals, what is most therapeutic is having their vitality and initiative recognized by another person. Therapists need to reach into the darker resources of people's internal world, slowly, sensitively, and delicately to break the isolation of the hidden self.

Primary maladaptive shame from internalized shame is probably the most frequently occurring emotion in therapy, and it needs to be experienced to be amenable to transformation by new input. Studies have found a relation between adult self-reported feelings of frequent shame and adult self-reported early experiences of physical and sexual abuse (Hoglund & Nicholas, 1995; Webb et al., 2007). Maltreatment also occurs by subtle forms of communication that come from parents' use of disciplinary methods that use shame to control children. Psychological maltreatment often leaves children with a deep sense of shame. Webb et al. (2007) studied 280 young adults and found that adults' experience of shame and depressive symptoms correlated positively with their reports of childhood experiences of psychological abuse, containing rejection, neglect, and isolation. Another study, without specifically examining psychological abuse or shaming behaviors, found a link between adult feelings of shame and high conflict in the family of origin (Pulakos, 1996). These kinds of experiences, through overt abuse or subtle family communications, can scar children, leaving them with an inherent sense that persists into adult life—a sense that something is wrong with them, that they are bad or an unwanted burden. Abused children often decide that the pain they feel from parental maltreatment is their fault and is deserved because of the *way they are*. Children have an overriding need to believe that their parents care about them, and this need often leads them to infer that there must be something basically wrong or bad about them. This feeling results in a pervasive, lifelong sense of shame.

A sense of the self as flawed or unworthy and maladaptive shame have been found to be significant predictors of many psychological difficulties, especially depression. A meta-analysis that examined more than 100 studies with more than 20,000 participants found that shame and pathological guilt were both predictive of symptoms of depression, whereas "shame-free" guilt was not. Shame is also highly prevalent in social anxiety and in other types of anxiety disorders (Moscovitch, 2009; Shahar et al., 2015); in eating disorders (Kelly et al., 2013; Troop et al., 2008); posttraumatic stress disorder (Paivio & Pascual-Leone, 2010); and borderline, narcissistic, and antisocial personality disorders (Goss & Allan, 2009; Kelly et al., 2013; Kramer et al., 2018; Ritter et al., 2014; Troop et al., 2008). It is also proposed as a common underlying experience leading to aggression and violent behavior (Velotti et al., 2014) and is hypothesized to underlie culture-specific disorders, such a fear of being shamed in public (Greenberg & Iwakabe, 2011).

In addition to distinguishing between the different shame processes, it also is important to distinguish between experiences of external and of internal shame. *External shame* is the feeling of being shamed by others or by perceptions of what is going on in the mind of the other about us in reaction to events. It involves the awareness that one has lost position in one's social group and comes from evolutionarily developed concern about the possibility of being ostracized by the group. This form of shame comes from outside the self and involves the painful awareness that others view the self negatively. *Internal shame* comes from inside the self and involves negative self-evaluation and self-criticism rather than imagining another person seeing or judging. It is something people do to themselves—one's own views of self and one's self-condemnation are more important than others' views of self. Internal shame is painful insofar as people condemn themselves; external shame is painful insofar as people possess knowledge that others condemn them. For example, it is possible for someone who is obese to be aware that obesity is highly externally shamed (e.g., one medical diagnostic label is "grossly obese") if they live in a society that frequently judges obese people as being greedy and lazy, but they may not feel personally, internally ashamed because they are happy with their appearance. Generally, however, the correlation between external and internal shame is high.

One cannot talk about shame without at least a note on *narcissism*, a self-centered personality style with an excessive interest in one's needs and a lack of empathy for others. Pathological narcissism is characterized by the emotions of shame and rage. Shame underlies narcissism; it is the dysphoric affect underlying states of narcissism and vulnerability (Morrison, 1989). It is linked to lack of pride, low self-esteem, and vulnerability (Morrison, 1989).

Narcissistic people have a weak self-structure, which they cover up with grandiosity as the main form of protection. At some point, the sense of shame felt by people with narcissistic self-organizations develops into rage or extreme hostility and a desire to destroy whoever seemingly wants to diminish their strong self-image (Martens, 2005). This process is referred to as the *shame–rage dynamic*. People who are narcissistic have great difficulty tolerating failure and have a fragile self-esteem. Failure then leads to intense shame; they externalize and place blame elsewhere and are filled with rage. This form of shame about failure or perceived slights is often felt as rejection: The person's self-importance has been dismissed, leaving them feeling that they cannot impress others with their self-image.

SHAME AS IT APPEARS IN THERAPY

Therapists need to work with different forms of shame in different ways. Based on clinical work and a qualitative study of 36 patients with depression (Greenberg & Paivio, 1997; Greenberg & Watson, 2006), we identified a number of situations in which different forms of shame benefited from different in-session interventions to facilitate client change. The major types of situations were (a) helping clients to become informed by their primary adaptive shame, (b) transforming a sense of primary maladaptive shame (core shame), and (c) overcoming secondary shame. Transforming a sense of core primary maladaptive shame arose in three forms: (a) internalized shame, (b) contempt and self-disgust, and (c) self-blocking. Secondary shame appeared in two forms: (a) self-critical cognitions related to not living up to standards and (b) overcoming societal shame. Differential interventions for each form are discussed briefly in the following section and elaborated in later chapters.

Working With Primary Adaptive Shame

Primary adaptive shame needs to be acknowledged in therapy because it provides clients with valuable information about socially acceptable behavior and provides action dispositions to guide appropriate conduct. Shame in response to violations of one's own intrinsic standards and values (e.g., shame at engaging in unacceptable behavior, shame at loss of control in public, shame at being a bad person in one's own eyes, shame at being a bad parent) is adaptive. Acknowledging, in therapy, actions that one feels ashamed of can be very difficult but also very cleansing and is a first step in change. In a study of therapy with couples who experienced the emotional injury of betrayal, the expression of shame by the injurer to a partner as part of an apology was found to be the most significant ingredient in rebuilding trust and promoting forgiveness and far more impactful than an apology (Dearing & Tangney, 2011; Woldarsky Meneses & Greenberg, 2011, 2014). When injured partners saw their partners experiencing and expressing shame—feeling bad in their own eyes—the injured partners were more likely to trust that the partner wouldn't betray them again. They also appeared to feel that seeing their partners suffer the pain of shame balanced the sense of injustice, as they both had suffered. The injuring partners generally at first defended their actions with anger, but expression of underlying adaptive shame in particular helped promote relational forgiveness by the injured partner (Woldarsky Meneses & Greenberg, 2011, 2014). Primary adaptive shame thus can be a healthy antidote to unwarranted anger and can help transform blaming or defensive anger into apologetic forgiveness seeking. In this way, shame provides submissive approach tendencies that can be conciliatory and relationally reparative.

Working With Primary Maladaptive Core Shame

Shame usually presents in therapy in its maladaptive form. The aim in therapy is to transform this maladaptive emotion into more adaptive emotions. As noted earlier, core maladaptive shame involves a sense of one's whole self as worthless, defective, or unacceptably flawed. Because of shame, people hide away from others' gaze and avoid social contact. When they socialize, they are overly submissive or passive and avoid expressing opinions or they say what they think people want to hear rather than expressing what they think or feel. Reducing this form of core shame helps prevent relapse of depression and other affective disorders.

Internalized Maladaptive Core Shame

Primary maladaptive core shame is shame that has been deeply internalized as feeling defective or rotten at the core. It generally arises from maltreatment, prior humiliation, or abuse and is at the core of a sense of self as inferior, worthless, and/or unlovable. Words such as *defective*, *inadequate*, and *worthless* are used to describe this feeling. Many people who were mistreated, abused, or denigrated feel that they were somehow responsible, bad, or defective—like spoiled goods. If caregivers are the source of the pain and blame, the children blame themselves. The issue of self-blame is chronic in many disorders and especially in some forms of abuse: People end up blaming themselves for what they did or did not do. People who in the past had been treated by significant others with disgust or contempt internalize these feelings, directing them toward themselves.

Therefore, a major problem for many abused clients is their guilt. They feel that they were responsible for what happened and blame themselves. Even though they were powerless and lacked control, they feel they either deserved the abuse or brought it on themselves. Abuse often is a closely guarded secret, resulting in pervasive *shame-anxiety* (i.e., anticipatory anxiety about feeling shame) and fear of intimacy. A pathogenic experience of the self as defective develops. For example, a client who as a girl had been sexually molested declares, "No one would want me now." Intervention with these clients, who often feel shamefully responsible for the abuse, involves helping them "put the blame where it belongs" and to externalize it by expressing anger at the wrongs done to them.

Internalized core maladaptive shame also often develops from experiences of rejection for being different and judged inferior. One client, for example, felt a searing sense of shame about her infertility, feeling as if she weren't a real woman. Another man was interested in flower arrangement and the arts rather than sports as an adolescent and was shamed by his father for not being the right kind of man. He reported in therapy that for 16 hours a day, he had this internal voice in his head, "I'm not enough of a man." Whenever anyone complimented him on his creativity or criticized him in any way, he was driven deeply into shame.

People also are shamed for belonging to a particular class, race, gender, or sexual orientation. Primary maladaptive core shame from social comparison and ostracism or humiliation is essentially only different from the internalized shame from childhood maltreatment in that the shame is not imposed by a primary attachment figure. People still internalize a core sense of self as inferior, unacceptable, deviant, or somehow deeply flawed (Dearing & Tangey, 2011).

Negative Self-Evaluation and Core Shame

The second form of maladaptive core shame comes from internalized negative self-evaluation generated by criticism accompanied by contempt and disgust directed at the self. Negative self-evaluation is often internalized from having been told "You are bad" and results in the person saying this to themselves. Core shame from internalized criticism and the negative affect conveyed in the criticism is applied to the whole self. Contempt toward the self that accompanies these negative evaluations leads to feeling worthless and ashamed and like a failure (Whelton & Greenberg, 2005). Therapy involves accessing the self's feeling of shame, of being rotten at the core, and then developing the self's capacity to assert against the criticism to develop compassion for the self rather than contempt.

This form of maladaptive core shame is found in situations in which people felt a lot of blame and self-contempt. For instance, people who grew up in harshly punishing environments often condemn themselves for having transgressed moral standards and feel debilitating shame; people who were invalidated live in fear of being denigrated. The problem is not distorted or unrealistic values and standards or inappropriate self-blame; rather, self-condemnations about what they had done endured long after the incidents and were generalized to the entire self. The therapeutic aim, then, is to facilitate self-compassion and forgiveness, and possibly remorse, rather than shame. In guilt, a person regrets specific behaviors, but the self remains more or less intact, with the attentional focus placed on the potential reparative actions. As noted previously, the action tendency in primary maladaptive shame is one of hiding and attacking oneself with criticisms and contempt with no possibility of making amends or forgiving the self. The inability to accept one's mistake and forgive oneself results in chronic depression, anxiety, and increased maladaptive avoidant and self-harming behaviors, such as substance abuse, that help to regulate the unbearable experience of shame. The treatment objective in these situations is to shift overgeneralized shame and self-condemnation to regrets about the behavior or mistake. From there, the therapist can help the client move from shame to guilt and then to self-understanding and compassion toward the self.

Blocking Shame
Blocking shame is the third form of maladaptive core shame. It comes from feeling shame about expressing one's feelings and needs: "I am ashamed of my feelings; if you see them, I will die." Blocking shame silences the self, possibly in the service of maintaining connection with significant others. This type of shame develops from a history of nonresponsiveness and punishment of children's development of healthy agency, autonomy, vitality, and expressiveness. A person feels shame about a primary disallowed emotion or need, such as feeling ashamed of one's sadness, anger, or excitement. Although blocking shame could be seen as secondary shame because it is an emotion (shame) about an emotion (anger or excitement or sadness), this form of primary maladaptive shame is about one's whole self being allowed to express. These more wounded clients have a "shame of being," of existing, and a sense of needing to hide to protect the self or to apologize for being. Some people who were treated in this way feel ashamed of showing any of their internal experience and any expression. Others are ashamed of expressing or experiencing specific emotions, such as feeling ashamed of feeling weak or needy, of feeling sexual or angry, or even of feeling joy. They feel mortified if they

express the feeling, and even though it may be felt in more circumscribed circumstances, when it is felt, it is about the whole self needing protection.

Feeling afraid that certain internal experiences might emerge can also lead to shame-anxiety, which is often indistinguishable from feeling vulnerable. Shame-anxiety is about being afraid that one's internal experience will be judged as unacceptable. Clients often censor their emotions, interrupting expression by tensing muscles, holding their breath, and becoming silent.

Naming that the person feels shame, saying what it's about or expressing the self in any way, helps refute the shame message that one doesn't deserve to exist, to have a particular feeling, or to express it. This is followed by accessing the need, emotion, and expression that was interrupted by the shame and allowing and accepting the underlying feeling.

People often experience great shame about sexual feelings in sexually restrictive societies. Sexual shame is one of the harder issues to work with. It is helpful to bring in the view of common humanity and the universal aspects of sexual experience to help clients start to work with it in a nonjudgmental way. Therapists need to help clients accept their sexual nature by validating its normality. Because there is deep shame around sexuality, permission can be so normalizing and can be a powerful antidote to shame. A good example of normalizing masturbation comes from an anecdote from a health classroom. The male instructor said, "Boys, I want you to know that 90% of males report masturbating." This comment led to great signs of relief on the adolescent boys' faces. Then he said, "And 10% of males lie." This is a good example of a de-shaming intervention. It helps break down real or assumed barriers to a person's desires, and when barriers are removed, shame loses an important foothold on their feelings.

These three forms of maladaptive shame—core maladaptive, self-critical core, and blocking—often are related. They can be seen as forming a spectrum of a shame-based syndrome, which generates a chronic sense of worthlessness and inferiority.

Working With Secondary Shame

In contrast to primary maladaptive shame, secondary shame is less stuck to the self. It arises in relation to certain domains of experience, certain events, or certain times. In these situations, people are critical of themselves for not living up to standards, for moral lapses, or for concern about social rejection.

Self-Critical Shame
Self-criticism probably is the most common dysfunctional secondary shame process. People chastise themselves for not having lived up to standards or

for their shortcomings. They judge themselves for their mistakes and suffer the burden of many "shoulds." This type of shame involves issues that arise only periodically, such as failing to be a good person friend or parent in some situation. Therefore, these feelings are situationally triggered rather than involving a pervasive sense of self. This cognitive–affective process generates feelings of inferiority or feeling less than.

Shame from self-critical process differs from maladaptive shame in that it is activated only periodically and in specific situations and does not apply to the whole self. However, if it is pervasive and occurs chronically across situations, it comes from a more central self-organization and involves symptoms of core primary maladaptive shame. In this form of shame, a part of the self is the critic, criticizing or judging certain behaviors or characteristics of another part of the self. The criticized part feels like a failure and feels ashamed but often reacts defensively or with hostility.

The therapeutic task in working with self-criticism is to activate the secondary shame in the session and then guide the client's emotional processing to the underlying more primary experience, which may be sadness of loneliness, fear of rejection or even adaptive anger. This process is accomplished by having the client enact the shame-producing self-criticism to activate the primary emotional response of the self to the criticisms. The self-critical process involves a judgment (e.g., you are bad for doing something judged as wrong or for having failed an expectation), and the criticized part of the self feels ashamed. Some situational examples include feeling ashamed that one failed an exam and not telling anyone, feeling ashamed of being divorced, and feeling ashamed of making a mistake. A self-critical process might also be felt as embarrassment, for example a guest feeling embarrassed about spilling a glass of wine at a dinner table.

In contrast to core maladaptive shame, which involves a pervasive sense of worthlessness, secondary shame occurs as a result of perceived failure affecting one's sense of self, such as losing a job, not being competent at one's job, failing as a parent, or sinning by getting divorced. This secondary shame also differs from guilt in that working to overcome it involves bypassing the secondary shame to get to underlying emotion that shame is protecting against, like sadness, fear, or anger, or if that is not possible, viewing the failure as an action of part of the self rather than the whole self.

Societal Shame
Societal shame is not self-criticism for a failure but rather occurs as a result of loss of social position and damage to one's identity or public image. Societal shame involves feeling humiliated in the eyes of others. People feel isolated because

the shame blocks them from seeking out others with whom to share their sense of loss and sadness, and they end up alienated. They are unable to rebuild their interpersonal network. Societal shame can result when people who are a threat to a community are branded as outcasts because they're not adhering to the community's norms. Some examples include having an abortion, losing a high-paying job, experiencing a personal defeat, or getting divorced, especially in groups that reject these situations as violations of their codes.

The therapeutic aim is to validate clients' worth and help them strengthen their self-esteem. Clients with societal shame are most sensitive to how they appear and feel humiliated in the eyes of others. Although societal shame is often situational, it can evoke past trauma and unresolved conflicts in some clients, as well as lack of confidence, of self-worth, and of a sense of efficacy. Therapists need to validate the pain of this shame and help clients stand up to or get rid of the critical voice so that they can deal with the underlying loss.

There is also much societal shame about the body that is, to differing degrees, internalized. An example presented earlier illustrates how obesity can be a core source of shame, but the images of the perfect body and the quest for beauty in the advertising industry affect all people and can leave them feeling not perfect enough. More often than men, women experience a lot of body image shame as a function of society's promotion of perfect female body images. This can lead to eating disorders, which are also more prevalent in women than in men. *Comparativitis* (i.e., comparing oneself with others) is a core source of shame, especially in media-dominated, appearance-obsessed cultures, which now pervade the world. Given the unrealistic standards for women's appearance set by culture or by the media, it is hard not to come up short and feel shame. Growing up in a culture that values a slender shape can lead to women feeling self-conscious and resorting to dieting. Failed attempts at dieting can become an additional source of shame. Furthermore, society has created shame about illness, aging, dependency, deprivation, unhappiness, and poverty. These are all subjects for therapeutic work to help people come back to themselves and accept themselves as they are, rather than living up to unattainable images of ways of being.

In looking at societal shame, it is important to distinguish stigma from shame. Feeling different is a universal experience that all people have, regardless of gender, race, ethnicity, or sexual orientation, but it's not always shame. Some people are hurt and angry about stereotype threat—basically, being treated differently because of whatever group they are a part of. They feel perfectly adequate but not accepted as part of the human family. For example, imagine that you grew up in a family that celebrated your identity, and it completely resonates with how you've always felt about yourself.

Then, you get into some other group, and suddenly they're treating you as if there's something wrong with you. You might feel more anger than shame, and you are resilient. That's a very different experience from being treated negatively after having grown up in an environment in which your identity was validated.

Not all stereotype threats are internalized. For instance, if shame is not actually present, it's important not to call the feeling "shame," as doing so further diminishes the person who is experiencing stigma or stereotype threat. The most appropriate interventions, then, for societal shame are empathic attunement, validation of the need to protect oneself, and emotional support. Therapeutic strategies for societal shame include getting in touch with sadness due to loss of part of the self, affirming the sense of confidence in the previously demoralized self, and accessing positive emotions such as joy, compassion, and pride in oneself.

CULTURAL, ETHNIC, RACIAL, SEXUAL, AND GENDER CHALLENGES IN WORKING WITH SHAME

Regardless of culture, when facing the prospect (or the reality) of being devalued, people feel a painful emotion, avoid acting to cause or increase devaluation, and conceal any information that could have a negative effect on their reputation. Even though this experience of shame is universal, what activates shame and how it is expressed are particularly sensitive to cultural differences. Therefore, to work effectively with shame, therapists need to understand people's belief systems and cultural norms around shame.

Even the word *shame* has nuanced meanings in different languages. For example, Mandarin appears to encode four different types of shame (Bedford, 2004). Shame can be felt in relation to the loss of reputation, failure to obtain an ideal, personal failure, or social failure, and it may have some guilt-like qualities, such as encouraging reparations. Interestingly, the Chinese character for shame comprises two parts: the character for "ear" and the character for "stop." The composition of the character seems to suggest that people have the ability to stop a wrong behavior when hearing other people criticize them.

Additionally, different cultures conceptualize the self in different ways. These conceptualizations affect the meaning of shame (Ha, 1995; Kitayama et al., 1995). Most Western countries in North America and Europe are independence-focused cultures in which people typically consider the self as discrete and separate from others. Shame is tied to a sense of flawed and isolated self. However, in more interdependence-focused Eastern cultures, people tend to see the self as interconnected and relational. In these cultures, the idea of a separate self, divorced from others and private, may not even fully make sense. Rather, the "I" is infused with a lot of "we." Shame that is relational in nature is less likely to reinforce a sense of a separate, flawed self that leads to isolation. So, "shame" may serve different functions, have different meanings, and operate differently depending on context.

When working with clients who are immigrants or from different cultures, it is important to understand their beliefs, values, and perspectives, especially regarding societal shame. Therapists need to inquire into clients' religious, spiritual, or tribal beliefs and their views of the world to understand their practices related to dealing with shame. For example, with a client from an immigrant family, it is important to understand the client's standing in the family and in the community. Community is often an important part of a person's identity, and so abiding by ascribed roles, such as walking behind one's husband or obeying one's elders, is important. Violations of these roles or norms can be shaming.

Further, immigrants and people from different cultures may feel shame about seeking mental health treatment. They may find it difficult to share shameful experiences with a professional of a different culture, and they may feel shame about their inability to speak English well. For many clients, Western views related to autonomy, control, and individual achievement, which are often implicit in Western therapies, may be quite contrary to the client's views and may be seen as threatening. In collectivist cultures, in contrast, group harmony and interdependence of individuals are emphasized (Markus & Kitayama, 1991), and thus a person's sense of self may be more closely related to one's membership in groups and to filling one's duty than in Western cultures, where independence, autonomy, and uniqueness of each individual is valued.

In interdependent cultures, shame is given a primary role in regulating social roles and behaviors. Furthermore, the expression of negative emotions such as anger, contempt, and sadness is suppressed, and positive emotions such as joy and interest are used instrumentally to maintain and strengthen the tie with other group members. Concern with status, hierarchy, and seniority may also lead to instrumental use of certain emotional expressions for role management. In addition, in some cultures, being humble and acting with reservation are considered virtuous and respectful, whereas the expression of negative emotions is considered disrespectful and disloyal (Dearing & Tangey, 2011). The spontaneous and direct expression of one's internal experience may be looked down upon. Therefore, people from interdependent cultures may express positive emotions frequently in social situations and suppress negative ones. Negative emotions may be more openly expressed within one's private or intimate relationships.

Humiliation and other public forms of shaming are often used in child-rearing, education, and other forms of social trainings, such as corporate trainings, and may be accepted as normative. Again, it is important for therapists to be aware that shame can play important different roles in different cultures (Ha, 1995). In many collectivist cultures, clients have problems resulting from societal shame as well as secondary shame generated by self-criticism. In Japan, for instance, a category of culture-based phobic disorders includes fear of potentially being shamed publicly or through the others' gaze, fear of unwanted exposure, and fear of one's own inappropriate personal behaviors.

Therapists need to ensure that their clients understand the rationales for working on emotion and recognize that accessing, expressing, experiencing, and understanding their shame will be better than hiding it. In working with clients from collectivist cultures, therapists need to ensure that they inform their clients that expression of negative emotions in front of the therapist is not only allowed but also encouraged for resolution of emotional problems. Clients from a collectivist culture may believe that they need to behave well or that they need to show respect to the therapist, who is in the position of authority. Because the therapist–client relationship is formal rather than personal, clients may feel that they need to put on a "social face" and refrain from disclosing negative emotions. They may also feel that it is good to show instrumental shame as a sign of respect. In addition, the expression of anger, pride, and contentment—emotions that counteract shame—may be very difficult or even prohibited in the culture if the client perceives the therapist as an authority figure. The therapist needs to directly address these and other challenges to help clients drop their social masks, share their primary shame experience, and access their adaptive emotions. It is therefore important that the therapist directly offer therapeutic rationales regarding the importance of openly expressing and experiencing a variety of emotions in therapy.

It is also very important for therapists to recognize that clients from racial, ethnic, and sexual minority groups possess a unique set of lived experiences of shame and that their experience of being shamed may differ markedly from the therapist's own experience and history of shame. For example, one South Asian client was told when she was young that she smelled and her family smelled. It is important to recognize that individuals from minoritized groups in a heterosexist/racist/White-privileged society are continuously subjected to shame related to systemic racism, prejudice, and stigmatization and may have internalized homophobia or racism. In addition, it should be understood that individuals from minoritized groups have to deal continuously with expectations of rejection and discrimination as well as with direct experiences of discrimination and violence. A therapist's failure to recognize the unique aspects of shame in someone from one of these subcultural groups can cause ruptures in the therapeutic alliance and hinder the effectiveness of therapeutic interventions.

In helping people deal on a personal level with racism, therapists need to help link them with environments that are going to be more affirming. If people are in environments in which they're not getting a lot of affirmation—maybe they're the only person of their racial ethnic group in their classroom or office—and hear messages that there's something wrong with them in some way, they might work on finding alternative settings in which they can be affirmed. They can also be helped to work within that environment to increase its awareness of the shaming messages that it might be communicating and help the environment to shift. Therapists thus need to work with increasing affirmation, not only in the therapeutic relationship but also in the context that people are in. Part of working with this type of shame is outing it—making it visible—and moving on to create not just relationally validating relationships but also empowerment processes in the individual. It is important to guide clients dealing with discrimination to use their voices, speak their truth, and be heard. Therapists need to make sure clients are aware of what has been silenced and to provide an emotionally safe space for that voice to speak.

People of color struggling in a predominantly White world to find themselves and develop their racial identities often first have to realize that they have identified with White culture. They then may begin to show an interest in their own racial groups. At this point individuals may withdraw from White culture to delve into their own racial exploration as part of the effort to define a new identity. People may then choose to identify with pride as members of their race(s), come to appreciate other cultures, and balance all aspects of their heritage of having been born into a multicultural world.

To respond to the damage caused by internalization of discrimination, the therapeutic aim is to help clients develop pride in their identities. For example, regarding sexual identity, some clients initially use multiple self-protective strategies to block recognition of personal homosexual feelings and need to be helped in therapy to face their feelings. Clients may use defenses to attempt to deny or minimize same-gender feelings, but these defenses demand a lot of effort. After a gradual recognition and tentative acceptance of same-gender feelings and as people come to accept that they are not heterosexually oriented, they begin to accept themselves and feel positive about their identity. Rather than merely tolerating it, they integrate this identity as an essential aspect of self.

Again, it is important to note that the EFT principles for working with shame remain the same regardless of culture, ethnicity, religion, or gender. Shame is the same for women and men, but the expectations in North America that activate shame vary across genders and are driven by different gender-based norms. In a qualitative study by Brené Brown (2012), women reported a complex web of different expectations among them. Women reported experiencing shame related to perfection or taking care of others, whereas men's shame had more to do with status. Gender differences should alert the therapist as to what to focus on when working with shame. Again, it is important, from an EFT perspective, to emphasize empathy over any theoretical notions. Therefore, by listening empathically to affect, the therapist is guided to the client's central concerns.

CONCLUSION

Shame comes in different forms. Awareness of differences between primary and secondary shame, adaptive and maladaptive shame, and cultural variations in expression of shame will sharpen therapists' skills in working with shame. Therapeutic intervention needs to be targeted specifically to working with adaptive shame, maladaptive core shame, and/or secondary shame. It is most important to understand how to help clients with maladaptive core shame. This issue is discussed further in the next chapters.

4 HELPING CLIENTS ARRIVE AT SHAME

Relational Validation and Acknowledgment

If we can share our story with someone who responds with empathy and understanding, shame can't survive.

—Brené Brown

The next four chapters, including this one, cover the treatment of shame. Three basic categories of shame treatment are discussed: relational validation and acknowledgment, regulation, and transformation. Generally, shame treatment always starts with relational validation and the attendant disclosure and acknowledgment of shame in the session. Once shame is acknowledged, it is important to regulate shame so it can be tolerated and made accessible to new experience. Shame regulation is thus discussed in Chapter 5. Chapter 6 relays the transformation of shame by the process of changing emotion with emotion and emphasizes that the transformative emotion is often anger and this anger often leads to sadness. Anger often brings subsequent grief at what was lost, and so the essence of transforming shame is gaining access to new emotions, anger, or a combination of anger and sadness. These three forms of intervention—relational validation, regulation, and transformation—do not necessarily occur in all cases or in a lockstep sequence, and each sometimes appears on its own.

---

https://doi.org/10.1037/0000393-004
Shame and Anger in Psychotherapy, by L. S. Greenberg
Copyright © 2024 by the American Psychological Association. All rights reserved.

RELATIONAL VALIDATION

When clients feel safe and accepted, they can take risks of disclosing and acknowledging the hidden shameful aspects of self so they can be open to new disconfirming experience in the session. Therapists' empathic affirmation of clients' vulnerability and provision of safety reduces clients' interpersonal shame and allows for greater tolerance of their anxiety about experiencing and expressing intrapersonal shame. When the client's initial vulnerability about disclosing their shame has passed and they feel confident that their experience is accepted, other interventions may be used.

Sharing feelings of shame brings great vulnerability and feelings of being exposed, which evokes fears of potential rejection or judgment, which then bring more shame (Dearing & Tangney, 2011). It's a sequence that is difficult to escape, but acceptance and validation by another person, especially someone important to you, can break this painful cycle. Shame, therefore, needs interpersonal validation (P. DeYoung, 2022; Kaufman, 1996). Therapists need to help clients to talk about what is painfully shameful and to name their shame. An understanding, supportive relationship is the essential aspect of the treatment of shame, not just a precondition to further work with shame. The therapeutic relationship enables a *healing interpersonal emotional experience*. Shame is created within relationships, and a relationship with another human being is needed to transform it.

In this chapter, I discuss three major ways I have found the relationship to be central in the treatment of shame. The first is the provision of a safe relationship with a therapist to promote disclosure. The second is through the provision of a corrective emotional experience, and the third is by helping clients acknowledge and experience shame in the session to make it accessible to transformation. This third aspect is how the relationship, by helping clients tolerate and regulate shame, makes the shame amenable to transformation. The chapter ends with a transcript of a session involving working relationally with shame, demonstrating how the therapist's provision of safety, presence, and acceptance facilitates disclosure.

PROVISION OF A SAFE RELATIONSHIP

In therapy, shame is ever-present as clients worry about what can be safely revealed and what should remain hidden—shame is an emotion rarely named but often felt. The therapy situation is also inherently shameful in that the client is in a subordinate weak position, feeling, in some way, like a failure by having to open themselves to someone in a stronger, more expert position. When talking is too shameful, an *empathic validating relationship* in which the therapist is present, accepting, and compassionate is crucial in helping clients feel safe in the session so that shame can be disclosed and then open to transformation (Dearing & Tangney, 2011). Clients have the opportunity to experience being accepted and understood when they reveal their flaws and shortcomings rather than to suffer the anticipated rejection or the judgment that they are defective or worthless. When the client can share their sense of despair and hopelessness surrounding the shame with the therapist, the therapist's understanding and validation of the pain under the hopelessness activates the client's unfulfilled yearnings for emotional contact and connection blocked by the shame, and it generates hope. This human contact with the therapist breaks the client's sense of isolation. Hope emerges when the client feels that their sense of hopelessness is understood.

Therapists therefore need to create relationships that are safe, respectful, and trusting enough so patients experiencing shame can be vulnerable, open up emotionally, and connect. This requires great attuned responsiveness and sensitivity on behalf of the therapist. Therapists need to have worked on their own shame or proneness to shame to remain connected and fearless in the face of clients' shame. Being present to clients' shame will be difficult if a therapist hasn't been able to tolerate their own shame. Reading about shame is also helpful to desensitize therapists to their shame.

The first aspect of helping clients arrive at shame is the safety of the relationship and acceptance by the therapist. Shame festers and grows with secrecy, silence, and negative judgments. The antidote to shame is authentic expression in a facilitative relationship. Ultimately, this requires clients being able to show up as they are and to say how it really is for them. To facilitate this, therapists need to be empathic, attuned to affect, and compassionate. To help clients show up, therapists need to show courage, disclosure, curiosity, and compassion in their relationships.

Central to working with shame, therapists need to validate the feelings and needs associated with that shame. A validating stance is essentially de-shaming. Validating statements are ones such as: "It must have left you feeling so humiliated to be treated like that by a father to his own son," "That must have been so shaming and so painful," and "You felt so afraid to cry because you would just be called a crybaby by all your family, but you were sad and needed to cry." Shame experience also needs to be normalized with the notion of a common humanity. Therapists need to normalize clients' desire to protect their dignity, and so when it is hard for clients to look at their therapists when they speak, therapists need to validate such experiences as expectable and to communicate that it is understandable that it is difficult to look at the therapist when feeling vulnerable.

Presence is the first key factor in therapists' way of working with client shame. Our therapeutic presence theory of relationships (Geller & Greenberg, 2002, 2012, 2023) suggests that the therapist's ability to be present, fully immersed in the moment, without judgment or expectation, and with and for the client facilitates healing. Presence involves a way of *being* with clients that ultimately optimizes the *doing* of therapy. As part of this theory, we have defined presence and developed a client and therapist questionnaire measure of therapist perceived presence as having the following five components:

1. Being completely in the moment
2. Bringing one's whole self into the encounter with the client physically, emotionally, cognitively, and spiritually
3. Being grounded in one's own body
4. Receptively taking in the verbal and bodily expression of the client's moment-by-moment emotional experience
5. Extending to meet the other in an empathic and congruent manner

Therapeutic presence involves being open and receptive to what is most poignant in the client's experience in the moment. This promotes an attunement to the inner world of the other that is based on sensing the other's experience as well as being aware of one's own experience and understanding the relationship between them. When therapists are present, they feel both grounded in their own bodies in the moment and in contact with themselves. Simultaneously they are open, receptive, and immersed in what is coming from the client. There is an increase of perceptual awareness and an experience of spaciousness. Therapeutic presence involves the intention of being with and for the client, in the service of healing.

Being present to a client's shame involves a constant process of the therapist being receptive and attuned to the client's moment-to-moment experience so that the client's shame can be sensed within by the therapist. This sense of the inner world of the other, felt in resonance with the client, allows the therapist to connect with the client's experience with empathy, acceptance, genuineness, compassion and sensitivity to all the nuances of shame. In our view, therapeutic presence is a precondition to empathy, a positive therapeutic alliance, and good therapeutic outcome (Geller & Greenberg, 2002, 2012, 2023; Geller et al., 2010; J. A. Hayes & Vinca, 2017; Pos et al., 2011).

Empathic attunement to affect is also important in working with shame because it is a core painful affect. Empathic attunement to affect goes beyond conveying understanding. It involves the body-based sensing of the client's inner world, feeling and experiencing what the client may be feeling as if one is the client, metaphorically being in their skin while maintaining oneself as separate (Rogers, 1959). Empathic attunement to affect goes beyond *empathic understanding*. The emphasis is on resonating with affect, which creates a sense for the client of feeling felt (Stern, 1985). The dyadic regulation of affect involves a two-person experience of *reciprocal affective resonance*, which results in a sense of connection between client and therapist. The focus is clearly on affective experience, not meaning. This type of connection promotes the co-regulation of affect (cf. Fosha, 2000).

Attunement to clients' affective states involves the therapist's ability to be in the moment and to mirror the clients' experiences in a manner that goes beyond words so the clients feel felt. In addition to communicating understanding, therapists also need to mirror their clients' manner of experience as conveyed by their body. Therapists need to respond to their clients' vocal and facial expressions, the way the clients hold their bodies, their postures, how they sit, their micromovements, breathing, vocal tone, and physiology. The therapist needs to match the client's pacing, the tempo of the interaction, and the client's state; their biorhythms become coordinated. This is expressed in a matching of language use, vocal tone, pauses, and other verbal behaviors (Watson, 2021). All of this occurs automatically.

Polyvagal theory (Porges, 2007, 2011) has illuminated how cues from people trigger the neuroception of safety in receivers, sending the message that it is safe to approach or not. There is a "face-to-heart connection" that functions continuously to support affect regulation in relationships. The therapist's face directly influences the client's parasympathetic nervous system. When cues from another person trigger the neuroception of safety in the receiver, it sends the message that it is safe to approach. In addition, eye contact releases oxytocin, the cuddle hormone, which provides comfort. Levinas (1969) proclaimed that the face is a source from which all meaning appears. The other's face, for Levinas, is an appeal, a call to action. When we address each other as subjects, not as objects, this way of seeing provides us with direct access to the meaning of others' experiences without having to rely on verbal communication. As living beings, we all have the capacity to engage directly with others, to perceive meaning directly in human expression, and to be able to grasp intuitively what the other needs from us.

Therapists need to cue clients that they are safe, and a large part of this cueing occurs nonverbally. With safety, a client's defenses lower, and therapeutic engagement becomes possible. It is through presence and attunement that therapists can activate their clients' neuroception of safety so they can process their shame. Safeness is cued by many aspects of therapists' behaviors.

Therapists need to be attuned and responsive to both nonverbal and verbal signs of in-session, shame-related experience. Nonverbal communication is probably the most important (Velotti et al., 2014). Cues that signal safety are things such as:

- Softness in eyes
- Prosody of voice, synchronizing with client's changing voice
- Show of interest
- Adequate provision of space
- Centered and grounded yet relaxed and open body posture
- Slow and even breathing
- Attention to the client and the present moment between them

It also is important for therapists to be aware of when they may be cueing non-safety as well as attuned to any small signs of shame that may arise in clients. Distraction, shifting or fidgeting, any hint of judgment, facial expression of disapproval, or even surprise can indicate some lack of interest or acceptance and may cue lack of safety.

Verbal narrative signals related to clients' feeling of safety also abound and need to be noticed and attended to. Examples include:

- Signals of self-criticism in language such as "something is wrong with me," "I feel stuck," "I felt stupid"
- Subtle cues of blaming or judging
- Comments about therapy, such as "I didn't want to come today," or jokes about "hating being here"
- Indications that it is somehow degrading to be in therapy, such as "Having to pay for help is humiliating"
- Talking about humiliating experiences intellectually rather than talking about the immediate experience

Client vocal quality is also a sign of potential shame or withdrawal. Examples include:

- High-pitched voice
- Monotone, or low-energy limited voice that is thin and wispy
- Any indication of the vocal stress of constriction
- Rapid speech or abrupt pauses

Client body language that conveys shame includes:

- Head lowered
- Shoulders slumped
- Chest narrowed or collapsed

- Freezing or throat closing
- Squirming or discomfort in seat
- Laughter
- Shrugging off that covers embarrassment

Facial expressions include:

- Downturned lips
- Downcast eyes
- Averted eye gaze
- Glazed look in face
- Blushing or flushing
- Facial touching
- Pursed lips
- Arched eyebrows (fear)

Therapists who are present are able to read shame cues and bring the client back to safety by doing such things as:

- Pausing and slowing down
- Naming where they are
- Using co-regulation techniques like breath entrainment
- Providing positive comments
- Responding with right-brain-based nonverbal communication

When therapists are present, they use their bodies to listen, which helps their clients regulate the intensity of their shame. Therapists need to pay attention to whether they have shamed the client by not understanding the client or have been misattuned and have missed something important. Again, trust is needed for clients to reveal to the therapist what they consider to be their deepest flaws and about what they are most ashamed. Shaming clients produces tears or ruptures in the working alliance. Healing these ruptures in the relationship and correcting current misunderstandings can be highly therapeutic (Dearing & Tangney, 2011).

Use of language is also important. Clients often do not use the word *shame*, as it is very intense, and so therapists need to use graded language, starting off with words like *diminished*, *smaller*, or *embarrassed* and building up (possibly) to the use of the word *shame*. The vocabulary for shame is substantial. Additional words that can be used are *uncomfortable, foolish, stupid, disrespected, helpless, powerless, weak, inferior, inept, unworthy,* or *inferior*. It is also important to note that it is not essential to use the word *shame*, but its use does sometimes help crystallize the person's experience. Shame resolution is discussed in detail in

Chapter 5. To acknowledge shame is, in itself, highly shaming and carries the implication that what the shame is about may in fact be true. For example, for a client to say, "I feel so ashamed of being stupid," opens the door to admit in front of another the possibility that one is actually stupid, with whatever implications this admission has for the person. A client who did use the word *shame* said, of her sexual abuse as a child, "I was ashamed of myself." But many clients did not use the word *shame*. For example, a male client said, "You know I feel very small, no confidence. I feel like, uh, nothing, like a big zero." Another client, talking about the impact of years of a father's abuse, said, "I felt so guilty to be alive." This client used the word *guilty* but said it with such great poignancy, dropping his face in shame, making it clear that it was actually maladaptive shame, akin to shame of being or existing.

Therapist empathic affirmation (Greenberg et al., 1993) is a specific intervention designed to be applied at a marker of vulnerability. In-session expressions of maladaptive shame are quintessential markers of client vulnerability. The therapist does not engage in empathic exploration focused on a leading edge to deepen experience and discover more but rather helps clients to stay with and tolerate the experience of shame, to open it to feeling the acceptance of the therapist and thus to access their own resilience. Emotions that emerge from revealing shame and having those emotions validated by the therapist are part of a growth-producing experience in that new adaptive emotions and action tendencies emerge, such as reaching out to connect to others or asserting one's desire to live (Greenberg, 2002; Greenberg et al., 1993).

People who suffer from core shame rarely allow themselves to experience positive emotions. They may feel too vulnerable to feel or express joy excitement out of the fear that any good feelings would be taken away. Therapy needs to help people access joy and pride in self and to open up and disclose to others.

PROVISION OF A CORRECTIVE EMOTIONAL EXPERIENCE

Interpersonal corrective emotional experiences (Alexander & French, 1946) are an antidote to shame. If, for example, you feel embarrassed or ashamed about having let down someone you care about and that person ends up connecting with you, accepting you, and possibly even forgiving you, the sense of acceptance from the other helps wash away the shame. Arriving at emotion and sharing vulnerable feelings with a therapist thus is the sine qua non of the treatment of shame (Kaufman, 1996).

Behind the pain of shame is a tremendous desire to be connected and accepted. Shame wants to make one hide but at the same time, within shame is the motivation to belong, to be connected, to be known and accepted (Leach & Cidam, 2015; Tignor & Colvin, 2017). We feel shame when we care deeply. When someone reaches out to you with empathy and compassion after you have revealed something about which you feel ashamed, it is a transformative experience, and you feel loved and accepted. Relational acceptance is a corrective emotional experience for shame.

The therapy relationship is an important source of healing of shame when it provides a corrective emotional experience. New emotional experience coming out of new interactions with the therapist can disconfirm expectations because the experienced acceptance contradicts the expectation of rejection. It is not a cognitive change of beliefs but the new emotional experience of acceptance that changes the shame. This is a corrective emotional experience, and it repairs traumatic earlier shaming relational experiences. Because dealing with one's weaknesses and vulnerability always involves some degree of shame or sense of failure, therapy offers multiple opportunities for the regulation of shame by providing security and soothing from the therapist's empathy. Corrective emotional experiences with the therapist happen in an ongoing fashion, as clients experience their feelings being attuned to and validated by their therapist.

Therapists also need to explore and understand the development of shame by delving into a client's historical context. They need to show empathy and compassion for how painful all this must have been. It is important to bring the historical sense of shame alive in the session, into the here and now of the client's experience. For shame not to fester in the client's internal world, it needs to be brought sensitively into the present. Shame needs to be processed directly, which means it needs to be experienced and symbolized with the therapist in the session. As stated, one of the most helpful ways of bringing shame into the room is therapist presence. In addition, curiosity and exploratory questions are helpful. Therapist empathy needs to be curious and promote exploration through gentle inquiry about what else may be happening internally or asking what else the client may be feeling.

Clients, however, often find it difficult to disclose certain aspects of their experience for fear that the therapist will be disgusted and repulsed, if not overtly then covertly. In these cases, therapists need to convey acceptance and work with clients to approach the hidden material in a graded manner. For example, a client who was too ashamed to talk about aspects of her sexual abuse was asked to write about it and then read it out loud in the session. Over time, she was able to make eye contact with the therapist and feel stronger as she continued to disclose. Similar to working with traumatic fear, the shame narrative needs to be disclosed in small steps so the client can experience mastery of the shame rather than a re-experience of its overwhelmingness. In this way, the client feels strength, agency, and dignity in disclosing rather than overwhelm and humiliation.

Additionally, specific new emotional experiences with the therapist that supply an undoing of specific patterns of interpersonal experience provide a corrective experience. People's core emotion schemes of shame change as a result of positive interpersonal experience. Clients often test the therapist by sharing a little shame-based vulnerability to see how the therapist responds and how safe it feels (Weiss et al., 1986). Clients who fear being shamed may test to see if the therapist will invalidate them for feeling inadequate or even for their rage. If the therapist validates the experience rather than judging or shaming the client, this corrective emotional experience helps undo past negative experience. The goal for clients, with the help of the safety in therapy, is to experience mastery in re-experiencing shame that they could not handle in the past. Clients in therapy thus need to re-experience a different more positive outcome. If the client expresses shame or anger to the therapist and is accepted and understood rather than being shamed or judged, they experience that they can assert without being put down or can open up without being rejected; this new experience promotes change.

The therapist, in addition, can be thought of as serving the function of a transitional conductor who promotes an experience for client of transitioning from shame to a more salutary state such as assertive anger or the sadness of grief. Anger would then undo shame. Good caregivers do this with infants in distress. The caregiver first calms the distressed feeling, accepting and validating the feeling: "There, there, that was scary." When the infant has calmed down from the soothing, the caregiver introduces some novel stimulus like a rattle or teddy bear, essentially to evoke a new emotion: "Look at this. Look at his cute nose." The child shifts emotional states, and life proceeds. The infant experiences two things—that emotional distress can be soothed and, even more important, that it is possible to transition from a negative emotional state to a more positive one.

A great deal of fragile shame-based clients have probably never experienced this combination of feeling soothed and transitioning to a better state. Instead, they have learned experientially that if they enter a shame state it sucks them in, and they don't know how to get out. When the therapist empathizes with and validates the client's shame and the pain of the shame with a statement like "just so hurtful, so diminishing, when what you really needed from your teacher was an understanding look, a supportive hand and some support and protection from this cruel humiliation by the other kids," the client has a new experience and begins to internalize the sense of support and validation. At this point a transition out of shame is possible. Therapy thus provides two new experiences: It is possible for painful emotional states of shame to be soothed, and it is possible to change the shame by transitioning to more positive emotional states.

FACILITATING THE ACKNOWLEDGMENT OF SHAME

It is important to note a difference in acknowledging and allowing or accessing shame. The first step and the one being referred to here is acknowledging shame, which is a form of knowing or naming. Accessing and allowing comes later. Accessing is a form of doing, actually having an embodied experience of shame and emotionally expressing it. Acknowledgment is more a form of enactment than knowing. The therapist first needs to work on acknowledging shame and only later can work on accessing it to transform it.

Often, helping clients have a sense of control over their approach to shame helps them to eventually acknowledge and experience it. In helping clients bring shame into the room so they can work on it, therapists can ask clients to get a working distance from the shame so as to be able to reflect on it. This can be facilitated by seeing the feeling as a part of them, not the whole of them, and helps move the client to "having the feeling" rather than "the feeling having the client." The client can then stop being entranced by the feeling and can look at it from a distance. The client needs to observe the emotion coursing through their body to symbolize the experience of it in words. For example, one can create a safe distance from an overwhelming sense of shame by adopting an observer's stance and then may be able to describe the fear as, say, a tight spring-like coil in one's stomach. This helps reduce the intensity. Externalizing shame by putting it out there and describing it helps clients objectify the shame, rather than identify with it, so they can begin symbolizing and transforming it. Therapists can also help undo the shutting down that can occur in shame by accessing movement, for instance by having clients change their postures by sitting up or looking at the therapist. Clients can be encouraged to shift attention to more than self—the world—and to look out, rather than being looked at.

In providing a corrective emotional experience, it is helpful to see that shame can be about attachment or about identity and so the corrective experience needs to fit the client's shame experience. Table 4.1 illustrates *attachment shame*, which is about exclusion/rejection and connection/belonging, and *identity shame*, which involves feelings of failure/worthlessness and is more about status/evaluation of worth than about connection. In addition,

TABLE 4.1. Comparing Attachment Shame With Identity Shame and Feelings of Guilt

Attachment shame	Identity shame	Connecting guilt (separate from shame)
Damage to connection	Damage to self and reputation (inward)	Hurt caused to the other (outward)
Feeling excluded, rejected, sad, lonely	Feeling paralyzed, anxious, empty	Feeling sorry, remorseful
Others' judgments of whole self—*who one is*	Negative self-judgments of the whole self—*who one is*	Judgments of own behavior—*what one did*
Action tendency is to withdraw, hide	Action tendency is to apologetically deny or avoid self-harm	Action tendency is to genuinely apologize, make reparations, make amends

making things more complex are experiences of guilt involving bad behavior and about hurt caused/repair that need to be distinguished from shame (Tangney, Miller, et al., 1996).

Further, it is important to understand that the emphasis of what the shame is about can be external or internal. External shame is concern about how others see us, and internal shame is more about how we see ourselves. It is helpful in providing corrective experiences that the therapist be attuned to whether the client is dealing with attachment or identity concerns and whether the focus is on how others see them or how they see themselves.

FACILITATING APPROACHING AND REVEALING SHAME

When relational safety is established, shame is acknowledged through disclosure. The aversion to shame is overcome, it is symbolized, and the painful feelings are named and begin to be experienced. Experiencing shame is at the center of the arriving phase. Therapists guide clients to attend to and acknowledge shame, disclose the feelings of shame, experience it in the room, cocreate a stance of willingness to develop curiosity toward it, and, finally, experience it to some degree.

Because shame is so painful, clients at first automatically deflect from experiencing it. Protecting against shame prevents clients from attending to their internal experience of it. Clients may "talk about" shaming experiences but avoid the actual discomfort of the bodily felt experience. It is important for therapists to reduce problematic protection against shame and promote experience, awareness, and acceptance of shame: You have to name it to tame it. The first step in problem solving is naming the shame and what it is about. Anything we resist persists, so acceptance is crucial, and naming is the first step in accepting. In addition, as mentioned earlier, therapists are not actually making people feel bad. They already feel bad, and therapists are helping them face and overcome the bad feeling.

Naming shame and related emotions and putting words to the bodily experience can help clients allow and tolerate the shame. People who use words to describe their internal states are more flexible and capable of regulating their emotions in an adaptive way (Kircanski et al., 2012; Ochsner et al., 2002). It is helpful for therapists to reach in and speak the unspoken for clients to help them name what they are feeling. Labeling intense shame helps keep the limbic system more in balance (decreasing amygdala activity) than does observing having an intensely emotional experience without naming it (Hariri et al., 2000; Lieberman et al., 2007).

Empathic Conjecture

A major method to help facilitate access to underlying emotion is empathic conjecture. This method involves the therapist offering a tentative guess at the client's immediate, implicit experience. This initial guess often is followed by a question as to whether the guess fits. The conjecture is based on knowledge of both the client and human nature in that situation. It uses a client's nonverbal behavior. The therapist is trying to help give the person words for things that they don't yet have words for. Therapists are not interpreting or declaring "it is this!" Rather, a conjecture is stated tentatively, recognizing that it may not fit, and is followed by a query as to whether it fits or not. For example, a client was talking about her anger at her brother who was addicted to drugs, in trouble with the law, and bringing disgrace on the family. The therapist became aware that the client did not appear angry but looked rather ashamed. The therapist saw the anger as secondary and protecting against shame, and guided the client toward her primary shame, saying, "I hear you are angry, but I also see the almost-shame expression on your face. Does that fit?" The client nodded and burst into tears.

When therapists recognize behaviors that cover shame, such as laughing at painful experiences or bravado about bad feelings, they can empathically conjecture about the underlying experience. A response to bravado about rejection might be "I hear the determination in your voice, like there's a part of you that puts on a brave front, but it sounds like another part of you is left feeling kind of insignificant." An empathic conjecture to the feelings of shame underlying a client's social anxiety might be: "It's like, if they saw you for who you really are, you feel they'd reject you and you would feel diminished," (Dearing & Tangney, 2011).

Drawing attention too quickly to shameful aspects of experience, however, often increases the client's tendency to retreat or to close off emotionally. Clients therefore need therapists to help them face their shame by gently guiding them to attend to their bodily felt experience and acknowledge their shame in small steps. Responses such as: "As you were talking about what happened to you, I noticed you looked away, and I imagined how diminishing that must have felt," will focus client's attention on their internal experience. Conjectures on the discomfort associated with feeling small, worthless, and humiliated in the presence of another by saying, "That must have hurt or been so humiliating," can be helpful. Empathically reflecting and normalizing how painful it is to feel small, worthless, and humiliated are also helpful. It is important for therapists to normalize a client's wish to protect their dignity and the inclination to look away from their therapists while they speak by saying such things as: "It is so humiliating when a boss criticizes someone in front of coworkers." The therapist needs to guide clients to attend to and acknowledge their shame. Interventions such as: "It's embarrassing to talk about such private things, but it's important," or "It's hard to ask for help, it can make one feel a bit like a child, but we all need help at times," validate the client's internal struggle and offer support.

Responses that help name the shame a client feels include: "Yes, as kids we all need so desperately to be accepted, to belong, and it feels so awfully shaming to be excluded like that," or "How humiliating to be exposed like that, caught on the toilet, with them laughing at and pointing fingers at you." Clients then might reveal how alone and rejected they felt as a child and how they so desperately wished that they were liked or loved in spite of their failings. Naming shameful feelings with a trusted other, putting into words what was felt, helps clients take an observer's perspective from a safe distance outside the emotional experience so that the shame no longer occupies his or her entire being (Dearing & Tangney, 2011). Seeing one's own shame from a safe distance helps self-compassion emerge.

Facilitating the Steps Toward the Client Experiencing Shame

Therapists must not only focus on the feeling of shame but also address how painful it is to feel shame. Acknowledgment of the hurt or pain provides an easy entry for clients to discuss what the pain is about, which of course is the shame. Client acknowledgment of core shame is helped by therapists keeping a gentle, consistent focus on the client's internal experience of pain and by empathically focusing on the underlying pain of the wounds to self-esteem and the pain of not belonging. Shame needs attention, and so does the pain of shame.

If secondary reactions are expressed by a client, the therapist can support these emotions through validation. For instance, if a client expresses reactive anger to cover shame at being humiliated, their anger can be supported by validating it because it is part of their experience. This validation, however, should be followed by empathizing with their underlying core experience of shame, and the anger should not be viewed as a primary emotion. An example of such a refocusing intervention that involves conjecturing about the underlying shame is: "Yes, so angry at being used in that way by him. No wonder you feel angry at being treated that way. Being used that way must have left you feeling so hurt, and so—what?—kind of unvalued—unimportant, or what?"

Focusing clients' attention on their shame can be very threatening for them, especially for clients with fragile self-esteem. Before activating shame, therapists need to assess clients' ego strength to ensure they will not feel overwhelmed by the therapist focusing on the dreaded shame. Therapists need to be sensitive and responsive to client fragility; they need to unobtrusively accept and respect the client's tendency to withdraw. It may be necessary, with fragile clients, to first build self-esteem before they can tolerate going into their shame experience. Therapists can suggest installing a safe place clients can go internally, where they can feel valued and secure before going into shame. Clients also need to be assured that they have control of when to come out of re-experiencing a shame experience and come into the present, to get the support of the therapist, or to go to their safe place to help regulate. Power sharing, taking a nonexpert stance, and communicating that therapists don't see clients as sick but rather as involved in the struggles of being human all help clients feel validated.

When clients are experiencing shame in the session, they may be too dysregulated to be able to process their shame productively. Often it is helpful to talk about the client's shame in the session following one in which it is too aroused by saying, for example, "Last week you felt so ashamed that you had used again and lied about it to your recovery group. Let's try to explore that a bit more in today's session." This type of statement is useful when the client is more regulated, stronger, and can more easily talk about what happened.

Shame is often so unbearable that it may be hidden not only from the therapist but also from the self through disclaiming the experience and action tendency, by changing the topic, or by secondary contempt, envy, or rage. To get to the shame, therapists need to first promote exploration of the feelings that are being expressed, such as anger and disappointment, and look for entries into the underlying shame experience. These underlying feelings need to be followed gently in a way that conveys interest and acceptance. Again, as clients experience their therapists as accepting and interested, they become more open and accepting of their shame. The shame then becomes gradually more bearable, and the client can begin to tolerate it. As the shame comes more and more into awareness, it can be explored and discussed.

What is needed by the client is to lean into the shame but not overidentify with it, to be present to what's going on but not be defined by it, and to have emotional curiosity about it. Acceptance of suffering—facing shame rather than running from it—is of great help in overcoming shame. Acknowledging shame and accepting it involves being able to observe it, acknowledge that it exists, welcome it, and accept it. People need to stand back from their shame, experience it as a wave that washes over them, and then move past it and move on. It is helpful to concentrate on different elements that make up the emotion, such as a specific sensation in one's body, or create some image to capture it.

Clients need the therapist's acceptance and attunement to enable this type of exploration. As much as the emphasis on activating unexpressed shame is needed to access it for reprocessing, therapists also need to work within the client's window of tolerance. So, working inside the client's zone of tolerance involves promoting arousal but not too much and not too little. Therapists need to start by talking about small or mid-intensity shame-related topics and show an interest in learning more about what was or is shameful. The aim is to help clients talk about their experience of shame.

In many cases, it is advisable to provide a rationale to explain the value of experiencing and disclosing shame. Clients come to therapy generally believing that their feelings are so painful and self-damaging that it is best to put their shame in a box and close the lid. The therapist's offer to face the shame, head on, is therefore counterintuitive. But when clients understand shame is a social emotion, they begin to understand that the only way to break free from it is to connect with others and share their shame. Shame, even more than feeling bad about oneself, actually motivates people to do something that allows them to reconnect with others. This is what shame was evolutionarily designed to do—allow people to reconnect with their tribes. So, what really is needed is to connect? Without a clear discussion of the rationale for experiencing shame and the creation of an alliance to go into the shame, the client may perceive the therapist as critical or coercive. When clients are reluctant to talk about shameful past experiences, therapists need to encourage them with responses such as: "I know it's painful, but it's so important to talk about it; otherwise, it stays in the dark, eats away at you, and keeps you so isolated," or "Shame is about not being seen by others, but it keeps you trapped. I'm inviting you to share what you feel ashamed about so we can try to help you deal with it."

Very often, shame is key in clients who were sexually abused. Perpetrators tell the child they [the child] really wanted the molestation and that they liked it, the victim's body may have responded, and they may have returned to re-engage. Their seducers hook them in with the client's own shame. In abuse cases involving a dominance/submission relationship and feelings of degradation, humiliation, and powerlessness, shame is central. The shame experience is exacerbated if parents have used shame as a way of controlling the child's behavior. In the therapeutic relationship, then, it's essential that the therapist create an atmosphere of acceptance, care, and compassion and that the therapist is sensitive to not re-shaming the client.

Additional Aspects of Responding to Shame

Focusing on clients' unmet needs related to shame is also very important. Therapist responses not only need to validate how the denigration and unmet yearning to belong left the client feeling so unworthy but also to affirm that they *deserved to have their needs met*. Shame results from an evaluation that the need for validation and worth has not been met or it has been violated. Implicit in shame is a need for validation. It is not enough to empathize with the shame and remark how painful it is. Therapists must also focus on the unmet need for validation, acceptance, and belonging. A feeling of having deserved to have the need met is a potential resource in the personality for overcoming the shame. When the client begins to feel they deserved respect rather than humiliation, the self is strengthened, and the shame begins to be transformed.

Adoption of any more knowing position by the therapist can be shame producing. Interpretation of patterns of interaction or of resistance, cognitive restructuring, and error correction can be shaming if they are experienced as criticism and invalidation. Very fragile, shame-prone clients have often, in their lives, experienced intrusive shaming or advice from others who have provided insights or suggestions during periods of shame that just made them feel more inadequate. These have invaded people's inner worlds and left them shamed. So, clients can be very sensitive to any type of invalidation. Small automatic elements of the therapist's manner or behavior can be needlessly shaming, such as terse phone calls to rearrange appointments or short emails. These may be experienced by clients as rejection, especially when they come from a therapist whom they have previously experienced, in sessions, as warm and concerned. Highly shame-prone clients require a greater emphasis on developing the relationship and a clearer here-and-now focus to deal with shame as it is occurring in the moment. Some of these cases also need an emphasis on recognizing shame triggers, stabilization of symptoms, and an increased emphasis on accessing resources to cope with strong emotions. Psychoeducation about shame also can be helpful, including normalizing shame by explaining that anyone would feel it and just naming it can be helpful to bring it out of hiding. In addition, it can be helpful to discuss the relationship between shame and anger and the negative effects of shame and withdrawal and to highlight the link between shame and symptoms such as self-harm, bingeing, and substance abuse.

Therapists' inner experiences of shame are also important. Therapists need to be aware of their own shame triggers, such as concerns about competence, self-doubt, and closeness. Awareness and use of internal experience is important for therapists to be aware of any of their own shame and because their responses are sometimes the only way for them to sense clients' underlying feelings. Clients also may shame their therapists or attack them for not understanding, for not being well trained, for being incompetent or uncaring, for not being like a previous therapist, for not being smart enough, or for being too smart—there are endless possibilities. Therapists need to be able to tolerate and contain these attacks without retaliating so they remain connected. The provision of safety helps clients face and explore their own experience of shame or contempt. When an ashamed–shaming interaction pattern occurs between client and therapist, the therapist needs to work to repair the problem by regulating it with the client, by understanding how the therapist has shamed the client, and also how it feels to be shamed. Close attunement to clients' shame at the nonverbal and affective level, rupture repair, and a focus on moment-by-moment process are all helpful in dealing with very shame-sensitive clients.

Client shame also can make therapy challenging because shame contributes to avoidance. If clients remain silent, it's hard to access relevant information, so shame can interfere with treatment. Unacknowledged shame prevents any direct focus on problems like trauma, depression, or anxiety. Trauma clients who are ashamed of their shame can't master their trauma because the shame prevents them from dealing with it. Often the sentiment "I would be weak," or "I need to soldier through it," prevents people from seeking treatment or disclosing vulnerabilities and can be a major barrier to seeking mental health care. Because of shame, clients often do not attend treatment, or they miss sessions and reject help. Shame also interferes with the exploration of difficulties and can lead to defensiveness and minimization of problems. In spite of these difficulties, treatment needs to provide a safe, compassionate, accepting relationship while explicitly focusing on shame.

CASE EXAMPLES

The following cases illustrate how the therapist's provision of safety, presence, and acceptance can help clients effectively arrive at, disclose, and eventually transform emotion.[1]

Case #1: Description

Anthony, a 45-year-old White lawyer, had a senior position in a prestigious law firm. He was continually worried about being humiliated for some kind of error that might bring him into disrepute in his firm. He had never had any bad reviews, feedback, or criticism and had never made any significant mistakes, but he was constantly worried about being found to be lacking and being shamed in front of his partners and employees. He talked about having often experienced shame in a variety of social and professional situations during his early adulthood. He was somewhat overweight and had been since childhood. He was teased at school and was singled out within his athletically oriented family as falling short of performance expectations. His parents were very controlling and repeatedly conveyed to him that his opinion didn't matter and what he was doing was silly. They communicated that one needed to be perfect, especially to the outside world. His experiences of being seen as nonathletic within a family that valued athleticism and being mocked by peers as slow and fat developed into a core feeling of inadequacy. These shameful emotions of not being good enough kept coming up at work in regard to his professional competence.

The first step in helping the client was in the context of an empathic style of relating. I communicated my understanding that he felt shame, which is a difficult emotion to deal with. This response was not intended, this early on in therapy, as a way of encouraging him to experience his shame but rather just to help him step back and identify the difficulty. I said things like: "I imagine it's difficult for you to talk about these things," and later, "So, it's so painful to feel the possibility of being seen in this way."

A little later, I reflected in a compassionate manner his tendency to skirt away from his feelings of shame: "I'm aware that it's not an easy topic for you to address." Trust was being built by communicating safety nonverbally, vocally, and facially and developing collaboration to delve a little bit more deeply, in a graded manner, into his shame. Together, we accessed his experience of

---

[1]The clinical material used in this book is adequately disguised to protect client confidentiality. Client identity has been maintained.

vigilance about making mistakes and being found to be incompetent. This helped us arrive at his fear of public exposure, and he began to talk about his never-processed feeling, since childhood, of being inferior and not being good enough. These were the underlying schematic emotions of shame and memories of inferiority that I encouraged him to start to connect with. This was a process. It was not a matter of a single insight connecting what was happening now to what happened when he was younger, nor was it a correction of his errors in thinking. Rather, it was a process in which the first step involved stepping back and identifying his difficulty.

Next, we turned to facing the threat of his emotions in general and of his shame more specifically. Initially, it was difficult for him to tolerate his own distress. Overcoming this block was achieved by focusing on his fear of disintegrating if he felt his shame and by offering him support and encouragement to face the dragon—his shame—by experiencing it. It was then important to symbolize his emotions in words to provide a sense of greater clarity. This work of emotional processing involves attending, symbolizing, congruent expression, and acceptance of emotion. Because Anthony was able to go into his shame but come back out to the safety of the therapeutic situation when it was too intense, he developed a sense of control and was able to regulate his emotions so that he could bring cognition to emotion and make sense of it.

Further, Anthony was helped to feel that he was an active agent, not a passive victim, of the emotion. He began experiencing "I felt ashamed," rather than "Shame happened to me." He learned that he had internalized his parents' invalidation and that his parents' voices in his head generated his shame. Finally, this shame began to transform as it differentiated into various aspects of his experience. Rather than being stuck in shame, he became more fluid, and other feelings and thoughts emerged. Emotional transformation took place through acceptance, experience, and transformation of his shame.

In summary, during our work together, we recognized the shame, the sense that something was wrong with him or something was defective, and we explored where the shame came from. We worked with awareness and symbolizing as well as expressing his emotions. He became emotionally more flexible: Not always having the same response to situations of his competence, not always feeling a fear of shame and hiding. In addition, working on his own, he was able to calm himself, which we had worked on in sessions. He developed a sense of confidence and self-control, earned security, and finally experienced joy as it came back into his life. We worked with shame, turning toward what was difficult and bringing it into the light of day to develop a sense of inner strength, security, and self-compassion. These are all wonderful strengths that can be gained in working with shame.

Helping Clients Arrive at Shame • 77

We see in Anthony's case that his core maladaptive shame was transformed more by a cumulative experience of the validating relationship with the therapist and the acknowledgment and eventual accessing and processing of his shame than by accessing anger. Rather than changing shame with anger, the corrective emotional experience with a validating compassionate therapist was curative, indicating different paths to the transformation of shame.

Case #2: Transcript

The following transcript comes from the final 15 minutes of a fourth session with Marcia, a 32-year-old Italian client who, from her appearance and manner, could be mistaken for a 17-year-old. She was working with an episode of shame in which she was reluctant to disclose something that was very filled with shame for her. She was recently divorced, had a 7-year-old child, and was herself, as a child, severely emotionally and physically abused and neglected. She presented as very shy and spoke in a very limited-energy voice; when she went into her painful experience, she didn't look at the therapist but rather looked down. The little she said made her sound more like a 5-year-old child than an adult. The transcript demonstrates how the therapist's presence and acceptance of the client's exquisite pain helped the client to overcome her reluctance, to come out of hiding and disclose something about which she felt ashamed.

CLIENT (C): Uhm-hm.

THERAPIST (T): Yeah, and I know this last thing has been like the last straw, in a sense, this thing with your brother, 'cause it just leaves you feeling like there's nobody I can rely on who won't betray me. I imagine that's it . . . *(silent pause 1 minute)*

C: (Slightly adjusts body position) It's hard to believe there's so many people in the world and you can be so alone.

T: (Nods, sighs) Yeah, and it could be very isolating. *(long, silent pause for 37 seconds)*

C: I don't really care about my feelings. I'm just kinda curious . . . *(long, silent pause for 30 seconds)*

T: And what do you find curious?

C: That I'm not even able to say to anybody what's really the problem.

T: (Nods) So, you're saying you're really not able to say to me what's really the problem – meaning you know what it is, but you're not saying?

c: Well, yeah, I think *(pause)*, well, I sort of said it.

t: Uhm-hm, did I not hear it?

c: (Looks down and to side, averts eye contact, folds into herself, cries silently)

t: So, it really touches the pain in you. Can you tell me?

c: (Hides her face with her arm, swallows, sobs silently)

t: Why don't you let the tears come? – You know, because there is so much hurt there and pain. What is it you said? Uhm-hm, 'cause you know it hurts to be so alone, to be so . . . (shakes head) It's not that. What is it?

c: (Crying, still hiding face behind her arm) *(pause for 31 seconds)*

t: Uhm-hm – Will you tell me? *(pause for 15 seconds)* What is it that it's so hard to tell? *(silent pause for 1 minute)* **(therapist remains present and attentive and breathes)** *(long silence 1 minute)* I know you said you can't ask, that you were told [as a child] you can only ask for water and that's all. *(Long silent pause)* I don't know if that is part of it or what? *(pause for 39 seconds)* I don't know if you can risk coming out and telling me . . .

c: (Uncovers face, reaches for tissue)

t: Will you? – No, you don't want to tell me? *(pause for 12 seconds)* What is it that stops you from telling?

c: (Takes big breath) *(pause for 13 seconds)* (whispers) Humiliation. (looking down)

t: Uhm-hm – somehow, you'll feel so diminished or shamed that I would – I don't know what, that I would look down on you? I would just see how you hurt? *(pause for 6 seconds)* Is it when you said that you don't know how to turn the heat on, did you feel humiliated? **(therapist guessing)** Somehow it's humiliating not knowing how to do things? *(pause for 8 seconds)* And that's part of what the problem is? I'm not quite sure what all of that means to you. *(pause for 24 seconds)* (C shifts body in chair, still looking down) But that's something I sure would like us to be able to talk about. I don't know exactly what this means. – Can you look at me? (Client looks up and glances sideways toward camera) *(pause)* (Client looks down) To see that I'm not judging – well, I guess you'd have to see for yourself how you felt *(pause for 31 seconds)* 'cause I think you do know how to do some things. . . . Pardon?

c: (Unintelligible very low childlike voice) . . . write it.

T: You can write it – is that what you said?

C: I can maybe write it.

T: Uhm-hm. Alright. That would be a good way of beginning. Would you do that?

C: (Slight nod) *(pause for 39 seconds)*

T: I'm not quite sure if you want to do that now, or you'll write it and bring it to me?

C: Maybe.

T: So, it's not that you want to write it now, or afterwards and leave it, or anything like that? *(silent pause for 22 seconds)* I think it would be really helpful for you and me if you would write it, share that with me . . . *(silent pause for 32 seconds)* Will you look at me? – I hate to see you hide. – You know you said somewhere I'm asking you to trust me and trust that it will help for you to be willing to tell me, and I know it's really hard for you to trust. *(silent pause for 25 seconds)* It's not that I've done that much to deserve your trust in many ways. I know you've been hurt by a lot by people. So, it's a big thing. *(pause for 20 seconds)* I hope you will do it. *(silent pause for 36 seconds)* Can you tell me something about where you are now? – Because we will need to end soon.

C: (In a very soft voice) You can go any time.

T: Yes, I know. *(silent pause for 9 seconds)* Will you write something? You don't want to – promise. *(silent pause for 30 seconds)* I don't know if you want to fill out these forms [post-session questionnaires]. I imagine it's quite a demand to even do that. *(silent pause for 21 seconds)* I think we should end. – I imagine your daughter's also waiting.

C: (In a whisper) Goodbye.

T: And we will meet next week?

C: (In a whisper) Possibly.

T: (Nods) Okay. Hope to see you.

In this session, the therapist was present, patient, warm, and empathic; his voice was gentle and soft, matching her fragile state, but he had a little more energy in his voice. The therapist realized only afterwards that her look at the camera was possibly indicating she didn't want to disclose on camera. After the camera was switched off at the end of this session, she told him that she self-harmed and this was what she was so ashamed of. She disclosed that when she couldn't do things and felt upset and frustrated, she stuck pins in her arms and banged her head against the floor. Having disclosed what she felt so ashamed of, she opened up more easily in the subsequent sessions, and a working alliance was formed to work on her traumatic past, which had left her feeling so worthless and unwanted. She reported feeling accepted and safe in therapy and that this, in addition to being able to disclose and talk about her shame, was very helpful.

This was a short-term time-limited research-based therapy. It ended after 16 sessions, at which time her presenting depression had lifted. She was still shy and could have benefited from ongoing therapy, but she had made a start on her inability to speak up for herself and be assertive. The corrective emotional experience with an empathically attuned, validating therapist led to the client's disclosure of her shame, which was curative. Helping her, in the safety of the therapeutic situation, access a sense of deserving to feel angry at her parents because of the abuse would have empowered her with some assertive anger, and that assertive anger would have acted as an antidote to her extremely pervasive sense of shame and her strong tendency to withdraw; it would have helped her process her grief at the loss of a happy childhood. But this possible path to transformation would have taken more emotional processing and a much longer therapy.

CONCLUSION

This chapter covered the three important means by which the therapeutic relationship helps arriving at emotion. The first was through provision of a safe relationship with a therapist who is present and empathically attuned to affect. The second was a corrective emotional experience of feeling soothed and accepted rather than judged or scorned, which is vital for clients to come out of shame. The third aspect involved experiencing the shame in the session with the therapist and acknowledging and accessing it to make it amenable to transformation.

Chapter 5 focuses on regulating shame at both the conscious level and the more fundamental automatic level. It reviews when to regulate deliberately with more left-hemispheric behavioral means. It also discusses when to regulate by development of more right-hemispheric implicit processes that occur at the neural level. Finally, Chapter 5 covers when not to regulate but rather to promote activation of shame and its expression.

5 REGULATING SHAME

The worst pain in the world is shame.

—Fiona Apple

This chapter includes discussion of both the deliberate and the automatic regulation of shame and the difference between them. I suggest deliberate shame regulation can provide clients with helpful coping skills but is a second-level process that manages shame after it has been activated. Automatic regulation of shame, on the other hand, is transformational and leads to the client no longer having shame. It is a form of affect regulation in which the shame is transformed at its point of generation.

Although it is important to access shame to make it amenable to transformation, shame can sometimes be too overwhelming and may need some form of regulation. Any feeling of shame that cannot be symbolized in awareness because it is so overwhelming needs regulation. Intense core shame needs to be downregulated to create a working distance from it. The inability to regulate shame can result in increased sympathetic nervous system arousal and the feeling of being overwhelmed by painful emotions. Alternatively, it

---

https://doi.org/10.1037/0000393-005
Shame and Anger in Psychotherapy, by L. S. Greenberg
Copyright © 2024 by the American Psychological Association. All rights reserved.

could lead to increased parasympathetic arousal and the feeling of becoming distant from the shame or even numb. Marcia, the client from the second case study in Chapter 4, was highly withdrawn but still in her zone of tolerance, as she was not going numb or dissociating. If shame is overactivated or is outside the client's zone of tolerance and no longer can be connected to cognition, then regulation is needed. It is important to help clients develop in-session regulation as well as skills to help downregulate shame outside the session. Adaptive emotion regulation involves experiencing the right emotion, at the right time, in the right way.

Talking about emotion regulation, however, introduces some ambiguity about the processes and the emotions that are being referred to. Emotion regulation in psychology and psychotherapy has predominantly come to mean deliberate control or management of emotion (Gross, 2001). Regulation is then a second-level process that occurs after the emotion has already been activated. Once a person feels shame, they recognize it and name it, and then can breathe, distract, or reappraise. Regulation can also be anticipatory, with the goal of preventing activation by avoiding a situation that might evoke shame. This process fundamentally involves reducing and reining in emotion. Emotion regulation has become central in modification-oriented therapies as a way of working with emotion. Helping clients to engage in emotion regulation involves teaching cognitive and behavioral skills, such as changing the situation, distraction, cognitive reappraisal, or self-calming. These methods are used to deal with managing and downregulating shame.

Affect regulation on the other hand, is another term used in the literature, predominantly by more intrapsychically oriented therapists. It refers to something quite different: the implicit modulation of emotion at its point of generation (Fonagy et al., 2002; Schore, 2003). It refers not to managing shame but rather to transforming shame so that it is no longer felt as dysregulating. This modulation occurs through processes such as the co-regulation of affect in the therapeutic relationship or by self-compassion to the original vulnerability. In this form of affect regulation, the emphasis is on accessing shame and transforming it—the person does not generate shame or experience it at a level that needs after-the-fact emotion management. This view of affect regulation focuses on regulating shame at the point of generation by transforming the automatic, underlying emotional process involved in the generation of shame. Both deliberate emotion regulation skills and automatic affect regulation processes are needed in managing shame. In an affective neuroscience perspective, emotion regulation is seen as automatically integrated with emotion generation (Cozolino, 2002) and is based on a one-factor view of regulation in which affect is regulated as it is generated. This view is different from a two-factor view of conscious, deliberate management in which shame often is initially generated and only later regulated.

Thus, there are both implicit (potentially more right-hemispheric) and explicit (more left-hemispheric) forms of emotion/affect regulation (Fonagy et al., 2002; Schore, 2003). Implicit regulation involves affect being regulated as it is constructed. In this form, a person would have the right amount of shame, at the right time, for the right reason to facilitate a socially competent response. In other words, either shame is being regulated as it is being activated or it no longer is activated. In line with Aristotle's (ca. 350 B.C.E./1926) sentiment that it is not easy "to be angry with the right person, and to the right degree, and at the right time, and for the right purpose, and in the right way," it takes a lot of skill to be emotionally balanced. Being emotionally balanced is challenging because emotion is not under deliberate conscious control, and the skill required is not developed through deliberate learning. Implicitly regulating shame thus means transforming shame at its source so the individual automatically feels an appropriate degree of shame, embarrassment, or modesty, at the right time, for the right reason and expresses it in the right way or possibly no longer even feels shame at all. Explicit regulation, on the other hand, is more deliberate, an after-the-fact form of regulation in which people learn to consciously manage or control an emotion that has already been evoked and is already dysregulated and will, or is likely to, overwhelm adaptive coping. This form of control leads to interventions such as anger management or, in the case of shame, teaching regulation skills such as breathing and distraction to reduce the already activated, overly intense shame.

For clients who are strongly shame-based and fragile, often a deficit in implicit forms of shame regulation is the problem. Deliberate behavioral and cognitive forms of regulation are useful for less fragile people who can use the skills to deliberately calm and soothe themselves to regulate their shame and for people in states of overwhelm. Over time, however, building implicit emotion regulation capacities best regulates affect so that people automatically do not feel shame or feel it at a significantly reduced level. The parasympathetic nervous system automatically regulates heart rate, breathing, and other sympathetic functions that speed up under the pain of shame so that one feels valued rather than worthless. One of the better ways to build this type of implicit transformation is therefore by directly experiencing aroused shame that is soothed relationally. Another way is to feel a self-generated emotion in relation to the cueing situation. For example, if one comes to feel empowered anger at, and deserving of respect from, an abusive parent, shame is no longer generated when one is criticized by one's boss. Clients need to have a new feeling to change the shame at its source; this new feeling is necessary to change the old feeling of shame.

Thus, shame can be regulated in different ways: by developing tolerance for it, by soothing it at a variety of different levels of emotion processing, or by managing it. Shame can be consciously and deliberately soothed once it is felt, or a person can change such that they no longer feel shame in situations which previously evoked shame.

DELIBERATE EMOTION REGULATION

When therapists are working with clients who are highly distressed and not coping well, helping them to find ways to consciously, or purposively, cope with managing their shame is often a first therapeutic step. Different types of treatment for emotion dysregulation target the dysregulation symptom. Medication, combined with effective psychotherapy, can improve sleep and stress management, which helps to reduce dysregulation. Psychoeducation can improve the quality of life for people with emotional dysregulation. Learning regulation skills is also useful to help people manage their shame and behave more competently.

At the more deliberate levels of regulation, promoting clients' abilities to receive and be compassionate to their emerging painful emotional experience helps them to tolerate their shame and to self-soothe. Clients who feel out of control can improve coping and limit distress by learning to distract when feeling shame (attentional regulation), consciously reappraise to change the meaning (cognitive regulation), take a warm bath to calm down (sensory regulation), engage in an opposite action (behavioral regulation), or change environments (situation regulation).

Distraction and distress tolerance skills are primary skills for regulating shame (Linehan, 1993). These skills include identifying triggers, avoiding triggers, creating a working distance from shame, tolerating shame, focusing on increasing positive emotions, self-soothing, relaxing, and mindful breathing. Tolerating shame includes becoming aware of shame, naming it, and diaphragmatic breathing. Breath regulation and the ability to observe one's own shame, letting it come and go, differ from being taken over by it and are crucial processes that help regulate shame and emotional distress.

Shame can be deliberately regulated by soothing and can function at different levels of processing. Soothing oneself physiologically involves activation of the parasympathetic nervous system, which helps regulate heart rate, breathing, and other sympathetic functions that accelerate under stress.

At a psychological level, promoting clients' abilities to receive and accept their emerging painful experience of shame is an important step toward tolerating shame and being able to soothe it. Some researchers have looked at what goes on in the brain when people feel an emotion like shame about a behavior they would like to change (Compas et al., 2017; Goldin et al., 2014) and have found that emotions such as shame can affect the prefrontal cortex, affecting its ability to regulate activity in the midbrain. Regulating shame so that it doesn't impair the prefrontal cortex helps people to regulate their behavior. When shame is overly intensified, the person may have difficulty staying open to the pain without shutting down (i.e., dorsal vagal shutdown) or may find it too painful to talk about. Therapists need to help clients feel safe first in their body and in their self. Long exhalations, yoga stretching, grounding visualization, and walking can all help.

Some clients may feel that certain behaviors seem to help them regulate their shame and keep their emotional balance, but those behaviors may actually be unhelpful and unhealthy. Behaviors such as using alcohol or other substances, compulsive sex, self-injury, avoiding or withdrawing from difficult situations, physical or verbal aggression, and excessive use of social media may help in the moment but do more damage in the long run. They may help people feel more positive in the moment, but they postpone ultimately facing shame and are not useful ways to regulate shame.

Stopping and taking a breath is one of the most crucial skills because it helps a person to take an observational perspective of their shame, to notice where the focus of their attention is directed, to identify what they are reacting to, and, most important, to observe their shame-related sensations, feelings, and thoughts. This skill facilitates taking a working distance from shame rather than being overwhelmed by it. Learning to pause between a shame reaction and an ensuing behavior is a very valuable skill.

The ability to regulate shame can be helped by mindfulness practices. Different forms of meditative practice, including yoga and tai chi, are often helpful in achieving an observer's perspective and providing distance from overwhelming maladaptive core shame. Along with regulating breath, observing emotions and letting them come and go, and generally being mindful of internal experience, it is helpful for clients to become aware of what is going on outside of their immediate internal emotional experience by redirecting their attention to the external environment.

Clients with dysregulated forms of shame, perhaps involving extreme withdrawal, contempt, or intense weeping combined with destructive acting out, benefit from developing skills to manage shame distress effectively, but deliberate use of skills to self-regulate is not easy. An important aspect of development of self-regulation skills is for clients to come to see that they can choose how to react to situations and they can deliberately choose to apply a skill they have learned to deal with their feelings. Choice, thus, is an important self-regulation skill that helps empower people to deal with their challenges and disruptions. Clients must, however, accept that they do not have full control over what they feel and so may not always succeed.

Therapists need to help clients to welcome, accept, and validate their shame and to practice these skills to embed them. These capacities can be difficult for people to develop. Therapists need to support and guide clients to accept their emotions in the same way they accept other aspects of themselves, such as their age, height, or allergies that they cannot change. Acceptance of what cannot be changed differs from approving or liking something. People don't have to like their acne or their allergies, but they can accept that they have them, and they can learn to manage them. Certain things are not easy to change, so coming to accept and possibly even appreciate what these things have to offer, rather than constantly fighting to change them, leads to feeling a lot better.

Acceptance of shame and facing it, rather than running away from it, can be of great help in regulating shame, but allowing one's shame takes strength and courage. Acceptance, in some ways, is more an attitude than a skill. Accepting shame involves acknowledging it, allowing it, observing it, and welcoming it. A person needs to step back from experiencing shame and instead experience the wave of sensation that sweeps through their torso and face, let it wash over them, and then move on to the next moments of experience. It is helpful to concentrate on a specific aspect of the emotion, rather than the whole thing. For instance, one could focus on the quality of sensation in the body—its shape, size, location, or color—or an image that captures some elements of it. One needs to observe the shame, the rushing of blood to the face, the looking down, the tendency to want to disappear, and to symbolize the experience of it in words. One can create a safe distance from shame by adopting an observer's stance and describing the shame as, say, a slumping of one's shoulders and torso (attempting to become smaller) and a sinking in the stomach.

It is helpful for people to recognize that they are not their shame and shame is a part, but not all, of who they are and what they feel. People are more than their shame. They do not necessarily have to have the shame govern their whole world and their sense of self, but rather they need to be able to sit with the emotion and observe it. People, however, need practice in welcoming, accepting, and validating shame.

As noted, when shame is too overwhelming or intense, it is important to find ways of calming and self-soothing. A specific method for a therapist to promote self-soothing is to guide distressed clients to imagine going to a safe place in their mind. A therapist may ask a client to access a place in their imagination where they feel safe; when they have an image of a safe place, the therapist may ask them to feel what it's like there. For example, a therapist might say, "Imagine yourself somewhere safe; where you feel safe, secure, and comforted. Where do you go? Can you describe what it's like? What do you feel there?" Imagery exercises like this one teach clients that they are capable of providing a safe place for themselves in their imagination. Teaching clients to access a safe place helps them build skills to be able to go to a more soothing place and achieve a calmer state when distressed. This process can be used to help clients soothe shame in the session and also can be given as homework to help cope with shame experiences outside the sessions. The skills can be taught and consciously cultivated to deliberately handle feelings of shame.

One of the most powerful tools of emotion regulation is having the ability to choose to regulate and then succeeding by taking an observer's perspective and naming one's emotion. It is important, however, to know the difference between primary and secondary shame and to know how to best address each in the most effective way.

Psychoeducation about emotion and the process of working on emotion can be most helpful to develop this knowledge. Psychoeducation draws on all that was discussed about shame in Chapter 1. Therapists can tell clients that shame is a normal part of being human and can describe what happens to people when they feel shame: Their minds might go blank, and they might feel confused, inferior, helpless, small, powerless, or exposed. Clients can learn to describe the bodily sensations that go along with shame: nausea or stomach upset; pain or tension; wanting to run away, withdraw, hide, or disappear from view. Facial and body expressions such as averting gaze, looking down, blushing, shoulders slumping, and chest caving may be described as normal manifestations of shame. Clients can be told that shame memories can sometimes flood in all at once or that they may feel they are reliving the original experience all over again. It also is helpful to highlight that shame has adaptive purposes, such as helping people to belong and preventing people from doing things that may result in being rejected by others. On the other hand, it should be stated that shame is often not adaptive. Rather, shame may result from having internalized past experiences of being devalued, humiliated, or abused. In these cases, shame leads to thoughts such as: "There's something wrong with me," "No one will ever love me," and "Other people see me negatively or look down on me."

Finally, how shame affects relationships can be discussed by emphasizing that shame makes people want to withdraw and hide. Withdrawing and hiding can protect people from humiliation, but the tendency to withdraw and hide may be detrimental to their ability to connect with people—when people hide what they feel is shameful, they end up feeling disconnected, isolated, or lonely. It can also be noted that disclosing feelings of shame often presents opportunities to be vulnerable with trusted others, which is one of the ways to build intimacy and make fulfilling relationships more likely.

WHEN TO DOWNREGULATE SHAME

Shame that cannot be connected to adaptive cognition because it is so overwhelming needs regulation. Too much shame, at too high an intensity, can be countertherapeutic. As noted previously, therapists need to help clients establish a working distance from overwhelming shame. When people can effectively distance themselves from their shame, the distance can help people to learn. However, simply suppressing feelings of shame can lead to a rebound effect, so total distancing from shame in many situations is not helpful. Thus, a crucial clinical skill is to understand when to help clients downregulate, distract, and modulate and when to help facilitate approach and intensification.

The time to work with deliberate downregulation is when a client's shame is outside their zone of tolerance. A two-step view of regulation is potentially useful when working with these more highly dysregulated clients. The first step involves teaching deliberate downregulation skills such as breathing, labeling, tolerance, and distraction. The second step is the development of automatic regulation by targeting underlying primary shame. Thus, if a client is panicking in an out-of-control fashion because of their shame or is despairing, self-harming or harming others, then distraction skills, calming, and distancing from shame are needed. In these situations, downregulation is the intervention of choice. This process is a second-level management process, in which emotions that are already aroused are acted on to control and contain them and thus to help people cope better. The primary shame is not being regulated as it is being generated; rather, the experienced shame is being managed in order to reduce its intensity. For example, when shame gets to an unmanageable level, self-soothing is helpful to manage the intensity of the feelings. The hope is that the experience of mastering the intensity of shame will rub off on the person and they will learn to engage in the same behaviors on other occasions. Clients can be given homework and be encouraged to practice these skills in real-world situations between sessions.

There are a number of indicators of when to deliberately intervene to downregulate shame. For instance, regulation is indicated when the relationship with the therapist is not yet strong enough to provide the safety needed for activation of shame. Shame regulation is also needed when a client feels overwhelmed by shame and when shame does not inform or promote adaptive action. When a client is in a crisis or is feeling overwhelmed and the shame does not promote adaptive action, crisis management involves downregulation. Other strong indicators for promoting downregulation of shame include a previous history of uncontrolled anger or violence in response to shame, experiences of disintegrating or being unable to cope, and having suicidal tendencies. In these situations, uncontrolled anger is a secondary emotion that protects against underlying shame; it is a sign that the shame is so painful that it may need to be downregulated before it can be worked with. Clients need coping skills if they are engaged in destructive coping, self-harm, or binge eating or drinking to deal with their shame, or if they use substances to self-medicate (Linehan, 1993). If the problem is a skill deficit, then shame regulation and problem-solving skills are needed. However, if clients are able to talk about their shame and their triggers in a more regulated fashion and are not overwhelmed by them, it is time to activate underlying shame and self-contempt to make them amenable to transformation, as discussed in Chapter 6.

IMPLICIT AFFECT REGULATION

Research has shown that development of a secure attachment relationship with a therapist, the development of the client's mentalization skills (Fonagy et al., 2002), and the ability to reflect on the contents of one's own and others' mental processes are helpful (Jurist, 2018). Problems of shame that occur in fragile people, the kind of shame that pervades their personalities, arise from a lack of implicit forms of regulation. These right-hemispheric processes cannot be modified by direct attempts. Highly fragile clients with personality disorders need to build implicit, automatic affect regulation capacities over time. Implicit forms of regulation cannot be explicitly trained or used as volitional skills, such as deliberate downregulation skills. Their development needs to be facilitated by other means, transforming shame at its point of inception so it is not overwhelming when it emerges. Following transformation, a person with borderline processes who self-harms to deflect from the painful feelings of shame will no longer feel the searing shame at perceived rejection and will no longer wish to self-harm.

The first process that helps a person to develop shame regulation is the ongoing ability and experience of symbolizing shame in awareness. A previously undifferentiated knot of emotional experiences becomes differentiated and symbolized by bringing cognition to emotion. Experiential therapies such as client-centered (Rogers, 1959) and focusing therapy (Gendlin, 1981) developed the Experiencing Scale (Klein et al., 1986), demonstrating empirically that deep experiencing predicts positive therapy outcome. The essence of deep experiencing is the process of symbolizing bodily felt feelings in words to be able to reflect on them to solve problems. More recently, Fonagy et al. (2002) argued that mentalizing the ability to understand one's own and others' mental states, a central process of change in psychoanalytic approaches, enables a person to comprehend the self's and others' intentions and affects. Fonagy and Target (2005) referred to this idea as having one's mind in mind. I refer to this idea as bringing cognition to emotion to make sense of it. Whatever one calls it, this process helps people to develop affect regulation at an implicit level. Being able to make sense of one's experience makes one master of it rather than a passive victim of it.

Implicit affect regulation develops most centrally through direct experience of aroused shame being soothed by right-hemispheric, nonverbal, relational, and automatic internal processes. Because implicit regulation occurs in the emotion-generation process, the emotion emerges in an adaptive fashion and doesn't need to be managed. The ability to self-soothe to regulate affect develops throughout life, initially by internalization of the soothing functions of the protective other (Stern, 1985); it is a core developmental process. One main way that shame regulation develops in therapy is through the internalization of the security of the therapeutic relationship and of the therapist's empathic attunement and responsiveness. The other main way is by clients feeling compassion to their own shame. The experience of compassion, empathy, and validation from the therapist or from a part of the self leads to the development of implicit shame regulation. This process is a developmental process, not a conscious learning one, and it occurs by changing emotion with emotion—in this case changing shame with the experience of feeling more valid and worthy. This, as I have said, comes by internalizing therapist acceptance and validation or experiencing a stronger part of the self providing compassion and care to the vulnerable shame-based part. In these ways, the internal capacity for implicit self-soothing is built. The development of implicit or automatic shame regulation capacities, over time, is important to help shame-prone clients transform their underlying sense of worthlessness or defectiveness into feeling free of shame.

Developing affect regulation is a process that is ever present, from infancy through old age. Therapy offers the opportunity to have a relationship with a therapist who will facilitate the ability to internalize the experience of security and offer validation that transforms the maladaptive core shame into a feeling of being accepted and valued. For example, clients have said to me that they hear my caring voice in their heads during the week and it helps them feel stronger. Having the experience of consistent empathy from another is transformative. Over time, empathy from the therapist is internalized as empathy for the self (Bohart & Greenberg, 1997), and a secure attachment with the therapist (Bowlby, 1988) is internalized into a sense of basic security (Mallinckrodt, 2010). The self becomes stronger, and the person is less fragile.

For example, I worked with a self-harming client who had a highly destructive internal voice that essentially told her she was disgusting, defective, and unlovable. Having seen how destructive this shame-producing voice was, I asked her (around Session 15, too early in the therapy with a client this fragile) if she could be compassionate to that all-too-consuming shame-based part of her experience. She astutely turned to me and said, "No, that's your job." One year later, having internalized my empathy and compassion to her childhood suffering and her sense of a secure attachment to me, she was able to transform her intense self-contemptuous voice into a more compassionate voice and to soothe her vulnerable, shame-based self. However, she could only be compassionate to herself after she had internalized enough validation, safety, compassion, and empathy from me to build this internal capacity for self-compassion. As another example of the gradual development of the internalization process is that early in the therapy process she talked about her inability to sit alone at home and read, resulting from her experiences of derealization, and experiences of "spacing out" because of feelings of isolation. Without ever addressing this symptom in therapy, after about 16 months or so she reported that she could sit comfortably alone at home and read. However, if I left the city to travel for any period of time, she could not sit alone and read. After about 2 years, she was able to read alone, regardless of my presence in the city.

For less fragile clients who have greater internal resources, regulation of their shame can be accelerated by accessing internal soothing and compassion from the self to the self without having to provide a long a period of relational soothing. Clients who have greater capacities to tolerate their shame can be helped to evoke childhood emotion memories of shame, humiliation, or abuse after initial relational safety has been established. The adult self can be helped to respond compassionately in the present to the shame and pain of the wounded self. Alternatively, compassion can be evoked, in a session, from an imagined soothing figure from the past who had offered the wounded child some of what was missing, and this person can be imagined as protecting the vulnerable self against the past threat and humiliation.

It is important to note that in this process of developing implicit self-soothing through intrapsychic processes, the client's self-compassion is not instructed but is evoked, and that needs to be done at the right time. The marker indicating when to engage in self-compassion dialogues is that clients have reached their core shame and in the session are experiencing the anguish of their shame related to past humiliation. This process is not an intervention to downregulate symptomatic or overwhelming shame deliberately but rather transforms previously unacknowledged shame that is only now being accessed as an underlying determinant of the client's depression, self-harm, or destructive behaviors.

TRANSFORMING SHAME WITH SELF-COMPASSION

In the spiritual traditions, the Buddha, for example, offered that you yourself, as much as anyone in the entire universe, deserve your own love and affection. According to the Dalai Lama (1995), compassion is an openness to suffering with the wish to relieve it. In the psychology literature, self-compassion relating to painful experiences contains self-kindness rather than self-judgment, common humanity rather than isolation, and mindfulness rather than overidentification (Germer & Neff, 2013). According to Neff (2011), self-compassion entails being warm and understanding toward ourselves when we suffer, fail, or feel inadequate rather than ignoring our pain or self-flagellating with self-criticism.

A good practice to offer clients is to take a self-compassion break. In this sort of break, a person invites themself to notice a place in the body where they feel stress or emotional discomfort and then say to themselves slowly,

- This is a moment of suffering. *(mindfulness)*
- Suffering is a part of life. *(common humanity)*
- Give myself what I need. *(self-kindness)*

Activating self-compassion can be complicated and requires safety and a very good attunement to clients in the moment. The therapist needs to read what is right for this client at this moment (immersion) as well as to consider the larger context of the person's issues and day-to-day life (expansion). The therapist also needs to be sensitive and attuned to what can be tolerated. For example, self-compassion may be possible right away with clients with low shame arousal, yet mindful awareness may initially be better with high-arousal clients, with a later shift to self-compassion.

SELF-SOOTHING

The development of transformational self-soothing differs from the development of coping self-soothing. Transformational soothing occurs implicitly and first involves the activation of the emotional suffering underlying the symptom. The shame is activated in the session to transform it, at its origins, into a more regulated state. This process differs from change through coping skills, which controls the shame after it has occurred. Painful emotions that never received the needed soothing in the past or the present can be changed by feeling compassion toward the self. Experiencing the previously disclaimed emotion allows the client to grieve the loss and soothe the anguish of the self. Soothing the painful evoked emotion can be provided by both the individual and the therapist. Coping self-soothing is a deliberate skill used to address symptomatic dysregulation that one needs to overcome, whereas the former brings soothing emotions in the present to unresolved painful emotions from the past. This soothing of unresolved pain helps transform threats from the past and strengthen the self by developing automatic soothing so emotion is experienced in a regulated or transformed way.

I have found that self-compassion is greatly facilitated at this point by having a chair dialogue, in which clients are asked how they as adults feel toward their currently evoked vulnerable ashamed self. The aim is to facilitate the activation of compassion for the self but not instruct it. This intervention is a specific way of directly facilitating the client's feeling so they experience compassion to the suffering self. In this process, clients are supported and encouraged to be caring and comforting to themselves. Therapists guide clients toward compassion, but they should only guide to places in a client's zone of proximal development, not too far ahead of their client's experience and not behind. They are facilitating development by accessing what is within but not yet formulated, rather than teaching a skill. For example, if from the position of the self responding to the shame a client says, "I feel sorry you had to suffer," or "I hear it was hard," the client is close to but not yet experiencing self-compassion. At this point, the therapist might guide, saying, "Can you tell your humiliated part what you feel toward her right now, as you say this?" This statement guides clients to attend to their evoked, lived experience and to express their compassion toward their shame, which differs from instructing compassion. For example, if the client speaking to the self's shame says contemptuously, "You've always been so weak, it doesn't help you at all," the therapist doesn't say, "It's important to be compassionate to your shame. Can you be compassionate to that part?" That statement would be outside the therapeutic zone of proximal development, and the dynamic self-organizing processes can't possibly shift so rapidly to a state of compassion in any genuine way. Clients can, and often will, voice compassion under this type of instruction, but they will not feel it. It is the true experience of compassion toward the self that transforms shame, not the behavior of saying or acting compassionate. The evocation of the experience of compassion toward the self for the past suffering is needed to undo shame (Greenberg, 2011; Tugade & Frederickson, 2004).

A therapist may start this self-compassion dialogue by inviting the client to imagine themselves as a child in a scene related to being maltreated by a parent or bullied and humiliated by others. The therapist then asks them to imagine their adult self or a protective other entering the scene and intervening to support/protect them as a child. For example, the therapist might say, "Describe the scene. What do you want to do for that little boy? What do you say to Mom and Dad on his behalf?" Then the therapist asks the client to again imagine themselves as a child and to feel what it's like now to receive care. As the child, they are guided to ask for anything that they might still need from the adult to help them feel better. Finally, the client is asked if they can take part in the protection and support and what that feels like.

It is helpful for therapists to ask questions covering different levels of experience:

- Sensory: "What do you see hear, smell, sense?"
- Emotional: "What do you feel? What's it like inside?"
- Cognitive: "What is going through your mind?"
- Behavioral: "What do you do? What is happening?"

It's important at this point to help the client imagine that kid back there. "How old were you? What were the circumstances? What was happening to you? What was it like to be a kid back then? You want to get the perspective of the kid back then, and to see that now, you really are a very different person. By differentiating what the kid went through and what you're going through right now, you try to vividly evoke the scenes from back then and say, 'Now, if you came across that scene right now—now that you're 50 years old and a much bigger person—what would you do?'" The client may respond with something like: "I would grab that kid and run out," or "I would punch that guy who's doing it." The internal differentiation is terribly important. The self-loathing and shame becomes the central issue in chronic trauma—not the event, but the relationship people have with their inner selves. Therapists need to help people make a clear differentiation between who they are right now and that kid back then.

In this process, the therapist might also ask a supportive adult, "What do you want to say or do for that little girl when you see her mom ignoring her?" In addition, the therapist might ask the adult to imagine taking the child to a safe place, saying, "Can you imagine taking her somewhere safe where you would take care of her and protect her? Where do you take her? Can you describe what you see around you? What do you want to say to her to make her feel safe?"

Before asking the adult to speak to the child self, it is important to check that the adult self feels something akin to compassion for the vulnerable child self. The therapist might ask, "How do you, the adult, feel toward that 9-year-old?" If the client expresses empathy, compassion, or support, such as: "I see her so sad and alone," the therapist then asks the client to enter the scene and either speak as the child or speak to the child. If the client appears to feel no compassion or support (e.g., "She is useless"), the therapist intervenes to access compassion by asking the client how she would respond to a child other than herself (i.e., a universal) who was suffering similar circumstances. If the client still feels no compassion, the therapist asks how a known supportive other would feel toward the child: "How would your best friend feel if she encountered this child or knew how much you were suffering?" If compassion is not accessed by any of these means, the therapist both expresses their own compassion for the child and validates that it's really hard for the client to have compassion for that vulnerable child self and then discusses what makes it difficult for the client to be compassionate. The therapist ends by saying that this difficulty is something they need to continue working on together.

When addressing their child self's shame, a client may feel contemptuous of the child for being fat, awkward, weak, or too needy, or the client may blame or hold them responsible for having allowed, for example, sexual abuse or for having responded physically. If the therapist asks how the adult feels about that child self who was molested or abused, clients will often say such things as: "She's disgusting. I hate that kid. I can't stand that kid. She was weak. She should have resisted him," or "He was dependent, weak. He didn't stand up to his father, didn't put up any resistance." Shame and self-loathing often become the central issue in chronic trauma. It's often not the actual event that is so damaging, but rather it's the person's relationship with themselves that becomes the problem.

Facilitating imaginal re-entry involves saying, in some way or another, "Can you go back into the scene as the adult you? What do you feel toward the child?" Then the therapist guides the client's experience in the therapeutic zone of proximal development to support and protect the vulnerable self. Therapists need, at all times, to stay in contact with clients' experience, asking them to tell the therapist what is happening in them in the moment or what is occurring in the scene or helping them to retell the trauma. The therapist might say, "I hear she's really scared, but there are no words, but this is what's happening. . . ." It can be very therapeutic to have the compassionate adult put words to what the inarticulate child may be seeing and experiencing. Therapists need to make sure the child self feels safe and protected by the support of the adult self and then facilitate the grieving and sadness that comes up about all that was missed. This process often results in the child self not only taking in the support and compassion of the caring other but also expressing healthy, adaptive anger to the humiliating, abusive other; asserting the needs of the child; or articulating what was not okay in the situation.

Finally, it is important to consolidate the changes in emotion-schematic memory by facilitating the making of new meaning and promoting new narratives (e.g., She wasn't bad; she was just a little girl and didn't do well in school because she was always scared). The new adaptive emotions (e.g., adaptive anger) and needs (e.g., need for positive attention and safety) that came up are validated, and the therapist may suggest homework to further strengthen new emotional experiences and narratives. This consolidation helps clients learn that they are capable of providing a safe place for themselves.

PILOT STUDIES OF THE SELF-SOOTHING PROCESS

In two qualitative observational studies using task analysis, researchers compared samples of resolvers engaged in self-compassion dialogues with nonresolvers (Goldman & Fox-Zurawic, 2012; Greenberg & Iwakabe, 2011). These studies found that resolvers were different from nonresolvers not because of their verbal expression of compassion to the self but rather because in the self-chair they reclaimed their unmet need and grieved the loss of not having the need met. Many people were able to enact being compassionate to themselves, but for significant change to happen, it seemed that the grief about unmet needs and past suffering was important. Mourning what was deserved but not received seemed to evoke a heartfelt compassion rather than a behavioral enactment of compassion and led to a more lasting sense of resilience.

The steps in the clients' resolution process are shown in Figure 5.1.

1. The first step begins with a marker indicating that the client is experiencing or has recently arrived at the anguish of emotional suffering. This is accompanied by a sense of familiar despair, that they are stuck in this feeling and it will never change.

2. Some clients go to the nonprogressive processes of fear of their shame or protest against the unfairness, saying things such as: "Why did this happen?"

FIGURE 5.1. Model of Self-Compassion Dialogue

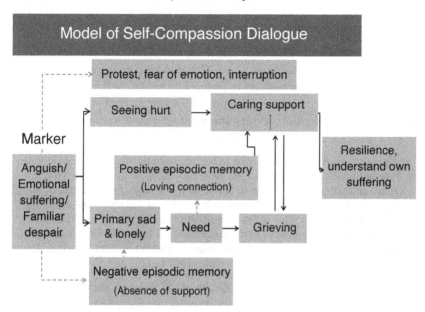

or "How can I be expected to give to myself what I never got?" These feelings need to be overcome to move to the next step.

3a. The next progressive step is to express the primary sadness of lonely abandonment and anger at not having the unmet needs met in the past.

3b. Some clients access negative episodic memories.

4. From the adult position, clients see the hurt and respond in an affiliative and caring manner.

5a. Clients access the previously disclaimed need and a sense of having deserved to have the need met.

5b. Some clients at this point may access positive memories of having had the need met on some occasions.

6. All resolved clients now get to the grief about what was missed and the evoked compassion and empathy for the wounded self's suffering and loss.

7. Partial resolution is achieved with an experience of feeling soothed and a bodily felt sense of relief.

8. Full resolution is signaled by a sense of resilience. No longer does the client experience the familiar despair but rather has hope for the future and a compassionate understanding of the self's shame.

Some clients have difficulty being compassionate to their own child self in response to an invitation such as: "Can you be yourself now as an adult entering the scene, and respond to yourself as a child? What do you want to say to them?" The therapist might then use a variety of other guiding statements. For example, after inviting the adult or supportive part of the self to enter the scene, the therapist might say,

> Where do you want to stand? Next to her, or maybe in front of her, maybe you take her hand? Do you want to tell me what's going on in the scene? Is there anything that you want to say to her or to say to anyone on her behalf? For example, there was nothing wrong with her; it was you that were wrong for how you treated her. What did she need that she didn't get? What was not OK? Do you want to take her out of the scene and take her somewhere safe where you take care of her and protect her? What do you want to say to her to help her heal from being so afraid (or so unlovable)?

When clients are guided to put things out in the real world or in a three-dimensional virtual reality space, the manner of processing changes. There is more opportunity to include nonverbal, spatial, and temporal processing. When the characters are laid out in space and experiences are re-enacted, the client can replay scenes from the past based on how they are right now. They are suddenly able to say, "My mother just stood there and didn't do anything." Enacting is different than sitting and talking about people from their past and who aren't present in the room. When these people actually come into the room, the whole dynamic changes, and the possibility having of more than the shame appears. While enacting the child self, clients simultaneously feel themselves as the child and not the child. Clients see that the other person was a large adult while they were just a little kid. They get in touch with what they did to survive, to deal with their circumstances, and with what they needed, and they begin to feel protective and supportive of the child.

It then can be helpful to work at a distance by suggesting speaking to a universal child. The therapist might say, "Imagine a vulnerable child in the universe. What would you say to him?" Speaking to a universal child allows a greater distance from the client's own automatically evoked contempt of their own child self.

Another possibility is going to a known child, saying, "I know that you really try to be there for your niece (or son/daughter). What would you say to your niece/son/daughter if they were going through this? Can you see them there and tell them?" The effort is to evoke compassion in an imagined situation with a real, known child.

Another option is to invoke a caring person rather than an adult self, saying, "Imagine your parent/significant other in the other chair, not as they were but as you needed them to be. Tell them what you need, then ask them for this. Then have them speak to you." The therapist could say this in various ways, such as: "Can you imagine what your father or mother would say to you now if they knew how you were suffering? If they had been in a better emotional state?" or "Can you be the father/mother of your dreams? What was it that you were yearning to hear?" or "Is there anyone in the past who has been caring and compassionate toward you, and what would they say to you?" (e.g., God, an uncle, a teacher).

CONCLUSION

This chapter shows that it is important to be aware of both emotion regulation and affect regulation and to see them as two different processes. Deliberate forms of cognitive and behavioral regulation of shame by left-hemispheric processes are useful as coping skills when people feel out of control. Deliberate emotion regulation helps people deliberately manage or control emotions once they are already on the road to dysregulation. Skills are taught and practiced. Implicit regulation, however, occurs at the point of emotion generation: Shame is regulated automatically when it emerges. This form of regulation is developed by symbolizing emotional experience in awareness and by internalizing the empathic soothing and secure attachment with the therapist. Affect regulation is helpful for more pervasive personality change; it can help reduce the likelihood that the person will be triggered by cues that previously evoked dysregulated shame.

Having discussed how clients arrive at and regulate shame, in Chapter 6 I move to the leaving stage of working with shame—transformation by synthesis of shame with another emotion—often anger, which has an action tendency to thrust forward and set boundaries, opposite of shame's action tendency to shrink into the ground and disappear. Chapter 6 shows that transformation is not the replacement of shame with anger but rather a synthesis that creates with something truly novel like confidence or calm.

6 TRANSFORMING SHAME

We need never be ashamed of our tears for they are rain upon the blinding dust of earth, overlying our hard hearts.
—Charles Dickens

Once a safe relationship has been formed and an alliance to work on shame has been established, the shame has been revealed to the therapist, and the shame is named and regulated, the focus of therapy shifts to helping bring the client's shame alive in the client's zone of tolerance, in the immediacy of the session, to make it amenable to processing and transformation. The focus on safety and empathic understanding moves to an exploratory and evocative emphasis. The aim is to help clients experience, symbolize, and differentiate the unspoken facets of their shame experience. Clients are guided to stay in touch with their felt sense and bodily experience of shame, and shame is evoked by stimulating methods such as chair dialogues and imagery. Shame left untreated grows stronger and can often lead clients to behaviors that bring even greater shame. Transformation of shame, not just acceptance, is essential to alleviate client suffering.

---
https://doi.org/10.1037/0000393-006
Shame and Anger in Psychotherapy, by L. S. Greenberg
Copyright © 2024 by the American Psychological Association. All rights reserved.

Work with core shame involves transforming shame-based emotion schemes, which is done by accessing the shame and changing it by retrieving new internal healthy resources and adaptive emotions. The arriving stage of work with shame, described in Chapter 4, involves acknowledging the shame in the session by focusing directly on it, naming it, and accepting it. Once that process is complete, clients need to experience their shame more vividly in the session to enable it to be processed. This full reclaiming of the shame at a bodily level makes the shame accessible for transformation by synthesis with newly accessed adaptive emotions.

After the client has arrived at the shame, the leaving stage begins. The shame and the pain of the shame are felt, and an emotionally driven self-preservation instinct, the organismic need for survival and relief from the pain, kicks in to guide the self-organizing process. The person begins to fight to survive, and a desire to want to live without the pain of the shame emerges because the shame is being viscerally felt. The will to survive, plus the reclaiming of one's right to have one's needs met, leads to a newfound sense of agency. The client feels more deserving and begins to feel angry at the unfairness of what occurred and to assert their right to be accepted and valued. This new, agentic, emotional experience of anger is synthesized with the maladaptive shame, and the client's feelings of worthlessness develop into a newfound, more worthy sense of self.

This chapter presents the steps involved in transformation in the leaving stage. It shows how new adaptive emotion is accessed and used to change shame and how the newly synthesized self-organization strengthens the self and leads to the formation of new narratives. The first and major step involves accessing the shame that has already been felt, feeling it and any accompanying painful feelings in the session. Then, the client reclaims the need embedded in the shame, which generates new emotions that synthesize with the shame and change it at a neural and schematic level. The next steps involve the validation of the more resilient emotional responses and the new, more confident self-organization that develops after undoing the shame with a new experience. This final step is the co-construction of new narratives.

This chapter presents the results of a study that analyzed the process of the transformation of shame in 23 clients (S. Miller, 2021). In this study, a model of the process of resolving shame in psychotherapy sessions was developed by initially observing a small number of cases involving the in-session overcoming of shame, isolating components involved in resolution, and developing an empirically based rational empirical model of the change process (Greenberg, 2007). The model was tested on a larger sample to identify the components that predicted resolution. This model illuminates some of the important process steps in helping to transform a shame-based self-organization into a more self-confident one and acts as a guide for therapist intervention.

The chapter ends with a discussion of interventions such as evocative imagery and psychodramatic enactments, which are useful in helping to access and transform shame (Elliott et al., 2004; Greenberg et al., 1993). Two-chair dialogues, in which clients enact the harshly negative, contemptuous, self-evaluative processes that produce shame, as well as empty-chair dialogues and imaginal re-entry into the shaming scenes, which are major interventions in emotion-focused therapy (EFT; Greenberg et al., 1993), are described. In these interventions, the client encounters either an internal, contemptuous, critical part of the self or a shaming other in an empty chair or in imagination. They are then able to express the shame and pain to the contemptuous self or humiliating other and to bring in new resources to help transform the shame.

TRANSFORMATION OF SHAME

As discussed previously, shame transformation involves activating new, adaptive, emotional responses and validating the new adaptive feelings and the emerging more confident self-organization (Greenberg, 2002, 2021). One of the best ways of changing shame is with an opposing and possibly stronger emotion that acts to transform it (Greenberg, 2021). Often the new emotion is assertive, empowered anger, but it can also be the sadness of grief or compassion for the shame of the pain. Most characteristically, sadness follows from empowered anger. Fueled by their anger, people feel more deserving and can grieve what was lost or never was and let go of trying to get the need met by the hurtful other. Once clients have accessed their core shame, the possibility of transforming the shame-based organization by mobilizing alternative emotional responses presents itself, based on accessing adaptive needs and goals that help expand clients' emotional-response repertoires. When withdrawal responses that are a part of a demoralized shame-based self-organization are coupled with new approach responses of standing up for oneself in empowered anger, reaching out for comfort in sadness, or the expansive tendencies of pride and other positive emotions, the effects of paralyzing shame are undone.

To promote transformation, therapists need to validate the emergence of adaptive emotions that arise spontaneously (Greenberg, 2002, 2021). It is also helpful for therapists to guide clients' attention to background or less focal, more adaptive feelings that are at some level felt but not attended to.

Complex dynamic self-organizing systems always have more available to awareness than is currently focused on. Experience is formed and can be changed by shifts in attentional allocation (James, 1890; J. Pascual-Leone & Johnson, 2021). Therefore, focusing on bodily felt sensation and feelings that are not yet fully formed can help new feelings to emerge.

Probably the most useful method of accessing a new emotion to facilitate the undoing of shame is to access and validate the unmet needs and goals embedded in the shame. Therapists need to ask clients what they and the painful shame need in order to feel better. Raising to consciousness the unmet need for validation and the goal of being accepted automatically evokes and heightens a sense of agency in the automatic self-organizing emotion system. The client becomes an agent who needs something, rather than a passive victim of shame. When a client in their shame state experiences that their needs for validation and acceptance are being confirmed by their therapist, they begin to sense that they deserved to have these previously unmet needs met. The sense of having been robbed and having lost what was needed spontaneously evokes assertive anger at not having gotten what they deserved and sadness at what they missed. Compassion for the self and pride at feeling worthy emerge.

As previously discussed, the emotional brain generates emotion by appraising situations in relation to need. When the deservingness of the need in the shame is experienced in awareness, the emotional brain automatically appraises that the need was not met. It generates an emotional response to the thwarting of a need or to loss, and it self-organizes to generate anger or sadness. In this process, it is important to distinguish a heartfelt need from a facilitative need. A *heartfelt need* is an organismic survival need that comes from the felt pain of aroused emotion. It has the quality of a deep sense of deservingness and arises as an organismic response to overcome the experienced pain. A *facilitative need* comes more from an intellectual understanding and is not as motivationally charged with the sense of urgency and deservingness that is felt in a heartfelt need. A facilitative need lubricates the chair dialogue at a cognitive level but is not as compelling as a heartfelt need, which can trigger an adaptive emotion designed to promote survival.

Expressive methods, such as enacting an emotion with one's body, can help clients experience a new emotion. For example, a client can be asked to sit up straight, put their feet on the ground, and speak louder to evoke anger. Remembering a time when they felt some other emotion, such as comfort or joy, can help clients change states and experience a more adaptive emotion. As mentioned, one of the main adaptive emotions that helps to transform shame is adaptive anger. Adaptive anger, discussed in detail in Chapter 8, is empowered anger. Adaptive anger often is followed by the sadness of grief at never having had a childhood need met, which is often followed by compassion for the suffering of the self. Adaptive anger promotes assertion of one's right and sets boundaries, while sadness provides an action tendency to reach out to connect. These new emotions help one to live life without shame (Greenberg, 2002; Greenberg et al., 1993).

People with core shame seldom feel positive emotions, especially not as fully as they could. Shame very often blocks positive emotions such as pride, joy, and interest (Nathanson, 1994; Tompkins, 1987). People with shame may feel too vulnerable to feel positive—they may fear that as soon as they start to enjoy positive feelings, they will be exposed and ostracized and lose the positive feelings. They may also feel unworthy of experiencing positive emotions and therefore hide their strengths and joys. Therapy needs to help shame-based clients feel joy and pride and share them with the therapist. Therapy can help shame-based clients reclaim and enjoy their strengths. A therapeutic focus on positive feelings helps validate them and may evoke other feelings attached to them.

Therapists can also ask clients to repeat or even exaggerate statements that are self-affirming and self-expressive, such as "I deserve to be loved," or "I am worthy," and to elaborate what these affirmations imply. This process helps clients to overcome constriction of the expression and their embarrassment at expressing these feelings. For example, inviting clients to take pride in and boast about their achievements helps them to express pride and gives them permission to feel it. In these situations, it is helpful to ask clients first to feel the positive feeling in their bodies; to feel the excitement and let it build; and then to show it on their faces, in their voice, and express it in their bodies (Greenberg & Watson, 2006).

At times, cognitive change can also bring about new feelings. To evoke new, more adaptive emotions, therapists can focus on different aspects of experience; for example, the therapist might guide a client to focus on what they didn't like about what their parents did. Instead of focusing on "I was a bad kid," the therapist can ask the client what they resented or what they needed. Talking with clients to help them change how they view a situation or to discuss the meaning of an emotional experience can help them experience new feelings (Gross, 2001). Therapists might also express a new emotion for a client when it is difficult for the client to feel it spontaneously. The therapist might genuinely feel moral outrage at the violation or sadness at the loss that the shamed client had to suffer but is unable to express, and the therapist can then express it on the client's behalf. A new client emotion can also be evoked in response to new interactions with the therapist. The therapist might, for example, self-disclose a sense of closeness and concern for the client's revelation of a shameful experience or a commonality that communicates acceptance. This disclosure can then evoke feelings of calmness and closeness that act as an antidote to expected shame and rejection.

TRANSFORMING SHAME BY EXPERIENCING PRIMARY ADAPTIVE ANGER

Often, shame is transformed by experiencing primary adaptive anger in therapy. This helps clients feel empowered to assert themselves and to stand up to abusers in imaginal confrontations and empowers them to challenge any self-blame and self-contempt they may experience (Harmon-Jones et al., 2008; Paivio, 1999). Shame and maladaptive self-blame can be transformed by accessing healthy feelings of adaptive anger at those who harmed the client. For example, the following transcript is from a session with a depressed male client.[1] Describing his relationship with his father, he says, "He abandoned me emotionally as a child after my mother had died." The client begins by stating that he felt he was at fault, he deserved to be rejected, and something was wrong with him. Exploration of this feeling gives rise to a sense of anger; noticing this, the therapist guides the client's attention toward those bodily sensed aspects of the emerging experience of anger. Through this process, his sense of worthlessness transforms into a more empowered sense of self-assertion.

CLIENT (C): He was cold and distant, never paying attention to me. I suffered, and I put myself through hell thinking it was my fault. I guess I have only myself to blame.

THERAPIST (T): So, there's this sense of you somehow not deserving his attention and love . . . *(empathic understanding)*

C: (Tears fill his eyes) I've had so many losses, all my life. It was so unfair. I've had to deal with it all on my own. I really am so furious at him for what he did.

T: Tell him what you feel. *(points to empty chair)* **(promote expression)**

C: (To his imagined father) I don't think you realize—everything has been so much harder because of you. All my relationships, because of the way you

---

[1]The clinical material used in this book is adequately disguised to protect client confidentiality. Client identity has been maintained.

treated me, have been hard. Every day, every week, every year I've had to fight through the things you made me feel . . .

T: Yeah. Tell him you resent . . .

C: I resent you for being so self-absorbed, so selfish, so inconsiderate, and dismissive, and—and *(long pause)* for just never seeing me, or putting my needs first. *(pause)* Not once. It's not that I always needed attention—oh, I'm just feeling he would never understand.

T: OK. Notice that, but try to stay with your resentment for a while longer. I know it's difficult, but tell him more about your resentment.

C: (Again, to his imagined father) It's hard to tell you directly, but it's just true: You were a bad father to me. You abandoned and neglected me—and I'm angry at you for that.

T: So, "I needed you to give me some love. And as a child I needed to be considered, my needs put first, at least sometimes." **(access unmet need)**

C: Yes. That's exactly it.

In this example, the client's maladaptive shame is transformed as primary feelings of anger and healthy entitlement are accessed and supported by the therapist. Over time, with repeated focus of this assertive anger during therapy, the client develops a sense of entitlement to having his needs met, and this sense becomes a new part of the client's sense of self. This sense of entitlement also leads to the sadness of loss at what was deserved but never received. Grieving the loss then leads to the client trying to let go, internally or externally, of having the unmet need met by the significant other and accepting what was.

Adaptive anger, however, needs to be distinguished from maladaptive rage that often accompanies narcissistic slights and feeling humiliated. Maladaptive rage is too intense, chronic, or destructive and inappropriate. Rage in reaction to minor insults or to failure experiences is not adaptive and doesn't help get primary needs met. Alternatively, therapists using emotion-focused therapy (EFT) help clients attend to, experience, and possibly intensify adaptive anger, which is empowering. The focus of such work is on asserting the self rather than destroying the other—on promoting "I" statements such as "I am angry that you beat my mother," and "I resent you were never there." The focus is not on "you" statements, such as "You should be shot," or "What kind of parent does that to a child? You were a useless parent." Maladaptive rage aimed at destroying the other is not intensified or encouraged but rather is bypassed. When adaptive anger is validated, clients tend to shift their focus to their internal experience of being hurt.

Introjected shaming messages that were associated with a client's core maladaptive shame, such as hearing "You're so selfish," or "Homosexuality is deviant," are accessed. The role of the therapist is to clarify the interpersonal origins of these messages, not to reinforce self-blame. These messages generally originated with significant others, such as parents, or people in authority positions in society. Once clients are able to stand up for themselves and feel supported by the therapist, they are encouraged to own that they no longer need to be governed by these messages. They are encouraged to understand that by having internalized these shaming messages, they have been agents in perpetuating their own suffering. As clients begin to see that their shame is internally generated, the focus then becomes the intrapersonal struggle for self-acceptance.

A TASK-ANALYTIC STUDY OF THE TRANSFORMATION OF SHAME

An investigation of shame resolution events was completed by Sara Miller (2021) in her doctoral dissertation at the York University Psychotherapy Research Lab. A model of transforming maladaptive shame in psychotherapy was developed, and its relation to therapy outcome was tested. This model was built using a task-analytic method (Greenberg, 2007), in which a number of resolution events were compared with events that failed to resolve and the components that discriminate these two groups apart were extracted.

Given that no observation is theory free (Kuhn, 1962; Nagel et al., 1973), we first laid out a rational model. This model of how shame is resolved in therapeutic sessions is based on EFT theory, research, clinical experience of working with shame in EFT, and the theoretical literature on shame. Then, a small number of good examples of resolution were compared with a few unresolved examples to extract the components that discriminated resolution from nonresolution performances on the task of resolving shame. The empirically derived steps were then synthesized with the rationally derived model.

The synthesized rational/empirical model of client resolution performance is shown in Figure 6.1. This model of client process includes states that were thought to be necessary in the resolution of shame as well as states that commonly arose but were not necessary or could even be detrimental to resolution, leading into possible therapeutic dead ends. The essential and nonessential components follow, with the essential components shown in bold font:

1a. **Express self-criticism and self-contempt** and/or
1b. **Access and narrate abuse memories**

FIGURE 6.1. Model of Resolution of Shame–Client Process

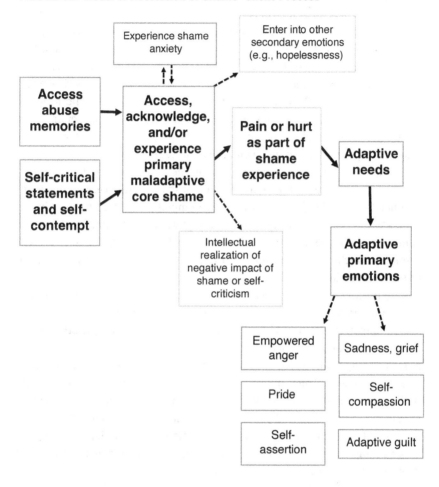

2. **Access primary maladaptive core shame**
3. Experience and articulate shame anxiety
4. Access the psychological pain of shame
5. Express secondary emotions such as global distress, hopelessness, helplessness, and other forms of anxiety over and above shame anxiety
6. Elaborate understanding of the impact of shame or of self-criticism/self-contempt at an intellectual level
7. **Express adaptive needs**
8. **Arrive at primary adaptive emotions and self-organizations**

An in-session shame event begins with a marker of shaming experience. The client expresses self-criticism, accompanied by self-contempt and/or narrated memories of core maladaptive shame related to significant trauma, abuse, neglect, or other interpersonal experiences. Next, and centrally important, is accessing, experiencing, acknowledging, and, in some form, symbolizing primary maladaptive shame in awareness. This is the core shame that needs to be transformed. The person might then experience and/or articulate shame anxiety. Along the way it may be expected that clients experience secondary emotions of global distress, hopelessness, helplessness, and forms of anxiety other than shame anxiety. Clients might have some understanding, at an intellectual level, of the negative impact of shame or of self-criticism/self-contempt but without much emotional arousal.

The next essential steps, emerging from the activated experience of maladaptive shame, are experiencing the pain of shame and accessing the adaptive needs for validation and acceptance embedded in the shame. Finally, clients who resolve will access primary adaptive emotions and develop more confident self-organizations. These more resilient states, which represent resolution, include adaptive anger, pride, and more complex emotions such as self-compassion.

The initial states on the path to resolution thus are self-criticism/self-contempt and abuse memories. Self-criticism is a criticism of the whole self and is often accompanied by contempt. Abuse memories, on the other hand, are of trauma, abuse, neglect, or other relational experiences that may have played an important a role in the development of the client's core maladaptive shame scheme. They are essential to the process of working productively with maladaptive shame, as they are the means to accessing and activating shame in the session to make it amenable to new input. Either or both states are possible as entry points, and some clients might experience one or the other during the session, while other clients might experience both. These components mark the beginning of a shame episode.

The next and most important step is accessing, experiencing, and, in some form, symbolizing primary maladaptive shame in awareness. This leads to the pain of shame, which is related to but distinct from feeling the shame itself. Clients acknowledged how painful the experience was, and this acknowledgment deepened the acceptance of the shame. Arrival at the lived experience of shame gave these clients access to the adaptive organismic needs for validation and acceptance, embedded in the shame.

It was hypothesized that a heartfelt need, but not a facilitative need, would be capable of triggering the emergence of adaptive emotion. A heartfelt need, as explained previously, has the quality of a deep sense of what was missed and a felt sense of having deserved to have had the need met. This feeling arises as an organismic response to overcome the pain. Finally, the clients arrived at primary adaptive emotions and developed more resilient self-organizations. The model of client process developed by task-analytic methods thus contained five hypothesized essential experiential states expected to occur in order: the initial states of self-criticism or abuse memories, activation of core maladaptive shame, the pain of shame, the heartfelt need, and resolution states.

The model of the emotional processing steps was then tested for its ability to predict reduction in depression at therapy termination. The sample included 23 psychotherapy clients with major depressive disorder who presented a core maladaptive shame scheme in early sessions. Videotaped sessions of 23 psychotherapies were coded using the Coding System for Emotional Processing of Maladaptive Shame developed for this study (CEMS; S. Miller, 2021), a psychotherapy process measure that incorporates and expands on elements of previously validated psychotherapy process research scales. The sessions on which to test the path from maladaptive shame to adaptive emotion were selected by identifying three sessions that contained chair work (because shame is most likely to be accessed at high levels of arousal in chair work) and had the highest rated score of in-session degree of resolution of shame (DRS) on a measure of resolution. The therapy outcome index used was pre–post difference scores on the Beck Depression Inventory (BDI; A. T. Beck et al., 1961), indicating change in depressive symptoms.

Multivariate regression analyses indicated that the number of utterances on rated maladaptive shame and on adaptive emotion together accounted for 30% of the variance in change scores on the BDI, whereas the addition of adaptive need to the analysis increased the explained variance to 36%. All clients who experienced a heightened emotional experience of both states over at least three utterances had good therapy outcomes. In addition, clients who had greater and more consistent progress through the model over the course of the session had greater pre–post change scores, and the sequence of states in the model was also found to be predictive of outcome.

The role of need was less definitive. Analyses revealed that a sufficient number of clients transitioned spontaneously from primary maladaptive shame to a primary adaptive emotion, without articulating a heartfelt need (rated as Level 3 or above on CEMS); this component was not statistically significant as a necessary transitional bridge. Articulating an adaptive need thus was not found to be a necessary step in the transformation from core maladaptive shame to the expression of an adaptive emotion; however, we found that articulating a lower level facilitative need (below Level 3 on CEMS), rather than a heartfelt need, served as a bridge between maladaptive and adaptive emotion. The sequence of maladaptive emotion to facilitative need to adaptive emotion occurred quite frequently, whereas the sequence involving a Level 3 heartfelt need occurred only rarely.

This study suggests that the transition from maladaptive to adaptive emotion often occurs spontaneously and a heartfelt need accompanied by a sense of deservingness, does not have to be fully articulated or accessed to trigger an adaptive emotion. It appears that (a) inquiring into clients' adaptive needs and asking them to express them is a helpful but not always necessary therapeutic tool for therapists to use, and (b) a client's expression of a need at a higher level of arousal is not essential in facilitating the emergence of adaptive emotion. However, most clients who reached adaptive emotion expression eventually accessed a heartfelt need rated as Level 3, but often after the adaptive emotion, a finding that suggests a circular relationship between these two states rather than a sequential one.

Analyses of the sequences also showed that accessing an adaptive emotion was significantly likely to be preceded by a client's experience of self-contempt followed by maladaptive shame, in that sequence. The primary adaptive emotions, in the session, that were found to be significant predictors of therapy outcome were pride, self-compassion, anger, and pride/anger (self-determination). The number of utterances indicative of assertion and self-care accounted for 51% of treatment outcome. Of note, clients who experienced one of these adaptive emotions also tended to experience the others. Furthermore, the number of client utterances of a Level 3 need was found to correlate significantly with therapy outcome, lending support to the therapeutic value if not necessity of heartfelt need expression.

In addition, clients who had a high proportion of early model states (e.g., self-contempt) across the therapy session had smaller change scores, whereas clients who manifested increasing experiences of later model states as the session advanced (e.g., primary adaptive emotion) had larger change scores. Results showed that progressing from lower model states to the higher level states was significantly related to reduction in BDI scores. It appears that the sequence of emotion states from secondary to primary maladaptive to adaptive emotion was significantly more likely than chance to happen in this order and that this sequence predicted outcome.

The most basic and the most clinically relevant finding, therefore, was that it is helpful to facilitate clients to deeply experience the two key emotion states of primary maladaptive shame followed by adaptive emotion to experience good outcomes. Clients who do not experience these two states are less likely to have good outcomes. In short, clients' deep access to maladaptive shame followed by primary adaptive emotion was significantly associated with alleviation of depressive symptomology at therapy termination.

The converse is also true, that poor outcome was associated with failure to access and deeply experience shame during the key best session.

It is interesting to note that clients in the study presented with a variety of concerns, including divorce, history of abuse or bereavement, unemployment, and marital difficulties, and all were diagnosed as depressed. Regardless of the content of the presenting concern, working through maladaptive shame according to the steps of the model significantly predicted good outcome. Not going through the process was significantly associated with poor outcome.

In addition, given that clients who more deeply and more frequently experienced shame and adaptive emotions had the largest gains at therapy termination, the findings of the study suggest that it is therapeutic to help clients stay with their painful experience of shame in order to resolve it, and it is important to access adaptive emotions such as pride, assertive anger, and self-compassion to help overcome maladaptive shame. These findings suggest that identifying a client's core maladaptive emotion scheme early in the course of therapy is clinically useful. The study also provides empirical support for the components that therapists need to facilitate to help clients who have underlying core maladaptive shame schemes transform to more resilient states.

THE PROCESS

The main components of interest in the model are elaborated in the following sections. This discussion is followed by a description of therapist interventions needed to facilitate the different process steps.

Shame Markers

Because shame hides itself, it is often buried in statements that are not obviously shame. In some instances, particular statements may not contain shame themselves, but the content serves as a signal that can alert therapists to be attuned to underlying shame in subsequent statements. For example, one client said, "My father had very high expectations of us kids. He was a perfectionist." This statement forecasts the emergence of shaming self-criticism. In the next statement, the client continued, "Nothing was ever good enough for him. I always felt I was falling short and felt not good enough." Another example of a client's indirect reference to shame was her description and reflection on her mother's statement that affected her sense of worthiness and her dignity: "My mother used to come to my house and would bring me clothes to wear because otherwise she would be embarrassed to be seen with me in public." Furthermore, experiences of being dismissed or being ignored can be shaming, as these experiences contain the idea that "you are not important enough for me to notice you." Feeling or being powerlessness, as reflected in one client's statement that "I just always felt so controlled, so regulated, powerless and useless," results in feelings of shame.

Powerlessness that engenders shame may have tones of self-contempt, implying that the self was impotent, incompetent, or unable, not that the situation was hopeless, difficult, or challenging. Helplessness that is about the self and not about the situation and perfectionism both may be related to feelings of shame. A person may use perfectionism and very high standards in an attempt to defend against an underlying feeling that they are inadequate, defective, or not good enough.

An example of a statement that doesn't directly disclose shame but contains underlying shame is "I feel like it's another failure." In another example, a client, speaking to his mother from experiencing chair, said, "You're not really, really interested in what—what it is that I'm talking about. I am not even important enough for you [my mother] to be interested in what I am saying to you." In another example, the client said, "I wanted you to take an interest in what I had to—there was some reason—to understand that I was worthwhile to listen to." The client was experiencing rejection that implies shame. In all these cases, it is important to gently move toward the shame and focus on it in both body and mind.

Accessing Primary Maladaptive Shame

Once a marker of a shame process has been identified, the client's primary adaptive shame and related self-organizations need to be accessed in the session. The client has to feel shame to change shame. Shame can be experienced in the session, in the moment, in different ways. It can arise because it was evoked by something that transpired in the session in response to memories of past events or because it was experienced while reliving a feeling of shame in a situation outside of the session.

To facilitate the articulation and experience of shame, therapists need to be attuned to clients' experience and especially aspects of their experience that have not yet been formulated, are difficult to symbolize, or have previously been disclaimed. Clients often know they feel shame, but they disclaim the experience of it because they fear that if they feel it, they will fall apart. The focus of therapy is on reclaiming the experience—on accepting, allowing, and exploring it—and facilitating the capacity to develop a language for describing the experience of shame. This lays a foundation for productive emotional processing of the core shame (Auszra et al., 2013). The goal is to be able to attend to it, own it, symbolize it, express it in a congruent manner, accept it, experience oneself as an agent rather than a victim of it, regulate it, and, finally, differentiate it.

The core maladaptive shame that is evoked, as described in Chapter 3, is about the self as defective, about having been humiliated, or about feeling over exposed. Body language and facial cues include averted gaze, head hanging down, and possibly blushing. The action tendency is to want to disappear or to cease to exist.

Shame Anxiety and Other Secondary Emotions

Along the path of working on shame, clients may experience anxiety or a fear of feeling shame. The client expresses anxiety about feeling shame, about being perceived by others as shameful, or about acting shamefully. Anxiety is activated in the session, and the focus of the anxiety is the feeling of shame. Prototypically, shame anxiety statements begin with some statement of anxiety that shame will be felt, such as "I'm afraid that I'll feel shame," "I'm worried that . . .," or "I'm anxious that. . . ." The client may talk about anxiety or about being exposed, embarrassed, or seen to be inadequate. One client stated, "I'm afraid to be a failure again." Another, when discussing his anxiety about attending a social event, said, "Um – you know I hope no one talks to me, ha, because then they'll find out that, you know, that I don't belong in here." Both clients were feeling anxious about feeling ashamed or being shameful.

Clients may also experience secondary or maladaptive emotions other than shame or shame anxiety in session. Secondary emotions often appear in the form of global distress, rejecting anger, hopelessness, helplessness, or complaint (i.e., a fusion of hurt and anger). In general, maladaptive emotions are fear or sadness regarding abandonment. For example, clients in a depressed population may express symptomatic distress, such as feeling depressed or fatigued, having difficulty sleeping, wanting to stay in bed all day, lacking purpose, or experiencing loss of meaning. When a client experiences secondary emotions in shame episodes, therapists should empathize with these feelings but refocus on the main process components of shame work.

Pain Arising From Shame

It is not uncommon for clients to experience deep pain when they access shame or articulate self-contempt. It is generally therapeutically productive to follow this pain, which acts as a compass that guides the process to the client's core concern. Processing emotional pain, rather than being stuck in it, helps get to the core wound. Pain is adaptive when it is a fresh new experience (such as allowing oneself to feel pain regarding past abuse, having previously blocked the pain).

The boundary separating shame and pain of shame is not always clear. However, because of its importance in working with maladaptive shame, we found it helpful to define the pain of shame as a discrete component in our model. Clients may use words such as *hurt, sad, pain, feeling broken*, or *shattered* to describe this experience of pain, or they may use metaphors of physical pain, such as "torn apart" or "left bleeding." Adaptive pain also borders on adaptive sadness/grief but differs in that it is the hurt of the shame rather than about loss as in grief.

Intellectual Acknowledgment of Impact

Clients may also acknowledge, realize, or explore the impact of the shame only on an intellectual level, without emotional arousal. They might focus on behavioral impacts (e.g., "When I criticize myself, I stay home all day"), somatic symptoms (e.g., "My self-criticism makes me so tense that I get headaches"), or cognitive processes (e.g., "I see now a pattern where I feel bad about myself and then I tell myself nothing will change"). Clients may express the feeling of insight with phrases such as "I see now that . . ." or "I realize now that. . . ." These feelings need to be acknowledged but bypassed to help access and reclaim their disclaimed need.

Progress Toward Resolution: Adaptive Needs and Emotions

As mentioned, need statements are not demands or complaints but rather are self-assertions of what the client needs. Typically, need statements begin with phrases such as "I needed . . ." or "When I was a child, I deserved. . . ." Statements that express a need more tentatively and less resolute in tone may be therapeutically useful. Ideal needs statements express heartfelt needs that come from aroused emotion and reflect that the client feels they are entitled to have those needs met. Examples of strong statements of need are "I deserve to be accepted" and "I deserve to be listened to." Another example comes from a client expressing to the mother in an empty chair: "I needed you to hug me when I was hurting, to understand when I was crying out for help."

The final step is arriving at primary adaptive emotions. This step includes arriving at complex states based on primary emotions and involve self-soothing, a sense of confidence, and strength or worthiness. The primary adaptive emotions we thought would be most important in transforming maladaptive shame were

- **Pride.** Pride can include such states as self-respect and self-confidence.

- **Self-compassion.** Self-compassion involves compassion, understanding, and/or forgiveness toward the self: "I can see that you're trying your best."

- **Anger.** Adaptive anger is a complex emotion to identify because people most often think of or define anger in secondary and maladaptive forms, which are therefore more likely to be observed and then confused with primary anger. Adaptive anger involves boundary setting and is not destructive. Statements such as "I am angry at you for..." and "I resent..." reflect adaptive anger provided they are not complaints or essentially whining. Adaptive anger should prototypically express "I am angry about it," not "I blame you for it." Again, to transform shame, clients have to access their empowering, primary adaptive anger in the safety of the therapy situation (not in the real world) by asserting themselves against abusers in imaginal confrontations and by challenging self-blame and contempt.

- **Pride/anger.** A mixture of pride and anger contains expressions of determination or agency or asserting one's agency.

- **Primary adaptive guilt.** Primary adaptive guilt is proportional to the perceived wrongdoing and motivates the person to take action to make amends to another or to repair damage. Primary adaptive guilt may be seen in the context of working with maladaptive shame, as some clients may move from shame into primary adaptive guilt. For example, some clients may denigrate themselves in relation to past actions without actually taking responsibility or making amends for those actions. A move to adaptive guilt—recognizing responsibility for wrongdoing and taking actions to repair damage—is adaptive.

- **Sadness/grief.** Primary adaptive sadness/grief often involves letting go of unmet needs with genuine acceptance (although with sadness) that they will not be met. As with pain (discussed later in this chapter), sadness/grief often has the quality of being about or in regard to another affect or experience. For example, a person may experience grief about their unmet needs.

THERAPEUTIC INTERVENTION

The model of change we have developed, like all models, does not claim to be true but is only an approximation to the truth. Some clients who had good therapy outcome did not process their emotion according to the model, suggesting that it is only a model and therapists should not ignore the unique and meaningful personal human story and experience of each person. Rather, the model provides a map that can assist therapists to locate the client's process in relation to a larger structure and suggest an empirically based route for the transformation of maladaptive shame by accessing a primary adaptive emotion. The categories in the model can assist therapists to understand different types of emotional processes in clients and can provide guidance as to the emotional states that would be most useful to facilitate at any given moment.

A therapist's basic question at each moment in session is "What do I do now?" This model provides a way of understanding the client's process and suggests how to facilitate next steps. Therapists are eager to learn intervention skills, but most important are the perceptual skills of being able to recognize when to do what. Perceptual skills enhance timing of interventions. The model helps to identify choice points and informs what to do and when to do it.

Figure 6.2 shows a descriptive model of therapist actions in line with the empirically derived model of resolution of shame. First, when a therapist identifies a marker of self-criticism or sees abuse memories emerging, they have an opportunity to intervene with an appropriate chair dialogue between self and self or self and other. Once shame emerges implicitly or overtly, the therapist needs to work toward its intensification to moderate to high degrees of arousal, as well as symbolization and differentiation of the shame. The therapist also needs to guide the client to process memories of past situations and feelings that were the original sources of shame. Along the way, the therapist needs to recognize tangents that lead away from the main focus of reprocessing the shame. Clients may narrate experiences of feeling anxious about being shamed. These are opportunities to work on how they produce the anxiety, using a two-chair anxiety split in which the client is asked to make themselves afraid of shame. However, the therapist needs to recognize that this is a waystation on the path to resolving shame and ultimately redirect the chair dialogue to the shame-producing criticisms rather than staying on the secondary anxiety-producing catastrophizing process.

Another flag indicating a tangent is the client entering a symptomatic secondary emotion such as hopelessness or helplessness. These emotions are to be acknowledged and validated but bypassed to get to the underlying experience. Therapists also need to acknowledge but not focus on clients' intellectual discussions of the negative impacts of shame on themselves and on their lives in an effort to problem solve or make "new year's resolutions,"

FIGURE 6.2. Model of Therapist Actions

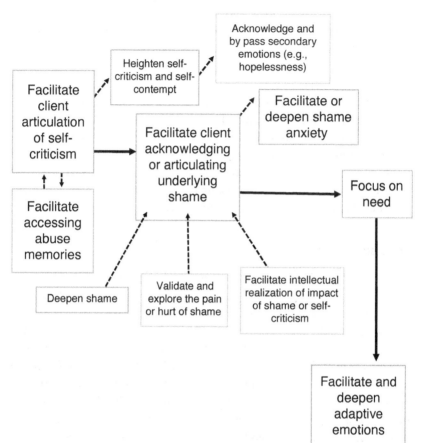

such as to stop being so self-critical or to stop ruminating and let go of their shameful memories. Therapists need to focus on the client's underlying feelings and needs rather than become mired in explanations and good intentions. The hurt that may arise spontaneously or has been evoked but still unspoken needs to be the focus of attention.

At this point, therapists need to capture the pain of it all and help the client stay with the pain, symbolizing what the shame is like in the body. This is the true sensory and physiological cost and pain of the shame. Once pain is being felt, therapists need to focus on the now-activated will of the client to overcome the suffering and to survive and live. Experiencing the wish to survive and experiencing that one's pain and needs are valid, the unconscious giant begins to feel angry or sad about the injustice and the loss of never having received what they in fact deserved. This leads to the conscious emergence of the adaptive emotions. Therapists need to validate and support the new emotions that emerge and the newly developed self-organization and to guide clients to change their narratives of the same old story in which they were stuck into a more positive outcome story (Angus & Greenberg, 2011).

Two major interventions for accessing shame are two-chair dialogues for self-critical splits and empty-chair dialogues for unfinished business. In two-chair dialogues, therapists ask clients to enact the two parts of themselves—the critic or judge who directs contemptuous statements to the self and the recipient of the contempt and disgust. In empty-chair dialogue, the client expresses unresolved feelings to the imagined other in an empty chair. This activates shame and provides access to unmet needs and new emotions.

Two-Chair Dialogues

Therapists can profitably work with shame-producing self-criticism (Greenberg et al., 1993) using two-chair dialogues. Resolution of self-critical splits has been related to good therapeutic outcomes (Greenberg, 1979, 2015; Greenberg & Webster, 1982). The process of resolving shame using this intervention begins by inviting clients to enact the "critic" in the "other" chair. The client criticizes or expresses contempt toward the self, criticizing the self's abilities and worth. Self-criticism and self-contempt lie on an intensity continuum, with self-contempt the more intense version of self-criticism. Criticism involves the evaluative aspect of this process but does not itself necessarily involve high emotional arousal. As emotional arousal increases, the client experiences and expresses more self-contempt (Whelton & Greenberg, 2005). The general interactional stance of the critic is hostile attack involving negative evaluation. Clients may also enact a *shame anxiety critic*, a voice that evokes anxiety about the possibility of being shamed or behaving shamefully in the future. Clients, for example, may make statements such as "People will laugh at you," "You'll make a fool of yourself," or "You'll look like an idiot."

When clients repeatedly berate themselves for not living up to expectations, the therapist can respond, "I hear how much that voice is saying, 'I don't like myself very much.' This must evoke such feelings of shame. I imagine it must be painful to be treated this way." Intervention involves specifying the shame-producing cognitions, highlighting the expressive quality of contempt, and heightening awareness of agency in the shame-producing process. The intervention focuses not only on the cognitive content of the critic's message but also on the facial and vocal contempt directed at the experiencing self and is designed to evoke the self's painful reaction to the harshness of the negative self-evaluation.

An important step in this process is heightening clients' awareness of their agency in the production of shame. Clients need to realize that their shame-producing messages are internally generated and, therefore, they can change them. The tendency to protest against and oppose the shaming message arises spontaneously in the self from another chair as a matter of survival. A negotiation between the two sides of the self then leads to a more self-accepting and self-soothing attitude toward the self and weakens the negative evaluations. This acceptance leads to the emergence of positive emotions such as pride and love in the self.

The two-chair self-critical process increases awareness of the specific internalized negative messages, the expressive quality of the critical voice, and the emotional impact of the internalized contempt. This process activates the shame of self-denigration as well as the damage to the client's self-esteem and makes them amenable to transformation. Shame is countered by supporting the emergence of the healthy part of self with feelings of assertiveness and pride.

As self-criticism and self-contempt arise in the moment, they activate underlying shame, related to the "defect" they are criticizing. In this way, self-criticism and shame are like two sides of the same coin. The client simultaneously experiences themself as critic and criticized. Nevertheless, these two processes are distinct, and it is best to separate and work with each independently as well as to work with their relationship to each other. The client's position in the chairs (critic or experiencing-self chair), the vocal quality, facial expression, and body posture as well as the exact content of the client's speech are factors that assist in differentiating the experience of shame from the more self-critical/self-contemptuous aspect of experience.

The critical chair uses blaming "you" language, in which the self is attacked and maligned for failings. Prototypically, this chair adopts an unfriendly, attacking interactional position. In this position, the person is talking about or to the self, not feeling as the self (e.g., "You're worthless, a blob, garbage, ugly, fat, lazy"). Clients often feel the underlying shame while voicing contempt, but they are speaking in "you" language and in a lecturing or scolding vocal tone, and they are identifying in body and mind mainly with an evaluating-attack position.

In the experiencing chair, clients use "I" language and, ideally, access feelings of shame. As the client explores their experience in the experiencing chair, shame emerges (e.g., "I just feel like such a failure" or "I feel small, diminished, or worthless"). Client statements beginning with "I feel" or "I felt" are signs that shame has emerged and the person has shifted out of the self-critical state. As an example, "You are such an idiot" (spoken toward the self-chair from the critic chair, with a strong lecturing vocal quality) is self-criticism, but "I feel foolish" (spoken in the self-chair, with a slumping posture, looking down, and with a quiet, fatigued vocal quality) is shame. It is important for the therapist to notice this subtle difference and promote separation between the doer and done-to position and to guide the client toward whatever it is that they are engaged in, shaming attack or diminishing shame.

As clients elaborate, their criticisms and self-contempt increase, and the underlying feeling of shame and pain begin to emerge. If the therapist is working skillfully, a prompt to switch back to the experiencing chair—given at the appropriate time, after the critic has really stung the self with contempt—accesses the client's underlying, vulnerable, feeling of shame. However, the self might "collapse" into agreement with the critical voice and into hopelessness. For example, in reaction to the critic, the self may say, "I agree with him," "He's right," or "There's no point in arguing with that." These responses represent withdrawal and collapsing of the self into hopelessness. They also are statements in the domain of cognition: "is true or not." Therapists ideally guide clients to operate in the domain of affect: "is good for me or bad for me" (i.e., how it feels), guiding toward how the client feels rather than promoting discussion of the factual reality of the criticisms.

Often therapists less experienced with this dialogue misguidedly encourage the cognitive process of arguing against the critic or encourage getting angry at the critic and telling it "Leave me alone." Although this strategy might sound good, as if people are standing up for themselves, usually it is secondary defensive anger at a cognitive level. Effective assertive feelings and needs must come from the experience of the painful shame, which provides access to the heartfelt need prompted by the motive to survive.

At times, the two processes (shame and self-contempt) are mixed, especially if the therapist is not facilitating the client's differentiation of them. EFT theory suggests that an important therapeutic objective is to assist the client to differentiate self-criticism and self-contempt from the underlying shame and to experience them differently. One client, for example, said from the critic chair, with a vicious tone of voice, "Your personality is garbage," and in the same vicious tone, "Nobody likes you because of the way you are," (Miller, 2021). This is a good example of shame producing self-contempt.

Empty-Chair Dialogue

The second type of affective-meaning state that leads into shame comes when a client narrates memories of past abuse or maltreatment to find new ways to come to terms with their unresolved bad feelings. In work with core maladaptive shame that involves maltreatment, empty-chair dialogue, in which the client confronts the other and expresses the previously unexpressed emotions, is helpful in overcoming shame (Greenberg, Rice, & Elliot, 1993). A number of research studies have found empty-chair dialogue to be very effective in helping people access unresolved feelings and resolve unfinished business (Greenberg & Malcolm, 2002; Paivio & Greenberg, 1995).

Working with shame-based survivors of maltreatment and abuse, who often feel responsible for the abuse, intervention involves externalizing the blame—putting the blame "where it belongs." In addition, for clients who have been abused, the abuse becomes a closely guarded secret and produces a lot of shame anxiety and fear of intimacy. Bringing it out in the dialogue acts as an antidote to the concealment.

In this dialogue, clients confront the humiliating or abusive other in their imagination, as if the person were sitting in the empty chair. This form of gestalt empty chair work involving imaginal confrontation for resolving unfinished business is helpful in accessing and resolving maladaptive shame (Greenberg, Rice, & Elliot, 1993). Empty-chair dialogue activates clients' internal views of significant others and facilitates their experience and expression of unresolved feelings and needs. Shifts in views of both the other and the self often occur, and resolution involves holding the other accountable or understanding or forgiving the other.

Work generally begins with the client's expression of a lot of secondary reactive emotions, especially protest, blame, or complaint. In empty-chair work, clients have to arrive at their painful emotions before they can leave them. In this process, significant unresolved feelings and unmet needs are first identified, then experienced as valid and voiced such that the emotions are symbolized and the action tendencies are reclaimed. The expression of the painful emotions and unmet needs to the imagined other leads to the emergence of a new way of experiencing the self and viewing the other.

Sometimes when a client experiences the underlying shame of violation or sadness of loss, it is as if the imagined person hears what the client needs, recognizes the legitimacy of the client's feelings and needs, and is responsive to the client's hurt. Then as the other person, the client experiences compassion and comfort, which transform the hurt and shame. However, when the imagined negative other is unable or unwilling to be responsive or to accept responsibility for the harm, a resolution of understanding is not possible. The client then needs to assert that they deserved to have their unmet needs met and hold the others accountable for their failures to provide. Acknowledging the pain of what happened and grieving the loss produces a new way of being. The self is strengthened, and the other is seen as weaker. In this process, a virtual reality is created in which memories are activated and can be transformed by a process in which memory reconsolidates with new input so that the client's experience of the past changes. This process helps clients establish the legitimacy of their need and explore ways to have their needs met in current and future relationships.

Experiences of abuse, neglect, and trauma (especially ongoing trauma as a child by important attachment figures), as well as experiences of rejection and/or ridicule by peers, frequently lead people to develop feelings of shame and worthlessness or feeling flawed (Miller, 2021). Some clients may first narrate and explore such abuse experiences and subsequently begin to access and articulate the shame from these experiences. Others arrive at memories of maltreatment during exploration of the historical and interpersonal roots of the client's self-criticism. Prototypically, clients then narrate memories of abuse, maltreatment, or neglect (what happened), explain the meaning of the experience (what it meant), and, less often, describe their experience of the maltreatment (what it felt like). This latter aspect, experiencing and symbolizing what was felt, needs to be focused on as therapy proceeds. The symbolization and exploration of what the person felt at the time (e.g., fear of feeling trapped, alone, unloved, vulnerable, terrified, confused, dread) begins the processing of the previously disclaimed emotion. The person will begin to re-experience some of these emotions, in the moment, in the session. Empty-chair dialogues help clients challenge the contempt and humiliation they received (Greenberg, Rice, & Elliott, 1993; Paivio et al., 2001); they are interventions of choice both to evoke shame and ultimately to empower clients to stand up to abusers in imaginal confrontations.

Narrating memories of abuse produces a large range of emotional body language and vocal qualities. For example, with a client discussing his father's violent outbursts, the therapist guided him to express his feelings to his father by saying, "Yeah – tell him what it was like for you when he lost control," to which the client said, after a long pause, "It made me give up – made me – it turned me off. It made me shut down, lose interest, I didn't care anymore – – didn't want to look forward to that, just . . .," and he trailed off.

The client accessed an autobiographical memory of experiencing his father's abuse and began to express his reactions to it and experience of it.

VALIDATION AND NARRATIVE CHANGE

Clients feel stronger, calmer, and more worthy having undone shame with anger at the unfairness, the sadness of grief, or self- or other compassion. At this point in the process, they will have developed a new experience of self by transformation by synthesis and will no longer have the tendency to run away or hide and can maintain eye contact. The therapist next needs to validate the newfound sense of self. Therapists no longer intervene to evoke shame, although they may use chair dialogues for clients to solidify the strengthened self and to express their newfound sense of self. Expression strengthens the neural pathways because the brain is always coding what the body does. By speaking out loud to the other part, albeit in a virtual reality, the person and the brain are repeating a new experience, and repetition is helpful to consolidate new learning. The main style of interaction at this stage, however, is dialogical, with the therapist empathizing and validating the client's newfound sense of self, inquiring how it feels and asking and giving feedback about what seems to have changed.

The aim, whether it be through anger, grief, or compassion, is to have a new bodily response and to be able to reflect on shame experiences and bring cognition to emotion in order to make sense of it. The client, with the help of the therapist, makes connections between different elements of their life, develops alternative explanations for their experiences, revises their views of themself, and develops a new story of their life and emotions. A therapeutic goal is to help clients develop these new past and future views of themselves. Therapists, therefore, help clients to develop narratives that emphasize their resilience and agency and to reconstruct their views of themselves. The self is no longer judged as incompetent but rather as capable and able to cope and grow, even if confronted with experiences that might previously have been perceived as threatening to survival.

An important final aspect of work in the transformation of shame is consolidation of a new narrative and construction of new meaning that confirms the client's identity. An old bad story changes into a story with a positive outcome, in which good things can happen. In addition to the change at the emotion schematic level is a process of narrative change, which both emanates from storying the new emotions and has been developing along the way by the process of reflection. In the course of therapy, clients have developed a working distance from their shame, symbolized their core maladaptive feelings of primary shame and worthlessness in awareness, and acknowledged that this is what they felt at their core—they have gained some reflective mastery over their shame. With the symbolization of their core shame feeling, they are able to create a separation from it and see it as a part of self rather than as their whole self. The feeling of shame becomes an object or product of the self, one that produces distress rather than engulfs the whole self. Shame, thus, is more easily regulated: "I'm a wretched person" has become "This is the wretched part of me, and I can see it and deal with it." This symbolization of parts creates a space for clients to reflect on themselves at a distance from the shameful experience. This piece can now be narrated at a conscious level, adding to the new bodily felt sense of confidence that emerged on an organismic experiential track from the will to survive and thrive. Change involves seeing the negative parts inside, understanding their origins and no longer accepting their old views of self and other. Clients then reconstruct their views of themselves and develop this. Now, the self is no longer viewed as a failure, but rather as competent and capable of success in the face of obstacles. They are able to thrive even when confronted with experiences that previously might have been perceived as shaming and threatening to survival.

7

CASE EXAMPLES

Let us not be ashamed to speak what we shame not to think.
—Michel de Montaigne

This chapter features transcripts of sessions of five different clients[1] involving work on shame. The first three are good-outcome cases: One focuses on shame from abuse and the other two shame from internalization of criticism. These three are followed by a poor-outcome case in which the shame was not resolved in the session. The last is a lengthier transcript of a more com moves to working with the internalized critical other.

---

[1]The clinical material used in this book is adequately disguised to protect client confidentiality. Client identity has been maintained.

https://doi.org/10.1037/0000393-007
Shame and Anger in Psychotherapy, by L. S. Greenberg
Copyright © 2024 by the American Psychological Association. All rights reserved.

CASE 1: ABUSE MEMORIES LEADING INTO SHAME (GOOD OUTCOME)

In this first example, Juan, a 28-year-old man of Latino origin, presented with anxiety and depression and expressed difficulty moving on in his life. He was artistically and literarily inclined, wanting to write as a reporter or author. As therapy progressed, it became clear that his relationship with his father was a source of great pain. Shame emerged as his core painful emotion, stemming from his experience of physical and emotional abuse at the hands of his father. It is of interest to note that no self-criticism had emerged in any of his sessions, and his shame developed purely from internalizing maltreatment.

In this transcript, from the 15th session, the client delves into the sense of worthlessness that his father's attitude toward him engendered. The episode begins with the narration of an abuse memory. His adaptive anger quickly transforms into accessing deep pain that he had walled off. His shame transforms into a sense of relief and worthiness once he allows his pain, has it validated, and can then draw on his empowered adaptive anger. His grief for the pain suffered and the feeling of empowered anger at being violated undo the feeling of shameful withdrawal and transform it into a sense of self-affirmation. The newly accessed anger and sadness of grief are the transformative emotions for this client. This therapy was successful, and the man came to forgive his father for wrongs done.

CLIENT (C): It was like a slow buildup, you know, he'd become more and more angry. It would take a while, but he would sit me down at the kitchen table and – – – – he'd pound his fist on the table to emphasize things and yell at me. He'd get closer to me. He'd pound his fist harder.

THERAPIST (T): Mm-hm.

C: He'd yell louder in my face . . . (sigh) *(narrating memory of abuse)*

T: Tell him what it was like for you sitting there while he pounded the table and got closer and yelled at you. – – Tell him how you felt. What was it like for you? *(focus on internal experience)*

C: (Sigh) I felt so small. (T: Mm-hm.) I felt like I just wanted to disappear, you know. *(core shame mixed with fear)*

T: Mm-hm. Just disappear.

C: I didn't want to be there, I didn't want to be anywhere, you know, I just didn't want to exist. *(pause for 3 minutes)*

T: Mm-hm. – – – Just like that feeling you talked about. Always waiting for something lurking around the corner. *(pause for 10 seconds)* So, it's like you broke my trust. (C: [Sigh]) Worse than that.

C: Always just failing really – – – – I don't know, guilty (T: Mm.) Ashamed. *(core shame)*

T: Mm. Ashamed.

C: I don't know why.

T: You don't know why you felt that way, or why you need to feel that way?

C: I don't know why I felt that way. You know, I just felt so bad. I felt like I didn't want to – like – – I felt like there was nothing I could do even if I did try.

T: Like there was no escape. – – – Nothing you could do would be right. (C: Mm-hm.) *(pause for 10 seconds)* Hm (incomprehensible) hurt me (incomprehensible) – – no – there's how awful it was to feel like nothing you could do would be accepted or loved or . . . (sigh) *(empathic exploration) (accessing core shame and then adaptive pain)*

C: Just felt so hopeless, you know. I just didn't – (clears throat) . . . (sigh) *(secondary hopelessness)*

T: How do you feel towards him? *(guides toward underlying emotion)*

C: Oh, I hate him. *(adaptive anger)*

T: Tell him.

C: I hate you.

T: Tell him.

C: (Sigh) I wish you were never in my life.

T: Hm. – – – – – – Tell him what you're—what you hate him about. What you are angry at him about. It's like "I'm angry at you for. . . ."

C: Making me hate myself and feel awful. *(shame)*

T: Mm-hm – – – – mm-hm – – mm-hm. – – Just let it come. It's okay.

C: (Client begins to sob) *(client enters into core pain for next few minutes)*

T: So painful.

C: (Crying intensifies)

T: Mm-hm, mm – – – – It's okay to let it come out. I'm here with you, around you. *(connection and support)*

C: (Crying)

T: Mm-hm.

C: (Sigh)

T: Mm-hm – – – so much pain, so many tears inside – hard to allow yourself.

C: (Looks to wall opposite of therapist and continues crying)

T: There's so much in there – – – – – – mm-hm – – – mm – – mm.

C: (Covers face, continues to look away, sigh) *(pause for 12 seconds)*

T: So sore inside it's like, you felt so squashed down.

C: (Sniffle, deep sigh) *(pause)* (deep sigh, weeping, continues to hide face)

T: You felt so unloved, it sounds like so painful. You needed safety. *(empathic affirmation, need validation)*

C: (Removes hand from face) *(pause for 10 seconds)* (sigh, looks up)

T: So much to endure . . .

C: Yeah, I felt so defeated and alone. I needed peace and safety, not explosions.

T: What are you feeling now?

C: I dunno. A kind of relief and exhausted.

T: I guess it was so much to carry all that anger and pain. So much especially as a kid, it wasn't yours to bear. *(narrative reconstruction)*

C: Yeah, I was a good kid. He was just a sick man. Kind of a bully probably because of all the crap from his life. But I deserved to exist free of the burden of all his stuff.

CASE 2: EXAMPLE OF SELF-CONTEMPT (GOOD OUTCOME)

In this example, Martha, a White 38-year-old woman who is married with three children, is dealing with her unresolved feelings about parental overintrusiveness and being a less favored child. She provides an example of her relationship with her mother, who brings an outfit for Martha to wear when the two go out so the mother won't be embarrassed to be seen with her in public.

This session is the tenth of a 14-session therapy with a very good outcome. Martha's shame was formed by her mother's invalidating attitude toward her and by her early experience of sexual abuse by the brother, denied by the parents. The abuse was revealed only in this tenth session. Up until this time, we had worked on her highly self-contemptuous internal voice. A few examples of the process enroute to accessing her shame are shown first.

The client starts by speaking from the experiencing chair in self-critical two-chair work. Her critic is both contemptuous and anxiety producing. She is speaking about her new job and is anxious about making errors.

C: And I won't be able to correct my mistake. I'll go to the branch, and I'm going to lose the job because if you don't balance your ledger (T: Right.) so many times, they don't want you, and I just kept that fear of I've got something good and I'm going to ruin it.

T: Okay, I want you to change chairs.

C: You want me to go over there?

T: Yeah. (client changes chairs to "critic" chair) So, tell her that – you've got something good, don't screw it up, and be that voice you were on that Tuesday.

C: Okay, I'm miserable. You're screwing it up. I knew you couldn't do it.

T: Yeah, it's a miserable, mean voice (C: Yeah.) and I guess it makes her feel kind of inadequate and (C: Right.) So, how does she do it? Do it. *(access critical voice)*

C: I don't know why you even bother trying at anything because you're not going to succeed. (T: Mm-hm.) Something's going to go wrong – haven't figured it out yet, but something's going to go wrong.

T: You're going to fail. (C: Yeah.) You're going . . .

C: Yes, you're heading down the street; you've fooled everybody that you've got a job with the company, and everybody's like wow, you're going to screw it up. (T: Ah.) You're not going to have enough money to feed the kids; you're not going to have enough money to make the loan payments. (T: Uh-huh.) You're going to die in this medical procedure. (T: Mm-hm.) Why are you going for this operation? Your loan won't go through in time, you'll miss your doctor's appointment, something will go wrong, and you won't get to the hospital on time, the surgery will be canceled, give it up, you know . . .

T: Give it up, stop trying.

C: Stop trying, exactly, just go back to your room, be depressed, be bummed out, shut the door, and don't function. You're pathetic, a loser . . . **(self-contempt)**

T: Uh-huh, don't even bother.

C: Yeah. Totally.

T: Because it's not going to work. Okay, change, and you're a loser . . .

C: (Changes chairs)

T: She's just told you, go to your room, be depressed, you're useless.

C: (Laughs)

T: How does that feel when you hear that? **(focus on activated experience)**

C: I feel awful.

T: What is awful like in your body? **(guide attention to bodily feeling)**

C: I dunno, sort like a sinking feeling inside. (looks down)

T: Can you just stay with that feeling and breathe?

C: (Curls up a little into a ball) **(action tendency)**

T: What's happening?

C: Like I want to get away, away from the pounding put-downs, the criticism.

T: Yeah, just like needing what? **(focus on need)**

C: I need, don't want these insults anymore. (looks up)

T: Yeah, tell her.

C: To hell with you! (laughs) **(moves into adaptive emotion based on deservingness)**

T: Tell her.

C: That's what I feel like.

T: So, why don't you tell her?

C: I want to overcome that. I'm really angry.

T: Yeah.

C: I don't need the constant failure thrown up in my face.

T: Yeah.

C: Not everything that's gone on wrong in my life is my fault. (T: Mm-hm.) Things happen, and I have to do what my mother-in-law told me and go forward. (T: Mm-hm.) And if I listen to you, then I'm going to go backwards.

A second example from Martha, later in the same session, shows how anger emerges as the antidote to shame and leads to self-worth. Generally, there are a number of chair dialogues throughout a therapy, each one hopefully leading to a little progress. Rome was not built in a day, and true change needs repetition. There often are two or three rounds of a dialogue in the same session, with the therapists circling back to the critical voice whenever it emerges in the process. This helps to activate more shame.

In this excerpt, Martha is in the critic chair. The therapist has asked Martha, as the critic, "What would happen if you stopped criticizing her?" to highlight the functions of the critic.

C: I'm afraid if I stop, you'll be proud of yourself, and that's wrong. (T: Mm-hm.) And uh . . .

T: Why is it wrong to be proud?

C: That's what I've always been taught.

T: Mm-hm, so tell her. "You have no right to be proud of yourself."

C: You've got no right to be proud of yourself. (T: Mm-hm.) You've screwed up in the past, and that's your track record, so – (T: Mm-hm.) that's what's going to happen. (T: Mm-hm.) And I have to make sure of it.

T: It's my job to make sure.

C: Yeah – (T: Mm.) (blows nose) and I don't really feel that any good will come at the end of you because I mean, you've messed everything up, so (T: Mm-hm.) how can you make it right.

The next excerpt is from the experiencing chair in the critic dialogue, a few minutes following the previous excerpt.

T: Mm-hm, and what happens for you when you hear that? It's almost like, can you tell her what happens, almost really destroys . . .

C: When I hear that – that, it just makes me want to cry. It makes me feel that it's going to be another bad experience to put on the chalkboard, and why didn't I kill myself when I was a teenager because then I wouldn't have to feel all this pain.

T: "So, it wipes me out." Can you tell her that, "It wipes me out when you're like that . . ."

C: You wipe me out when you're like that.

T: Yeah, crushing.

C: It makes me feel – like a nobody.

T: Yeah.

C: It makes me feel worthless and . . .

T: Yeah.

C: And not functioning, and I want to be, that I want to be normal . . .

T: Yeah, and really hard to change that.

C: And I'm afraid that somebody at the bank will find out my battle with this, (sniffs) and if I listen to you, it's going to show, and I'm going to fail. (cries) *(shame anxiety)*

A few seconds later, Martha is in the experiencing chair and accesses her core shame. She responds to the critic blaming her:

C: I hate that feeling.

T: What is it? *(naming the feeling)*

C: (Crying) That's when you told me it was my fault that I was sexually abused, and I hate that feeling, I feel so guilty. So bad, worthless. Like it was my fault.

T: Tell them [parents] what it was like when they brushed it off and said it was just brotherly love. *(therapist guides her to turn the anger outward that has been turned inward)*

C: I felt so, confused, unsupported, angry, but most of all just alone.

T: Yeah, tell them.

C: I felt all alone in the world without support, rejected, cut off . . .

T: Tell them what you needed.

C: I need you to hear me, to understand, and to do something about it. I needed support.

T: What do you feel as you say this? *(focuses on experience of expressing the need)*

C: Sad and angry. Like, how could you do this? You left me out in the cold, a child asking for support. You abandoned me.

T: Yes. You deserved to be heard. Tell them what you needed. *(oscillating between feeling and need to intensify both)*

C: I'm furious. I needed your protection, not turning a blind eye. I'd like to . . .

T: Yes, what would you like to do? *(focus on action tendency—in extreme violation, expression of rage is helpful as a beginning)*

C: I'm furious. I needed your protection, not turning a blind eye, I'd like to just smash you.

T: Go ahead, just imagine smashing them.

C: More I'd like someone to come in and tell them how they should have handled it.

T: Who would you like to come in?

At this point, we went into an imaginal re-entry in which I, as a protective adult and psychologist, went into the scene in which she was around 14 years old, telling her parents what had been happening with her brother. I instructed them to support her and educated her parents on the problems with denying the brother's sexual abuse.

CASE 3: BEING DISMISSED AS INTERNALIZED SHAME (GOOD OUTCOME)

The third case example involves a 47-year-old White male client whose mother was very dismissive and belittling; he referred to his mother as a "barracuda." This transcript offers an example of how being dismissed, ignored, or ostracized can be shaming because it contains the implication that "you are not worthy of my regard or attention; you are insignificant." The client's strongest access of shame comes in the context of expressing his need to feel worthwhile, indicative of not feeling worthy. There is kind of a fusion of shame and need, indicating how shame often is implied rather than outwardly stated. Some of the following transcript is from before the emergence of shame, as an example of how shame can underlie difficulties that are not obviously shame. After he accesses shame, we see an example of emotion changing emotion as he moves into anger.

This section begins with the therapist attempting to set up an empty-chair dialogue with the client's mother and the client having some difficulty engaging with her.

T: You could tell her, "It's really hard to talk to you – – – – it's really hard to talk to you like this." *(creates contact with the mother from where the client is at)*

C: Yeah, it's hard to talk to you because you – (T: Uh-huh.) you're not really, really interested in what, what it is that I'm talking about.

T: So, there's this . . .

C: Um, I mean, if I really was to do this, she'd be on the defensive, and "What are you talking about, what are you talking about? What do you mean? I didn't do that," and "Oh, so that's the way you think about me," (breath in) – ah, just being totally defensive as opposed to listening. Um (T: So, you . . .) just to tr – just to try and understand how I feel (breath in), not necessarily (breath out) to accept responsibility for everything, but at least . . .

T: Just listen.

C: Yeah, at least hearing and acknowledging that that's the way I feel.

T: So, "I feel . . ."

C: I, yeah, feel . . .

T: "Even trying to talk to you because I know that you're not really going to hear me . . ."

C: Well, yeah, she's, you know, I mean . . .

T: "You're not gonna hear me."

C: You're not gonna hear me.

T: "You never . . ."

C: You don't . . .

T: "Hear me".

C: You never had, you never will, you don't know how to listen, to care enough . . .

T: "You don't, you didn't care . . ." *(conjectures about deeper feeling)*

C: (Breath in)

T: "You didn't care for me . . ."

C: Well, you think you cared as much as you needed to, you had your own rules about caring, and they just don't necessarily apply to me, the way I feel.

T: What did you want her to do, really (incomprehensible), can you tell her that, "I wanted you . . ." *(guiding to facilitative need)*

C: I wanted you to listen, to try and understand how it is that I felt. (T: Yeah.) Um, whether I had reason to feel that way or not or, you know, was making something, mountain out of a molehill or whatever (sigh) ah . . .

T: "I wanted you to hear me, I wanted you to listen to me."

C: Well, I wanted you to understand how I felt. (T: Mm, mm-hm.) And allow me to express it. (T: Mm, mm-hm.) That's the only, if the only way was to – talk to me about it, fine, which requires you to listen but, I mean, listening entails more than just what two people say to each other, a hell of a lot more.

T: Tell her, "I wanted you to understand me and . . ."

C: Yeah, and take an interest that I had to, there was some reason – – to understand that I was worthwhile listening to. *(need that contains underlying acknowledgment of shame)*

T: "I wanted you to, I wanted you to see me as worthwhile." (C: Yeah.) Can you say that again, "I wanted you to see me as worthwhile . . ." *(repetition for amplification)*

C: I wanted you to see me as worthwhile. *(need that contains underlying acknowledgment of shame)*

T: Can you say that again . . .

C: I wanted you to see me as worthwhile, not being dismissed as you have all my life. *(implied shame)*

T: "I wanted you to see me, I want you to see me, I want you to see me as worthwhile."

C: I want you to see me as a person. *(shame/need)* (T: Ah.) Not an extension of you, not as one of the children.

T: "I want you to see me . . ."

C: A problem to be endured or dismissed.

T: "I wanted you to see me for who I was . . ." *(intensification and need)*

C: Yeah, see me.

T: Tell her, "I wanted you to see . . ."

C: I wanted you to see me! (tearful sniff)

T: What's happening as you say this? *(important to focus on what is felt in the moment when need is expressed)*

C: *(Pause for 9 seconds)* (sigh) Ah, a little anger creeps up. *(shift to anger)*

T: So, tell her, "I feel angry when I'm trying to tell you this now, I feel the anger creeping up." *(makes sure to catch the anger as it arises)*

C: Well, actually I feel a lot! of anger but ah . . .

T: Tell her that. "I feel a lot! of anger."

C: I feel a lot! of anger.

T: "You never saw me . . ."

C: You never saw me, you still don't, and (breath in) you don't really want to.

T: "So, I feel angry . . ."

C: "Which makes – me angry."

T: Angry.

C: As well, so I guess I'm angry for the past, I'm angry for the present, and with no indication you're going to change, I'm angry for the future, and I'm tired of being angry. (T: Mm.) So, I guess, it's a sense of retaliation, and in some way, I'm going to dismiss you now, you often do whatever, whatever mind games you want, just do it in your own yard.

T: "I feel very angry with you for not seeing me or not knowing me, I feel angry . . ." *(consolidating anger)*

C: I feel angry, really angry for you not seeing me, understanding me.

T: "Knowing me . . ."

C: (Sigh) for not knowing me and not wanting! to know me.

This client went on to work through his anger at his mother and at his critical voice, internalized from both her explicit criticisms and her nonverbal denigrating manner. His anger was his liberation undoing his shame. He also grieved the loss of the mother he wished he had and felt compassion to the young boy who had to endure his mother's denigration. This all helped him feel worthy and less anxious about falling short or being dismissed.

CASE 4: UNABLE TO ACCESS STRONG SELF-CONTEMPT OR MOVE INTO SHAME (POOR OUTCOME)

This case includes a 37-year-old female client with a therapist. For most of the therapy, the client engages in mid-level self-criticism without accessing either strong self-contempt or moving into shame. There are also alliance issues. She tells the therapist in this session, "I think it is just so senseless even coming here." This is the beginning of the "best" chair-work of the therapy, and the therapist is unable to help the client access her core criticisms and her shame-based sense of self.

T: Right, right, so there is like, I hear that there is a sort of frustrating, and there is some very real circumstances, and there is this sort of a part of you that is really driving yourself hard and almost like, you know, are not doing a good enough job, you are not, um, (C: Ah.) trying hard enough, you are not, you need to get it more, almost, does that sound like accurate, Melinda? It's like sort of a voice. It's – in you, sort of driving yourself very hard and saying that the job that you are doing that somehow is not good enough.

C: Well, criticizing myself really for not doing anything.

T: Right, right.

C: Essentially . . .

T: Right, right.

C: Diddling away my time . . . *(Here we have what I call a "coach" critic criticizing her for having a problem. This is not a core criticism of her character.)*

T: Right, right. *(The three previous therapist responses have been minimal validation responses without deepening.)*

C: Um, and um, and not really going, going for the biggest resistance, I go, I make this, make the choices of doing what is easiest right now . . .

T: Right, right, so I am wondering if you could, if you could sort of just, sounds like it is a very powerful important voice that is driving a lot of what is going on and sort of really bringing you down as well, in the midst of all this when you really need to sort of use your resources to focus – I am wondering if you could just sort of do the thing you told me now about, um, you know, the critical voice, I am wondering if you could just be that part? The part that is critical, ok? – Th – that saying what you're doing is useless, you are doing nothing, whatever, whatever it is – I don't want to put words in your mouth. *(Therapist responses do not guide the client to the core problem, which is not being able to do things. Need to focus on how she stops herself from getting things done. The therapist might say, "So it's hard to make decisions; what happens inside that makes it hard to decide?" to try to get at the more core problem process.)*

C: Um...

T: You can just really get in touch with that and just sort of trying to imagine over here in this chair (pointing to the empty chair) that you are there, the other part. It is the part, how do you make Melinda ok? How do you make her feel bad? What is this that you say to her? What is the message you are tell – you are giving her now? To make her feel like she is useless? Or she is... *(Work is not on characterological criticism like you are too stupid, weak, etc.; rather, it is a second-level criticism: You are bad for not doing things.)*

C: Well, essentially, she is no good...

T: Can you tell her "you are no good?" What is it...

C: You are no good, you are no good, you are, um, you are wasting your time, you are wasting your energy, (T: Um-mm.) you are, um, like a lost baby in the woods, (T: Um-mm, um-mm.) and, um, and you know how it is, how important it is to (T: Um-mm.) to get some things done, I'm not even saying all things done.

T: That's right.

C: But to get ahead, you cannot stand on your, one spot all the time.

T: Right, right, so you are not getting anything done now... *(The therapist continues in a misdirected dialogue.)*

C: Well, I would not consider it really anything of importance that you are getting done. (T: Um-mm.) You are just staying afloat.

T: Right, you are saying to her, "You are no good." Can you tell her what is no good about her? What is... *(still promoting criticizing self for having the problem—the problem is her indecisiveness, not criticizing herself for this)*

In the next example, the therapist continues to focus on the client's second-level criticism but tries to move to a more specific criticism, which is good because it sometimes helps to get to a character criticism. Unfortunately, it doesn't work here, and the therapist stays with the second-level blaming process:

C: Well, indecisiveness is one, (T: Um-mm.) um, um – – – not, not taking hold of things and carrying them through, (T: Um-mm.) any, any, um, little discouragement . . .

T: Um-mm, so you get defeated very easily, you are saying to her? Is that right? That you get defeated easily? As soon as something comes in the way?

C: Yeah, yeah, I get defeated easily. (T: Um-mm.) I almost use it as an excuse not to do it if, (T: Right) if something a little bit . . .

T: Right, so can you say that to her, "You, you are just, you are making excuses?" (pointing to the empty chair) Whatever it is, the criticism that you, sort of drives you, what is it that you say to her? To make her feel useless?

C: *(Pause for 15 seconds)* I do not know if I can put it in words. (T: Um-mm.) It is . . .

T: Can you give her an example of how she is being sort of useless and ineffective lately?

C: *(Pause for 6 seconds)* Well, what did you do yesterday? (T: Um-mm.) – – – – you did gardening – – and you lined up couple of appointments that you know are not going to lead anywhere, but at least they are appointments. (T: Um-mm.) You made some food – – tasteless food . . .

T: Right, right. *(This is a missed opportunity. If the therapist said, "Tell her why they won't lead anywhere," this might have moved to some statement of a character weakness like "because you are no good at gardening or you are too stupid.")*

C: Just to feed you, feeding (T: Um-mm.) and, um . . .

T: So, she cannot even cook, is that what you are saying?

C: (Laughing) Can cook, but it was not particularly edible, enjoyable . . .

T: Yeah, right, right, so it means you wasted your time, didn't even make anything good to eat. *(Therapist stays stuck in the second level of criticism. The client's problematic process that needs to be focused on is what happens internally that stops her from getting anything done. It could be an anxiety process, a hopelessness process, or an inadequacy process.)*

C: Exactly, I mean you took your time to cook, and it doesn't even taste good . . .

T: Right, right.

C: (Laughing) And in the meanwhile you are rebelling that you have to cook, and you have to be on beck and call. (T: Um-mm.) What is going on?

T: Right.

C: It is like no situation is right (T: Right.) for me right now.

T: Right.

C: It is like ill-fitting clothes. (T: Um-mm.) Not even clothes feel good.

T: Right, right, so there is . . .

C: They pull here, they stretch, stretch there . . .

T: Right, so you are saying to her noth – nothing in your life right now is going good?

C: Yeah. (T: So, the message . . .) It's like you have, you have to, this, um, you have to shed your skin and get the new layer.

In this process, the therapist is unable to help the client get to a core character criticism and the contempt or anxiety associated with it. Without these core emotions, the client is unable to activate the core shame in the session and make it accessible to transformation. The client must arrive at her shame before she can leave it.

CASE 5: DEPRESSED MAN (GOOD OUTCOME)

Ending this chapter on a more successful note, this example involves a severely depressed 51-year-old man in his 25th session. He came in for his session on a Monday morning after a weekend in which he hadn't left his apartment and had hardly eaten other than having some alcohol, but not to a point of inebriation. He is in the critical chair in a dialogue with himself. The therapist, by facilitating the client's extremely harsh critic, activates his hopelessness and his feeling of worthlessness and incompetence (shame). The therapist, rather than trying to reappraise or look on the bright side, amplifies his sense of hopelessness and emptiness.

This example shows how the power of empathic mirroring of affect, in the spirit of "the only way out is through," helps break the client's sense of isolation.

Once this feeling is felt, the client finds his own resilience and begins to feel angry at having been judged by his ex-girlfriend. Accessing a feeling of having deserved to be valued, he accesses his anger at her and expresses it to her in an empty-chair dialogue. This leads him to feel stronger and more worthwhile.

C: You're not motivated, you're not – you're not proactive. *(being seen raises his vitality and he becomes more resilient)*

T: The core is somehow you don't have self-confidence. So, the issue is how do you rob him of his confidence? Here he is, he goes, he does a yoga class, he gets applause, so he has some competence but somehow you make him feel like he's – you know, we did this a long time ago. Like, I can't quite remember, but it's like, you just don't have what it takes or you're not good enough, like when we were talking about filming in Africa. *(therapist shifts him from the coach critic to a more core character criticism)*

C: Mm-hm.

T: There's some kind of a voice that comes in and smashes his confidence and puts him down, makes him feel like he's not good enough – something. So, how do you do that to yourself?

C: Yeah well, there's – there's a hopelessness that it's not gonna work out, it's not gonna be sustained.

T: Is there anything that you do?

C: Anything that you do won't work out.

T: Why?

C: 'Cause you don't have the strength or the – the confidence to – to keep it going. You allow yourself to be defeated.

T: So, make him not have the self-confidence. See, there's some kind of process. And here you are, doing yoga. Make yourself not confident. What do you say? You can't do it? You're not good enough? *(The process has now shifted from "you don't do anything" to "you're not good enough," which makes him anxious.)*

C: Yeah, you're not – you're not good enough. You don't, uh – you're unsure of yourself, you're not, uh . . .

T: Make him unsure of himself.

C: You're not clear, you're uh, on the other hand, you're not really special. You're not uh, um – so many other people that are better than you, that uh, have confidence and – and you're not – you're not special.

T: How is he not special? What – What part? *(differentiating to get to core criticism)*

C: I don't know.

T: What's not special?

C: Well, just . . .

T: Just him, totally.

C: The total of what you have to offer.

T: Okay, yeah, so its sort of – it's like a bla – it's not even specific. It's not like you don't know how to do this pose or your breathing isn't – It's more like *you* are not special, you are not good enough, as a whole. *(reflecting that he feels the whole self is bad)*

C: Mm-hm.

T: Where does this come from? I mean, you suffered this all your life. *(seeking origins of criticism)*

C: I don't know.

T: You're not good enough. You're not special. You're not as good as others. I mean, this is the kind of voice that – Is that what it is? I mean that's what you . . .

C: I – I – I think so, yeah. Um, I think feeling – feeling, uh, say 'round – Brenda, feeling let down, that the criticism what – what – what came from her just – just I – I don't know, just, is an example of – of really where I'm at. I mean, if she wants to be with me then I must be okay, but if she doesn't, then these things that I'm concerned about, you know, verifies it.

T: Yeah, so say that to him, right. "She's proof. If you were worthwhile, she would have wanted to be with you." *(following the client empathically without preconceptions or inferences about the origins)*

C: Yeah, she's proof that if you had it together and were – were worthwhile, to, you know, to be with she would have – she would be with you.

T: Uh-huh, so that's an important piece of what so smashed you, right, and what smashes you at the end of the relationships. It's like, "It's proof that you're, that you're" – what?

C: That you're, um, you know, inferior and you're – you're, you're nothing, you know nothing, you're not a man, you're nothing special. *(shame)*

T: "No one wants you because you're not good enough, you're not special enough." *(emphasizing core criticism)*

C: Yeah, you can be replaced.

T: "You have nothing special to offer."

C: Yeah, you have nothing special to offer. You can be replaced easily.

T: And he has nothing special to offer because he is not a success or – what?

C: Because he's not a success. Because he's, yeah, he's not a success. Um, sort of like a, you know, just being blown around in the wind. Anyone can say anything or do anything, and uh, you take it on. You, uh, you place so much importance in what people think about you. You have no backbone.

T: Yeah, you haven't said that. You have no backbone, right. Let's change. So, this is what you're dealing with. What happens? I mean, you're nothing because she rejects you. You're a f – it's living proof that you're not special, you have nothing. You have no backbone. What does that do to you inside? *(shifts attention to the bodily felt experience of the effect of these criticisms and nonverbally expressed contempt in face and voice)*

C: I just feel a pain in my – my chest.

T: Uh huh, uh-huh. (change chairs) So now, how do you deal with it? I mean, firstly it gives you the pain. *(having accessed core criticism and contempt, shift position to access experiencing self)*

C: It makes me want to quit.

T: Right, right. So, I just want to give up.

C: Yeah, I just want to give up.

T: It's a feeling of like I can't – I can't beat you, or I can't – This is the defeat. I just feel defeated. *(reflects feeling to stay focused on differentiating it)*

C: Mm-hm, there's no room for mistakes. There's, I guess, you know . . .

T: It must feel so harshly, kind of, treated, but then you just want to curl up into a ball, probably. Is that what it's like? *(conjectures about primary maladaptive emotion's action tendency)*

C: Yeah, well, that I have to get away.

T: Yeah, yeah, "that I've got to get away."

C: So, tell him, right. I try to run away from this, from you. Yes, I have to get away and start fresh. You know, I can't stay here. It'll kill me.

T: "You'll kill me." *(emphasizes that is the critical part of the self doing this)*

C: You'll kill me.

T: "'Cause I just can't take this battering anymore. This . . ." *(focuses attention back on self's experience)*

C: I can't – can't take this, well, yeah, this battering, this constant criticism. Having to prove myself over and over again.

T: So, what do you want or need from this? 'Cause this is a part of you, ultimately. *(having accessed core shame, now accesses need from the critic)*

C: I need someone who looks at me as I am.

T: Uh-huh.

C: And not judge whatever is going on as good or bad. It just – just is.

T: What do you need from yourself? 'Cause this someone, this voice is actually you.

C: I need you to be strong, to, um – to stand up for yourself, take charge of your life. *(The client breaks out of the structure of the two-chair dialogue of critic and criticized by telling critic to be strong.)*

T: Uh-huh. It's almost like, "I need you to be strong for me and help me take charge." 'Cause you know, this part is quite strong actually. It uses all its strength to beat you up. What actually happens inside? I mean I know this is very. *(guides client back to speak from the experiencing self)*

C: I feel – I just feel so weak. So, like I can, you know, I don't have any frame, any bones inside to hold me up. I just, you know, it's an effort just to stand straight.

T: Yeah, yeah. So, let's just go into that place, that weakness right, rather than – 'cause I know that's what it feels like. It's kind of like, it must be sucking your energy from the inside. Tell me, I'm just come over here. Tell me about this weak state, right. *(Following "you have to feel it to heal," therapist focuses attention on painful feelings of core hopelessness and sense of incompetence, which is shame based.)*

C: It's um – it's uh, it's like everything is an effort, just to – to shower and – and – and get dressed and uh . . .

T: Just to sort of get up and get yourself together. It's just like dragging lead almost. *(empathic affirmation of vulnerability)*

C: Yeah, yeah. I mean I – I – I do well at the, you know, when I take yoga, but nothing is consistent. You know, again, everything – It's just moving along but there's no purpose, no focus.

T: Right, so it's hard to . . .

C: It's meaningless. The future seems meaningless. It's like why? Why – why am I doing all those things?

T: Right, right, there's no sense of this really going anywhere that's gonna have any meaning. "I just feel kind of void or everything is nothing. My life has no meaning, I don't know why I'm doing it. I don't seem to be going anywhere?" Right, I mean, it's . . . *(empathic mirroring to break the clients sense of isolation)*

C: You know, or if I get there, and if I am teaching, you know, a number of classes or – or whatever, it, well, I'm thinking, well, so what?

T: So, "I'm doing this but it's going nowhere, or so what? So what? It has no real meaning. Because somehow my life, I feel empty. I feel without a purpose, without a connection."

C: Yeah, yeah, there's – there's no peace. I don't know what's driving me and – and I can't put it into words now what was driving me before. Uh, where it just appeared like enthusiasm, or, and . . .

T: Now there's just nothing. "I just don't have that kind of 'oomph' or that charge for doing anything so everything's a drag, an incredible energy drain to get myself moving. 'Cause it's like for what?" *(continued empathic mirroring)*

C: Yeah.

T: But somehow there's just this core energylessness, right?

C: Yeah.

T: And at the core all – as you said the – ripple of meaninglessness is some sort of sense of there's no purpose, "I have no purpose. I don't know what I'm aiming at, doing it for. I feel like kind of in an emptiness." So, we have to grapple with that feeling. I mean I understand it's there, and it's an awful feeling.

C: Yeah, and I – I guess part of it is that, um, having the Christmas break I felt free, you know, no responsibility then – then coming back and – and not – yeah, I wasn't feeling well last week, um, I think I went to the doctors

Thursday. Anyway I had a sinus infection and, uh, but my friend says it's probably stress related, but the anxiety like around going to teach, I go "what?" Do I want to put myself through this and have to take medication to do that to make a pittance per week? I go "well what's – and . . ."

T: But it's kind of like I have this image of you sort of look out at the horizon and you see nothing. *(continued empathic mirroring plus intensification)*

C: Yeah.

T: There's like nothing there, so, there's nothing to pull me forward. It just all feels like a vast open nothingness, and it's so hard to get up and go. Nothing to energize or sustain me.

C: Mm-hm, and that's – that's part of the fear. When I – when I think of returning to teaching, it's like I did it, I got through it and – and got positive feedback, now I don't want to do it anymore. But it's like I can't – can't sustain anything. It's either like I don't give myself room to – to be human or to fail or I expect I'm going to fail or and I – I imagine that's the same way in relationships of these great beginnings but – but . . . *(puts words to the feeling)*

T: I can't sustain it.

C: Sustaining it. And it just gets to be proven like – like with Bren. And I – I was thinking the other day about this – this confidence, well, after I taught the yoga class, and I thought what's, well, you know, she – she lacked confidence and she was, you know, not uh, you know, was insecure and couldn't get her assignments done on time and struggling and struggling with it but like, like, I was like so what? That's part of it.

T: Yeah, yeah.

C: And then I think why did I get so much criticism for it? And – and that feeling too, where things get labeled and – and that feeling of being – not being established is uh, you know a friend of mine went through that once too. *(beginning of resilience)*

T: And somehow what Bren said to me still gets me. It's so hard to sort of feel worthwhile in the face of those criticisms, in the face of those put-downs. *(reflection)*

C: Yeah, yeah.

T: It's like that pierces into my core and just deflates me totally. *(feeling, stays with core vulnerable)*

C: Yeah, being – being tested all – that's, you know, I know I wasn't a saint either. I hurt her feelings many times. But I'm thinking, her pushing me to get this, me to do this yoga class when – as soon as I got back for – for her sisters and – and was a test to see how see how I – much I learned and how I – and – and I went up there and taught it and didn't even prepare for it, you know? *(anger emerges spontaneously generated by automatic processes)*

T: What would you want to say to her? "Get off my back." *(encourages expression of anger)*

C: Yeah, like it was such bullshit to do that. Or you know, I'm mad at myself or like, in spite of everything I – I think I should have enough sense to say hey, you know.

T: Right, right, right.

C: I don't read enough? Excuse me? Well there's the door, goodbye. You're like, you're nuts.

T: But somehow – let's bring her in here because this is important. Tell her, right. There's no good being mad at yourself, you're mad at her. Tell her you're mad at her. *(shifts to a dialogue with ex to promote expression of anger)*

C: Yeah I'm – I'm really pissed off that . . .

T: You actually see her here, right? *(create contact with her image to intensify emotion)*

C: Yeah, that you tested me, that you – you judged me, and you had an agenda and – and weren't clear in your communication. You kept asking me about me all the time, you know, and how I was doing, what I was going to do because you wanted me to ask how you were doing and what you were going to do, instead of being clear and asking for something it was you know, it was basically a mind fuck.

T: Right, right, right, tell her, "you mind-fucked me."

C: You mind-fucked me.

T: Right, and tell her what you're angry at her for. "I'm angry at you testing me . . ." *(promotes expression)*

C: I'm angry at you testing me.

T: "I'm angry at you judging me . . ."

C: And judging me and putting me in situations, uh, that were un – really just unfair. It was bullshit and expecting me to – to – to be something, and – and – and some superman or something, someone, you know, to fill, you know, to fill what was missing in you. Just being so unclear about everything. Leading me on.

T: Tell her something like, "I won't pro – have to prove myself to you." I won't – this, I mean this is a problem you do. Right, but, tell her "I'm not here to prove myself to you."

C: I'm not here to prove myself to you about, uh, about anything. You know, I, um, wow . . .

T: What, what happens.

C: I – I just can't – I can't figure out what uh, I mean it seems like there's so much stuff that I uh . . .

T: What?

C: I can't – I can't put it into words.

T: Let's try and put some of it into words. What is it? *(promotes symbolizing in words)*

C: Just feel that you suck the life out of me, you – you took what you could and got what you could and – and uh . . .

T: It's like, "You threw me away."

C: And just, yeah, just threw me away.

T: Uh-huh.

C: But made me responsible for it. It was something that I wasn't doing, something, something that I couldn't be, and no matter what I did, you found reason to criticize or you had an excuse.

T: Now I want you to make her responsible, not you responsible. Tell her what she did wrong. Hold her accountable for how she wronged you. Tell her.

C: You used me. And – and if it were the other you know, way around, you know, you would say I abused you when you abused me . . .

T: Right, right.

C: You took advantage of my feelings uh or my – my good nature. You – you – you know you led me on, you, you know, were unwilling to communicate. You silently judged and sized me up and criticized me and tested me and . . .

T: "And then you discarded me . . ."

C: And then you just discarded me like it was, you know, like I didn't exist.

T: Mm-hm, mm-hm.

C: Pushed me to be something, pushed me to – to go and do this, this yoga training, pushed me to get another apartment, pushed me to do this and to teach and have a career and – and – and – and – and but you had no intention, no intention of – of staying around. It was just like some test, something you needed to do to fill something that was missing in you.

T: Now I want to try to tell her, "I take back your right to judge me," or "I won't give you the power to determine who I am." You know, 'cause that's some of the difficulty. You give up this power. I want you to take it back. Tell her my definition isn't dependent on you. This is what's so hard for you. **(guide him to set boundaries and begin a new narrative reclaiming his power and worth)**

C: So, I take back, what?

T: Yeah, take back your power from her. Try saying, "My definition is not dependent on you."

C: My definition is not dependent on you.

T: Now what happens?

C: I wanna – I take back my power, my self-worth, my self-esteem.

T: "I won't give you the right."

C: Yes. I won't give you the right or – or the – the power to – to judge me, to determine who I am.

T: And what do you actually feel when you say this?

C: Well, I feel – feel angry, I feel very resentful.

T: Right, tell her some more, "I resent that you . . ."

C: I resent that you took advantage of me. I resent the fact that you judged me, that you found every excuse imaginable to opt out of this relationship. That you, you know, you know in the guys being so – so open and so loving and supportive to – to me and people around you, that it's your own shit that you – you take no responsibility in what you – what you did.

T: Right, right, tell her what you wanted her to take responsibility for. **(co-construction of a new narrative)**

C: I want you to take responsibility in – in leading me on, in – in forcing me to – to, um, make – make decisions or do things that you wanted to be – that you – you appeared to be a part of and that you really – and then turn around and say oh, we're just – just friends or you know, all the phone calls on us being together and sleeping together, oh, you were just checking in. It was – meant nothing to you.

T: So, "I reject you and what you did to me." Try that.

C: I reject you and what you did to me.

T: Right. Try, "I won't let your rejection smash me or define me as worthless."

C: I won't let your rejection smash me, beat me down, or define me as being worthless.

T: And when you say that, what do you experience?

C: Well, I feel – feel some strength but I'm – I'm also getting that anything that's related to her, and I know she just happens to be the one right now. *(emergence of a new synthesized feeling of strength and pride)*

T: Right, right.

C: That I'm resisting, possibly some of it is resisting teaching yoga, anything that – that's connected to her, pushing me to do, I'm resisting. And it's in some ways it's – it's um, well a lot of ways it's – it's validating, it's making her right.

T: Yeah.

C: Uh, but – but it – but it – it is the feeling that no, I'm not gonna do this because you pushed me to do this so I'm backing – backing off and backing off of – of coaching more, of – of – of teaching and, uh . . .

T: So, "I'm still letting you influence me."

C: Yeah, and I can't determine whether it's something I really wanted to do . . .

T: Yes, yes.

C: Or that I was doing to please you, to keep you happy.

T: Yeah, I think that's an important thing you're saying, but now you have to determine why she continues to influence you. It's like, I just want to get away from anything that you've had – that you've tainted 'cause I don't know if it's me, if it's you, what it is. How can you not let her determine your life now? What do you have to do? *(creation of new meaning and action possibilities)*

C: I don't know, I don't know. Meet somebody else, uh, you know, be successful.

T: I guess you've also got to choose what you want to do. Not worry about. – Tell her why it's hard to get rid of her. "It's hard to get rid of you . . ."

C: It's hard to get rid of you because I – I believed you.

T: Yeah, and that – I mean that's a very, yeah . . .

C: Sorry?

T: That's very profound, I mean, that's exactly it. Because I believed you. To the degree that you believe her, you remain sort of defeated and hopeless. To the degree that you stand up to her, you begin to mobilize, right, you get stronger.

C: Mm-hm.

T: Try again. "I won't give you the power to determine who I am."

C: I won't give you the power to determine who I am.

T: But that's what's hard, right? 'Cause you do sort of give her that power. *(cycles back to check on what may block his anger)*

C: Mm-hm.

T: This is the big struggle. Tell her again what you're angry at 'cause that's your greatest ally, your anger. To help you not feel so defeated. Tell her "I'm angry at you." *(consolidates anger)*

C: I'm angry because you led me on. Because your communication, you were unclear. You always had some agenda, uh, and weren't clear about what you wanted. And I'm angry that you judged me, and criticized me, and compared me to other people and your father, and then – then just denied it like – like it was something with me, I heard things wrong, incorrectly.

T: So, "I'm angry that you tested me, that you judged me . . ."

C: You constantly tested me and were judging me and . . .

T: "And then you threw me away . . ."

C: And then just – just threw me away, just – just like that. I'm angry that you – you involved yourself in my life so much and pretended to be and then said oh, and just denied any – any real connection, discounted any real connection.

T: Tell her "I don't have to meet your expectations to be okay." *(co-constructing a new narrative)*

C: I don't have to meet your expectations to be okay.

T: "And what I needed was support to bring the best out in me, not criticism . . ."

C: Yes, and what I needed from you was support to bring the best – best out in me, not – not criticism. I didn't judge you when you had, uh, you know, lacked confidence, and you couldn't get your assignments done, or couldn't quit smoking, or you couldn't quit drinking. I hung in there. Now you're living basically off your friend and it's, you know, you do this to, what I've seen, you do this to a number of people. Get involved in their lives and have them make major changes in their life then blame them for, you know, not meeting your expectation, and then you sort of move on and uh, you know, leave this trail of – of – of people behind you like it's, you know, like it, you know, and take no responsibility in it.

T: So, what's happening now? We're gonna need to end soon. What do you feel?

C: Well, I feel a little more alive.

T: Yeah, yeah. I mean the issue is how to maintain the sense of your own rights, your own worth. This is not such a worthless, defeated place. You know, I have a hunch. Put your mother there and tell her what you needed from her way back then. *(ties back to origins which have been previously discussed and is part of the case formulation that he felt emotionally abandoned by his mother at a young age)*

C: I needed you to support me, to, you know, put your arms around me, and talk to me, tell me that you loved me, to – to really open up and let me know how you were feeling.

T: Right, "I needed that kind of support and connection, and when I don't have it, I feel very much like I'm a 13 year old, kind of without knowing what's going on, empty, confused." I mean, I think that is what happens, right.

C: Mm-hm, yeah, the feeling I have with my mother or back then was, yeah, there was no – no connection and there wasn't any connection and I feel the same way with women, that it can go so far . . .

T: Yeah.

C: And what – what I'm angry at now, I'm getting if I, you know, in hindsight, just did what I intuitively felt like doing in the relationship with Brenda we'd maybe still be together instead of compromising and – and – and allowing her criticism, taking on all her stuff to – to totally defeat me.

T: Mm-hm, it's kind of like if I felt comfortable just voicing my own feeling and saying what was going on.

C: Like yeah, like I believed every – everything and attached so much importance to things.

T: But I think you're saying like with your mother and in your family, nobody ever spoke. You never said what was really going on. Somehow, you've always not really spoken from what's really happening. And then you take on what she said and all kinds of. . . . But now it's like up to you to choose rather than run away from her, and things contaminated by her, so how do you choose? *(co-constructing a new narrative based on his new feeling of self-worth)*

C: That I don't know.

CONCLUSION

In this chapter, transcripts of actual sessions demonstrate the moment-by-moment processes in working on shame events in therapy. The process of four good outcome cases and one poor outcome case were reviewed. These transcripts show how to work with shame by validating and acknowledging it, helping it be tolerated and sufficiently regulated so as to make it amenable to transformation by accessing new emotions.

This chapter illustrates how central anger is in undoing shame by synthesizing with it to form a truly novel emotional state. In transformation by synthesis, anger does not replace shame. which would not necessarily be therapeutic, as the person would end up feeling anger in place of feeling ashamed. That is not an adaptive solution. Rather, the action tendency of assertion blends with the action tendency of withdrawal, and the emotion schemes of anger synthesize with the emotion schemes of shame. These changes lead the client to feel more solid, worthwhile, self-accepting, calm, and peaceful. This change in self-organization leads to a more functional and adaptive narrative that helps consolidate the change in conscious awareness.

The chapters to come focus on accessing interrupted anger. The emphasis in emotion-focused therapy is on accessing previously unexpressed adaptive anger rather than on anger management training, which downregulates anger. I discuss how to help clients access and accept their previously unacknowledged adaptive anger. As I have said, they have to overcome their myriad ways of blocking their anger, their fear of their own anger and how it might overwhelm them or destroy relationships, and the guilt of expressing it, especially to parents.

8 THE MANY SHADES OF ANGER

I was angry with my friend:
I told my wrath, my wrath did end.
I was angry with my foe:
I told it not, my wrath did grow.

—William Blake

This chapter includes discussion of different types of anger as well as gender and cultural issues related to working with anger in psychotherapy. I focus on the nature and function of anger and its different manifestations, including the process assessment of anger as primary, secondary, or instrumental and as adaptive or maladaptive. I also discuss the importance of anger as an adaptive emotion and show how, in contrast with the emphasis on the downregulation of anger, the activation of previously unexpressed anger is an important therapeutic process change.

Anger is often viewed as a disruptive emotion, but most fundamentally, it is as an adaptive emotion that signals boundary intrusion or a block on one's path. Anger promotes self-protective action or mobilizes a person to

https://doi.org/10.1037/0000393-008
Shame and Anger in Psychotherapy, by L. S. Greenberg
Copyright © 2024 by the American Psychological Association. All rights reserved.

overcome the block. The action tendency of anger helps the person respond in a constructive manner to violation through assertive action or by aggression. Much has been written about anger control, but anger suppression is also an important therapeutic problem. Many disorders involve interrupted anger. Although anger and irritability can be symptoms of blaming depressions, many depressions have underlying primary feelings of anger that are not adaptively expressed. For example, suppressed rage is often at the base of somatization. Anger inhibition, submissive behavior, and poor assertiveness are linked with depression (Akhavan, 2001; Harmon-Jones et al., 2002), and many depressed clients show signs of anger and resentment (Fava et al., 1990; Brody et al., 1999). When anger is not expressed, it increases stress and contributes to depression and many other disorders (Gilbert, 2006; Watson & Greenberg, 2017).

Feminist writers have asserted that anger can be empowering. Chemaly (2018) argued that anger is "a critically useful and positive emotion" that "warns us, as humans, that something is wrong and needs to change" when "being threatened with indignity, physical harm, humiliation and unfairness" and, therefore, is "a powerful force for political good." Furthermore, she stated that women and minorities are not permitted to be angry to the same extent as are White men. In a similar vein, Traister (2019) argued that holding back anger has been an impediment to the progress of women's rights. She highlighted the ways that a double standard perpetuated against women by all sexes has a disastrous and stultifying effect on women. Thus, unexpressed anger has a sociopolitical effect as well as an effect on psychological disorders.

Gilbert and Gilbert (2003) used the term *arrested anger* to refer to aroused anger that is blocked and not expressed. They described how, in situations of aroused anger, the organism's physiological response is one of either fight or flight and argued that this response generally is automatic, originating in the amygdala. In an automatic fight reaction, the person expresses anger toward the triggering stimulus, and the need in the aroused anger to protect boundaries or overcome the obstacle, ideally, is met. This response allows the person to move on to meet the next most urgent situation. In the opposite case of interrupted anger, individuals continually block their fight reactions and end up preventing need satisfaction. They are left feeling hopeless and powerless, which leads to wanting to give up and ultimately to depression. In this context, interrupted anger can be understood as anger that is activated at a physiological level but is repeatedly not expressed or not experienced.

This and following chapters focus mainly on interrupted anger and its treatment. I see arrested anger as involving a process of interrupting the experience and/or expression of emotion by actively blocking, either automatically or deliberately. I discuss how, in the safety of the therapy situation, overcoming blocks to the expression of previously unexpressed anger can promote a sense of worth and empowerment and can counter the tendency to submit. As with the treatment of shame in earlier chapters, differential treatment of different types of anger is offered. Different methods for dealing with interrupted anger, rejecting anger, dysregulated anger, and rage are discussed.

The process of experiencing and expressing anger can be classified into three main categories: anger in, anger out, and anger control (Snell et al., 1995). People who tend to internalize anger usually suppress angry feelings and thoughts. In contrast, people who externalize their anger in an anger-out tendency react to provocations with angry and sometimes aggressive behaviors. Last, people who are able to control their anger can monitor their experiencing and, depending on the situation, can either express or prevent the expression of anger.

Injunctions against anger or anxiety about its experience and expression can cause anger to be suppressed. Suppressing primary adaptive reactions of anger that result from being treated unfairly, violation or hurt, or sufficient loss may lead to unhealthy overcontrol or to physiological symptoms such as headaches and high blood pressure as well as emotional symptoms such as resignation, hopelessness, and anxiety. Suppressed anger can also lead to relational problems, including difficulty asserting oneself and an inability to set boundaries, as well as withdrawal or despair. Individuals who continuously suppress their anger lose touch with their own needs and wants. They feel hopeless and powerless to get their needs met, and they feel sad or resentful. These feelings are symptom of many types of disorders; often they are symptomatic secondary feelings that protect the person from underlying, disallowed, primary feelings of anger. Adaptive anger that is interrupted is a primary feeling that provides important orientation and information, and it needs to be accessed and acknowledged in therapy sometimes to overcome secondary emotion (e.g., hopelessness) and at other times to transform underlying maladaptive emotion (e.g., shame).

Bridewell and Chang (1997) examined the role of anger in, anger out, and anger control as predictors of depressive symptoms. They reported that internalizing anger was a better predictor of depressive symptoms than lack of anger control or the tendency to externalize anger. Clients who interrupt their anger internalize anger and become critical or contemptuous of themselves. In discussing the implications for treatment, the authors suggested that it is therefore valuable to modify clients' tendencies to internalize their anger.

ANGER: ITS NATURE AND FUNCTION

Anger is a basic emotion honed by evolution to promote survival. It is characterized by feelings of antagonism toward someone or something who was perceived to have thwarted or wronged one. For a person to be angry at another, they must believe the other is responsible for something that violated them and must want to do something to the other about it. Anger's strength can vary. When it is mild, it may be relatively easy to override; it is harder to override anger when it is intense.

As an innate response to frustration, anger is an adaptive feeling when it informs people about their need for protection from harm. It's a perfectly normal response to frustrating or difficult situations, but it can also be destructive and can lead to rejecting behavior and rage. Anger involves the action tendency to puff up, grow larger, and thrust forward to defend one's boundaries and therefore can lead to acting out through violence or to blowing up, especially when it is suppressed. Importantly, however, anger must be distinguished from aggression: It signals aggression but is not the behavior of aggression, which comes from further cognitive processing and decision making.

In anger, the physiological response involves an elevated heart rate, muscular tension, and possibly feeling hot because sugar is released in the bloodstream (Izard, 1993). The expressive component may involve a frown or going red in the face; the voice becomes louder and could even result in yelling. Body movements such as growing larger and clenching one's fists are also possible. The subjective feeling of anger includes a sense of irritation or feeling violated, mistreated, or wronged in relation to a specific event or events.

Anger appears in many shades: hot anger and cold anger, destructive and empowering anger, hate and annoyance. Its intensity can vary from irritation or indignation to rage or fury. Anger can be seen as varying not just in intensity (how strong is the anger) but also in frequency (how often a person gets angry), duration (how long the person stays angry), latency (how quickly a person angers), and threshold (how sensitive to evocation; Fernandez, 2013; Fernandez & Johnson, 2016; Fernandez et al., 2010). An angry mood also differs from an angry reaction. An angry mood is a feeling that lasts for a time and is generally less intense than an angry reaction. A person with an angry temperament is not someone who is reacting with anger but is a person whose anger is recurrent and pervasive.

English and other languages have many words that express the different shades of anger. In English, *resentment* is probably therapeutically one of the more important words for a specific experience of anger. Resentment needs to be distinguished from currently activated anger (Spielberger et al., 1995). Anger arises in direct response to violation, unfairness, or being thwarted and is an acute response that serves the adaptive purpose of asserting one's rights. In contrast, resentment involves long-lasting bitterness to a perceived wrong and is more subtle. It lingers—it can be chronic and long-lasting—and is harbored internally. If it involves someone close or trusted, it is often made more complex by feelings of betrayal. People react with anger but harbor resentment. The complexity of resentment as a human emotion is reflected in the difficulty found in translating it into many other languages: Some simply don't have a parallel word and may use a phrase rather than a word to express it.

In English, *resentment* is therapeutically a very helpful term because it carries the notion of a long-lasting anger that eats away at the person and is the source of much psychological distress. People feel angry when provoked, but when they recount the experience in therapy, at a distance from the provoking situation, the experience is more like a slow-burning, smouldering feeling. The word *resentment* catches what they are feeling in the session better than *anger*.

Irritability is another word that expresses a form of anger characterized by a feeling of agitation and a tendency to be easily upset or annoyed. *Frustration* is also a word that often comes up in therapy to denote anger. People find it hard to say, "I'm angry," but easy to say, "I'm frustrated." Often, if I say to clients, "Sounds like that left you feeling angry," they reply, "I'm not angry, just frustrated," but this is often a way of watering down anger. For example, when I was a young and an engineer, I could not acknowledge anger and would sulk. To say I was angry implied vulnerability and that I could be hurt, and I was trying to be invincible. My late wife and my therapy training eventually disavowed me of that self-protective defense. Acknowledging anger is difficult, and people are socialized in many ways to not express anger. Unacknowledged anger often comes out as blame, which is the main interpersonal manifestation of anger.

Anger can also mix with other emotions. Anger has been dubbed a member of a hostile trio, along with contempt and disgust (Harmon-Jones et al., 2008). Contempt, as discussed in Chapter 3, comes from dis-smell moving up to a superior position. Disgust is from distaste and a rejection of what is bad. All involve rejection in some form. Hatred is a passionate or intense dislike but probably includes disgust, as does loathing. It is also worth repeating here that anger is not aggression.

Thus, all anger is not the same. Some anger is adaptive and evolved to aid survival, and its suppression is not physically or psychologically healthy. Anger can strengthen one's position in bargaining, enhance competitiveness in sport, and mobilize bodily resources for retaliatory action. It can help people pursue goals and be happier and healthier in the long run. Anger can bring about change. Expressing empowered or assertive anger also can make people feel better about themselves, more optimistic, more in control, and more likely to take risks. Anger can also be pleasurable, even though it might simultaneously be painful. Anger isn't good or bad. It just is. It's what one does with anger that matters. Like anything else, it can build or destroy.

As Timulak and Keogh (2022) pointed out, assertive anger is even better viewed as protective anger. Healthy anger is self-affirming and brings inner strength and confidence. Healthy anger can be distinguished from secondary anger that is much more a reaction to inner vulnerability ("I'm angry because I'm hurt"). Protective anger is much more measured than reactive anger. It is not as high in physiological arousal; rather, it is characterized by a firmness ("I won't let you hurt me anymore") and is not an expansive anger that encroaches on others. It is an antidote to vulnerability and is felt in the service of meeting unmet needs ("I am valuable").

Healthy anger is adaptive, appropriate to the situation, and a reaction to unfairness or to barriers that block goal attainment. It needs to be contrasted with and distinguished from maladaptive anger, which is excessive and destructive. Maladaptive anger is most unhelpful; it manifests as rage, which is unjustified, uncontrolled, undifferentiated, and unprocessed. Maladaptive anger is the source of many problems in human functioning and can be highly destructive in relationships. It often covers other feelings and can be displaced onto someone or something else, like kicking the proverbial cat.

It is important in working with the expression of anger to clearly distinguish adaptive, empowering anger at maltreatment from maladaptive rage associated with narcissistic slights or secondary reactions to feeling inferior or humiliated. Maladaptive rage is overly intense, chronic, destructive and/or inappropriate, and often reactive to minor insult or failure experience. Because maladaptive rage is aimed at destroying the other, it needs to be acknowledged but not intensified. To empower clients, therapists need to facilitate them to pay attention to and intensify the experience of adaptive anger at unfairness. The focus is on asserting the self and setting boundaries, rather than destroying the other.

Secondary anger is a reactive expression that masks underlying hurt. This expression is what people most imagine when they think of anger, and how anger is predominantly characterized, as bad. Excessive anger, of course, can and does cause problems. Increased blood pressure and other physical changes associated with highly aroused anger harm physical and mental health. Anger can make it difficult to think clearly; it engenders a loss of perspective and the inability to make good judgments.

Anger, therefore, needs to be viewed differentially and assessed based on its function. This is no easy task. Some anger is manipulative or destructive or threatening, and its expression can be harmful as it drives people away, resulting in loss of support. Other forms can distract people from pain and threatening feelings, provoke fear in others, or allow one to gain control, and some anger is adaptive and helps people to attain goals.

Even if a person thinks their current angry response to someone, for example, for being late or forgotten, is a justified adaptive feeling of anger, the person still needs to figure out how to express this anger in a constructive fashion. Aristotle, in the Nicomachean ethics (Aristotle, ca. 350 B.C.E./2009) offered that a good-tempered person can at times get angry, but it is not an easy task to find the golden mean of expression. To paraphrase his famous statement, it may be easy for people to get angry, but it is not easy to get angry at the right person, at the right time, to the right degree, with the right motive, and in the right way.

It also may not be wise to express adaptive anger at all, especially impulsively. However, the inability to deal constructively with anger can be a major source of difficulty leading to feelings of incompetence or to submissiveness and hopelessness. Dealing with anger is complicated in life and in therapy. In line with the emotion assessment approach used in emotion-focused therapy (EFT), anger can be primary, secondary, or instrumental as well as adaptive or maladaptive. Working with anger thus involves differential process assessments of the type of anger that is occurring.

ANGER SUBTYPES

The EFT conceptualization of emotions classifies emotion as primary, secondary, or instrumental and as adaptive and maladaptive (Greenberg, 2002). Anger does not belong exclusively to any one of these categories, and it can travel between the categories depending on its specific activation. Those who see anger as always secondary to hurt miss the importance of the adaptive aspects of anger and the negative role of interrupted anger.

Primary Adaptive Anger

Anger can be an adaptive or a maladaptive immediate reaction to an external event. *Primary anger* is irreducible to preceding emotions or cognitions. It is a direct reaction to an evoking situation, not mediated by thought. *Primary adaptive anger* provides an orientation to the environment by means of an action tendency (Frijda, 1986) that helps manage the situation one finds oneself in. In addition, it informs people of unfair treatment, boundary violation, and goal frustration. Adaptive anger changes dynamically in response to changing circumstances. Primary adaptive anger changes when its adaptive function has been served. It does not linger longer than needed to right the wrong or overcome the obstacle.

Primary adaptive anger is something people feel for a reason. It disposes one to act a certain way to solve problems, such as asserting against a boundary intrusion or mobilizing to overcome an obstacle. People need to listen to what their anger is telling them about being treated unfairly and to respect what is it saying, rather than to avoid or protect against what it is telling them. Their anger is sending them a message that their boundaries are being violated, they are being treated unfairly, their rights are being violated, their wants or needs are not being met, or progress toward a goal is being frustrated. Anger may also signal that the person is overextending. Anger aids people to say, "Enough! I won't take it anymore!" Anger aids in the setting of limits and empowers people to say, "No" (Greenberg, 2002).

Primary Maladaptive Anger

Like primary adaptive anger, *primary maladaptive anger* is an immediate reaction to external events that is unmediated by cognition, but it differs in that it is a reaction formed in and responding to the past, in the present. Primary maladaptive anger is often developed from a damaging learning history which causes reactions that do not fit the current situation, often because of traumatic learning and past violations. For example, it is maladaptive if a person reacts angrily to true, nonexploitative kindness. Anger in response to kindness or intimacy can come from prior boundary violations or from a history of believing nobody does anything for free. The person's anger at violation may have been adaptive in the past but is no longer adaptive in the present, such as when a slightly louder voice from another person leads to an explosive angry reaction.

Core anger is maladaptive when it no longer protects a person from harm or violation and is destructive. Rage and destructive anger often come from a history of witnessing or having suffered violence, and it causes problems in relationships. Some people rage at others without knowing why. They are volatile in many situations, have hair-trigger tempers, and become easily irritated without control. This type of intense arousal is often connected to past events, and people often try to shut down such arousal. When people who have suffered from violence in their past become angry, their anger can trigger explosions. Often clients' maladaptive anger is not about what they are angry at; it is about their previously unmet needs. Once they come to see this, they can begin to process their feelings and needs in a new way to help curb their rage.

Some forms of anger associated with posttraumatic stress disorder (PTSD) are typical examples of a primary maladaptive anger response. Trauma often generates maladaptive anger (Paivio & Pascual-Leone, 2010; A. Pascual-Leone & Paivio, 2013) because it is easy for people to become overwhelmed by the intensity of emotion during trauma. Memories are stored with very high sensory and perceptual processing and low verbal encoding of meaning (Brewin, 2001), and so it is difficult for people to articulate and make sense of their emotions. In most traumatic situations, the person often feels angry but is a powerless victim, and their adaptive anger at violation cannot be expressed. People shut down their anger as a coping strategy in the original situation and generalize this strategy to later situations. When the suppression fails, the rage breaks through. People with PTSD, therefore, can oscillate between numb passivity and explosive rage. Anger suppression serves as necessary protection at the time of the trauma; however, chronic subsequent blocking of anger prevents processing of the anger and fear and often can produce problems of over- or underregulation.

A personal history that results in a core sense of self as being unworthy, vulnerable, and unsafe and generates primary maladaptive emotional reactions of fear and shame can lead to hair-trigger primary maladaptive anger. For people who have hair-trigger anger reactions, anger was their primary protection when as a child they were, for example, locked in a closet by parents or bullied by peers, and they swore they would never let those things happen again. When learning that anger protects has been so strongly repetitive, it becomes so overlearned that it becomes second nature to react with anger to minor threats. It is as though now anger is the person's first automatic reaction—a primary maladaptive response, which can lead to destructive anger. But despite this response being overlearned, if the therapist can help a person get past their anger, they will find an underlying vulnerable emotion such as fear or shame as the most primary bad feeling. So primary maladaptive anger, although a primary response in the present, at a deeper level was initially a secondary reaction in the past to a primary threat. In "honor cultures," any threat to one's identity or family is responded to with anger and may be seen as requiring retaliation; this learned maladaptive response is congruent with the culture. Again, it is a primary response, but the underlying issue is threat, so in some way it is a semi-primary or secondary emotion because initially the person experienced shame or fear, which are more fundamental. Therefore, in working with this form of anger, a therapist needs to see it as the client's most basic response in the present but work toward accessing the underlying shame or fear from the past.

Secondary Anger

Secondary anger is a reaction to primary emotions. It often protects people from their primary emotion, which they fear will lead them to fall apart, disintegrate, and not be able to cope (Greenberg, 2021). The underlying emotion is seen as dangerous and intolerable and as leading to too much vulnerability. This type of anger is incongruent with the current situation in that it doesn't promote need satisfaction or goal attainment. Thus, if I'm angry when I feel hurt and sad at a partner's nonresponsiveness, an angry response of blaming or distancing does not help me meet my need for closeness.

Secondary anger is a much more common form of anger in therapy with nonviolent people. Secondary anger predominantly protects against the vulnerability of shame or fear or against the sadness of lonely abandonment. Thus, nonadaptive anger is not often a person's primary emotion because situations that evoke primary shame or fear often are followed by a secondary reaction of protective, defensive anger. Secondary anger is often a response to feeling diminished or to a blow to self-esteem, and it can cause a lot of interpersonal difficulties. This anger often feels justified in the moment. The person feels slighted or wronged, loses contact with all the good things received from the other person, and remembers only the slight. The more fragile the person's self-esteem, the more easily they lose contact with the positive parts of their relationships. The person feels only the diminishment and sees the other person as all bad. People may later feel apologetic about their anger, but their shame or guilt does not lead to change in their self-esteem, and they remain fragile and vulnerable to slights.

Secondary anger can also be a reaction to prior cognitive processes, so it can be the result of negative automatic thoughts. For example, secondary anger can result from hostile attributions or faulty appraisals. Why do these negative thoughts occur? According to EFT theory, the negative cognitions are a secondary phenomenon, secondary to underlying primary emotions such as shame, fear, or sadness. Thus, the anger-producing attribution or faulty appraisal that one was slighted or wronged is secondary to the automatic primary feeling of shame evoked by the situation.

Secondary anger to avoid more vulnerable (primary) experiences can lead to hostility and rage. An unfortunate example has been described as the shame–rage cycle, a common underlying process in domestic violence

(Scheff & Retzinger, 1991). It is important to remember, however, that while anger is a feeling, aggression is a behavior, and turning anger into action requires processing in addition to simply feeling angry. Another type of secondary anger results from the deterioration of what may have initially been adaptive anger. Over time, the arousal in the person's anger feeds on itself, and what started off as mild anger burgeons into rage by means of uncontrollable arousal.

Instrumental Anger

Finally, *instrumental anger* is expressed to obtain a desired reaction from others. This type of anger is used, consciously or automatically, to make others feel, think, or behave in a certain way and to achieve a measure of control over others, such as by expressing anger to intimidate others. People act angry but do not feel angry in a congruent fashion. Instrumental anger serves as a strategic or manipulative function and is an indirect way of getting what one wants without having to express authentic feelings or needs.

ANGER ASSESSMENT

Anger can be classified in any of these categories, depending on its function, at any given time. To arrive at a clear understanding of the function of anger, the therapist must conduct an *emotion assessment*, an ongoing process that requires attention to a variety of verbal and nonverbal sources of information and includes an evaluation of the client's capacity for emotion regulation (Greenberg, 2015, 2021). Emotion assessment consists of a moment-by-moment understanding of the client's emotions as they unfold. The therapist, keeping their fingers on the client's emotional pulse, follows the client's idiosyncratic experience, listening for the ebb and flow of anger as it rises and falls, and constantly trying to understand the client's unique subjective experience.

This process involves attending to vocal quality and other aspects of nonverbal communication. For example, complaints or protests, which are fusions of anger and sadness (Greenberg, 2021), are often identified through the voice and need to be differentiated into pure anger and pure sadness. In complaints, primary anger at having been robbed of something one deserved is fused with primary sadness at having suffered a loss, and neither emotion is processed. Therapists need to help clients differentiate the two emotions so that each can be experienced and expressed clearly rather than as a fused and confused experience. Once adaptive anger is validated, therapists need to shift the client's focus to the internal experience of being wounded and hurt, which opens the door to sadness of loss and to the deconstruction of beliefs that the self is bad and defective.

Therapists also need to use their cultural knowledge of anger to understand when clients are feeling angry. This involves the therapist's theoretical and personal knowledge of universal human emotional responses to specific situations as well as cultural differences and rules of expression. The therapist understands, for example, that being treated unfairly evokes anger and being slighted or treated disrespectfully frequently generates secondary anger covering shame. Knowledge of this person over time in therapy and case formulation helps the therapist understand the client's core painful emotions and their emotion styles. Knowledge of a client's learning history is also crucial for accurately assessing the type of anger. Does this person have a learning history in which angry outbursts got them their way or protected them, or is this the first time that anger is being expressed? It is very helpful in treating anger to distinguish old, stale secondary anger from novel, fresh adaptive anger.

Different ways of responding to clients' anger are needed for the different types and causes of anger. For example, anger at having been rejected or disappointed in love is not the same as anger at having been violated or an angry reaction to another person's anger. Each needs to be treated differently. Revenge anger attempts to get back at or harm a loved one are maladaptive responses to being hurt or disappointed by that person. They don't help one get what they need.

ANGER PROBLEMS

Clients who meet diagnostic criteria associated with many mental health disorders often present with symptoms of anger and feelings of irritability. People with diagnoses of substance abuse disorders, bipolar disorders, adjustment disorder, intermittent explosive disorder, posttraumatic stress disorder, personality disorders, and schizophrenia or other psychotic disorders often have anger problems. Anger is generally seen as a disruptive symptom that needs to be alleviated (Kassinove & Tafrate, 2002) or as a maladaptive attempt at coping with stress, resulting in conflict and personal discomfort (Cox et al., 1999; Novaco, 1975). Anger problems include the inability to recognize that one is angry; recognizing but not being able to express anger; expressing anger with too much intensity; starting off at an acceptable level of anger but getting carried away into blaming or attacking; and being chronically angry and overreactive.

I put forth that access to adaptive, interrupted anger is as much needed in therapy as is control of secondary anger and anger management. It is also important to emphasize that expressing anger in the safety of the therapy hour is very different from expressing anger in one's life. In therapy, expression of anger can be liberating; in life, it can lead to all kinds of interpersonal and personal problems. As much as feeling anger can be a useful signal of a problem, venting anger will not provide a solution. In life, emotional intelligence involves expressing anger in the right way at the right time. Primary maladaptive anger is destructive and needs to be transformed at its source, which is the injury to the person's sense of worth.

ANGER IN RELATIONSHIPS

Anger can be a major problem in a couple's interaction because anger expression, especially expression of blaming anger, can hurt partners and produce misunderstanding. For couples, expressing anger too intensely often leads to escalating cycles of attack and defense or counterattacks, which prevent listening and collaboration. One partner, for example, might express secondary blaming anger and be critical when the underlying primary experience is really one of feeling sad and unsupported or invalidated. The other partner's secondary protective defensive response might then be feeling angry or sullenly withdrawing, or it might be a compliant "good kid" response; underneath, however, this partner would be feeling primarily unloved, not desired, and not valued (Greenberg & Goldman, 2008). In this case, secondary anger obscures what is really being felt.

Direct expression of primary adaptive anger at intrusion is important, as it can help solve the problem it signals. It is better to skillfully disclose one is angry than to harbor resentment and build a wall filled with bricks of resentment. Healthy expression of anger often means not reacting angrily, yelling, or blaming, but rather disclosing that one is angry. The mark of adaptive anger, as discussed, is disclosing it at the right intensity, in the right way, for the right reason. Moderation is the golden mean (Aristotle, ca. 350 B.C.E./1926).

AWARENESS AND EXPRESSION OF ANGER

Awareness of anger and expression of anger are two very different phenomena and involve different processes. Awareness involves attending to how one's body feels and being able to describe in words what one is experiencing rather than behaviorally acting out the anger. It is a form of knowing. The goal of awareness is to be informed. Expressing anger, in contrast, generally has a goal of informing others and attempting to influence them; it is a form of doing. Effective expression of anger requires great interpersonal skills. Even if a person is skilled in communicating anger, they can never predict the other person's reaction. The skill also involves knowing what to do after someone has expressed anger or experiences a sense of being wronged. Emotional competence involves a person's ability to handle other people's reactions to the person's expression of emotion. People should not express anger unless they are able to deal with what comes after the expression. Expressing anger to another usually involves a complex interaction. Rather than reacting impulsively and explosively or overcontrolling and suppressing anger, it is generally best to steer a middle course, which involves integrating emotion and reason by using social and cultural know-how in expressing emotion. This is often more complex than solving math problems and requires emotional intelligence (Greenberg, 2002).

INTERRUPTED ANGER

Much has been written suggesting that anger regulation requires teaching anger management skills, but suppression of anger is an equally problematic phenomenon. Anger is an innate response to frustration and violation. It is neither right nor wrong, nor is it good or bad. Rather, it provides information. It tells people about their needs, such as the need for protection against violation. Anger has adaptive value and pushes people to action. However, it can also be destructive, such as when it leads to aggression and violence or when it is suppressed rather than expressed.

In states of *interrupted anger*, the client's expressions indicate that anger is present in the body at some level but is not expressed explicitly. Rather, it comes out in the form of complaint, blame, bitterness, hopelessness, resignation, cutting remarks, silences, or other nonverbal cues. Emotionally, the person may experience a sense of collapsing, hopelessness, helplessness, despair, defeat, alienation, resignation, powerlessness relating to lack of entitlement, or fear.

The resolution to this state involves a sense of empowerment and self-affirmation. Clients then experience a stronger sense of self and feel entitled to their feelings and needs. They feel greater self-confidence and more assertive, and they define new goals projecting to the future. With access to their assertive anger, clients often experience a positive view of themselves; feel strong, in control, worthwhile, and lovable; have hope for the future and are optimistic.

ANGER MANAGEMENT

Proponents of cognitive behavior therapy work with managing anger that is too intense, misplaced, and disruptive (Kassinove & Tafrate, 2002) or that is a maladaptive attempt at coping with stress, resulting in conflict and personal discomfort (Consedine et al., 2002; Cox et al., 1999; Novaco, 1975). Therapeutic work involves encouraging clients to inhibit their anger (Bushman, 2002; Mayne, 1999). Anger management, which involves anger control and inhibition, is a key intervention strategy for therapeutic sessions, with numerous programs developed to train clients in anger management skills (Toohey, 2021). The negative effects of anger and the need for management is reflected in ideas like one attributed to Thomas Jefferson: "When angry count to ten before you speak. If very angry, count to one hundred."

These views emphasize the benefits of and the need for anger management and regulation. They capture the imagination and make sense to many, but difficulties arise with a blanket application of this view. When healthy assertion is thwarted, the person experiences adaptive anger, but when anger is thwarted, the person experiences hostility and possibly becomes aggressive. When clients experience an anger-driven wish to harm, therapists need to understand the wrongs that clients feel they have suffered and to empathize with the need to retaliate rather than seeing this anger as needing to be inhibited. Clients want revenge to get justice or to feel empowered rather than feel their underlying shame or vulnerability. To help clients get out of their shame/blame revenge cycle, therapists need to get to the underlying vulnerability. In addition, when people act out their anger in therapy by venting, they don't feel their anger. Getting angry and then yelling or crying immediately discharges the tension but, in these situations, people don't viscerally feel their anger or the texture of it. To make sense of their anger, people need to be helped to feel their anger and not immediately discharge it. Hostility is not all there is—it is just the surface secondary reaction. Beneath rage and hostility is often a longing and a need to belong or to be recognized. One needs to search beneath the rage to find a place of tender vulnerability and the feelings of shame.

An important difficulty in therapy, however, occurs when healthy, self-assertive anger in significant attachment relationships is interrupted (Greenberg & Woldarsky Meneses, 2019), leading to unfinished business with someone who was significant in the person's life. This form of unresolved of anger is the source of a lot of psychological distress for many people. All people can probably recall some interpersonal injuries that still make them feel angry.

There is a real difference between events that still make us feel angry and those that merely irritate or annoy. Unresolved anger leads to corrosive resentment that can remain unprocessed for a lifetime. As time passes, some feelings of anger wax and wane; they eventually pass away and are no longer anger. Certain other experiences, however, do not fade. They often boil and bubble inside. These experiences need to be addressed in therapy.

Anger that lasts over time is often directed at significant others, such as anger arising from parental maltreatment, a spouse's betrayal or abandonment, parents' divorce, a father's humiliation, or an unprotective mother. This anger persists into the present. It affects current relationships and prevents loving relationships from developing. Even though many of the situational details are forgotten, the emotions remain, and the person feels them repeatedly as if the event were occurring right now. This happens because the major violation was so arousing and overwhelming that the person was unable to process their emotions and cope effectively with the intensity of the hurt and anger at the time. They were unable to make sense of it and assimilate it into their understanding of the world. Instead, it was stored in emotional memory as an intense feeling.

Self-assertive anger, as discussed previously, is an empowering emotion; it promotes the experience of one's self as an active agent who can influence the environment and others. Self-assertive anger is a fundamentally important emotion in the process of resolving fear, sadness, and shame in unfinished business, and blocked or split-off anger is among the most common difficulties that lead to impasses in resolution (Greenberg & Woldarsky Meneses, 2019). When people block, they generally end up feeling hopeless and helpless, become depressed, and may react with destructive anger that doesn't fit the situation or isn't well timed. Unresolved feelings may be aimed at an internalized representation of a harsh significant other or at a bad self.

ANGER RESEARCH

Expression of previously suppressed anger in therapy can be beneficial. A number of studies have shown that when anger serves its primary biological-adaptive function of boundary setting, expressing it has a positive effect (Harmon-Jones et al., 2006; Rubin, 1970; Sicoli, 2005). When anger is interrupted, stress increases; research also suggests that interrupted anger contributes to depression (Akhavan, 2001; Gilbert, 2006; Harmon-Jones et al., 2002). Further evidence suggests that the emotion suppression is associated with an increase in negative emotionality, increased problems with physical health, and greater stress (Dalgleish et al., 2009; Kiecolt-Glaser et al., 2002; Pennebaker, 1995, 1997; Pennebaker & Francis, 1996). Previously depressed clients reported more anger suppression and greater fear of expressing anger than people who had never been depressed. Jack (1991) developed a theory of "silencing the self," noting that women who were depressed silenced themselves with an internal voice, mainly to maintain and protect relationships, especially intimate ones. Many depressed women silence their feelings, suppress their anger, and are agreeable so they do not jeopardize close relationships (Brody et al., 1999; Jack, 1991).

Symptomatic hopelessness and helplessness are nonresilient responses to unexpressed anger toward others (e.g., the "wrongdoer") or to the person themself. These symptomatic experiences are secondary emotions that involve closing down or giving up, and they represent a protective reaction, often against anger. Overcontrolling or blocking the expression of anger at threats prevents the possibility of assertive action. This, in turn, amplifies a feeling of weakness and disempowerment and can thus engender even more anger, as illustrated by the "bottle-up–blow-up syndrome," in which a compliant spouse who suppresses anger suddenly explodes in rage or violence (Greenberg & Paivio, 1997).

On the other hand, when anger is viewed as an adaptive emotion that provides information (Greenberg, 2002) and self-protective action and aids in overcoming obstructed goals and perceived threats, it is potentially energizing and provides a feeling of power (Masters, 1999). Accessing unacknowledged primary anger, which is often accompanied by secondary feelings of hopelessness, helplessness, sadness, resignation, and alienation, is thus an important change process in therapy that helps to energize people. The secondary feelings define a marker of a global sense of interrupted anger and disempowerment. During therapy, successful clients who acknowledge, differentiate, and accept the primary emotions of anger move toward a greater assertive expression through expression of needs and development of agency. This, in turn, results in the resolution of different symptoms such as depression, anxiety, trauma, and interpersonal problems. The suppression of anger is a problem of interrupted anger. Alternatively, it can be most therapeutic when a person in a state of interrupted anger can re-own and even intensify that anger rather than downregulating the anger experience and expression.

An important question to ask, then, is why healthy anger is so often interrupted in adults. As with shame, one reason is that social norms and rules such as "anger is bad" and "you shouldn't be angry" are fairly strong. Children learn these rules at an early age. Parents do not generally respond to anger with empathy, and they are not usually good emotion coaches who help children deal with anger constructively. In fact, they probably cannot deal with their own anger in a healthy fashion. The lessons about controlling anger start young and are well learned by adolescence.

In addition, negative learning experiences in childhood leave painful emotional memories about anger. Children who grow up in a violent environment learn that anger is destructive, and their own anger is often interrupted by secondary fear. When children are abused and traumatized, they tend to direct their healthy anger about being wronged at themselves, not at their parents (Abbass, 2015; Greenberg & Woldarsky Meneses, 2019). This inward direction of anger protects their attachment to parents. However, when the adaptive reactions of anger cannot be directed outwardly in childhood, they are either disowned or directed against the self, strengthening the child's experience of the self as bad and producing guilt and shame.

A number of studies provide evidence for the value of anger expression in therapy. For example, Van Velsor and Cox (2001) found that, for survivors of sexual abuse, anger expression develops self-efficacy, promotes the development of healing memories, and helps attribute blame. Brody et al. (1999) also suggested that the constructive expression of anger is helpful in the treatment of depression. In a skills-training program informed by dialectical behavior therapy (DBT), the frequency of assertive anger was found to increase for therapy completers and to statistically mediate a decrease in symptoms at the end of treatment (Kramer et al., 2016). Assertive behaviors, emotions, and attitudes are facilitated in DBT treatments and are understood as the core of efficient coping with distress (Linehan et al., 2007).

Several studies support the benefits of adaptive anger expression in EFT and similar approaches. In a study of clients with depression, Mohr et al. (1991) found that anger expression was significantly associated with conflict resolution and with reduction of hurt. Additional support for the benefits of anger expression comes from a study in which more than half (64%) of the clients in trauma treatment, upon entering therapy, identified anger-related problems among the top concerns for which they wanted help (Ralston, 2006). Of these, the most frequently identified problems were unresolved anger toward perpetrators of abuse and difficulties stemming from limited access to anger experience (e.g., powerlessness, nonassertiveness). Holowaty and Paivio (2012) asked clients to retrospectively identify aspects of therapy they found most helpful and when these events occurred in therapy. Analyses of the videotaped therapy sessions indicated that the client-identified helpful events were characterized by a high level of arousal and that anger was the predominantly expressed emotion in half of these events.

Another study directly examined the contributions of anger expression to the resolution of child abuse trauma (Paivio, 2013). Client dialogues during the imagined confrontation procedure (99 videotaped episodes taken from 33 different clients) were analyzed using criteria for healthy anger expression. Results indicated a moderately large relationship between healthy anger expression and both the resolution of abuse issues and interpersonal dimensions of change, particularly at 12 months after treatment. Together, these results provide support for the assertion that healthy anger expression in key therapy situations can have a beneficial effect on outcome.

Research has also indicated that facilitating the experience and expression of anger within two-chair dialogues for self-criticism and unfinished interpersonal business in empty-chair dialogues (Greenberg & Foerster, 1996; Greenberg & Malcolm, 2002; Sicoli, 2005) leads to productive psychotherapy outcome. Additionally, Beutler and colleagues (1988, 1991) found that empty-chair dialogues are especially effective when working with clients with overcontrolled anger. Sicoli's (2005) research on overcoming hopelessness in depression indicated that resolvers were more likely to be aware of, express, and allow anger as well as to express wants and needs, all of which helped achieve a resilient stance. Sicoli found that the client's capacity to adaptively express anger in the session counteracted feelings of hopelessness and appeared to change depression.

Studies of psychodynamic interpersonal therapy indicate that anger expression is important in the process of change (Mackay et al., 2002). Clients who, in response to interventions to focus on their feelings, successfully stayed with the feeling of anger attained higher levels of emotional arousal. This arousal related significantly to a decrease in clients' pathological symptoms and interpersonal problems.

Although expression of anger in therapy sessions has been found to relate to positive therapy outcomes, simply arousing and venting anger in therapy is not always beneficial. In some circumstances, it might become nontherapeutic and even lead to aggressiveness (Olatunji et al., 2007). In a number of analogue studies on catharsis and anger, Bohart (1980) found that high levels of in-session arousal and discharge of anger did not lead to reduction of anger, and nor did intellectual and rational analysis of anger. Aroused anger that remained unprocessed led to signs of increased aggressiveness, whereas arousal of anger and its expression in conjunction with the exploration of its meaning led to anger resolution. Therefore, it appeared that anger expression combined with cognitive processing helped to resolve anger.

Taken together, these studies offer support for the hypothesis that arousing, expressing, and transforming anger in therapy promotes therapeutic change. It is thus clear not only that anger control is important for therapeutic change but also that arousal, expression, and understanding of anger, and mobilization of a sense of deserving to have the need in the anger met, help people let go of the anger and resolve "unfinished business" (Greenberg, Rice, & Elliott, 1993). When anger is inhibited, the individual often feels hopeless about getting needs met and in unexpected moments may react with anger that is out of proportion to the provocation (Siegman & Snow, 1997).

GENDER AND CULTURE

Anger and its expression are influenced by context, and gender and culture are two of the main factors that influence how people view and deal with anger. Working with accessing and transforming emotion in general, and anger more specifically, requires a special effort to reflect themes that are germane to both the gender identity of the person and the culture in which they are embedded. Some core aspects, such as the evolutionary function to protect boundaries and overcome obstacles, remain the same regardless of gender and culture, but some differ. For example, the role of anger and how it is expressed and received is different for people of different genders or races/ethnicities. The treatment of anger must be sensitive to gender and cultural differences in help seeking and completion of therapy.

Anger and Gender

Anger and related problems of aggression and violence occur in men and women, and anger also occurs in men and women in psychotherapy. People of all genders are candidates for appropriate anger treatment. A gender-informed treatment needs to account for the fact that people of different genders also differ, in some ways, in anger experience and expression (Fernandez & Malley-Morrison, 2013).

Kring (2000) noted that conventional wisdom suggests anger is much more a male than a female emotion. Higher levels of male anger may result when men are socialized for competitive and combative roles that encourage the expression of anger while women are socialized for more nurturing, caring, and supportive roles. When anger is discouraged in women, they may turn their anger inwards, resulting in more depression (Ross & Van Willigen, 1996). Men, in contrast, tend to transform all negative or painful emotions into anger. There may be some truth to the ideas that women suppress anger and men inhibit their anger far less, but these stereotypes might reflect extreme ends of functioning in society.

Reviewing empirical studies in the wider arena, Sharkin (1993) maintained that there are few significant gender differences in anger. Averill (1983) reported no significant gender difference in frequency or intensity of anger in college students and community residents, although women were four times more likely than men to cry when angry. Research has also indicated that men's anger tends to occur in short outbursts that are intense but relatively brief and occasional, whereas anger in women is less intense but more prolonged and frequent (Fernandez & Scott, 2009). Archer (2004), in a meta-analysis of gender differences in aggression and anger, found that men exceed women in direct physical aggression and less so in verbal aggression, while women exceed men in indirect aggression such as gossip, social ostracism, and silent treatment (Buss & Durkee, 1957).

The gender difference in indirect expression of anger seems to persist across age and culture. It is not the amount of anger but its expression that most differentiates people of different genders. Research also suggests that men express anger more with other men as opponents than with women, whereas women express anger with men more than with women (Archer, 2004). It has been suggested that women in North America are socialized to see the direct expression of anger as a threat to relationships, possibly resulting in social rejection, so anger is silenced or expressed indirectly (Hatch & Forgays, 2001). This tendency in North American women, then, needs direct attention in therapy. In addition, preferences for type of therapy also differ as a function of gender identity. On average, men are more receptive to behavioral and informational aspects of therapy, whereas women are inclined to prefer the verbal and emotionally oriented aspects. Given that emotion-focused therapies tend to be preferred by women and that men are potentially less receptive to therapy than women are, a special effort is needed to engage and retain male-identifying clients with dysfunctional anger.

Anger and Culture

Like gender, culture is an inescapable aspect of clients in therapy, and in multicultural societies throughout the world, the ideal is a multicultural therapy. Matsumoto et al. (2010) asserted that expressions of anger can be found across cultures, albeit with some culture-specific modifications and variability. As mentioned previously, anger has an evolutionary role that serves as an adaptive response to a perceived threat, and this applies across cultures. As a result, a culturally sensitive treatment of anger, based on observations of important differences in anger display rules across cultures, is important (Ramirez et al., 2002). In one vivid example, culturally sensitive care for a

Muslim patient required understanding that, for Muslims, a major illness is considered God's will and therefore the expression of anger at the illness would be deemed inappropriate (Lawrence & Rozmus, 2001).

Race also exerts a strong influence on emotional expression, especially in the context of racism. Expressing emotion is dangerous for members of marginalized racial or ethnic groups (Smart Richman & Leary, 2009; Wingfield, 2010). Many Black children, for example, are socialized not to express anger so they are not judged as violent. It can be dangerous for Black men to express anger or even be assertive in public, and it is potentially lethal to be assertive with law enforcement officers, as witnessed by the recent tragic events in America. The terrible paradox for people of color is that anger, which is a healthy response to injustice and violation, is denied, particularly to Black people, who have the most cause to feel angry about systemic racism and social injustice. When working with anger, therapists need to understand that because of racial stereotyping, it can be dangerous for Black clients to express anger. People of color are at much greater risk of having force used against them if they express anger, whereas White individuals can more often express anger without fear of being penalized.

It also has been found that many Black woman are brought up in historical and culture-bound expectations of strength that often create unrealistic expectations and demands on them to help others while ignoring their own distress (Beauboeuf-Lafontant, 2007; S. A. Thomas & González-Prendes, 2009; Thompkins, 2004). This creates a double bind for these women: They may experience anger and resentment related to the lack of attention to their needs and at the same time may feel that expressing dissatisfaction or anger and complaining is a sign of weakness. Some research suggests that when coping with acute racism, Black women express less anger, and at a lower rate, than Black men do (Pittman, 2011).

Almost all Black people, however, are subjected to anti-Black oppression, making the experience of rage almost inevitable. Rage is a normal and even expected response to the painful degradation of racial oppression. Black individuals are routinely forced to suffer their pain and humiliation in silence, which creates an optimal context for the cultivation of rage. Carter and Forsyth (2010) found that the most frequent reactions to racial discrimination were feeling disrespected and angry, followed by feeling insulted, disappointed, frustrated, outraged, hurt, and shocked.

When anger is suppressed and internalized, it can present as despair or depression. Internalized rage can contribute to health deterioration, substance abuse, and suicidal ideation. Suppressed rage can also be externalized into explosive volatility. Pittman's (2011) research indicated that the use of anger by Black individuals to cope with racial discrimination negatively affected their general well-being and caused psychological distress. Both experienced anger and anger inhibition have been found to be significant predictors of circulatory disease (CD) for Black adults, with the relation between experienced anger and CD mediated by anger inhibition. Cultural factors thus play a role in the development of an anger-inhibitory style, and this trait may pose a serious risk factor for CD.

Shame is also an important effect of racism that leads to suppression of anger. Direct experiences with racial discrimination are associated with higher levels of shame (Carter & Forsyth, 2010; C. G. DeYoung, 2015; Dickerson & Kemeny, 2004; Kaufman, 1996; R. S. Miller, 1997; Tangney & Dearing, 2002). Shame is a part of the social dominance and racial hierarchy apparatus of any society. Social devaluation and the experience of contempt from others, as well as the internalization of those external perceptions, lead to shame. The experience of otherness is impossible for people of color living in a predominantly White society to avoid. Black men are routinely exposed to degradation, and their attempts to navigate the degradation can result in internalized feelings of inferiority (i.e., shame) and powerlessness. They are often objects of condemnation, receiving incessant messages that they are failures not only because of their actions but also simply because they are Black. Black men may experience shame because they cannot transcend anti-Black racism. Poverty as a function of racism also adds to the mix, as not being able to financially provide for their families can produce shame. In addition, the inability to protect themselves from police violence can produce a sense of shame (e.g., feeling weak and helpless), while encountering the ongoing threat to one's bodily integrity can lead to withdrawal for self-protection. Given the role of anger to set boundaries and overcome barriers, anger would be an adaptive response to shame-producing experiences. However, anger has had to be inhibited for reasons of safety and social acceptability, which leaves people of color with a lot of interrupted anger.

Clinicians working with Black men need to understand the contextual aspects of the sources of anger and shame and, sometimes, the overcompensatory efforts that they may use to prove their worth. Often this results in unhealthy overworking or overly high effort in order to control or manage their environment. Therapists, then, need to help them engage in healthier coping that aids empowerment by focusing on other fulfilling aspects of their lives, independent of their employment success. A contextualized emotion-focused approach is therefore recommended for therapists working with Black men, and the realities of Black male experience need to be integrated into the therapy. Similarly, of course, with Black women, and with all people of color, where the ability to navigate White spaces and deal with the dehumanizing objectification while still operating as an integrated human being of worth, needs always to be recognized.

Therapists should be constantly aware of contextual factors when working with people of color and need to negotiate ways to acknowledge clients' collective experience of unfairness and oppression while not denying the person's individuality and idiosyncratic personal experience. Therapists need to bear witness to the person's experience of injustice and right to anger without increasing alienation and feelings of otherness. In addition to being good facilitators of change, therapists need to become agents of social change by raising awareness of systemic racism and understanding how it affects the individual. It is important for therapists to understand that many White people see color as a factor that helps to explain the behavior of Black men and women. The simple reality exists that skin color matters in the interpretation of human interaction.

Although it has been shown that Black Americans are exposed to racial discrimination more than other ethnic or racial groups are (Chou et al., 2012), Indigenous people, Latino, and Asian Americans also suffer from discrimination. Therapy needs to help clients work through the emotional wounds caused by racial trauma so they can gain awareness and cope with systemic racism while supporting clients' resistance to, and protection from, the external forces that cause ethno-racial trauma and ultimately find relief.

Asian cultural norms and display rules also shape individuals' culturally approved expressions of anger. For instance, Mauss et al. (2010) reported that Asian American women experienced less anger and displayed less intense forms of anger expression than European American women did. Emotional expression within a culture is mediated by whether the culture has a collectivist orientation of harmony and interdependence or an orientation toward independence and self-determination. Collectivist societies are less likely to approve the overt and amplified expression of anger than individualistic societies are. Practitioners, however, should avoid making overarching generalizations based on this dimension and thereby overlook intraculture variability based on socioeconomic, religious, and educational, differences which also influence emotional expression of anger.

Culture-sensitive regulation of anger must attend to salient aspects of the client's culture as well as to the uniqueness of the individual and recognize the role that cultural norms and display rules play in the expression of emotions in general and anger in particular. To overlook this is to risk making stereotypical generalizations about groups of people and thus ignore the uniqueness of the person.

CONCLUSION

This chapter discussed the nature and function of anger and its assessment in psychotherapy. It highlighted the idea that interrupted anger is as much of a problem as dysregulation of anger, which has received so much attention of late with anger management. Anger, as much as it can be a disruptive emotion, is most fundamentally an adaptive internal signal that promotes self-protective action and a constructive response to violation. Additionally, this chapter reviewed the research on the negative effects of interrupted anger and the positive effects of anger expression in life and in therapy. It ended with gender and cultural considerations that need attention when working with anger.

Chapter 9 includes a look at activating interrupted anger by helping clients become aware of how they actively interrupt their experience and expression of adaptive anger. In addition, it covers methods for undoing these self-interruptive processes to provide clients access to their healthy adaptive anger.

9 ACTIVATING INTERRUPTED ANGER

You should be angry. You must not be bitter. Bitterness is like cancer. It eats upon the host. It doesn't do anything to the object of its displeasure. So use that anger.

—Maya Angelou

This chapter is focused on accessing interrupted anger to help clients become more empowered and discusses ways to help clients express interrupted anger. Disowned, interrupted anger underlies many presenting symptoms such as depression, anxiety, and interpersonal problems (Akhavan, 2001; Gilbert, 2006; Harmon-Jones et al., 2002). Our clinical work on interrupted anger has demonstrated a definite therapeutic benefit to accessing previously disowned, interrupted, adaptive anger. Based on that work, this chapter presents a clinically derived set of treatment steps for helping clients undo the interruptions, offering clinical evidence supporting the activation of anger as an important therapeutic change process. Chapter 10 then uses research projects to illustrate how interrupted anger is overcome in therapy and considers the clinical efficacy of this process.

---

https://doi.org/10.1037/0000393-009
Shame and Anger in Psychotherapy, by L. S. Greenberg
Copyright © 2024 by the American Psychological Association. All rights reserved.

This chapter illustrates the difference between accessing interrupted anger in therapy, which involves facilitating anger expression, and management of symptomatic, dysregulated anger, which involves controlling anger expression. The chapter discusses how to recognize when to use each approach by specifying the type of anger that is being treated. One type of anger involves too little primary adaptive anger, whereas the second involves too much symptomatic secondary or too much primary maladaptive anger.

Many clients need help to allow and accept underlying adaptive anger that has been blocked rather than to manage anger. To allow and accept underlying adaptive anger, clients first have to become aware that they are blocking anger and of the myriad ways they deflect, suppress, and interrupt anger expression. They then need to be helped to overcome these blocks by addressing both their fear of anger and their shame or guilt about expressing it. Finally, they are able to experience and express their previously disowned anger. In activating interrupted anger, clients need to feel their anger in their bodies and not just talk about it.

Working to access primary adaptive anger involves quite a different mindset than that involved in working with core maladaptive shame (see Chapter 6). Although arriving at disclaimed emotion is similar whether the emotion is shame or anger, when therapists work with interrupted anger they are facilitating arrival at a blocked *primary adaptive emotion* for its good information, whereas with shame, therapists are generally accessing a *primary maladaptive emotion* to help transform it by changing emotion with emotion. When accessing interrupted anger, therapists are not working to change the anger; they are working to help clients overcome their blocks to it and to accept and express their anger in the safety of the therapeutic situation. The therapist is trying to help the client feel entitled to feel angry. Therapists' validation of their clients' deservingness of healthy, previously unmet needs helps generate empowered anger while validating clients' newly felt anger and the emerging more empowered self-organizations helps them re-story their narratives.

When working on interrupted anger, clients need to be helped to allow and accept their adaptive anger. To overcome the blocks that interfere with self-acceptance, clients have to undo the tendency to deflect and suppress the experience of unacknowledged anger. One significant block to expressing anger is shame or shame anxiety. A person doesn't express assertive anger because they anticipate they will feel embarrassed or foolish, look like they have lost control, or reveal that they are hurt; instead, they interrupt. They are anxious that they would feel ashamed if they expressed anger. Therapists therefore need to acknowledge the client's anger and validate its legitimacy to help overcome the tendency to feel embarrassed or ashamed. Interventions may include comments such as "It's important to accept your anger" and "It's hard to be angry but this is here in the session for you to allow your anger, it's not to express it in the real world. It's about accepting what you feel and getting what it is saying." The therapist encourages the client to express empowered anger; the therapist can express curiosity about the client's adaptive anger by asking, "How does it feel inside your body? Do you feel it in a specific place in your body? Your face? Your stomach?" or "Are there images? Does it have a voice? Words? Is it saying something?" The therapist may also ask, "Are you willing to stay with it for a while? It may be painful to feel it a little more, but it will help us get to know it better." When primary anger has been arrived at, the scene is set to express it and its need and to develop new approach responses associated with empowered anger.

STEPS INVOLVED IN TREATING INTERRUPTED ANGER

After establishing relational safety, making a process diagnosis that there is interrupted anger, and developing an alliance to work on interrupted anger, the treatment steps for working with interrupted anger involve (a) facilitating recognition of the interruption of anger, (b) undoing the interruption of anger, (c) accessing interrupted anger and unmet needs, (d) facilitating grief at the loss of what was deserved but never received, and finally (e) constructing a new narrative based on newly experienced anger. These steps facilitate "arriving" at anger and involve acknowledging, accessing, tolerating, symbolizing, and regulating it. In this process, new, adaptive feelings of anger at violation are validated, their expression in the session is facilitated, narratives are reconstructed to develop more positive outcome stories, and assertive expression in the world is encouraged where appropriate. This chapter also shows how important it is to assess the type of anger being expressed and when it is expressed, and to recognize that anger may not be all that clients are feeling when they express anger.

THE RELATIONAL CONTEXT

Influenced by both client-centered (Rogers, 1959), and Gestalt therapy (Perls et al., 1951), emotion-focused therapy (EFT) is a relationally and interpersonally based experiential therapy (Greenberg, Rice, & Elliott, 1993). To reiterate, therapist presence (Geller & Greenberg, 2012) and empathic attunement to affect (Greenberg, 2021) are at the core of therapeutic work.

In addition, there is a strong task component in which the therapist is guiding the client's emotional process to clarify and make sense of emotion processing difficulties. In line with the client-centered therapy tradition, EFT holds that the therapist's role is to provide a curative relational environment conducive to productive emotional processing through presence (genuineness), empathy (understanding), and unconditional positive regard (valuing). This overall approach is applicable to working with anger.

Often, however, therapists find it hard to genuinely empathize with clients' anger and accept it, especially when it is secondary or maladaptive. Perhaps the greatest obstacle to including emotional process work in the treatment of anger is the therapist's own aversion to this frightening and potentially destructive emotion. Very few individuals wish to be exposed to another person's anger or rage. When anger or the behaviors associated with it are frightening to therapists, there can be a rush to change what the client is experiencing and expressing. The therapist might deliberately, or possibly without awareness, shut down the client's anger. If the client's anger has been dangerous, it is natural for the therapist to want the client not to be angry during the session. However, previously unexpressed anger must be evoked to effect change and shouldn't be confused with destructive anger. In cases of dysregulated, destructive anger, anger management is needed first; however, while helping to down-regulate anger, therapists need to validate the client's anger as understandable and promote acceptance of what is happening in the moment to maintain the safe relationship and to melt or not activate self-protective defenses.

The first step in accessing interrupted anger, then, involves developing a safe, supportive, validating, empathic, and affectively attuned relationship. When relational safety has been established, the focus with clients who have interrupted anger needs shifts to overcoming the fear of accessing previously unexpressed anger. An alliance needs to be formed with clients to work on becoming aware that they are interrupting their anger, then to work on how they are interrupting, and finally to help them express their interrupted anger. Once anger has been accessed, interventions focus on helping clients stay in touch with their experience of assertive anger, accept it, and symbolize these feelings in the immediacy of the session.

A strong alliance and a safe and trusting therapeutic relationship are developed through a warm bond and agreement on goals and tasks. The bond is developed mainly through empathy, which involves understanding clients' experience from their point of view. The relationship is both an essential context for intervention and an active ingredient of change. Empathic attunement to affect provides a corrective emotional experience by providing accurate mirroring of affective states, accurate labeling, and appropriate expression of emotions; it acts as a form of co-regulation of distress. In addition to facilitation of affect regulation, empathy provides the environment for other forms of process-guiding interventions that promote productive emotional processing.

A comfortable, nonjudgmental atmosphere that provides support and communicates understanding of the person's anger allows the client to feel validated and understood as a unique individual with idiosyncratic experiences. This facilitates an increased trust in the therapist, and the client feels increasingly empowered to explore and express previously unacknowledged anger and the associated unmet needs. Human beings have a deep need for recognition (Greenberg & Goldman, 2008). Recognition by the therapist makes clients' feelings, intentions, and actions meaningful. Being seen by the therapist is growth enhancing—negative views of self that were learned in past relationships, such as "I am unworthy or unlovable," are changed by the experience of being recognized. Being seen and valued relationally challenges these views and makes the client feel worthy. With validation, acceptance, and understanding, the client's difficulties with anger slowly begin to come into focus, as do their previously unmet needs. This leads ultimately to a self-reorganization.

PROCESS DIAGNOSIS

To develop a focus for the treatment of a client's interrupted anger, the therapist engages in a "process diagnosis" (Greenberg, Rice, & Elliott, 1993) of the client's current manner of processing anger. For instance, the therapist needs to consider whether the client is expressing primary anger at unfairness or secondary blaming anger masking hurt. Perhaps the client is expressing dominant instrumental anger or anger that is fused with sadness and expressed as complaint. Is the client expressing hopelessness or resignation because their anger, even though it is somewhat discernable, is interrupted anger? Is there anger in the voice or body movement but not in the content, or are there signs of interruption, such as changing the topic, shifting eye gaze, sighing, or a change in breathing? Based on these moment-by-moment formulations of what the client is currently experiencing, the therapist chooses to focus on a specific processing task (e.g., attending, experiential search, active expression, or interpersonal contact), with the goal of promoting contact with the interrupted anger.

What therapists do is based first on what they observe (Greenberg, 2015). Therefore, identifying and differentiating the client's emotional experience is central. The therapist works with the client to identify whether the client's immediate anger is primary or secondary and whether it is adaptive or maladaptive. These two important distinctions help in understanding the client's anger. Then the therapist looks at whether the client is processing the anger productively. Does the client's verbal content match the nonverbal behavior (i.e., is it congruent)? Is the anger being accepted or evaluated negatively? Does the client feel they are the agent of the emotion, or is the anger happening to them? What is the client's level of emotional regulation (e.g., overcontrolled or underregulated)? In answering these questions, therapists and clients gain a better way of processing their anger.

If anger is secondary, the therapist first empathizes with the client's experience, acknowledging their sense of being wronged and validating their immediate experience of anger. As noted previously, this helps clients feel understood and prevents defensiveness. Then, the therapist moves beyond the validation of anger to deepen emotional experiencing, using empathic exploration to explore emerging strands of associated feelings, thoughts, and needs through empathic attunement to client experiencing underneath the secondary anger.

If a client is expressing instrumental anger, which is a learned response to regulate others' behavior for secondary gains, the therapist should not try to arouse or experientially explore this type of anger. Rather, the therapist should help the client become aware of the aims underlying their expression by providing feedback that indicates what the therapist understands or conjectures about the client's underlying aims. The goal in working with instrumental anger is to help clients understand their own needs and motivations and help them find alternative ways of achieving their goals.

CRITERIA FOR HEALTHY ANGER EXPRESSION

Criteria for healthy expression of anger is necessary when recommending the therapeutic value of anger intensification. A general principle is that anger activation is only appropriate for accessing interrupted adaptive anger at violation. Activation of anger is not appropriate for individuals who are overwhelmed by their anger and have anger control problems. The purpose of anger activation is to access the adaptive information associated with healthy anger. This aids in the construction of more adaptive meaning regarding self, others, and traumatic events.

For therapists to promote the expression of previously unacknowledged or interrupted anger, the following guidelines are helpful to ensure that the expression is healthy and empowering (Paivio & Pascual-Leone, 2010;

A. Pascual-Leone et al., 2013). First, anger should be directed outward toward the appropriate target, rather than inward toward the self or to a third party. Next, to make the information and action tendency inherent in the anger available to guide clients, it needs to be viscerally experienced, not talked about in a conceptual manner. Anger then must be differentiated from other emotions, experienced in pure form and not contaminated by emotions such as sadness, fear, or guilt. Anger expression mixed with sadness makes for complaint and, if mixed with fear, does not provide the bodily felt sense of strength nor the cognitive, motivational, and action-tendency support that the experience of primary adaptive anger provides. An example of this important process of differentiating anger from hurt is provided in the following transcript, which shows a client in an unfinished business dialogue with his father moving from hurt to anger at being hurt.

THERAPIST (T): How does it feel when your father talks to you like that?

CLIENT (C): It hurts me.

T: Tell him directly!

C: It hurts me when you talk to me like that.

T: And how does it feel to be hurt?

C: (With burgeoning anger in his voice) I don't like being hurt, it feels really bad.

T: So, the hurt feels bad and brings up some anger. Tell him directly! Tell him what you resent. *(The therapist separates the anger from the hurt and guides toward the anger.)*

C: (Angry) I resent being hurt by you. I want you to stop doing that. I don't deserve to be treated badly. Do you understand?! *(accesses anger)*

For anger to be healthy, clients must experience themselves as agents of their anger and take responsibility for their feelings. Anger should be expressed assertively with ownership of experience rather than reactively, aggressively, passively, or indirectly. This is helped by expressing *I-anger* ("I am angry at you") rather than *you-anger* ("you made me angry"). Clients thus are encouraged to use "I" statements rather than referring to themselves in third person, blaming and complaining, or attacking or insulting the other.

For anger to be experienced rather than talked about, its expression must be direct, for example, by expressing needs as demands and expectations (e.g., "I demand," "I expect," "I want that," instead of "I need") and anger in terms of boundary setting or rejection (e.g., "I refuse," "I will not under any circumstances," "I don't want," instead of "I can't"). Expressing differences can be helpful to promote differentiation (e.g., "Tell your mother that you are different from her. Explain to her in what ways you are different from her"). Expressing resentment helps to hold and strengthen anger (e.g., "Most of all I resent you for . . .," "I blame you for . . .").

In addition, for anger to be healthy, the intensity of the anger must match the evoking situation and the extent of the experienced injustice or block. Intensity of expression is reflected in voice tone, body posture, facial expression, and choice of words. Any disproportionate intensity of anger that overwhelms with rage or the opposite, that is lacking in conviction or energy, lacks the necessary information and action orientation to respond adaptively to the situation that is being worked on in the session.

STEPS IN THE TREATMENT OF INTERRUPTED ANGER

Once relational safety has been established, interrupted anger has been identified, and an alliance to work on it has been established, the therapist begins the process of working with interrupted anger. The first step, as mentioned, involves facilitating recognition of the interruption of anger. This is followed by undoing the interruption of anger to access the anger and unmet needs. Having allowed and accepted the anger, the client often experiences a process of facilitating grief at the loss of what was deserved but never received and then finally constructs a new narrative based on the newly experienced anger. The steps designed to facilitate arriving at allowing, expressing, and processing interrupted anger are elaborated in the next sections.

Facilitating Recognition of the Interruption of Anger

The first step in working on undoing interrupted anger involves helping clients see that they are interrupting their anger. Only when they see themselves interrupting can they begin working on how they interrupt. The therapist thus listens for markers that indicate clients are blocking their anger and for the presence of persistent unresolved needs and feelings toward a significant other that suggest anger at unfairness (Greenberg, 2021).

The therapist brings interruptive processes to the client's awareness by making process observations, saying things like "I noticed you went silent there. What just happened?" Interruptive processes include changing the topic, intellectualizing, numbing, minimizing, going blank, or rationally controlling anger as well as expressing feelings of helplessness, resignation, or depression instead of anger. Focusing externally on events or people, in the form of chronic blame (which signals an underlying resentment) or complaint (a fusion of sadness and anger), are other forms of interruption. All these forms of interruption need to be brought gently into awareness.

Interruptions often appear during the client's narrative while they are addressing vulnerable experiences from the past. Self-interruption is essentially giving oneself the instruction, "Don't feel. Don't need." There can also be purely automatic physiological processes, such as tension in the chest, or a headache, or a pain in the neck. Nonverbal markers of interruption are abrupt changes or the disappearance of the emotion that was about to emerge as well as changes in respiratory rhythm, facial expression, and body tension, accompanied by changes in content. Resignation and hopelessness in the face of core emotional needs not being met are other important indicators of interruption. "What's the use" or "Why even bother" accompanied by sighing or shrugging shoulders often conveys this feeling. Pointing out all these signs and especially the nonverbal aspects helps to bring the experience of interruption alive in the session. When, for example, anger is blocked, the therapist might draw the client's attention to how they tighten their neck muscles or point out how their breathing has changed. In addition, when clients express hostile self-criticism, self-blame, or self-hate (A. Pascual-Leone et al., 2013), it is important for the therapist to recognize that this anger is usually anger turned inward and that it is therapeutic to help the client to express it outwardly and to put it where it belongs, toward others who have injured the client.

Undoing the Interruption of Anger: Two-Chair Enactment

A major therapeutic task used to successfully resolve interrupted anger is two-chair enactment for self-interruption. This task involves having one part of the self enact interrupting the anger of another part of the self in a dialogue with an empty chair (Greenberg, 2021; Greenberg, Rice, & Elliott, 1993).

In work with interrupted anger, the early goal of therapy is to help the client take ownership of their role in interrupting their anger, which in turn allows them to begin to reduce the fear of expressing anger in the session and to develop a desire to change. Clients are invited to articulate the injunctions they use and to enact the bodily actions and muscular constrictions involved in the interruption. Enacting the suppressing actions, such as tightening the chest and holding one's breath, eventually provokes a response from the suppressed anger, often a reaction of opposing the suppression. On experiencing the distress caused by the interruption, the angry part of the self that is interrupted anger asserts itself against the injunctions and undoes the muscular constrictions of the interrupter so that the interrupted anger can spontaneously emerge. This intervention turns an automatic passive process of interruption into an active process of doing it to oneself, which heightens clients' awareness of how they interrupt themselves. The aim is to help undo these interruptive processes so that emotions can be accessed and processed.

Because talking to oneself in an empty chair is an unusual activity, the therapist needs to provide a lot of structure to help the client deal with self-consciousness and awkwardness. To begin this intervention, the therapist encourages the client to enact a part of the self interrupting the expression of anger and invites the client to begin the dialogue in the chair.

Two-chair enactment involves four main steps (Greenberg, 2021):

1. Bringing the client's attention to the interruption as it is occurring (e.g., by noting that the client just looked away or smiled when talking about feeling wronged).

2. Turning the automatic to deliberate (passive into active) by asking, "How do you stop yourself or interrupt yourself?" This question starts an awareness task to elaborate conscious experience and specify how the person interrupts.

3. Encouraging the client to enact what they do when interrupting (e.g., doing it with their hands or to a pillow) or finding some other way to engage them in an activity that allows them to experience themself as the agent of the interruption.

4. Finally, accessing what is being suppressed. New emotion emerges only after the client experiences themself as the agent of the interruptive process and experiences that the cost of interrupting (emotional pain) outweighs the benefit of the interruption (self-protection).

To summarize, therapists need to help clients discover first *that* they interrupt, then they need to explore *how* they interrupt. Recognizing the protective function of the interruption, experiencing the fear that drives the self-protective interruption, and overcoming it ultimately leads to the anger that has been interrupted. Validation of clients' fears of their anger and acknowledgment of the protective function of the interruption helps them feel safer to approach their anger. Accessing the nonverbal body component of the interruption of anger is often important. Therapists need to help clients locate muscular tension and blocking points and discover how they are producing them. Identifying the verbal, cognitive part of the experience is also important. This process involves helping people symbolize in awareness what they say to themselves and then have them actually say it to themselves.

Expressing Interrupted Anger and Unmet Need

Before promoting expression of anger, therapists need to ensure that clients have enough internal support to allow and tolerate the blocked anger. Clients may be afraid of facing their anger and may become tense at the prospect. Therapists need to empathize with the fear and provide support, understanding that the block serves a protective function. In addition to relational support, internal supports are built by taking a slow, step-by-step approach to allowing the emotion, which helps clients tolerate their anxiety. This type of graded approach is most useful in helping clients to approach and tolerate their anger. The therapist also helps clients regulate their breathing, put their feet on the ground, and describe what they are experiencing to increase contact with sensory reality. All of these strategies help clients mobilize more internal support.

For very anxious and fragile clients whose self-experience is not solid enough to tolerate and take ownership of anger, it can be helpful to talk about the anger in more distant terms and invite the client to observe their experience rather than immerse themselves in it. The therapist can talk about the anger in the third person, such as referring to "that anger in the body" and can invite the client to observe it. A helpful question that promotes the experience of self-assertive anger focuses on the action tendency of the energy: "What would this energy in your body do if it was free do what it wanted?" To create a safe distance, the therapist can go one step further and externalize the energy: "What would the energy do if it didn't belong to you but was the anger of a wild animal?"

Clients who do not feel entitled to be angry, then, can be helped by being introduced to gradually stronger anger expression. Therapists can offer clients increasingly stronger words and phrases that promote the experience of hurt and anger. For example, a therapist might encourage the client to first use mild statements such as "feeling wronged," "feeling disappointed," or "I'm annoyed," before moving to "feeling angry" and then to "feeling furious" or to express anger more indirectly, beginning with "I feel hurt it was unfair," then moving to "I don't like being treated this way," and finally more pointedly expressing "This makes me really angry," and then "I'm outraged and beside myself." The therapist can invite clients to repeat the same phrase offered by the therapist and, in the spirit of an experiment, to use stronger and stronger words and see how it feels.

When clients disclaim feelings of anger at violation, therapists can use empathic exploration and conjectures and experiential questions to help them acknowledge the experience. For example, the therapist might say, "Sounds like you felt that was pretty unfair," or even "What did you need that you were robbed of?" Or therapists can focus on client nonverbal behavior that emerges spontaneously and then encourage clients to put words to these actions, for example, by saying, "What's in that tone of voice—is it 'how dare you'?" In this form of graded increase in intensity, clients are encouraged to adopt congruent body postures and facial expressions. Explicit teaching about emotions and emotional processes can also be helpful. This is typically integrated into the process of exploring current or past issues rather than presented as an explicit exercise.

Once clients have experienced themselves as agents who interrupt their emotions, therapists help them get in touch with the emotions that have been disclaimed, thus recovering their information and healing power. This process involves supporting and following the experience in the experiential self until the experiential self becomes more empowered. When, after working on a self-interruption, a client feels more deserving and says, for example, "I do deserve it; I didn't do anything wrong," the therapist guides the client to express these newly accessed feelings and needs first back toward the interrupter and possibly later toward a significant other who was the source of the process of interruption.

Undoing interruption can be done via strategies other than two-chair enactments as well, including empathic exploration, imagery, experiential focusing, and other interventions (Elliott et al., 2004). Basically, the therapist follows the client's narrative content, listening for the most emotionally relevant experience and then guiding the process to the client's pain. What is important to realize is that people are always doing the best they can, trying to survive and be happy, and so it is important to empathize with what they are feeling and to try to accept and understand both their anger and their need to interrupt it. Self-interruptions are self-protections to be validated, not defenses to be challenged.

Therapists can use their own experience to express the client's interrupted anger and model anger expression to help clients access interrupted anger (Greenberg, 2015). A therapist can, for example, describe what a parent's treatment of a child evokes in them: "Being controlled by my father in this way would have made me angry. Does it make you angry?" Alternatively, the therapist can describe the sensations and reactions they notice in their own bodies: "As I'm listening to you, I feel this tension in my arms and hands and almost pulling a fist. What happens for you?"

It is also important to help clients reclaim the needs embedded in their anger. Research has shown that mobilizing unmet needs is one of the most helpful ways to activate an adaptive emotion (Greenberg, 2021; A. Pascual-Leone & Greenberg, 2007). Clients' acknowledgment that they need and, in fact, deserve validation activates adaptive emotions such as anger at invalidation and possibly an ensuing sense of pride and self-worth. Needs and action tendencies provide direction. In assertive anger, the need for nonviolation and the boundary-setting action tendencies provide orientation and direction and mobilize a sense of agency in the person. Therapists, therefore, need to help clients get to their need.

When clients habitually mask and interrupt their anger with secondary emotions (e.g., guilt, fear, sadness), it is important to validate these secondary emotions so as not to raise defensive anxiety and then focus on the underlying anger. In these moments, it is important for the therapist to guide the process by saying such things as "I see the extent to which being angry and losing control scares you. No wonder it is so; I know your story," "Your anger is important. Maybe we can give it a little more space today," "As you tell this, a whole lot of emotions are coming up. Sadness, guilt, but also anger. Let's focus on your anger today; I can hear it clearly in your voice," or "That really hurt, but I also hear anger in your voice."

Expressing Anger: Empty-Chair Dialogue

Empty-chair dialogue for unfinished business is an important intervention for accessing and expressing interrupted anger (Greenberg & Woldarsky Meneses, 2019). Once a safe therapeutic relationship has been established, therapists invite clients to imagine significant others at whose hands they have suffered abandonments, invalidations, maltreatment, and abuse in front of them in an empty chair. They are then encouraged to express their feelings directly to the other. This initially can evoke fear and avoidance of internal experience as well as shame and self-blame (e.g., "I was such a bad kid. No wonder she yelled so much"). These interruptions can then become the focus of intervention until the underlying anger is accessed. After some of the hurt, fear, and shame are processed, traumatic feelings and memories often occur. Clients then become better able to freely express previously inhibited feelings directly to the imagined other. The client is supported by the therapist to express adaptive anger at unfairness, abandonment, maltreatment, or abuse in an uninhibited fashion. Appropriate expression of anger encourages assertive expression of interpersonal needs, self-empowerment, and boundary definition (Greenberg, Rice, & Elliott, 1993). Helping the client to access the primary anger that is out of awareness also allows them to access the underlying network of meaning that has kept it blocked, which will consequently lead to the exploration of other underlying emotions and expression of feelings.

It is important to guide clients' processing to their underlying feeling and not stay engaged with the narrative content of the angry feeling. In guiding clients to their underlying feelings, the therapist is not telling them what their underlying feelings are but rather is guiding them to put their attention into that place where they feel their feelings and to see what they are feeling now. The therapist may be curious and may help to differentiate what is being felt by saying something like, "So, it sounds like you get taken over by a sort of cold, rejecting anger," or may facilitate exploration of the anger with questions such as "What is that, that you feel in your body as you feel angry?" The therapist may also empathically conjecture: "I hear you feel sad and alone when you mother never asks about you or you kids, but I guess it leaves you also kind of mad at her?"

Therapists need to make the distinction for clients between experiencing anger and acting out anger (Greenberg, 2015). Self-asserting anger is a purely internal experience. Acting out anger is a behavior that can be destructive, especially relationally. Clients who have grown up in violent environments often associate anger with violence and powerlessness. With these clients, it is important for the therapist to point out the distinction between feeling and behavior. To feel anger within oneself and to understand when one has been treated badly or hurt is an extremely important skill. This is a way to protect or set interpersonal boundaries. Acting out this anger, or even expressing it in relationships, is something completely different.

Psychoeducation also can be helpful to promote healthy expression of interrupted anger. Therapists can point out that adaptive anger is an important, useful emotion that has a strong impact on thoughts, behaviors, and interpersonal relationships. In addition, therapists can discuss anger's role in helping achieve one's goals and in protecting oneself and that anger gives a sense of self-efficacy.

To promote blocked and split-off anger, it may be worthwhile to give the client experiential homework (e.g., expressive writing; Pennebaker, 1995). To sharpen awareness of interrupted anger, the client can be invited to observe and describe situations during the week in which burgeoning anger was interrupted. For example, a therapist might ask a client to pay attention to how their anger is interrupted by sadness. Homework might also consist of clients writing down their experience in certain situations and then thinking about how a best friend would have felt in the same situation. These types of distancing exercises can help clients develop an awareness of the adaptive emotions that are missing from their behavioral repertoire.

Facilitating Grief at Loss

After anger has been accessed, it is important to explore what else clients feel in addition to anger. When clients suffer from suppressed or hopeless anger, the goal is not only to access the core anger but also to process more adaptive primary emotions of sadness and compassion and possibly also maladaptive primary shame, fear, and sad loneliness that often are at the core of much disease and to which primary adaptive anger is a healthy antidote. The ultimate goal in working with primary suppressed anger is to help clients access the dysfunctional emotion schematic network that is at the core of their interrupted anger. This may be a "weak-me" sense of self that is insecure or a "bad-me" worthless sense of self that was learned in early development (Greenberg, Rice, & Elliott, 1993). Both of these senses of self may lead to difficulties in allowing and adaptively expressing anger.

Anger and sadness are usually strongly linked in overcoming interrupted anger. After reclaiming their adaptive anger at having been wronged, people feel angry that they were robbed of getting their needs met, but they also feel sad that they missed getting their needs met. Therapists, thus, need to help clients grieve the loss of what they needed but never got. Sadness at missing having their needs met and grief at the loss of what was missed is an important step in the process of resolving interrupted anger and needs to be facilitated by inviting clients to grieve lost relationships, lost childhoods, lost time, and lost possibilities, even to grieve not having been able to express anger. Clients' sadness at this point is no longer the sadness of lonely abandonment but rather a sadness of mourning the losses caused by attachment ruptures and identity violations. The sadness of grief differs from the sadness of lonely abandonment because grief is sorrow and regret for a loss and has no complaint or protest. Grief also involves acknowledgment and assimilation of the personal meaning of the loss.

In chair dialogues, as a result of grieving the loss, the other or the interrupter changes, and acceptance and understanding, and a sense of relief and calmness follow. Clients are finally able to accept the reality of what happened to them, and they begin to look for avenues to move on. Therapists can then focus on helping clients accept how their loss has changed their life and facilitate letting go of wishing that their loss didn't occur. Clients are helped to accept that their lives have forever changed and it is time to seek out new meaning. Acceptance is not resignation; rather, it is creating a space to bring that past with you and allowing space for the way that pain and loss have shaped who you are. Grief allows people to become more deeply connected to themselves.

Constructing New Narratives

Finally, clients need to be able to make meaning from their anger and their losses and to re-story their experience. The process of expressing anger is not one of cathartic venting, nor of acting out the anger, but rather productive expression that includes some elaboration and exploration of meaning.

Anger-inhibited clients often experience adaptive anger in a tentative and incomplete manner, so they need help in articulating a new narrative based on their earned right to be angry. Their anger needs to be incorporated so that they can use this emotion to their advantage. It is helpful for the therapist to identify, name, and assign importance to the elements that indicate assertive anger: "I hear a new energy in your voice; do you notice it too? I think this energy might be important. Is it okay if we stay with it for a moment and you try to experience it more in awareness?" The therapist then supports the client in bringing the elements of anger that are present but not yet organized into a coherent form in a co-constructive process so the client can use them. It is like putting together disorganized pieces of a puzzle—only when the pieces are organized in a coherent whole does the picture become clear. A new narrative is thus formed.

Meaning making and experiencing emotion are complex, intertwined processes that play crucial roles in an individual's change (Angus & Greenberg, 2011; Greenberg & Angus, 2004). Emotions happen to a client who is the main character in a narrative, and the client's stories provide the context for understanding their experienced emotions. Articulating, organizing, and ordering the clients anger into a coherent narrative thus are important in consolidating change. The newly experienced expression of anger needs to be formed into a new narrative, and therapists need to help co-construct empowered narratives to change old narratives of disempowerment.

EXAMPLE OF RESOLVING INTERRUPTED ANGER IN THERAPY: CASE DESCRIPTION

This chapter concludes with an example of an episode of working to resolve anger in therapy. This case is adapted from *Emotion-Focused Therapy: Coaching Clients to Work Through Their Feelings* (Greenberg, 2015). The names and some details have been changed.[1]

---

[1] The clinical material used in this book is adequately disguised to protect client confidentiality. Client identity has been maintained.

Natalia, a European woman in her 40s, had been divorced almost 23 years and had two adult children. She came into therapy with relationship difficulties, unable to get into a close relationship and feeling that she pushed people away. She said she would like to be in a relationship "before I get much older," but she was afraid of getting hurt and having her life shattered, as had happened with her first husband all those years ago. She narrated how, without warning, one morning her husband said goodbye at breakfast and walked out on her and their two small children. She went into a state of shock at the time and from then on struggled to cope. She said she had managed by controlling her emotions and hadn't allowed herself any feelings since then. She had suppressed her anger and her pain from the abandonment because she feared that she would fall apart and not be able to cope. Well-intentioned friends told her, "Don't shed one tear over that bastard; he's not worth it," which reinforced her "be strong" coping strategy. She said she had not dealt with her feelings in all these years.

She had succeeded in her life since then but had never dealt satisfactorily with the loss of her marriage and still had many unresolved emotions. She had not grieved the loss of her marriage, nor had she allowed herself to fully experience and allow her anger at her ex-husband for the pain and hardship of the abandonment. She was not only angry at the desertion but also angry that he had always been such a "selfish bastard" and had never really cared for her. Therapy offered her a safe environment to process all these feelings and overcome her fears of an intimate relationship.

As a first step, the client allowed her long-suppressed anger at her ex-husband. This was an experiential process, not simply intellectually acknowledging her anger by saying, "I'm angry at him." She knew this and had uttered these words many times before. Rather, now in therapy, she felt her anger in a full-bodied way, experiencing the smouldering anger in her stomach, feeling it rise up in volcanic bursts. Once she permitted herself to feel, a floodgate of suppressed and overcontrolled feelings opened—feelings of anger, sadness, shame, and even fear. During the seventh session she recounted a detailed narrative of the day he walked out on her. She exclaimed in anger, "And he just walked away. I hate him for that! I hate him for that!" I invited her to imagine her husband in an empty chair and to express this to him directly. She proceeded to say, "I hate what you did; I really hate you! I hate you; I really hate you." When asked how she felt, she replied, "I feel better. I feel better that I hate him."

Feeling empowered by her anger, she reflected on her marital experience, saying that she and the children "didn't deserve what he gave us. If I had been a bad mother and a bad wife I could understand, but I wasn't. I loved him." Speaking to her imagined husband in an empty chair in front of her, she said, "I loved you, and you didn't deserve it—you didn't deserve for me to love you, and my love turned to hate, and I hate you now, I hate you! I hate you for all those years I've wasted, trying to make something that wasn't there." After integrating what she had said to him, she began to expand on what she felt.

I responded to her sense of wasted time and validated her sense of loss. She said, "Yes, it was a big loss, and the loss is what hurts me, the loss, and the wasted years, and for somebody that wasn't worth it. He wasn't even worth it; how could anyone waste that much time on somebody who's not worth it?" Her pain arose spontaneously, and she began to weep deeply for her loss, for the betrayal and the devastation that left her so intensely vulnerable. I validated how painful it must have been and that her pain "must feel almost unbearable."

She felt that her sense of having been terribly wronged was validated, and for the first time since that awful night, she felt she had deserved better and allowed herself to fully feel and express her feelings of being wronged. She sobbed, "How can anybody hurt someone else so much? How can they, and then walk away without even feeling any emotion out of it? My conscience would tell me if I'm hurting somebody—it is unforgivable—and he is just nothing in my eyes, just nothing." Looking at the empty chair and clenching her fists, she yelled, "I hate you. How can anybody hate anybody so much; I didn't think I had that much hate in me."

At this point, I asked her if she felt an urge in her body to hit and offered her a pillow to do so if she chose to express her rage in the safe confines of the therapy room. She expressed her anger and rage and experienced the satisfaction that her anger desired. She imagined exposing him to all their family and friends for what a selfish person he had truly been. She expressed contempt at how poor a father he had been. At the end of this therapeutic experience, the client said, "I felt the pain; the anger again, as if it were all happening again, only more intensely." She said it was her fear of being hurt again that prevented her from entering into new relationships and she now felt stronger, empowered by her anger, to manage herself and her emotions in an intimate relationship. She also talked about her anger at herself for being unable to stand up to her ex-husband and felt shame that there must have been something wrong with her: "How could anyone put up with that and keep coming back for more?" She proceeded to explore and confirm her current strengths, saying, "I recognize now that I'm no longer that young mother with little children who was so dependent and vulnerable."

Empowered by the legitimacy of her anger, she was able to draw on her current resources to challenge and change the belief that she was helpless and the fear that she might repeat this desperation or lack of assertion in another relationship. At the end of treatment, she felt stronger and had constructed a new view of herself as able to maintain her autonomy in a new relationship. She felt her fear would no longer dominate her.

This therapy demonstrates that overcontrolled anger can turn into highly problematic emotional memories. The client's strategy of closing up, although possibly helpful in the short run, was not healthy in the long run. Control sometimes seems to work, but only when the hurt and anger are minor. If a person blocks legitimate anger, not only do they cut themselves off from others but they also block important information from within. Unexpressed anger that remains unresolved burns within a person as bricks of resentment and becomes a barrier to intimacy. These bricks of resentment, imperceptible at first, soon combine to form a nearly impenetrable wall of anger and distance.

This example does not mean that anger should always be expressed or that this form of therapeutic expression is called for in everyday life. It does, however, point to the damage of unexpressed, overcontrolled anger. Anger expression at violation is sometimes necessary to protect one's health and relationships, including present relationships and the possibility of future ones.

The type of anger expression in therapy in which this client was engaged was not done for cathartic reasons to get rid of some excess discharge. Her anger was not just sitting in some storage tank, waiting to be drained off. Repeatedly venting her anger over many sessions to further drain it off would not be helpful. Many academics are critical of the worth of expressing anger in therapy, thinking it either will reinforce anger or will not promote insight. They fail to see that the true therapeutic purpose of this form of expression is to validate the feeling, to be informed by it, and for it to change meaning (Greenberg & Safran, 1987).

Allowing herself to experience this degree of anger was a way for this client to acknowledge the extent of the violation and to put in motion a lot of important other change processes that would have been difficult to promote without her first feeling entitled to and expressing her anger. This type of anger awareness and expression informs and mobilizes. Expressing anger in a healthy way in therapy results in empowerment.

CONCLUSION

This chapter discussed the clinical steps involved in overcoming interrupted anger and looked at the process of resolution. Interventions involved in working with interrupted anger were presented, including two-chair enactment for undoing the interruption of anger and empty-chair dialogue for resolving anger-related unfinished business. The chapter concluded with a presentation of a case example involving resolution of interrupted anger in therapy.

Activating previously unacknowledged anger has been shown to be important in the treatment of depression and anxiety. People who interrupt their anger experience tremendous discomfort and possibly shame regarding their anger; anger and shame are intimately related. As covered in earlier chapters, shame can shut down anger, but also, as discussed in this chapter and illustrated by the case example, when clients can access empowered anger because they feel entitled to have needs met, anger serves as an antidote to shame and helps transform it.

Experiencing anger, however, can be powerfully inconsistent with how people wish to view themselves. The slightest arousal of anger may be experienced as a powerful threat to their self-image so they interrupt, suppress, or minimize such feelings, resulting in depressive symptoms. Often people fear that anger will lead to rejection or damage to attachment relationships, and so they shut down their anger. For people with panic and anxiety, their anger often is not in awareness, and becoming aware of their anger can create intense anxiety for fear of disrupting important relationships. For all these reasons, it is important to help clients access their interrupted anger in the safety of the therapeutic situation.

In Chapter 10, I present the results of a discovery-oriented study that led to building a model of how clients resolved their anger in therapy and a study that validated this model. The model lays out the components of competence and the steps taken by clients in their process of resolution.

10
A MODEL OF THE RESOLUTION OF INTERRUPTED ANGER AND ITS VALIDATION

Holding on to anger is like grasping a hot coal with the intent of throwing it at someone else; you are the one who gets burned.

—Buddha

An empirical investigation of the role of anger in therapeutic change was carried out in a number of studies at the York University Psychotherapy Research Lab (Sicoli, 2005; Tarba, 2007; Tregoubov, 2006). These projects analyzed cases involving overcoming interrupted anger in therapy and extracted the components of clients' performance that led to successful resolution. This work led to the development of a model of the client steps in undoing interrupted anger, discussed in detail in this chapter. This chapter also presents transcript examples that demonstrate both the resolution process and effective therapist interventions. To demonstrate that expressing previously interrupted anger predicted good outcome, this chapter reports the results of a study relating the main components of the model to therapy outcome, showing that clients who manifested the components in their sessions had significantly better outcomes than those who did not.

---

https://doi.org/10.1037/0000393-010
Shame and Anger in Psychotherapy, by L. S. Greenberg
Copyright © 2024 by the American Psychological Association. All rights reserved.

These studies added rigorous observation to the clinically based model outlined in the previous chapter and tested its predictive power. Similar to our study of the resolution of episodes of shame, we used a task analysis of the ways in which clients overcame interrupted anger to construct a rational/empirical model of the process of resolution (Greenberg, 2007). In addition, the components of the model were related to reduction in depression at therapy outcome (Tarba, 2015). More specifically, how the expression of interrupted anger helped clients overcome feelings of hopelessness, helplessness, sadness, resignation, and alienation was investigated.

The model-building aspect of the task analysis (Tarba, 2007) intensively analyzed the process of resolution in five clients with depression—three successful and two unsuccessful cases. This discovery-oriented investigation elucidated how the expression of anger helped clients reach a more resilient state that helped undo depression.

A second study (Tarba, 2015) validated the model with a sample of 23 clients. All the clients had interrupted anger at parents and/or at current or former spouses or partners as a result of emotional neglect and mistreatment. Clients were selected for intensive analysis if they manifested feelings of disempowerment in the first few sessions. The clients all showed some overall indications of interrupted anger from the start of therapy but also had a session where they clearly interrupted the expression and experience of anger.

A *marker of interrupted anger* was defined as follows: The client's expression indicates that anger is present at some level, but it is not expressed explicitly and comes out in the form of complaint, blame, bitterness, hopelessness, resignation, cutting remarks, silences, and other nonverbal cues. The following features characterized this component of the model:

1. Emotionally, the client showed a sense of collapsing, hopelessness, helplessness, despair, defeat, sense of no control, alienation, resignation, and/or powerlessness (relates to lack of entitlement or fear).

2. Verbally, the client used passive or negative verbs (e.g., "I can't"), stereotypical expressions (e.g., "What's the point?" "You know?"), and/or passive voice and third person in a generic way (e.g., "The entire situation was created by my father," "He did all of these things, and on top of it, he imposed rules on us").

3. Behaviorally, indicators were faded voice, sighs, pauses, laughter incongruent with the situation, muscular tension, slight frowning, and clenching of the jaw.

A *marker of resolution* was defined as follows: The client experiences a stronger sense of self, with feelings of empowerment and entitlement for their own feelings and needs, self-confidence, and assertiveness, and defines goals for the future. Clients may experience a positive view of themselves (e.g., feel strong, in control, worthwhile, lovable) with hope and optimism. The following features characterized this component:

1. A sense of empowerment, entitlement, confidence, self-assuredness, ownership, hope, power, and humor.
2. The use of active verbs in an active voice (e.g., "I started," "I will do") and/or use of first person as an expression of agency (e.g., "I" instead of "he," "she," or "them").
3. A stronger voice; fine modulations of voice; erect position of the trunk; relaxed facial expression; smiles and/or laughter; richer mimic, expression, and body movements.
4. A report of engaging in or planning to engage in future-directed activities that signal a sense of empowerment and hope.

Given that no observation is theory free (Kuhn, 1962; Nagel et al., 1973), we first laid out the rational model—how we thought resolution might be achieved based on theory, clinical experience, and what had already been observed in Tregoubov's (2006) early research on one good and one poor case. Three new resolution cases were then inspected and compared to two new non-resolution cases of working on interrupted anger (Tarba, 2007). All examples were in chair dialogues. The successful cases were also compared to the rational model to see what needed to be changed in the rational model.

We found that, between the initial marker of interrupted anger and the final marker of empowerment/self-affirmation, six essential components were involved in the resolution process:

1. Undifferentiated/fused anger and sadness with complaint and hopelessness
2. Expressing anger and standing up
3. Expressing a heartfelt need
4. Considering an alternative way of seeing reality
5. Sadness and grief
6. Empathic understanding for another or the self being validated

Additional **nonessential steps** in the model included:

1. Self-interruptive processes (fear, beliefs, and shutting down)
2. Avoidance of confrontations of imagined others in the session
3. Validation from other/critic

Figure 10.1 presents the rational/empirical model derived from rigorous observations of these clients. The main resolution processes involving direct

206 • Shame and Anger in Psychotherapy

FIGURE 10.1. Rational-Empirical Model of Resolution of Interrupted Anger

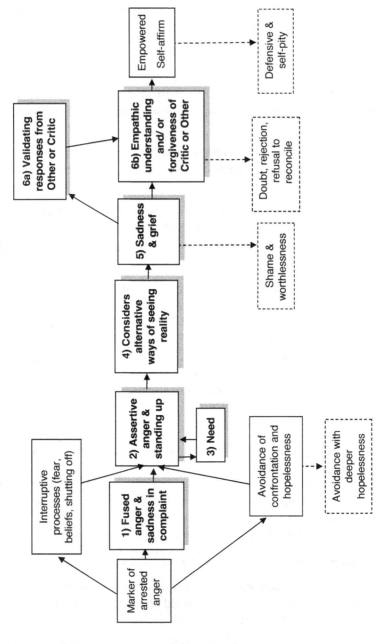

Note. Adapted from *Relating a Model of Resolution of Arrested Anger to Outcome in Emotion-focused Therapy of Depression* [Unpublished doctoral dissertation], by L. R. Tarba, 2015, York University. Copyright 2015, by L. R. Tarba. Adapted with permission.

responses of clients to an empty chair are outlined in the center of the diagram. Highlighted boxes denote essential components (i.e., found only in clients who resolve) and broken lines (– – –) denote components characteristic of clients who do not resolve. The components are presented in the sequence in which they tended to occur.

It is important to note that the actual process is nonlinear but progressive: The clients cycle from one component to another and back again. Thus, every so often they return to the previous mode of functioning but without remaining stuck; they overcome it and move to the next component, and they advance from lower to higher stages of resolution.

There is no one-to-one correspondence between the treatment steps and the steps in the model client resolution process because the treatment steps focus on clinical intervention and clinical experience as opposed to explication of client processes. While there is overlap, intervention requires a different focus. For example, in Chapter 9, we elaborated in detail how to work on interruption, which is not essential in clients' resolution processes because not all clients block sufficiently strongly to need this type of major intervention. That said, it is a useful tool in the therapist's tool kit and was therefore elaborated in the treatment steps. Understanding the necessary components of the client resolution process helps inform intervention and orient the therapist as to what is happening in the client.

ESSENTIAL COMPONENTS OF THE MODEL

Each component of the resolution model that emerged after a marker of interrupted anger appeared is described in the following sections and is exemplified by excerpts from transcripts of psychotherapy sessions.

Step 1: Undifferentiated Anger and Sadness With Complaint (Victim Stance)

The client starts to open up in front of the therapist and explains, generally in a complaining voice, or protests that a significant other—one or both parents, a sibling or partner, or, on occasion, their own internal critic—has mistreated them or has disapproved of them. The other's hurtful behavior is described from a passive, victimized stance rather than from an empowered or assertive stance. Mixed feelings of anger and sadness are present but remain at a conceptual level or are fused into blame or complaint. The core underlying emotions are neither recognized nor accessed at a deeper experiential level.

In chair dialogues, a client's complaints are not expressed directly to the other and appear as a mixture of sadness and implicit resentment. There is a sense of dissatisfaction, often uttered in a plaintive, whining way, as lamentations or protest. Feelings of anger and sadness remain undifferentiated, and for the most part the other's wrongdoing is insinuated or the accusations are indirect or implicit in the complaint. Any feelings that are expressed tend to be reactive or defensive in nature. Two types of blaming anger can be identified in clients' sessions: blaming-approach anger, often with a question (e.g., "Why didn't you try more?," You were never there for me,") and blaming-distancing anger (e.g., "It's your fault, and I don't want to see you," "You make me sick; leave me alone"). Complaints are easily recognized by the use of "why": "Why did you leave us?" "Why did you abuse me?" These fusions of sadness and anger need to be differentiated.

In the following example of undifferentiated sadness and anger taken from transcripts of tapes from the York Psychotherapy research centre archives[1], the client is talking about her relationship with her parents, showing mixed feelings of anger for not being supported and sadness for the loss of acceptance mixed with regret.

THERAPIST (T): It's almost like I need you to acknowledge that even though I'm not like you I'm still okay. I'm not what you expect or . . . *(therapist reflecting client's meaning)*

CLIENT (C): – Yeah, like, just – I – I don't know, I want that recognition like I have really, they really never gave me any recognition like for anything *(generic memory)*, like, I just never could do anything right, like, no, it got to a point it was, like, okay, um – this is just, this is just it – like, I figured just do your own thing *(implicit anger)* and, but yet it's so hard, like, to – to keep on doing that while not being able to come to terms with them, and just like the whole thing, like, that I closed myself off to this so much, like I *(implicit sadness)*, I don't want to fight, like, this ongoing battle of back and forth and back and forth like you should and no and – like every time, like, I have the nerve like to come forward with something and say okay this is you know, this is what I do, well, I know it doesn't fit into like your, what you think is the best for me or your expectations, but you know, like I gave it a try but it never works. They never accept it *(complaint)*.

---

[1] The clinical material used in this book is adequately disguised to protect client confidentiality. Client identity has been maintained.

Step 2: Expressing Assertive Anger and Standing Up

The client, having started with complaint combined with hopelessness and fused feelings of anger and sadness, moves to the expression of primary anger, usually related to the impact of mistreatment by a significant other or contempt by voice of the internal critic. The primary adaptive emotion of anger is separated from sadness and is vividly expressed. Instead of complaining in a whiny, hopeless voice without directing feelings of frustration to a specific target, the client starts to make contact with whoever is in the other chair. Anger about a past situation, which the client was previously unable to express overtly, is expressed. Anger is related to themes of criticism or invalidation (e.g., dismissal, disrespect, humiliation, boundary violation) or abandonment (e.g., feeling neglected or rejected).

Usually, clients who resolve the difficulty through expression of interrupted anger tend to start by expressing feelings of rejecting anger in a blaming voice (e.g., "You are bad"), but they soon change to more consistently expressing assertive anger (e.g., "I am mad"). The client asserts, sets a boundary, stands up, speaks up, doesn't accept the situation as it is, and expresses more freely. Clients' voices clearly express a sense of conviction concerning how wronged they felt plus a sense of entitlement that they deserved to have their needs for love and respect met.

Most depressed or anxious clients who are successful in the resolution process express blaming-approach anger combined with an associated need for understanding, connection, support, and being valued or loved. Blaming anger, which has the quality of distancing, withdrawing, or rejecting, is present at times but is much less frequent than blaming-approach anger. Blaming-distancing anger seems to be the predominant feeling for non-resolution clients. For clients who resolve, blaming anger is followed by assertive anger.

As discussed in earlier chapters, accessing and expressing anger is a crucial aspect of resolution because it allows the client to acknowledge hurt and to further protect themselves from it. Also, by naming or labeling anger, the person becomes able to reflect on it, understand it, and regulate it if needed. The client's narratives or memories become more specific and contextualized rather than global and generic, and emotional arousal is heightened. The material is experienced at a deeper level and emotion is aroused rather than just talked about. Primary anger is clearly differentiated and vividly expressed at a moderate to high level of arousal. The heightened feelings of anger relate to having been abandoned, discounted, rejected or criticized, disrespected, or humiliated. The client feels entitled to being angry, feels more in control, and feels comfortable expressing anger in the presence of the therapist. Anger is verbally labeled and expressed directly to the other.

There is a direct expression of assertive anger. The client speaks in the first person ("I"). Blaming anger is expressed in the second person ("you") with a raised voice, frowning, and a clenching of the fist or angry gestures.

In the following example of anger expression, the client is talking to her imagined father in an empty-chair dialogue. She starts with blaming-distancing anger and then moves to assertive anger.

T: Right. What happens in the face of that, right? Stay with him.

C: Oh, I get very angry. *(assertive anger)* (T: Un-huh.) Oh, I do, and I just tell him, I now, more so, I don't see him as much but there was a time when . . .

T: Tell him.

C: I think you're a terrible father, and you're an asshole – that's what I would say to him. My sisters would be like . . . (gasp, laugh) *(blaming-distancing anger)*

T: You sound very angry.

C: Oh, very angry. Yeah, there's no need for it. *(assertive anger)*

T: Un-hum. What do you feel now? Try to imagine him here. Let's try to see him, I mean.

C: I'd like – Well, I felt they never should have had children. I always wondered that 'cause you could tell by the way they were toward – really I get – didn't want children. They didn't want girls. I know my dad didn't want girls, and he got four of them, so maybe that was god's way of punishing him (laughs) but you know . . .

T: Tell him.

C: Yeah, I'm angry you shouldn't have had – had children because you know they were so – he was so – you're so into yourself. *(assertive anger)*

T: Right.

Step 3: Need Expression

In this step, clients engage in expressing a core, heartfelt need to the other or critic (e.g., "I need your support and understanding," "I need to feel loved," "I need to feel important to you"). The need is usually related to an important theme (e.g., being valued or loved) and differs from superficial expressions of everyday needs. The want, request, or wish is made in a non-blaming way and with a sense of hope that the other/critic will be able and willing to respond to it. Often, clients express their needs naturally, immediately after anger is addressed, directly to the other or critic. Sometimes the therapist introduces or facilitates the need expression. The client's request to the other chair for a need to be met is made in a self-focused, internal voice, and the client uses the word *need* or a synonym.

In the initial stages of therapy, a need is expressed minimally and is followed immediately by hopelessness, defeat, or doubt that the need will be heard. As therapy progresses, clients start to feel more and more empowered and entitled to have their needs met, and they assert them with an increasingly stronger voice. Hopeless responses are slowly replaced with assertive anger and by consideration of alternative ways of seeing reality, which represents the next important component.

In the following example, the client is talking to her imagined husband in an empty chair. She asks him to learn from past mistakes in relation to her and to show understanding and to care for her.

T: What would – what would you – what do you want from Peter right now? – Maybe you can tell him, and then we can – we can say goodbye to him for – for now. What would you like to – say? – What do you want from him?

C: (Sniffs) I'd like him to really think about – – some of his actions – and how they have – – – – impacted on me – and to learn from that – – and not to do it any more.

T: Okay. Is there anything else you want?

C: *(Pause for 6 seconds)* I guess I would like him to *(pause for 6 seconds)* think of me as a more fragile human being. **(need to be acknowledged as vulnerable)**

T: Okay – so you're not – you're not as strong – kind of hard-willed person all the time.

C: That I've been passing off. (laughs)

T: Yeah. – Could you tell him that?

C: *(Pause for 22 seconds)* I'd like you to, ah – – be a – more understanding of my – (sniffs) emotions – – and be a little bit more caring. **(need for understanding and care)**

Step 4: Consideration of Alternative Ways of Seeing Reality (Self, Other, or Situation)

Having expressed anger and needs, the client progresses to more reflective calm. At this step, clients have different perspectives and can evaluate reality in new ways. They have reorganized emotion schemes and can now see the other, self, or situation in a more differentiated way (e.g., with both good and bad qualities). This stage of reflection and understanding resembles the process of de-escalation in interpersonal conflict, during which automatic fight/flight reactions subside and calm sets in. In addition, clients begin accepting some responsibility for their own flaws and for their own part in the difficulties.

There are generally three important ways in which clients gain an alternative perspective. One occurs by seeing the other in a more positive manner, becoming more understanding (e.g., mother's view of life is different but valid), acknowledging the circumstances of the other (e.g., difficulty raising a seventh child because they were overwhelmed, parent financial security), or recognizing that intentions were good even if the effects were bad (e.g., to help them succeed). A second is understanding the negative treatment in interactional terms by recognizing personal contributions to the negative relationship interaction, not speaking up, being overly needing of approval, or not protecting oneself. Clients recognize that although the other harmed them, the way they related to the other allowed it to happen. A third way is by feeling adaptive guilt about harm they may have.

Thus, through this process, clients understand the others' perspective and take some responsibility for their own contributions. The emergence of a differentiated narrative helps the client progress toward resolution. This is important because by considering alternative ways of seeing self, other, and situations, a client becomes capable and ready to surpass the stage of pure anger. Through empathy and/or forgiveness, the client is able to advance toward resolution. In this step, the level of emotion is not high, but new meaning is being constructed, as reflected by moderate to high scores on the experiencing scale. The client's voice is internally focused, indicating the creation of meaning from current experience. A complaining voice is no longer present, the client is much calmer, has a sense of acceptance and understanding, and is no longer emotionally distressed. This step is sometimes followed by clients' expressions of vulnerability.

The next example shows the client talking to her mother. She agrees with her mother and assumes responsibility for past inconsiderate actions.

C: – (sniff) (*pause for 9 seconds*) I feel better – ah (*pause for 12 seconds*) I guess I'm repeating, ah (*pause for 10 seconds*) what my parents did **(under-**

stands own behavior) – um, doing the best, um – with the knowledge that was available to them at that time.

T: Mm-hm.

C: And I was doing the same thing – – um – – it's true I shouldn't, ah – – – for the people who mean a lot to me – I should sort of, ah, stand up more for them – and don't let things – um – sort of – slide and think they'll get better on their own – because they don't. *(acknowledges necessity to change behavior)*

T: So, you kind of agree with her. (C: Yeah.) She's right, eh? Can you say that to her, "I – I agree . . ."

C: I agree with you that you're right, I shouldn't let things slide and should stand up. *(agrees with mother)*

T: Okay, is there anything . . .

C: For the things that are important to me, and for the people that are important to me. (sniffs)

Step 5: Sadness and Grief

This step is characterized by the primary emotion of sadness at missing having had needs met and grief at the loss of what was missed. Unlike the initial stages of therapy, at this step sadness is differentiated from anger and is experienced, symbolized, and expressed separately and in adaptive ways. The full expression of anger in a previous step allows clients to feel empowered, to exert agency, and to move forward, acknowledging the painfulness in the lack of love or the invalidation. A number of clients in our study grieved losses of time, of possibilities, and, ultimately, of relationships.

At this point, clients start by accessing feelings of "pure" sadness caused by identity invalidation or attachment injuries. It is important to note that the sadness of grief differs from the sadness of lonely abandonment. Grief involves the access and expression of deep sadness, but it has no complaint or protest; rather, it involves acknowledgment and reflection on the meaning of the loss. By grieving, clients not only experience deep pain and sadness but also stay with the feeling of loss, understand its meaning, and begin reconstructing their lives in the absence of what was lost. It is also important to note that grief has feelings of sadness of loss at its core, not shame or the loss of approval or love. Some clients might experience extreme sadness for having been abandoned, neglected, or rejected, which automatically implies a need for the other's love, but this sadness of lonely abandonment needs to be followed by a process of sorrow or grieving for the loss of the other or of the relationship.

Sadness is usually labeled verbally as "hurt," "pain," or a synonym. Grief is expressed as regret for a loss, and the word *miss* is often important (e.g., "I miss your love . . .") and addressed directly to the other. Again, it is important that first-person pronouns are used to express sadness when grieving: singular "I" or plural "we" (e.g., "I felt sad") rather than third person (e.g., "It was sad"). Sadness and grief are characterized by the look of sadness on the face or crying and weeping. The experiential and arousal levels are heightened while the voice is lowered, internal, and focused.

The client in the following example dialogues with a sister in an empty chair. She expresses that her sister's disapproval and invalidation had hurt her tremendously, and she grieves the loss of her relationship.

C: Yeah. It's like she's pushing me away. It's like she's pushing me away. You know, and I guess I became very hurt by it because we used to be. I become very hurt by it.

T: Now, I want you to go to the hurt place. Let's not talk about it. (C: Yeah.) See if you can go inside.

C: Oh, I'm still hurt by it. I think about it all the time. I probably think about her every day. *(acknowledges sadness)*

T: Oh, really.

C: Yeah, oh yeah, because it bothers me.

T: So, where do you feel the hurt?

C: In my – I guess it's sort of like, you know, you get that tightness in your throat?

T: Yes, yes. So, do you feel it now?

C: Yeah, yeah, yeah.

T: I want you to try to speak to her from the hurt. Tell her.

C: Well, you've really hurt me. You've been so . . . *(expresses sadness and hurt)*

T: Tell her "I . . ."

C: I feel really hurt by the things you've said. I feel really hurt by your disapproval. By you think you're better than me. I feel really hurt by the things you've said about me to other people. I feel really hurt because for years while

I was going around telling people how close we were, you were going around telling people what an asshole I was. *(hurt)*

T: Let's stay with it rather than all these words.

C: Okay. I'm sad about it because there was a time, you know, that we were very close and we did everything together and . . . *(sadness of loss)*

T: Tell her what you miss.

C: I miss our friendship. I miss the things we used to do together. *(grieving)*

T: I want you to see her.

C: I miss, you know, I guess – it's hard. I miss it, but I don't. I miss what it was, I think. I miss what it was, and I realize that people go on with their lives and they – but, you know . . .

T: Tell her again, "I miss what I had with you."

C: Yeah, I miss what I had with you, and I realize that, you know, things change as time goes on but I never thought they would change like this. *(grief for lost relationship)* I never thought that we would become to the point where we didn't like each other. *(sadness of grief)*

Step 6a & 6b: Validation by the Other and/or Empathic Understanding and/or Forgiveness

This step is broken into two substeps. Step 6a describes what the other does, while Step 6b describes what the self does. Both, however, achieve a similar aim of resolving the conflict.

Step 6a: Validation by the Other

Upon hearing the client expressing feelings of sadness or grief, the other/critic responds with compassion, support, a sincere desire to amend the damage done, and promises for future. Rather than criticizing and invalidating the client's behavior, the other/critic shows understanding and affective attunement to the client's feelings, perception, and meaning given to an interpersonal event. Also, the other/critic moves beyond simply addressing nonhostile requests and encouragements to understanding and accepting the client's experience, softening their expression, and "returning" an understanding of their own experience.

In the following segment, the client enacts her mother in an empty-chair dialogue. The mother responds with validation to her daughter's expression of hurt.

T: Okay – can you come back here? (C switches) Okay – – seems like A.'s – – said a lot – – she's hurting. What do you want to say to her?

C: *(Pause for 18 seconds)* It's not true that you should feel this way, A., because I do love you and – – – – I guess I'm wrong in the way I've been showing it – – and just that you – – you give so easily – that we take it for granted that you're always there. *(validates)*

T: Mm-hm. – – You take her for granted – – 'cause she is always there. – – – Can you say that to her – again?

C: I have been taking you for granted – and it's – it's not right *(pause for 8 seconds)* *(validation)* I'll try to change, but I'm going to need a lot of help – and it's going to take some time I guess. (sniffs)

T: Okay – what would – what would you like from her – to help you with that?

C: *(Pause for 7 seconds)* I guess I'd like her to continue being understanding – – and still be there for us, the way you have been. *(validation)*

T: So, you still want her to be there – – can you say it again? "I still want you to be there for us . . ."

C: – I still want you to be there for us. I know that you are the only one that is always there – – – – (T: And . . .) and we really haven't shown it – – how much it really means to us. *(validation)*

Step 6b: Empathic Understanding of the Other and Forgiveness

Having accessed underlying painful feelings of pain and/or grief, the client explores past experiences in an open manner and accepts what is occurring in the present relationship or lets go of past unresolved feelings. The other is understood emotionally, and the person may have compassion and empathy for the other. The reality of the other is not only seen but "felt," and thus the client begins to move toward letting go. Forgiveness may also take place. Anger toward the other/critic is transformed into acceptance, and the person feels calm and relieved.

Verbally, the client uses verbs related to "letting go," "accepting," and "understanding." The verbal expression becomes richer and more nuanced. A more relaxed body posture suggests a sense of relief, calmness, and serenity.

In the following dialogue between the client and her inner critic, the client asserts the validity of her actions, and the critic responds empathically.

T: Okay, come over here. (C: (Sniff)) – – What – what do you want to say to that?

C: (Sigh) *(pause for 7 seconds)* I tried, (T: Mm-hm.) um – I thought at the time that was the best thing . . .

T: Mm-hm.

C: But I guess it wasn't – it wasn't good enough, but at the time I thought that was the best.

T: Tell her what it was like for you.

C: *(Pause for 6 seconds)* It hurt a lot, and I wanted to protect them, and I thought at the time that if I interfered more, or said more, (sniff) it would make him even angrier and make things – the situation worse.

T: Mm – so you thought . . .

C: So, I . . .

T: You'd make things worse – if you interfered – (C: Mm-hm.) so you . . .

C: So, I backed off – and – ah – hoping he'd cool off – and ah – calm down – – and sometimes that worked and sometimes it didn't.

T: Mm-hm, so you – you did the best you could – can you say that to her?

C: I did the best that I could at that time and – under the circumstances **(defends herself)** and, um – – (sniff) – and that's all I did – could have done – was the best . . . (sniff)

T: – Anything else you're feeling?

C: (Sniff) No.

T: – Okay. – Come back here – – – okay. – She says she did the best she could – she tried . . .

C: *(Pause for 20 seconds)* (sigh) (sniff) (sigh) I guess you can't ask for any more then, when somebody's thinking they are giving their best . . .

T: Mm-hm – – so what do you want to say to her?

C: (Sigh) Maybe you're being too hard on yourself **(empathy)** (T: Mm-hm.) – um – – and you should allow yourself to be human – and can make mistakes at times – and to be able to, ah – to forgive yourself – and then maybe you could also – if you ask your son for forgiveness and he wants to give it to you, to accept it – and go on from there and heal from that. (sniff) *(empathy)*

T: Mm-hm – – – so it sounds like you kind of understand her – understand her a bit more why she – did the best she could.

C: (Sniff) (sigh) I guess it's a lot like, she thought her parents did – they did the best under the circumstances – and she doesn't hold any grudges against them for – for doing their best – even though it wasn't always . . .

T: So, you understand she did her best?

C: I guess so . . .

NONESSENTIAL COMPONENTS AND HINDRANCES

There were two main hindrances to resolving interrupted anger. The first was avoiding facing the people who hurt them, the second was interruption by resignation and helplessness.

Avoidance of Confrontation and Hopelessness

This component is characterized by clients' not wanting to talk to others as well as restraint from expressing feelings or confronting others. More specifically, clients describe feelings of dread talking to or imagining the other in chair dialogues; sometimes they also describe feelings of tension and confusion in the presence of the imagined other. Often clients acknowledge their tendency to withdraw when hurt rather than to confront or express, and they express their need to distance from problems and people when feeling overwhelmed.

The avoidance of confrontation is more self-protective than rejecting. Clients explicitly express hopelessness and doubt related to the other's capacity to understand or relate to clients' feelings, but this does not represent the main feature of this component. Cognitively, clients acknowledge they have a tendency to withdraw when hurt or to keep distance when overwhelmed. This initial stage, however, facilitates further processes and foresees resolution: Clients become aware of their avoidance, acknowledge their withdrawal tendencies, and thus become more comfortable with the possibility of confrontation. Clients articulate that they want to deal with the avoidance, get over their mixed feelings, and overcome the avoidance.

In the following example, the client is talking to the therapist about her sister and what makes her avoid her sister, and confrontations, more generally.

C: (Sigh) Ah – I'm sort of also in a way dreading – with the Christmas holidays coming up – and the conflict that I'm having with my sister – and what's going to be happening with it. *(avoidance, generic)* – – um – I know that I have to deal with her – and speak to her about it – – and – I'm afraid to approach it. *(fear of confrontation)*

T: Mm-hm.

C: I've always been – so careful never to talk – I guess not to get into confrontations with anybody, because – not to say anything that's going to hurt their feelings or – – or that someday – because sometimes people in anger and annoyance come out and say things that they really shouldn't be saying – that can cause people a lot of pain, so I go out of my way not to say anything to anybody rather than – – you know, rather than say something. *(acknowledges avoidance of confrontations)*

T: So, you're very careful.

C: Very.

T: Careful to make sure you don't upset anybody.

Interruptive Processes (Fear, Beliefs, Shutting Off Processes)

Blocks tend to be more frequent and intense in the initial stages of therapy before primary emotions of anger/hurt are expressed. Interruptive processes interfere with clients' ability to productively process their anger and hurt. When self-interrupting, they become more detached and are unable to respond. The dread of looking at their feelings creates an inability to explore further. Self-interruptive events or processes may take the form of resignation, hopelessness, and fear of being rejected, criticized, discouraged, distrusted, or of not being in control. Self-related beliefs such as not being entitled to be angry or that giving in to emotions is weak are also prevalent, along with socially learned attitudes that it is not acceptable to be angry. At a body level, interruption manifests as shutting down, emotional numbness, incongruent laughter, and silences. The interruptions may take place either when the client is on the verge of accessing or deepening a primary feeling or after the acknowledgment and expression of a core emotion by minimization (e.g., "it is not important") or intellectual justification (e.g., "I feel . . .

because . . ." or "It's better not to feel because . . ."). Blocks are characterized by low depth of experiencing and by unproductive processing. The voice quality is external and detached.

In the following example, the client is talking to the therapist about her difficulty in approaching people she likes because she fears rejection.

T: Yeah, because you don't ask, because you're risking rejection, but you never ask, so you're sort of just stuck in that lonely place or that confusing place, kind of like you have to take the risk to get out of that place, is that what you're saying?

C: Well, I guess the really big thing right now is that, um – I have made a number of, like, attempts like to – uh, no, I find it difficult – I always have this fear of rejection. *(acknowledge fear)* Like there are always like people I'd be interested to get to know, and I'm just having such a difficult to say afterwards, um, well, how about, uh, going for a coffee now. Like with my volunteer work, for instance, I mean there are a number of people I'd really kind of would – would like to get more friendly with, like really have them as, as friends, and I'm just so – yeah, so afraid of saying how about, like, having a bite to eat or having a coffee or going for a beer or whatever. *(difficult to approach people)*

T: So, it's like you want to say it and something holds you back.

C: Yeah, I'm just so afraid of getting no (laughs) and then not, but there might be like a very simple explanation, you know, like, well, but I – I don't really want to make people say, well, but then nobody ever would say I'm not interested (laughs), but it's almost like I only can do it once and then I just feel this complete rejection, and I won't try again ever out of fear, like I'm going to get a no the second time or the third time, it's like . . . *(fear of rejection)*

NON-RESOLUTION COMPONENTS

In the process of building the model, the emphasis was on components of competence, the steps needed to get to resolution. Some observations that were made of clients who didn't resolve were not highlighted in the model but are discussed in the following sections describing non-resolution components. Looking at what these clients did that prevented them from attaining the required competencies is helpful and suggests what therapists need to work on to move these clients into a resolution process.

Avoid Facing the People Who Hurt Them and Experience a Deeper Sense of Hopelessness

Non-resolution clients are hopeless about their future (e.g., "it won't help," "I don't think it will amount to anything," "What's the point?"), and they talk about significant others with doubt and hopelessness (e.g., "I don't know if he/she has the capacity to understand," "Why should I be in therapy; it doesn't change him/her"). This overwhelming amount of hopelessness makes non-resolution clients shut down or give up in an attempt to protect themselves against dreaded feelings of shame or anxiety of being rejected and abandoned.

Furthermore, instead of directly expressing the need to deal with problems and get over their mixed feelings in an agentic way, non-resolution clients express false hopes that the other will change, the situation will get better by itself, or a miracle will come to solve the problems or save them. A certain level of hopelessness is also present for clients who resolve, but it does not have the same overbearing effects as for non-resolution clients.

Therapists need to persist in encouraging clients to face the people who hurt them rather than accepting their clients' hopeless stance and feeling hopeless themselves. Work on how the client creates hopelessness with a two-chair self-interruptive dialogue (e.g., "How do you create this hopeless feeling? Come over here and be a part that makes you feel hopeless,") may be helpful.

Shame and Worthlessness

For non-resolution clients, anger and needs expression, if it occurs, is often followed by feelings of shame and worthlessness rather than assertion. Although feelings of shame may be present also in the sessions of clients who resolve, in tandem with need expression, they are transformed into an adaptive emotion by accessing it and assuming responsibility for their own mistakes. For non-resolution clients, shame does not transform into an adaptive emotion because these clients are overly passive and dependent in relation to exploring their experience and the real sources of their shame. Non-resolution clients remain undecided between the benefits and consequences of assertively expressing productive anger and assuming their own responsibility by accessing guilt.

Therapists need to work on helping clients reclaim their experience of shame and re-own the disowned feeling. Using "I" language to help clients feel a sense of agency (e.g., "I feel ashamed") rather than a passive stance (e.g., "It made me feel ashamed") is a small step in the right direction.

Encouragement and relational support are also helpful to overcome the fear that their shame experience will overwhelm them.

Doubt, Rejection of the Other/Critic, Refusal to Reconcile

Non-resolution clients respond to the other/critic's invalidations, as well as to encouragements and nonhostile requests made in the interest of the client, with doubt, rejection, denial, disbelief, disagreement, and refusal to reconcile. They often say, "I don't trust him/her," "I don't want to be/talk to/see him/her," or "It's only your fault." On the contrary, clients who resolve depression tend to soften their expression in the late stages of therapy and to come to a more accepting and understanding view of themselves and the other. Even though non-resolution clients seem able to express anger (i.e., blaming anger rather than productive anger), they do not reorganize and accept reality using a more complex and nuanced view of the self and other/critic.

Therapists can support clients, not by trying to help them see the positive in others but by helping clients change to be where they are and express that they do not trust the other and will never reconcile. Elaborating this stance may have a paradoxical effect of leading to a more conciliatory stance.

Defensiveness, Hopelessness, and Self-Pity

By the end of therapy, the most dominant attitude of non-resolution clients is related to feeling hopeless and/or defending their position as justified from the victim's perspective. As therapy gets close to its end and depressive feelings are still present, clients start to engage in detached analyses of the problem in a manner that is out of touch with their feelings, attack or belittle significant others, or justify their position by recounting how they've been hurt and mistreated. The reality of the other is neither seen nor "felt," and clients remain stuck in their own view of it. There is a general sense of tension, aggravation, and uneasiness. Hopelessness takes more covert forms: skepticism, detachment, or sarcastic remarks regarding self, others, and the future. Feelings of anger are not changed with acceptance and understanding; rather, the client vacillates between different unproductive, unresolved forms of anger (e.g., interrupted anger, secondary anger, and blaming-distancing anger).

This endpoint will not be arrived at if the non-resolution steps leading up to it are changed, as the shame will instead be accessed. If the client and therapist feel this stuck, they need to engage in alliance work through inspection and review of the bond and the agreement on task and goals.

SUMMARY

Based on this intensive study of the process of resolution of interrupted anger, it seems that the fundamental shift consists in moving from a victim stance (e.g., "My problem is caused by external factors—others or situations—and is out of my control,") to an assertive stance (e.g., "I am the agent of change"). In other words, instead of attributing responsibility for the felt emotions and for the resolution of problematic situations or depression to external sources, the client takes full responsibility in the process of change and starts to work through their emotions in a productive, agentic way. This attitude is most obvious in the process when clients replace blaming anger with assertiveness and move from their subjective reality to considering alternative, more nuanced, and complex ways of seeing self, the other, or the situations.

The focus, thus, becomes taking responsibility for one's agency in the construction of one's personal reality. That is not to say the client has to take responsibility for everything that has been done or happened in the past, which would be tantamount to self-blame and victimization. Rather, clients engage in a collaborative effort emerging from the exploration into how their own processes contributed to their distress. By being aware of their agency and having a sense of personal responsibility, clients become agents in the creation of their experience and begin to gain control over their experience, moving from a position of passive victim to one of assertive agent.

Another essential shift takes place when clients differentiate between anger and sadness. Anger and sadness are often experienced together, and it is helpful to ensure that these two primary emotional states are experienced, symbolized, and expressed separately. Clients' engagement in exploring primary adaptive feelings of sadness and abandonment was crucial for the resolution of interrupted anger in the studied cases. While anger undoes despair and transforms blame and hopelessness into assertiveness, sadness promotes grief, acceptance, and transformation of anger. Accessing healthy adaptive sadness that reaches out for comfort and validation, similar to accessing primary adaptive anger, helps clients transform rejection and doubt into healthier, adaptive boundary setting. The experience of sadness and the process of grief helped resolution clients let go of and integrate aspects of the loss and become more resilient. These clients transformed their weak and deprived self-image into a view of themselves as strong, worthwhile, and lovable.

Nevertheless, overcoming the victim stance in the process of transforming blaming anger and hopelessness into assertiveness, on one hand, and accessing primary adaptive sadness in the process of becoming strong and self-affirmed, on the other, is not always easily attainable. Perhaps the most instructive lessons about the process of resolution are found in the processes of non-resolution clients. Overall, the responses of the non-resolution clients were marked by a pervasive sense of shame, a fundamental lack of trust, and blaming anger toward the significant other. Shame, related as it is to deep feelings of worthlessness instilled in a person during childhood and having a core feeling of being "bad" or "wrong," prevented these clients from resolving. Non-resolution clients in this study were unable to connect with their core feeling of worth. They remained detached and unaware of the effects of shame on their behavior, social contacts, and needs expression. Non-resolution clients became defensive and self-justificatory, did not access and accept core feelings, did not grieve, and rather became self-pitying or angry at themselves. By the end of therapy, they returned to blaming anger directed at the other/critic, which was characteristic of their early therapy sessions.

VALIDATION OF THE MODEL

The model of the resolution of interrupted anger was tested on 23 clients to see whether the model components of in-session client performances, including the expression of assertive anger, predicted outcome in depressed clients with early in-therapy signs of interrupted anger (Tarba, 2015). The five essential components investigated were (a) marker of interrupted anger, (b) the expression of assertive anger, (c) empathic understanding of the other/self-critic, (d) expression of primary adaptive sadness, and (e) letting go/forgiving.

At the beginning of the study, measures of the components were developed, and the presence of the hypothesized components was related to outcome. Regressions analyses showed that the five components of resolution, taken together, significantly predicted changes in depression scores (64% of the overall variance explained). In addition, expression of assertive anger was a unique independent predictor of change in depression (43% of variance explained), as was letting go/forgiving (22% variance explained). No other components were independent predictors of outcome. This study confirmed the therapeutic value of overcoming interrupted anger by expressing and processing primary adaptive anger in overcoming depression.

CONCLUSION

This chapter presented the results of a task analysis of the process of resolving interrupted anger. Expressing previously interrupted anger involved a multi-step process of differentiating the fused anger and sadness of complaint and expressing empowered anger and the heartfelt need in it. Resolution did not simply involve the expression of anger but entailed seeing things in a new way, grieving what was lost, and possibly showing empathic understanding for the significant other or feeling validated by the other or by one's own critical voice.

Chapter 11 presents a study of two different paths to help facilitate different ways of dealing with resolving anger. One was a more of a modification-oriented path offered by cognitive behavioral therapists, while the other was a more acceptance-related path offered by humanistic therapists.

11
WORKING WITH NONADAPTIVE ANGER

Anger is an acid that can do more harm to the vessel in which it is stored than to anything on which it is poured.

—Mark Twain

This chapter focuses on how to work with both secondary anger and primary maladaptive anger from an emotion-focused perspective. In both cases, therapists need to understand them, validate them, and help the client move on from them. While the chapter touches on methods of downregulating anger, these methods are well covered in the anger management literature (Fernandez, 2013) and are not the focus here. Instead, this chapter concentrates on alternative methods of working with unproductive anger. It also discusses when it is advisable to access anger and when to regulate it. As mentioned, the assessment of the type of anger and timing are some of the most important factors in guiding intervention.

This chapter covers how to work with secondary anger to get to its underlying determinants and how to work with primary maladaptive anger to understand it and transform it. Shame is probably the major underlying

---

https://doi.org/10.1037/0000393-011
Shame and Anger in Psychotherapy, by L. S. Greenberg
Copyright © 2024 by the American Psychological Association. All rights reserved.

determinant of most nonadaptive anger, although fear can also be an underlying determinant. Anger is one of the most prevalent forms of protection against the painful emotion of shame. Shame is so painful that people will often do anything they can to avoid it, and rage is often what ensues. People explode indignantly to protect their self-esteem or yell at their partners to not feel inadequate. Insulted people often become furious rather than process the pain of the insult. In all these situations, secondary reactive anger or even destructive rage hides primary maladaptive shame. In addition to discussing how to help clients access underlying vulnerable emotions like shame and fear, this chapter focuses on accepting one's anger and developing compassion for it as a way of changing anger with the opposing emotion of compassion. The chapter concludes with a discussion of how to regulate anger.

The chapter highlights the clinical implications of a qualitative study that looked at two different ways of working with anger expression in therapy—one focused on regulation, the other on acceptance. Therapists using cognitive behavior therapy (CBT) helped clients learn ways to calm themselves when angry. Anger management helped clients identify when they were feeling overwhelmed by anger and develop strategies for quelling their anger. Therapists with emotion-focused orientations promoted clients' acceptance of anger and the exploration of underlying threats and fears of loss of control.

DOWNREGULATION OF ANGER

Emotion downregulation is a major way that modification-oriented therapists work with dysregulated anger. Downregulation refers to the process by which individuals influence the nature, frequency, intensity, and expression of their own emotional experience (Gross & John, 2003). Difficulties with regulation are seen as arising from poor control of eliciting cues, difficulty in accessing emotional experience, and insufficient upward or downward control of experience and expression. People who are unaware of what elicits their anger cannot control the evoking cues. Anger can be experienced as overwhelming or it can be overcontrolled to the point of suppression. In all instances of dysregulation, the orienting action tendencies of adaptive anger cannot serve its assertive and self-protective function.

When a client's anger is overwhelming and out of control, the client needs to develop regulation skills before exploring underlying determinants. The first step in emotion regulation is to learn to accurately identify emotions and to understand the function of emotions when they occur. Therapists need to help clients recognize that emotions occur for a reason and are not invalid overreactions. Most clients with anger problems rarely just observe their emotions objectively. Rather, when an emotion becomes intense, they often engage in behaviors to change what they experience by means of avoidance (e.g., drug use, lashing out at someone, self-harm). In the short term, these behavioral strategies "work" by decreasing the intensity of the emotion, which then increases the likelihood that the new behavior will be practiced in a similar scenario in the future. The downside is, these individuals never learn that if they just observe without acting on the emotion, the emotion will naturally lessen in intensity even without action (Bishop et al., 2004). This latter skill of observing, however, also can be taught with the message that emotions are not something to always run away from and avoid. Simply noticing the emotion could change one's relationship to the experience of the emotion.

A central component of working on downregulation is engaging in a behavioral analysis, which includes identifying vulnerability factors, the prompting event, links between the prompting event and the problem behavior, the nature of the problem behavior itself, and consequences (Linehan, 1993). Conducting a behavioral analysis usually first involves creating a detailed account of what the behavior looks like in terms of frequency and intensity. The therapist then helps the client identify what triggered the problem behavior and the factors that made the individual more vulnerable to the effects of the evoking event on the particular day or in that particular moment, such as a fight that morning with a partner or being tired or stressed. Finally, consequences of the angry behavior are explored, such as first feeling powerful but then feeling shame over losing control. What the client could have done differently along the way and what skills could have been applied are then discussed.

Opposite action is a primary skill suggested by dialectical behavior therapy (DBT); it is used when individuals want to change the emotion they are currently experiencing (Linehan, 1993; Rizvi & Linehan, 2005). It works most effectively when the emotion, or the intensity of the emotion, is neither warranted nor effective in the context. In essence, the skill involves identifying the action urge associated with the current emotional experience and acting in ways that are opposite to that urge. For example, if someone experiences anger at a boss for assigning her an unappealing project, she might have the urge to verbally attack the boss. However, if verbally attacking the boss is ineffective for the client (i.e., by creating a worse working environment or impeding promotional opportunities), then she might want to change the anger through opposite action. Engaging in opposite action might be acting kind to the boss, throwing herself wholeheartedly into expressing kindness, making eye contact, and refraining from verbal attacks. Using opposite action would also involve thinking kind thoughts about the boss since holding on to negative appraisals would only serve to prolong feelings of anger. The skill needs to be practiced until the intensity of her anger decreases.

Action urges most associated with anger are to lash out or attack the person eliciting the anger (physically or verbally). Thus, the standard opposite actions for anger are to either gently avoid the person or to "be decent," which means to approach the person with decency, compassion, and kindness, if possible. For example, if a client is angry at her sister, whom she perceives as having favored another sibling over her, and that anger has the potential to ruin a family event because the behavioral urge associated with anger is to verbally attack the sister, then an effective choice might be to practice opposite action. In this case, the client might gently avoid the sister and engage with other relatives, or in being decent, she might respond civilly to the sister's questions, pay her sister a compliment, or even hug her.

DIFFERENT FORMS OF REGULATION

Deliberate forms of regulation, both behavioral and cognitive, are more generally governed by left-hemispheric processes. These forms of regulation are helpful for people whose anger is out of control. When individuals are dealing with dysfunctional anger, it is important to build, over time, automatic emotion-regulation capacities that occur at the implicit level (Shore, 2003). A lot has been written about teaching anger management skills, and many programs exist (Toohey, 2021), but psychoeducational and cognitive behavioral methods are not necessarily effective for all individuals. This is especially true for people who have long periods of intense emotional arousal or for who do not want to give up their anger because, from their perspective, it has served them well by protecting them and providing them with strength.

One further drawback of anger management is that therapists' attempts to have clients downregulate their anger could convey that the client is bad and being angry is a pathological response that needs to be controlled (Fernandez, 2013; Kassinove & Tafrate, 2002; Toohey, 2021). This message may evoke shame and opposition or exacerbate shame that is possibly the root cause of the anger (A. Pascual-Leone et al., 2013) and lead to the client getting even angrier. In addition, judging anger as bad is contrary to an emotion-focused approach in which acceptance and the withholding of judgments of feelings, by both therapist and client, is seen as central to receiving the message emotion is sending and getting the resources it provides.

The most significant problem with psychoeducation and skill-training methods to downregulate anger is that they rely on the individual's desire in the moment to give up the anger. A major problem of deliberate control is that once anger is evoked, there is often an extended period during which cognition is governed by emotion. In this period, anger allows only thoughts that justify or confirm the person's anger, and the person has no motivation to use deliberate skills of downregulation (Short, 2001). Anger management methods are useful for coping with anger, but their utility needs to be put in perspective.

The difficulty with efforts to deliberately manage anger is that during episodes of emotional arousal, the mind enters a refractory period that makes it difficult to take in any information that does not maintain or justify—or is contrary to—the emotion being experienced (Frijda, 1988). In my clinical experience and observation of many clients, trying to help clients deliberately inhibit anger does not work well for people who experience rapid and intense arousal of anger because anger management skills are extremely difficult to implement when dysfunctional anger is active. A significant problem with any method that requires the use of conscious thought and reason to regulate anger is that it requires low arousal of emotion during the time of needed application (Shore, 2003). Anger that results from faulty reasoning or negative thinking can be controlled using reason and deliberate management, but the type of anger that generally leads to significant dysfunction occurs too quickly in response to the cues that trigger it.

It appears that people with anger problems and/or who come to treatment for domestic violence have anger or outbursts of rage, most often protecting against shame, that overtake them long before they have time to think (A. Pascual-Leone et al., 2013). Amygdala-based anger and threat responses, what LeDoux (1996) dubbed low-road, fast processing, initially bypass the cortical regions of the brain. Anger has control precedence over functioning (Frijda, 1988) and protects against vulnerable feelings, most notably shame. This anger affects all mental processes, including attention, memory, perception, learning, and inhibition of emotion; all of this occurs before conscious recognition or explicit reflection on the underlying shame (LeDoux, 2003; Phelps & LeDoux, 2005). Similarly, emotion influences attribution and explanatory processes (Forgas & Locke, 2005). Emotions can control thought for many hours, especially for people with severe emotional disorders. This can lead to major distortions in memory and in people's judgments, decision making, and perception of both their behavior and the actions of others (Forgas & Bower, 1987).

Some form of downregulation is necessary when clients are overwhelmed by their anger, when the anger is destructive in their lives, and when the anger is outside their zone of tolerance and cognition can no longer be brought to emotion to make sense of it. If clients fly into irrational rages and later regret what they did, it's time to develop skills to downregulate. When clients have limited capacity for emotion regulation, intervention needs to include the explicit use of emotion-regulation strategies such as breath regulation, physical forms of relaxation, time outs, or distraction, all of which have been clearly spelled out in the CBT literature (e.g., Deffenbacher, 2011; Fernandez, 2010). These strategies are discussed toward the end of this chapter. Clinical and research evidence, however, suggest that psycho-educationally based, cognitive-behavioral methods often fail to promote lasting change or to prevent relapses and violence (Short, 2001). Therefore, something in addition to anger management is often needed in dealing with destructive anger.

AN EMOTION-FOCUSED APPROACH

In the preceding chapters, I have argued that it is therapeutic to increase arousal to facilitate access to interrupted adaptive anger and that it is helpful to raise awareness of anger of which clients may not be aware. How then, should one work with secondary and maladaptive anger? These types of anger need to be worked with differently, not simply accessed.

Working With Secondary Anger

Secondary symptomatic anger that is a reaction to a more painful primary emotion, such as shame, fear, or sadness, needs to be validated but then bypassed to get at the underlying primary feeling. For example, the shame of not mattering and/or sadness of loss from a rejection might rapidly lead to anger at the rejecting person. The emotion of anger may be preferable because it is less painful than feeling vulnerable. Anger is preferred because it makes the person feel more powerful and right, as opposed to worthless, powerless, or shamefully wrong. Secondary anger protects against underlying feelings of threat, shame, vulnerability, not mattering, or desperation. This anger, however, is not the feeling a therapist wants to elaborate or amplify. Rather, it is best to move the focus to the underlying shame or threat; the underlying affective processes need to be raised to awareness and the different maladaptive aspects explored and transformed.

The first step in working with problem anger is assessing clients' ability to attend to and symbolize their internal experience. When a client's anger is not totally overwhelming, the therapist needs to work to help the client first become aware of and accept their anger so they can begin to identify the internal and external factors that lead to anger maintenance and escalation. Helping clients become aware of their anger also aids in the development of an alliance with the therapist and the ability to start working on the anger.

Clients' awareness of their internal experience needs to increase for them to gain understanding of their anger (e.g., T: "So, it sounds like when you think your kids don't respect you and dwell on that, you feel yourself getting more and more angry. What happens internally? What do you feel in your body and how does that affect what you think?"). Emotion-focused therapy (EFT) focuses on exploring and creating meaning rather than on challenging maladaptive cognitions or teaching skills. When anger at perceived disrespect is a defense against hurt or shame, the therapist directs client attention to the primary experience (e.g., T: "So, it triggers some sense that you're a bad father, incompetent? That must hurt a lot. Let's stay with that.").

Therapeutic work on emotion in an emotion-focused approach is based on the view that people need to accept who they are before they can begin to change who they are. So, anger needs to be accepted before it can be changed. To work effectively with anger from an acceptance perspective, one always has to first validate a client's anger. This is the "arrival" stage of treatment. Later work involves leaving the anger by ultimately transforming the fear and shame as well as the hurt that leads to blame, which underlies the secondary anger and the destructive rage.

Emotion-focused treatments that focus on dysregulated anger need some type of work on the emotional processes involved in regulating dysregulated anger rather than on cognitive or behavioral processes. As illustrated throughout this book, a general principle in working with emotion is that emotion is an effective means of changing emotion (Davidson, 2000; Fredrickson et al., 2000; Greenberg, 2002). In addition, awareness and symbolization of bodily felt experience in words has been shown to downregulate emotional arousal (Kircanski et al., 2012; Lieberman et al., 2007; Schore, 2003). Increase in emotional awareness promotes self-regulation of amygdala-based anger. From an emotion-focused perspective, a key principle of anger management is that access to other emotions and to a greater range of emotions not only downregulates anger but also leads to a greater ability to reflect on anger, make sense of anger, and use reasoned thought to guide responsible behavior.

It is thus important to determine whether anger is a primary or a secondary emotion, as this distinction has important treatment implications. Ultimately, work to transform the underlying emotion is needed. In working with secondary anger, the therapy needs to access the root cause of the anger rather than only treating the anger symptom. Transformation of the underlying cause of the anger, rather than its management, is then needed. In this way, problems of excessive anger are not overcorrected by seeking to control the anger; rather, secondary anger is transformed by no longer being felt.

Working With Primary Maladaptive Anger

Primary maladaptive anger, in contrast to secondary anger, must be explored in detail to be understood. The therapist needs to understand the client's reasons for anger and to show compassion to anger's aim of self-protection. This helps the client develop self-compassion. Clients may also need to grieve for the way they suffered, which led to anger being such a primary way of self-protection. A person with chronic maladaptive anger problems who is engaged in hostile blaming and rejection needs to learn how to attend to their sense of shame or of loss and the sadness of grief instead of focusing on their anger. This is the path to healing the attachment and identity injuries that stem, often, from child maltreatment and lead to so much anger. In doing so, however, it is important to validate anger as a legitimate response to maltreatment and to illustrate that anger should not be controlled or deflected from but initially should be acknowledged. Thus, therapy validates clients' experiences of maladaptive anger. It finds ways to help them symbolize and express it appropriately and enables them to get to other feelings.

Evidence suggests that anger and pride are opposing emotions, in that anger is more closely connected to failure and pride is more closely associated with experiences of success (Tausch & Becker, 2013). So, helping clients access pride about strengths and successes is also an effective strategy. Deeper emotional exploration sometimes reveals that anger has served people as a universal response and that it replaces other emotions that individuals wish to avoid, such as shame, fear, or sadness. In many instances, men have a highly restricted range of emotional expression, and increasing their range of emotions helps reduce anger as their only form of response (Thomas, 1989).

Work with primary maladaptive anger, which often stems from prior abuse, begins with guiding clients to closely observe what is happening in their bodies, ultimately followed by the activation of new emotions, which then lead to the development of new ways of thinking and acting. Early in the process, the therapist needs to guide the client to attend to their anger at violation, betrayal, and maltreatment as well as their unmet needs and action tendencies. Memory evocation strategies can be used to help the client become aware of the triggers of problem anger. A therapist might say, "As you get angry now, it sounds like you really needed his support, not his continual criticisms," or "I imagine that you must have felt so powerless watching your father beat up on your mother, you being a small child unable to do anything." In these instances, it can be helpful to direct clients' attention to their bodily experiences associated with anger, such as tension, or trembling of anxiety, heaviness of sadness, or hiding in shame to help them be able to symbolize what they feel rather than simply to react.

AN ANALYSIS OF TWO WAYS OF WORKING WITH ANGER EXPRESSION IN THERAPY

A group from University of Massachusetts (Kannan et al., 2011) investigated the process by which therapists of different orientations worked with anger expression in therapy. This research provides insight in two different ways of working with anger—modification versus exploration. Eight female clients, seven White and one Black, were treated by six therapists. Three therapists were mainly CBT and modification oriented, and three were emotion-focused, humanistic, and feminist in orientation. The more behaviorally oriented CBT therapists focused on promoting coping while the more internally oriented therapists focused on internal exploration and experiencing. Six events, one with each therapist, were identified as having clear markers of the presence of anger in the session and of resolution of anger by the end of the session. The marker of anger was an overt statement of anger, the client's explicit agreement with the therapist's naming anger, or a loud and angry tone of voice. Resolution of anger was identified by reduction in anger by the end and a shift in the meaning of anger. Resolution also included a new meaning or emotional state linked to the experience of anger, a change in manner of coping with anger, or the reduction of anger. These judgments were made by group consensus among the five judges.

Two processes leading to resolution were identified, one followed by the more cognitive and behaviorally oriented CBT therapists and the other by more emotionally oriented therapists. There was some overlap, but it is more instructive to see how they differed. The main difference was that cognitive behaviorists tended to promote a coping-strategy approach, whereas the emotionally oriented therapists explored the anger in depth.

In CBT, clients were directed in ways of anger management and helped to explore ways in which they could calm themselves when angry. These clients were helped to identify when they were feeling overwhelmed by anger, and the emphasis was then placed on strategies for quelling their anger. Therapists with the more emotion-focused orientation promoted clients' acceptance of anger and the exploration of underlying threats, shame, and fear of loss of control. These EFT therapists also coached clients in ways of coping with states of high arousal. The main objective of EFT therapists, however, was to promote the exploration and development of the personal meaning of disavowed anger experience, rather than on skills training per se. The emotionally oriented therapists mainly explored their clients' understanding of their anger by means of process-guiding statements such as "Let's try and slow down," or "What is that saying to you?" Staying with the experience of anger and symbolizing its meaning led to clarity about the threat signaled by the anger. The focus was thus on acceptance and shifting the focus to the underlying threat.

The path to change of anger across both approaches consisted of six stages: 1) exploration of the anger marker, 2) clarifying the threat and owning emotions, 3) tying anger to the past, 4) reframing the problem, 5) exploring options, and finally 6) integrating change. Both sets of therapists had a lot in common in most stages, but differences between the two sets of therapists emerged, mainly in Stages 2 and 5. In these stages, the emotion-focused therapists focused more internally. More detail about the six stages follows.

Stage 1, exploration of the anger marker, involved verbal description of the anger event. Typically, the emotion of anger was named as such by the client and/or the therapist. The exploration of the anger episode intensified the sense of being wronged.

Stage 2, clarifying the threat and owning emotions, possessed two main directions that depended on the type of treatment, although both approaches involved exploring anger in connection to a fear or worry (Kannan et al., 2011). Clients in CBT explored their fears of being overwhelmed and losing control and worked on identifying and evaluating the source of the threat that was activating their anger. The focus of the exploration appeared to be on what they were angry about, and the CBT therapists guided clients to see that their anger was a reaction to an irrational threat. In contrast, the clients in the emotion-focused treatments focused on exploring their fear of being hurt. The humanistic therapists focused clients' attention inwards on the self rather than to an external threat and guided attention to the clients' feelings, needs, and meanings. For instance, one humanistic therapist said, "I'm hearing a lot about him and how he needs to take care of himself during this period of time. . . . But you haven't said anything about what you need." The main focus underlying these explorations appeared to be on what internal feeling or needs are leading to this anger.

In Stage 3, tying anger to the past, both approaches focused on the relationship between the current and past threats and looked at means of coping with the threat. Through this process, CBT therapists led clients to notice that their anger was often a reaction to an external threat, while humanists facilitated their clients' awareness of their more primary internal feelings underlying their anger, which was seen as a secondary reaction.

Stage 4 involved reframing the problem. When clients seemed to better understand the cause of their anger, both sets of therapists reframed the problem in terms of how to better cope with their anger. Typically, the EFT therapists moved on from this point to consider how to deal with underlying hurt, while the CBT therapists focused on how to deal with the experience of being overwhelmed with anger within an evoking situation.

Stages 5 and 6 involved exploring options and integrating change. Exploration typically took one of two directions, depending on the approach. In Stage 5, clients with CBT therapists examined how to regulate their angry reactions, while those with emotion-oriented therapists explored becoming more assertive and more entitled to express their feelings and needs. In CBT, clients evaluated ways they could respond to their own increased arousal. Options included relaxation, time outs away from the situation, and self-monitoring of arousal. In contrast, clients in the emotion-focused treatments were guided to deal with their hurt caused in the interpersonal situation. They explored responses such as empathizing with the other, self-soothing, and setting boundaries. Recognition of the hurt underlying the anger often would lead clients to become empowered and led them to consider ways to assert their needs (Kannan et al., 2011). In Stage 5, CBT clients looked at how to regulate their angry reactions. In contrast, the clients in the emotionally focused treatments accessed and responded to their own hurt. Often recognizing the hurt underlying the anger led clients to feel empowered and become more assertive about their needs. In Stage 6, some clients from both groups explored other emotions, examining how they interacted with anger, while others talked about how their anger was a protective force or planned what to do when anger occurred in the future.

Therapists in this study construed their clients' anger as a reaction to (a) feeling overwhelmed and unable to control their anger or (b) a relational threat in which they were being hurt or wronged by another. In the cognitive behavior therapies, the emphasis was on coping with anger, downregulating, and teaching skills to do this. In contrast, it appeared that in the emotion-focused treatments, anger was construed not as an unhealthy or pathological emotion but rather as a useful portal to understanding underlying emotional experiences. These therapists worked to encourage self-discovery, acceptance, and the expression of emotion rather than suppressing or distancing from difficult emotion. The aim was to help the client have a therapeutic anger experience in which they benefited from their anger.

As noted previously, the two treatment approaches had commonalities. The approaches were quite similar in initially identifying anger markers, and they appeared similar as they approached resolution. All therapists generally were supportive and maintained a strong alliance, despite the charged emotion. Therapists on both paths focused clients on the legitimacy of the need for self-care and self-protection. Therapists of both approaches guided the clients to redefine their problems as psychologically based reactions that they could control—either as a fear of being overwhelmed or a fear of their hurt. Clients ended both treatments with a new understanding of their experience of anger and began to feel more comfortable (Kannan et al., 2011).

ACCEPTING ANGER

As seen in the previously discussed work with anger, to be therapeutic, emotion-focused therapists need to help clients develop the capacity to accept, tolerate, and experience anger rather than deny it. Sometimes, however, people's anger can be so painful that they want to act out or close down, so being able to tolerate the distress and sit with it is important.

People have to learn to endure the discomfort that comes from not acting on their anger but instead observe what it feels like in their bodies. For example, a client who felt ashamed of smashing things in anger and lashing out at family and friends felt his anger was out of control. Going back to a memory of being humiliated and taunted by bullies before they beat him up, he became aware, in therapy, of an impulse to lash out and strike back that originated from this experience. The therapist encouraged him to follow this impulse in the sessions by pushing against a pillow on the chair in front of him and to describe his bodily experience and physical sensations while doing this. With repetition of his aggressive actions and increasing his awareness in small doses, he slowly came to appreciate the protective function of this anger and began to process his underlying fear and shame and to work on transforming them. Completing incomplete protective actions of anger in this manner, in awareness and in small experiments of expression, helps to develop affect regulation and opens the path to underlying emotions.

Thus, therapists need to help clients accept their anger and then experience some compassion for themselves. This can be facilitated by saying things such as "How difficult it is that you have to experience the suffering of anger. Can you just sit with it for a bit?" Helping clients change their habits of anger means they first have to accept and endure the discomfort that occurs when they refrain from the usual ways they react by blowing up. Clients and therapists need to recognize clients' anger experiences and validate that they, or some other person, may be feeling this way. Clients need to be helped to examine their own feelings and to accept and be curious about them so they can truly understand and make meaning from them. It is very helpful for clients to empathically understand their own feelings. Many people have never learned to recognize, name, and talk about their anger or other emotions.

Clients also need to be helped to learn no to condemn nor judge their anger. They need to learn to avoid labeling their feelings as good or bad and their thoughts as right or wrong. Rather, they need to observe their experience and others' experience nonjudgmentally. Clients need to know that their unwanted anger comes from an evolutionarily developed response to threat and is there to protect them. When, however, the threat is an internal vulnerability, it is more complicated to recognize. The underlying feeling, rather than what provoked it, needs to be worked on. Clients need help to make sense of how they feel, have what they feel validated, and be aware that their anger is a response to their own underlying vulnerable feeling.

As stated, an important approach to working with problems of dysregulated anger is not only acceptance of anger but also feeling compassion for the self rather than blaming the self (Kolts et al., 2018). Clients often feel it is their own fault that they are unreasonably angry, and they thus feel they are bad. They then experience shame or get mired in self-blame. Alternatively, clients may search for ways to justify their anger and related behaviors, or they may ignore them. These ways of dealing with anger prevent them from taking responsibility for their anger. Helping clients to understand anger often is not exactly their fault but rather is produced by the way evolution has shaped their brains helps to reduce self-blame. It helps for clients to understand that once patterns of angry responding are set, they take root in the brain and can be activated almost automatically. So, accepting rather than blaming the self for being angry is an important attitudinal change.

Being able to observe one's anger and the attendant negative thoughts as they arise, in the moment, and accepting anger thus is important. Therapists need to guide clients to focus their attention on their breath and guide them to breathe deeply so that the air enters their diaphragms. Then they need to guide clients to be aware of their stomach rising and falling as they breathe in and out and to notice what happens. The idea is simply to watch one's breath and to notice when one's attention moves away. When one's attention has left the breath, it is important to simply bring it back gently, again and again, to one's breath. It is also important not to judge thoughts and emotions that might come up and just notice them as mental events.

Learning to notice emotions, bodily sensations, and thoughts as they rise up helps people create a working distance from anger. Pausing and watching one's breath and observing when one's attention leaves the breath by getting distracted by an internal or external sensation, caught up in an emotion, or lost in thoughts keeps one more balanced. Awareness of anger as it arises gives people the chance to take a step back and decide what to do with it rather than lashing out or shutting down. In this way, they can influence their behavior rather than being controlled by their anger. People can learn to interrupt their anger by learning to recognize what is occurring in their minds that signals anger, although this is very difficult to do. The first step is awareness (often referred to as mindfulness), which helps people guide their attention, under their own control, to place it where they want it and keep it there. Awareness leads to the possibility of choice. People can possibly control the "spotlight" of attention by guiding attention to where it can be less fueling and more calming.

It is next important to develop compassion for oneself and others. Anger is related to threat, but compassion is related to caring. When people feel compassionate, they feel caring and kind rather than defensive and angry. Directing compassion toward oneself helps clients to self-soothe and to feel safer, and it facilitates work with the underlying distressing feelings that fuel anger. Feeling compassion for others helps people understand others' actions and helps reduce their own experience of anger. Compassion may be a new and different way of dealing with emotional pain and suffering. A compassionate approach acknowledges that life presents various difficulties and that all people suffer painful emotions such as fear, shame, sadness, anger, and grief in their lives. These are not viewed as weaknesses but rather normal, universal human experiences.

With practice, clients may be able to develop new habits of observing their episodes of anger. Careful observation facilitates awareness of anger as it emerges and before it gets out of control. This helps clients understand the threats and situations that tend to trigger them. Once they are aware of anger as it arises and can tolerate and be compassionate toward it, they are ready to leave it by transforming the anger they have arrived at into another state. An exercise to work on transformation (Greenberg, 2015) is adapted here to use with anger.

Step 1

Trigger: Pick a time when you got angry in an out-of-control fashion. Briefly describe the situation that triggered anger or irritation. What was the threat?

Step 2

Emotions: What were you feeling during the situation?

Attend to the maladaptive anger sensations in your body. Welcome and accept them.

- How intense was your anger (1–10)?
- How intense is it now (1–10)?
- Do you need to regulate your anger or create distance from it? If so, how?

Thoughts: What things did you tell yourself?

- What are the negative things you are saying to yourself? What are the thoughts going through your mind?

- What is the tone of the voices in your head and what feelings do they express (usually contempt or hostility)?
- Where do these voices come from?

Behaviors: What did you do? What actions did you take?

Step 3
- What is the basic threat and what is the unmet need, goal, or concern your anger is addressing?
- What do you need either from yourself or from others to undo the threat?
- Accept this and validate that you deserved to have this unmet need met.

Step 4
- Notice what else you may be feeling in your body now that you feel entitled to having your need met.
- Identify a new more adaptive emotional response to the anger, like sadness or compassion or whatever comes up for you. Give this feeling a voice. Imagine a situation in which you feel that helpful emotion. Enter this feeling or situation. Can you be compassionate to yourself?

Step 5
Bring new adaptive feelings and needs into contact with your maladaptive anger state.
- Allow your healthy need to confront the negative thoughts in your head.
- Integrate your new feelings and strengths and newly found resources into your sense of self.

Exercises and practice are helpful for clients with whom an alliance has been established to overcome their anger, but some clients may not easily want to change their relationship with their anger. An important aspect of therapeutic work with anger involves clients' ability to let go of it. Anger, because of the neurochemistry it involves, may make clients feel powerful, and they may be concerned that giving up power will make them vulnerable or lose their motivation to achieve. Some may be reluctant to give up their anger as it may have been their companion for a long time. Focusing on clients' fear of change is then a necessary step.

MEMORY RECONSOLIDATION

Anger may be activated by events that trigger implicit memories developed during prior emotional experiences. Memories can then produce experience without the person remembering what happened in the past that is activating the experience. Many of our behaviors and feelings are automatic; for example, our bodies remember how to ride a bicycle and emotions come up when we hear a specific song. When memory is implicit, people often don't recognize that the anger they are feeling in the present is a reflection of patterns laid down in the past. People then may have strong emotional reactions of anger that are not well understood and seem out of proportion to the present situation.

Emotion memory structures automatically influence the arousal of emotion, so if a past memory trace is changed in the present, future responses will also be transformed (Högberg et al., 2011; Moscovitch & Nadel, 1999). When an emotional memory is reactivated, it temporarily enters into a labile state during which the emotional memory is amenable to change. This process is referred to as memory reconsolidation. It is therapeutically helpful to encourage clients to recall past episodes of anger (Short, 2001). When the experience of anger embedded in the memory has been processed and an additional opposing emotion (e.g., compassion or sadness) is simultaneously activated, aspects of the memory change so that the next time the incident is experienced, the client's experience is also changed.

Emotional memories of anger, therefore, need to be activated during treatment in order to change them. Certain emotions transform anger because they oppose the action tendencies and the bodily experience of anger. Probably the strongest opposing emotions are compassion, joy, and pride. Compassion, as illustrated, offers a vastly different reaction to suffering and emotional pain than the way clients have traditionally responded to distress.

Learning to accept and be compassionate to oneself is a practice that takes time. Every time a person does anything, cells in their brains are activated together and become interconnected, forming into patterns and networks. With repeated emotional distress, pathways become formed in the brain, like walking the same way over and over wears down a path. Having new experience and developing new ways of responding lays down new pathways. Practice strengthens these new paths as the old ones decay over time through non-use. Just as if we stop walking on an old path and walk a new way, a new path is slowly formed while the old one gradually grows over. This process takes time, but if people continue new ways of being, the new path will be formed and the old one will slowly erode. Eventually, then, one has trained one's attention and a new habit, one that has been actively chosen, will have formed.

Creating a soothing space can be helpful to developing a way of calming one's response to threat and is a good alternative to anger and the laying down of new pathways. In an imagery-based process, therapists can guide clients to create a safe place in their mind—a place that gives them feelings of safety and calm. These feelings can be difficult to generate for clients when they are angry, but the attempt, the action of trying and opening up a sense of the safe place, is the important thing. The therapist may begin by saying,

> Imagine a place where you feel completely comfortable, safe, and at ease. It may be a beautiful wood, by a lake, or a beautiful beach with a blue sea, or a comfortable, cozy room by a log fire. These are examples or possible places, but the focus is on developing a feeling of safeness for you. Once you have found your safe place, focus on the feelings of safety, comfort, and being valued, just as you. When you bring your safe place to mind, allow your body to relax. Let your face have a soft smile of the pleasure at being here. Feel how safe you feel and how this place comforts you. Explore your feelings when you imagine this place is happy that you are there.

These types of experiences, repeated over sessions and as homework, help people develop the capacity to soothe themselves when they get into anger-activating situations. Once internalized, they can even help prevent the activation of anger.

CONCLUSION

Experiential techniques that promote activation and acceptance of anger need to be used alongside cognitive and behavioral interventions that manage and regulate anger. In addition, because there are discernibly different types of anger, differential treatment is warranted. Coping with overwhelming anger requires downregulation; interrupted anger involves accessing the anger; secondary symptomatic anger requires accessing the underlying, primary vulnerable emotions; and maladaptive anger requires understanding and transforming the underlying original determinant of the maladaptive anger.

Anger treatment needs to become more inclusive, rather than having divergent schools of therapy attending to only part of the terrain. Therapists need to select methods to fit the client and the emotional state or the anger stage the client is in and to sequence interventions to fit the situation. The result of a more differentiated approach to the treatment of anger would provide a more comprehensive but programmatic approach to the regulation of anger.

12 CASE EXAMPLE

Never feel bad for being assertive, speaking your mind, and putting your foot down. What you think is anger, others see as a good solid display of self-esteem.
—Alison James

This chapter follows the therapy of Gisella, a 37-year-old married woman of Italian descent with two children, to provide a look at how a therapy unfolds over time[1]. Gisella presented with clinical depression and anxiety and had interpersonal problems with her husband and with her parents. The therapy involved 15 sessions that took place over 5 months. The therapist was a 34-year-old female psychologist.

In this chapter, portions of some earlier sessions are presented to provide a real flavor of how the process unfolds. These transcripts are followed by a narrative description of the later sessions. Analysis of the transcripts demonstrates that the therapist is a moment-by-moment emotional-processing facilitator and demonstrates how every therapist response has an influence on the client's manner of emotional and narrative processing in the next moment.

---

[1] The clinical material used in this book is adequately disguised to protect client confidentiality. Client identity has been maintained.

https://doi.org/10.1037/0000393-012
Shame and Anger in Psychotherapy, by L. S. Greenberg
Copyright © 2024 by the American Psychological Association. All rights reserved.

The transcript includes running descriptions of the therapist's responses, and the codes of the narrative process coding system (NPCS; Angus & Greenberg, 2011), a research tool for coding narrative process, are used at times to describe the client process. The three codes in this system are *external*, *reflexive*, and *internal*. Essentially, in the external mode a client is talking about *what happened*, in a reflexive mode the client is talking about *what it means*, and in an internal mode *what it feels like*. The emphasis in emotion-focused therapy is guiding clients to an internal mode of processing.

A SILENCED VOICE

At the time of therapy, Gisella was living with her husband (V), who had a gambling problem. As therapy progressed, it became clear that her father also had a gambling problem. It was apparent in the first session that she was struggling with interrupted anger in relation to her husband and her family, as well as some shame. As a result, the focus over the course of therapy was on the client's difficulty in setting boundaries with her husband and her enmeshment with her family of origin.

Gisella was an emotionally available client. She had no issue accessing her emotions, but not all emotions were available to her, and adaptive anger was not one of them. Initially, she expressed a lot of secondary sadness of hopelessness in a somewhat dysregulated fashion, as well as helplessness and fear. Over the course of therapy, she progressively gained access to more adaptive feelings of anger and grief. She also differentiated from her significant others and asserted her own voice. She became more able to assert herself against her own critical/demanding voice and against her husband's and her internalized father's voice, which were all shame inducing. She changed the way she related to her husband in the imaginary in-session dialogues, and she recognized how the way she was raised had contributed to her marital difficulties and resulted in her losing her own voice. She became more aware of her needs and, from there, worked on overcoming the internal processes that hindered her getting her needs met. Toward the end of the therapy, Gisella reported she had made changes in her life, including symptomatic changes and a clear remission of her depression, and had developed a different way of dealing with her husband. Her measures of depression, general symptoms, and interpersonal functioning all changed significantly by termination and follow-up (Greenberg & Watson, 1998).

SESSION 1

The therapy begins with the client unfolding her narrative, facilitated by the therapist's empathic understanding. The following excerpt tracks how the therapist's empathic responses, by their internal focus, guide the client's processing to become more internal. The therapist asks for a specific example and then shifts the focus from an external mode of processing what happened to an internal mode of what it felt like.

THERAPIST (T): Uh-huh, is there something, like, are you thinking of something that's happened recently or . . . *(request example)*

CLIENT (C): Um, – – – well, you know, he'll, say he'll [husband] go out and, you know, in the meantime there's other things that you know, he could be doing at home. (T: Mm-hm.) And my mood would change because I, um, automatically think he's, you know, going to, uh, out to gamble or have a game of cards or whatever. (T: Uh-huh.) And my mood, just, it triggers, yeah, feelings are, um, well, they recur, they haven't gone away, they're just more suppressed than all of them, they're always there, yeah. (T: Mm-hm.) Um – – I excuse him and you know, think, well, it's a disease, and he can't help it (T: Uh-huh.) and that's it, and I leave it as that, like I don't express it to him. *(unfolds narrative with mainly an external focus on what happens)*

T: Uh-huh, but it's there, like it feels like a pretty heavy burden, is that it? *(focus on internal experience of what it feels like, also empathically checks understanding)*

C: Yes, it does, when it happens it does, because again, the – the mood triggers, and I might just, you know, out of the blue, just start yelling at the kids to pick up their things . . . *(continues to unfold her narrative but in an external mode elaborating what she does)*

Facilitated by the therapist's empathic following and a focus on the internal, the client later elaborates the internal narrative of what she feels, saying she feels ignored and diminished but is afraid to challenge him.

C: Just, you know (crying), don't – don't I count, what I say, doesn't it mean anything? *(internal narrative)*

T: Uh-huh, feels like somehow he's not considering you, feeling you don't count. *(focus on internal experience)*

C: Yeah (sniff), as just – I'm just his wife I guess (sniff) and just to be there as a provider. *(unfolds the narrative in a reflexive narrative mode on what it means rather than in an internal mode of what it feels like)*

T: Uh-huh, it's almost like my voice is just as important. *(exploratory empathy on implicit experience)*

C: Yeah, that's right, um, or he believes, you know, he's the man (crying). Maybe that's the way he was brought up, but my voice is important too, um . . . *(emotion is aroused focus is initially external [on husband] but shifts to her experience)*

Gisella elaborates that she is afraid to fight it out because he'll raise his voice and so she simmers down. She further explains that she doesn't say what she feels for fear that he would walk out and leave the house and so she is afraid to stand up for herself. Talking in the third person, she continues:

C: So, you're going to start a fight, and, um, he can end up, say, going out of the house or leaving and, you know, he's mentioned, when I get into that kind of a mood where I ignore him he gets back into the gambling, you know, he's, say, you made me go back into it.

T: Oh I see, so it's like if you rock the boat and he leaves, then you feel blamed. *(empathic understanding focused on internal experience of feeling blamed)*

C: It's almost like, I feel like it's my fault. (crying) *(internal narrative and symbolizes internal experience)*

T: Uh-huh, and that's what sort of feels really painful about this. (C: Yeah.) Like so much rests on you. *(follows the pain with empathic understanding)*

C: Yeah, and it shouldn't, I'm not responsible for his actions. (crying) *(focuses on her internal experience)*

T: Uh-huh, you kind of know that, but it still feels like you have to just tiptoe around because otherwise he, you know, you move this way, you move that way, and he'll be off again. *(empathic exploration of implicit experience of feeling of having to tiptoe or else)*

C: It's sort of, isn't it like, you know, if you come from a dysfunctional family and everybody's quiet about it, or and then there's one person that, you know, kind of erupts the family (laugh) or questions or doesn't obey or do . . . *(third person reflexive processing of meaning)*

T: Mm-hm. So it's – I guess it feels like again, you – you shouldn't rock the boat, afraid of rocking it. *(exploratory understanding of internal experience)*

C: Yeah, yeah, that's right, I am afraid. It's like I should just keep it a secret and – and life goes on. *(shifts attention to internal experience)*

A little later in the session, Gisella is talking about her feelings in relation to her husband, and the therapist maintains a consistent, gentle focus on the internal, slowly guiding the client to attend inward.

T: Mm-hm, so even when you talk about it, it's like a lot of, there's old feelings come up again, right. *(focus on internal)*

C: Yeah, (sniff), and I try, I try not to – to think about it, or to – to make myself go back into it, but it just (sniff), just happens. *(focus on internal)*

T: So, it's like even right now when you talk about it, some of those feelings come up. (C: Yeah.) What's it like, it's like feeling hurt almost, I'm not sure? *(focus on internal feeling with exploratory question)*

C: Um, I guess rejection. *(focus on internal feeling)*

T: Uh-huh, you feel rejected. *(focus on internal feeling)*

C: Yeah, and, um, not – well, I shouldn't say not loved, – – or maybe not – – – I don't know, maybe not cared, you know, it's an illness . . . *(focus on internal feeling and meaning of his behavior)*

T: Uh-huh, even if you kind of know it's an illness and he doesn't mean it, it's like you're pretty close to him and you still end up feeling as it's somehow, it's directed at you, somehow it's "He doesn't really care and I feel unloved." *(focus on internal feeling)*

C: Yeah, it – it feels like that, unloved, but then on the other hand, you know, he does care, but I – I, it's really confusing. *(states a conflict)*

T: Uh-huh, it's kind of like you know he cares, you know. *(empathic understanding)*

C: Yeah, but he still does it. *(external)*

T: It feels more like not being heard. *(focus on internal feeling)*

C: Mm-hm, that you know, he wants his family and – and – and everything but, then he still goes to the other . . . *(external)*

T: Uh-huh, and then you end up feeling neglected. *(focus on internal feeling)*

C: Yeah, neglected or rejected or, um, just there for the purpose of – of being there as the provider for the kids and . . . *(shifts to internal feeling)*

T: Mm-hm, so kind of just left all alone holding the bag. *(focus on internal feeling)*

C: Yeah, yeah, I guess I – I take a lot, I hold a lot on my shoulders, which (T: Mm-hm.) um – – I excuse him and, you know, think, well, it's a disease and he can't help it. (T: Uh-huh.) And that's it, and I leave it as that, like I don't express it to him. *(focus on internal experience and meaning)*

T: Uh-huh, but it's there, like, it feels like a pretty heavy burden, is that it? *(focus on internal feeling checking question)*

C: And that's, there's no way of escaping that, feeling trapped. (T: Yeah.) Yeah. *(focus on internal feeling)*

T: So, it – it's like the feeling of being kind of locked in. *(focus on internal feeling)*

C: Yeah, more as, uh, isolated (T: Uh-huh.) You know I can't do anything about it, it's happening but I . . . *(differentiates internal feeling)*

T: So, you start feeling almost feeling helpless. *(focus on internal feeling)*

C: That's right, I'm, um, I'm helpless about it, I can't do anything. *(focus on internal feeling)*

Throughout the session, the therapist responds with empathic understanding and attunement to affect. Gisella expresses a range of emotions in the session—feeling hopeless, helpless, and sad; feeling rejected, unloved, and isolated. She finds it difficult to stay with her core sadness of loneliness and often shifts into secondary sadness of hopelessness. She also expresses some anger and resentment, but these rapidly shift into feeling hurt and helpless. Her core emotional pain appears to be the sadness of feeling isolated, not listened to, rejected, and ultimately unloved. She comments that the roots of her resentment lie in her childhood when she experienced her father as controlling, particularly when he would shout at her. She feels similarly controlled when her husband criticizes her, shouts at her, and threatens to leave the house to gamble. This prevents her from standing up for herself and asserting her needs, to grow and to have her own voice. This is an early indicator of an internal split between a part that wants to express how she feels toward her husband and a part that stays silent. It is clear from this first session that, among other feelings, she feels angry, but the anger is interrupted because she is afraid it would rock the boat. The session ends with an agreement to work together to help her deal with all the feelings that she has silenced.

SESSION 2

At the beginning of the session, the client recalls memories of her childhood and the expectation put upon her by her mother to mind her younger brothers.

She believes she missed out on having a childhood. The client expresses a mixture of sadness, hurt, and resentment in relation to her mother; at times, these feelings are emotionally overwhelming. She feels that her mother never gave her support, and she now pushes her mother away but says she feels bad:

C: Yeah. (crying) I feel bad. (sniff) *(high emotional arousal)*

T: You feel bad for pushing her out. *(focus on internal feeling)*

C: Mm-hm, yes. (crying, sniff)

T: So, it's, like, kind of – – – feeling comes up. *(focusing on a bodily felt sense)*

C: I feel, like, that I'm punishing her (crying), and I don't know if it's . . . (sniff) *(focus on internal feeling)*

T: Take a breath. *(grounding with breath)*

C: But then again, it's not really fair. (crying) She's only human (sniff) – but I'm pretty hard on her – – I guess I'm hard on myself and I'm hard on the person, um . . .

T: It feels like your feelings towards her are pretty strong. *(focus on internal)*

C: Yeah, I get really angry and frustrated inside and, you know, why do I let her treat me like this, and then I'm, it's like, oh no, I can't talk like that to my mother, it's like . . .

T: Uh-huh, there's a voice that says, "You shouldn't be disrespectful to your mother," is that what it is? *(focus on interruption)*

C: Yeah, yeah, disrespectful or, you know, she has her own problems and she's going through enough, she doesn't need to hear it from me.

The client says she needs to forgive her mother because she is only human and has had a hard time herself. And the therapist, hearing her sadness, says,

T: But it sounds like it also brings up other feelings, it sounds like . . . *(guiding toward underlying feeling)*

C: Sadness. *(focus on internal feeling)*

T: Uh-huh, uh-huh, sadness. (*pause for 11 seconds*) Just take a moment, stay with the sadness. *(focus on internal feeling)*

C: (Sigh) Um, being controlled . . . *(differentiates internal feeling)*

In the remainder of the session, the client expresses secondary emotions of helplessness and hopelessness, believing that nobody understands what she is going through and that she is going through it alone: "It's like nobody understands, it's – it's me that's going through it and there's no point asking for help or support (sniff)." She says,

C: I just kind of walk around and, you know, just pretend, I guess I pretend myself that it's – it's not really happening, but it is. *(focus on external)*

T: Uh-huh, so is there something about that pretending that is painful or something. *(exploratory focus on internal feeling)*

C: Yeah, it is, it is, because I know inside, you know, she's in pain. *(focus on meaning)*

T: Uh-huh, uh-huh, so when you talk about her pain, that also kind of brings up your own . . . (C: Yeah.) so maybe that's where . . . *(focus on internal feeling)*

C: Well, I don't want to get close (T: Oh, I see.) Um – – I guess it's being afraid or . . . *(focus on internal feeling)*

T: Afraid? *(focus on internal feeling)*

C: Um, it's like not trusting. (T: Uh-huh.) I guess because there's – there's pain, that's, like, it's like, that's all I know, like, if you trust – – I don't know, it – it's hard to explain it, um, *(pause for 6 seconds)* it's like nobody understands, it's – it's me that's going through it, and there's no point asking for help or support. (sniff) *(focus on internal feeling and creating meaning)*

T: Oh, I see, so it's like, maybe, you know, you've tried that, you've asked for support or . . . *(empathic understanding)*

C: Yeah, and then I kind of get stabbed in the back. (T: I see.) It's not being able to trust anybody. *(expresses on internal feeling)*

T: I see. So, it's like all of this pain inside, and then feeling like I can't rely on anybody else. *(focus on internal feeling & meaning)*

The client later expresses her need to feel deserving of love and support. This is the result of brief expressions of adaptive self-soothing emotions and assertive anger, which had been interrupted. The client expresses adaptive assertive anger to her mother's lack of responsiveness to her throughout her life. This anger is self-protective and begins a separation and boundary-setting process. The client was also able to take a reflective stance toward her experience, allowing her anger to be present yet regulated and, therefore, useful for self-assertion. The session ends with her relaying an incident that occurred the day before. She says she didn't know why she came out with it but that she said to her husband, "You know, sometimes you guys expect me to be, um, Mother Theresa." She says that at home she doesn't talk about what she feels but if she suddenly lets her feelings out, her husband and children don't know what's got into her because it seems so crazy. By this point, it was clear that she was struggling with interrupted anger as well as sadness and was silencing herself.

SESSION 3

In the early part of this session, the client's narrative relates to her sad loneliness and her experience growing up in a family culture that promoted coping by avoiding emotional experience. The client identifies with her mother's pain in that her mother continues to be in a difficult domestic situation with her husband, in which her mother's need for emotional support is ignored by the client's father. The client says she believes that she learned how to suppress her own emotions from her father, as this was his way of coping with distress. She describes feeling angry at him as she sees how his behavior has led to her own difficulties in expressing emotion. The therapist suggests an empty-chair dialogue for unfinished business with her father to offer an opportunity to express the anger she has toward him. In these dialogues, therapist actions are indicated and note the difference between two different forms of intervention, one to promote awareness and another to promote expression of emotion.

T: Let's try an experiment if you are willing, with your dad, because what you're describing is a very strong feeling of anger towards him and, so that if you were to bring him in here that might, I mean, bring him in here in an imagined way, it would give you a chance to actually express it towards him. Would you be willing to do it?

C: Yeah, okay.

T: Okay, and I'll sort of show you, I'll tell you how to – yeah, I'll put a chair here, and, and what I want you to do is – first of all, can you actually imagine him being here, in a sense, in your mind, bring him in here. (C: Okay.) *(structuring the experiment)*

T: Can you get a sense of him? (C: Mm-hm.) What – what do you feel when you can see him. (C: (Crying)) It just feels that way. (C: (Crying)) Uh-huh, do you feel scared or, what? *(focus on bodily sense of seeing him)*

C: Yes, scared. (crying) Scared. I feel that I always had to be a good girl in front of him.

T: Uh-huh, sounds like you have things to say. Say more. Tell him. *(guiding to expression of emotion)*

C: Yeah, well, I'm not accepted.

T: Uh-huh, you're not okay as you are? (C: Yes.) Can you tell him that? Tell him "I don't feel accepted by you." *(naming a shame-based feeling and guiding her to express her emotions)*

C: (Sigh) Um. *(pause for 6 seconds)* (sigh) Um, it seems to me I'm blocking. It's gone out of my mind again. *(an interruption emerges)*

T: Uh-huh, okay, so just stay where you're at. Don't try to be something you're not, but what do you feel now, what comes up now. *(guiding to awareness of emotion)*

C: Um, I don't, I don't want to face it, or um him.

T: You don't want to face him?

C: Well, yes and no, again, as I was saying, um, you know, him wanting to be, no, I'm sorry, um, not feeling comfortable in front of him and . . .

T: That's what you feel now, uncomfortable? (C: Yeah, um.) Uncomfortable. *(focus on awareness of emotion)*

C: Being that good little girl and – and, if I'm not, then I'm, you know, no good.

T: Tell him what you feel about this. *(focus on expression of emotion)*

She begins to express some anger to the father about the pain that he causes her mother. At this point in the dialogue, the therapist asks for the central message she internalized from her father:

T: Uh-huh, so just, what's the message, just put away your pain and your . . . *(awareness of other's message)*

C: Yeah, it's not allowed – it's not allowed in my family.

T: Okay, so tell her, "You're not allowed to have your feelings." *(focus on interruption of emotion)*

C: Yeah, you're not allowed to feel what you're really feeling, and you're not allowed (crying) to feel your pain. (sniff)

When the client is asked how she responds to this message, she expresses fear—a fear that she won't be accepted by him and a fear of his anger. This fear leads her to hide her feelings, with the result that she feels "phony." She then begins to take an understanding stance toward him, knowing he too has had his difficulties. She oscillates between a little bit of self-assertion and empathy for him and others and has difficulty holding onto her own feelings and needs. In the dialogue, the father apologizes and acts contrite, saying the client was right and he should see her mother's pain more. This brings sadness to the client, and she rapidly and repeatedly organizes as sad and helpless. She expresses her core pain of maladaptive loneliness from her sense of loneliness growing up and the resulting sense of emptiness. She stays with the emotion and explores the meaning inherent in it; she does not collapse to a secondary emotional response of sad hopelessness. These needs are for acceptance, to be listened to, to be supported, to be understood, and to find closeness. In essence, there is a longing for the connection that was never there.

T: Mm-hm, and this brings out sadness. (C: Yeah.) Stay with the sadness. Can you tell your dad about the sad feelings? *(expression of emotion)*

C: You've never told me that you love me. And I would have liked to hear that word more often.

A little while later the client expresses anger at not having had her needs met. The therapist validates her feelings and needs:

T: So, tell him what you feel, what do you feel towards him? *(awareness of emotion)*

C: Um, I feel angry with the way, um, you mistreated my mother.

T: "I resent the way you treated Mom. You didn't take her into account." *(validation of emotion)*

C: Um, I resent the way you treated Mom, and I think that's why she's caught up in her own problems right now in her life.

As the therapist maintains a focus on the client's anger that is present in the dialogue, the client asserts self-protective anger, which promotes a sense of boundary-setting separation:

C: It's not my fault that you gambled!

T: What do you feel inside when you say that? *(awareness of emotion)*

C: Separate, away from him, like I'm my own self.

T: So, tell him, "I'm me, and I've got my own feelings." *(expression of emotion)*

C: I am me, and these feelings belong to me, and if I want to tell you, I will.

As the dialogue between the client and her father continues, some key moments generate self-soothing emotions, such as when she experiences her imagined father as acknowledging the hurt he has caused while assuring that it was unintentional. Toward the end of the session, and as a result of expressing her feelings toward her father, she is able to let go of some of her anger, saying that she doesn't have to carry it around anymore. She now sees her father as someone who carries a lot of sadness and who is alone in the world, not really having anyone to talk to. She can recognize the impact of the hurt he caused her and also grieve for the relationship that could have been but never was. The grieving has a letting-go quality. The client says she feels peaceful and loves the father.

Picking up from earlier in the conversation, the therapist asks her to stay with her sadness and express it to the father:

T: Mm-hm, and this brings out sadness. (C: Yeah.) Stay with the sadness. (*pause for 10 seconds*) Can you tell your dad about the sad feelings? **(express feelings)**

C: You've never told me that you love me, and I would have liked to hear that word more often. (T: Yeah.) But I would have like a reassurance in whatever choice I make . . .

T: "I would have liked your reassurance that I was, I was okay."

C: Yeah. It's just, it would have been nice to hear and it feels good.

SESSION 4

Session 4 continues with the exploration of the client's distress in relation to her husband's behavior toward her. As the client moves through different emotional states, her core painful sadness is explored and further elaborated. More primary maladaptive emotions, such as shame and loneliness, are accessed in relation to her husband's mistreatment of her. Her ability to experience her core emotional pain of feeling alone, rejected, and not loved in the session and to express the needs implicit in them leads her to express more assertive anger and compassion for herself.

Early in the session, in response to the therapist's query into how she was doing, she says she's a little bit angry this week at her husband: "There's a bit of anger (crying) – uh, uh, a bit of disappointment again," and "It's so obvious, the gambling has become so obvious now." The therapist responds empathically that she's feeling let down, and the client excuses her husband's behavior by saying she understands he can't control his gambling but then says he should do something about it. At this point she is quite tearful. She then elaborates that he said he was going to get back into the 12-step program and follow it, but he just did it to kind of get her to come back home, and then he did whatever he felt like. She relays an incident during the week in which she was so mad that she cut up the credit card in front of him and says he's so uncontrolled that he doesn't really realize what he's doing.

The client then enters into a self-critical shaming process regarding her lack of ability to connect to her husband. On one hand, she feels she is to blame for his behavior: "Yeah, I say to myself, is it my fault that I haven't tried hard enough?" The client describes being afraid of her husband and how she feels about his treatment of her. She fears that if he realizes he has let her down, his feelings may be hurt and things will get worse. She is protecting herself from rejection and from things worsening. Her disclaimed core primary feelings are fear of rejection, isolation, and sad loneliness. She does, however, say, "I – I guess I fear him, like I – I – I look at him as my father and – – I have fear," but at this point it's more conceptual than experiential.

The therapist focuses the remainder of the session on an empty-chair dialogue for unfinished business with her husband to facilitate exploring the client's core emotional scheme of the sadness of loneliness and feelings of being unloved. Initially, the client talks about being angry at her husband; however, this is voiced in a timid way without arousal. Facilitated by the therapist's empathic exploration and validation, the client expresses her primary maladaptive loneliness, a feeling of being unloved and unsupported. However, the client soon moves away from experiencing this core painful emotion pain and engages in a self-interruptive process by expressing a fear that he may become angry at her. The following lengthy portion of the transcript shows her overcoming the self-interruption:

T: Okay, well, let's try – can you imagine him here? *(setting up a dialogue and guides her to make imaginal contact with him to create experience)*

C: (Sigh) Oh, yeah . . .

T: Do you have a sense of him? What's – what's he doing right now, or what do you see? *(amplifies the contact)*

C: (Sigh) *(pause for 7 seconds)* Sad.

T: Uh-huh, he looks sad. (C: Yeah.) Uh-huh, and what do you feel towards him right now? *(present-centered focus on emotion)*

C: Um – – – – I'm angry – um . . .

T: Tell him. Tell him "I'm angry at you." *(promotes expression)*

C: I'm angry at you – for, um – – not putting your – effort into it – for not trying and, well, you try, but then you – you bail out. (T: Uh-huh.) I'm angry at you for not letting other people help you. (T: Uh-huh.) Um – you believe that you just – just want to do it yourself and – and push everybody else aside.

T: Uh-huh. "I'm angry at you for, for not trying," right. *(empathically validates)*

C: Yeah. Not putting the effort – and – at least, you know, for a while until – – not keeping it up. You just want to pull out – as soon as things get better you just pull out – you figure you don't need the help anymore or you can do it on your own. I feel unloved, um, and not supported. I don't feel supported by you.

T: Uh-huh. Tell him what it's like to feel like that. *(promotes expression)*

C: Um – – it's lonely, and – – – and it hurts and I feel, um, like, I'm in a cage and I – I just can't get out. *(the client is approaching the core maladaptive feelings)*

T: Uh-huh. Tell him about that trapped feeling. *(elaborate and differentiate the feeling)*

C: Um – – – – I feel like there's these iron bars or something – I just – I can't seem to – even though my heart tells me that I would, I should get out and – and do what I feel is right, when you're up here in front of me it's, like, stop, don't go anywhere.

T: That's what you say to yourself, "Stop, don't go anywhere"? *(reflects the self-interruption)*

C: Yeah, because he's, he's going to get angry or he's going to become angry with me or, you know, I have got to think what I'm doing is right (T: Mm-hm.) – so you're going to – – if I – if I'm all worked up to do that thing, you change my mind – like my mind totally goes the opposite way . . .

T: Come over here for a second. Um, okay, so what you're tell – let's take a look at how you stop her . . .

C: Right, right.

T: Scare her. How do you do it. How would you do it? (C: Um, now.) Or I'm not sure if it's V. or you're you. – It's something. What I'm saying is that somehow you stop yourself from getting angry at him. *(guides her to become the agent of the interruption)*

C: Okay, it could be me in that voice.

T: Okay so, become that for – for now and be this part of you. And stop her from getting angry at him. *(become the doer rather than the done-to)*

C: Um. No, you shouldn't do that – um, you should just – – – you know, stay home and be with the kids and – take care of the kids and – your time will just come later – you know, right now the main priority is – – is your children, and . . .

T: So think of the children, that's part of it, right? What else? *(validates and encourages)*

C: Yeah, yeah. You know, you don't deserve to be doing that or – um . . .

T: You don't deserve to be, free, is that what you're saying?

C: Yeah, to do what you think is right.

T: She doesn't deserve that. (C: No.) Tell her that – – that she's just – – she's not worth it, or . . . *(intensifies)*

C: Um. *(pause for 6 seconds)*. Well, here, you know my mother – um – always stayed home and – and dealt with the family first and then – – – – and – and – you just can't do that – you know – it's – you should be home and that's what comes first.

T: So, you know – that's what you've been taught and that's what you believe. *(reflects to maintain relational understanding and connection)*

C: Yeah, yeah. you're a bad person if you do, or . . .

T: I see, so if you – what if you leave or if you express yourself, even? *(promote articulation of catastrophizing)*

C: Um – – well, when I do, when she does express herself, she's either laughed at, or . . .

T: Oh, I see, so tell her "If you don't express yourself you'll be laughed at." *(guides back to express in the dialogue)*

C: Don't express yourself because you're just going to be laughed at (T: Uh-huh.) and not listened to.

T: (Cough) That's what we were saying before, and – and some of it is – is – what, like, a message here – don't try, don't, don't express yourself. *(reflects for emphasis)*

C: You'll be – if you express yourself, no one's going to listen to you, or just – kind of – yeah, yeah, but – you know, you don't count, your feelings don't count.

T: Uh-huh, tell her that. "Your feelings don't matter." *(express)*

C: You're, your feelings, it's okay what – anybody does to you.

T: OK. Switch. – – What do you feel when he tells you that you won't be listened to anyway and that your feelings won't matter. *(switches to the experiencing chair to access emotion)*

C: (Sigh) Um – – – yes, they do matter. *(The client stands up for herself.)*

T: Tell her that – "I, I do matter." *(supports expression)*

C: I, I do matter.

T: What do you feel about that? *(This is important to access the feeling of doing this, not simply the behavior but the client's true experience.)*

C: (Crying) Sad. *(Although the words were assertive, the affect is vulnerable.)*

T: Stay with the sadness – it's fairly strong. Tell him about the sadness. *(The therapist is empathically attuned to affect and follows the pain.)*

C: Um – – – I want to believe that I can really do it.

T: You want to . . . *(follows the emergence of need/want)*

C: I want to believe in myself.

T: Uh-huh, who are you saying that to? *(clarifies to follow her experience)* Tell him "I want . . ." *(express need/want)*

C: I want you to take me seriously (T: Uh-huh.) – – – and when you don't it's very painful.

T: Uh-huh. Tell him about the pain. *(We see here a hallmark of emotion-focused therapy, going into the pain to make it accessible to new input, not skipping over it or promoting good intentions.)*

C: Um (sniff) – – – it gets lonely (crying) and – and – I – I just feel like I'm (sigh) there to provide for you and the kids and not to share anything else. (sniff)

T: Mm-hm, right, so that's hard not being loved, it's hard being isolated. *(Now the therapist empathizes with and validates the core painful emotion.)*

C: Yes. Um – – I don't like your protectiveness and your jealousy.

T: So, what do you feel towards him when you say that, "I don't like you." (C: Um.) Tell him that, what happens when he does things like that. *(follows emerging anger)*

C: Um, he – I don't trust you, all of a sudden I don't trust you and – – I don't want to live with somebody like that. It's very uncomfortable.

T: Mm-hm. I don't want to live with you when you do what? *(specifying question)*

C: When you become controlling or jealous or when you don't trust me.

As the client experiences the effect of her self-interruption, she accesses her more primary maladaptive emotions of sadness, hurt, and loneliness about how she is being treated. This allows the client to express a need for separation and distancing from her husband. There is some anger accompanying these needs; however, it appears that the client cannot easily tolerate this anger, and she soon collapses into secondary emotions of complaint, consisting of fused anger and sadness.

The therapist guides the client to stay with her anger and express it, which leads to a more congruent expression of anger and the need for love, support, respect, and acceptance. A few minutes later in the dialogue, she says,

C: Yeah, you're not – you're just not there for me.

T: Tell him what you feel about that. *(express)*

C: Um, you're not supportive at home and it makes me angry and . . .

T: Tell him about that anger. Tell him how you're angry, tell him what you resent, is it "I resent you not being home . . ." *(promote anger expression with "I" statements)*

C: Yeah, yeah. I resent you not being – – being home – and doing something with me or the children, um, and when you're there you think you've really put in, you know, your day's work, but really it's nothing – it's not good enough to me or the kids.

T: So, "I resent you not . . ." *(repetition)*

C: Not being there, yeah, just – if there's something to do, you just – you don't say I need your help, you just nag about it that I should be taking care of everything and being supermom.

T: Uh-huh. So, "I resent you not putting in fifty percent . . ." *(repetition)*

C: Effort, around the house, or with the children.

T: "And I resent you leaving me with so much responsibility." *(repetition and elaboration)* (C: Yes, yeah.) Tell him about the resentment. *(express and elaborate)*

C: Um – – – there's days when I – I hate you and I (crying) – I just don't want to be with you (sniff) – – – I feel very lonely and . . .

T: Tell him about this lonely feeling. *(follows the emerging feelings, and express and elaborate)*

C: No one to share my day with. (crying, sigh)

T: "I feel all alone." What do you feel towards him right now? *(differentiate and deepen by focusing on present experience)*

C: I'm angry. *(self organizes as angry)*

T: Yeah, tell him, "I'm angry, I resent . . ." *(expression)*

C: I'm angry at you (crying) – you always – treat me like a child. (crying) (T: Uh-huh.) You never take me seriously and never make me feel like a woman.

T: Uh-huh, "I want you to take me seriously." – – Tell him. *(focus on want/need to deepen)*

C: I want to, to take me seriously!

T: And tell him what you resent. (C: (Sigh)) "There's a lot of feeling here and I . . ." *(focus back on anger to deepen)*

C: Um, there's days when I resent even marrying you.

T: Tell him that. "Sometimes I resent ever marrying you." *(expression)*

C: Sometimes I (cough) resent marrying you.

T: What's it like when you say this to him? *(experiential question to elaborate)*

C: (Sigh) It's really easy.

T: Tell him more about the resentment. "I resent ever being with you . . ." *(express anger)*

C: You don't deserve me – I – I know I deserve better than this. (sigh)

T: Uh-huh, tell him that again. *(repetition and expression of heartfelt need)*

C: You, you don't deserve! me, I – I deserve better.

T: Uh-huh, tell him what you deserve. – Tell him what you want, what you want from him. *(expression and differentiation of heartfelt need)*

C: I deserve love and compassion and (sniff), to be treated, and accepted for what I am.

T: Uh-huh, what do you feel as you say this, you want this acceptance? *(focus on the experience of expressing the words to guide attention to present experience)*

C: (Sigh) Um – – what do I feel? I feel sad.

T: Mm-hm. When you say that to him, can you see him over here? *(promote contact)*

C: Um, yeah – – – I really feel like – he's saying "That's all I can give you. It's the best I can do."

T: Okay, that's him speaking, right?

C: Yeah, "That's the best I can do."

T: Come over here. – – – Tell her, "That's the best, it's as much as I can give you." *(This is to amplify the negative voice to activate more of the painful feeling.)*

C: This is – – as much as I can give you, this is the best that I can do for you that – that I feel comfortable with.

T: Uh-huh – – "This is all I can give," right? (C: Yeah.) "This is as much as I've got." (C: Yeah.) Tell her that. *(express)*

C: This is the best that I can give you – that I – that I have to offer.

T: Uh-huh, okay, come back over here. He said, "This is all I've got; this is what I can give." What do you feel? Inside. *(focus internally)*

C: That's not good enough.

T: Tell him what you want. *(express need/want)*

C: I want your honesty, to be able to trust you, um, to love me.

T: Uh-huh, what do you feel as if you said, you see, I hear a certain kind of a – longing in your voice when you say, "I want you to love me." *(focus on nonverbal expression to raise awareness and promote congruent expression)*

C: I want you to love me.

T: What happens inside when you say that? *(promote awareness and symbolization)*

C: *(Pause for 7 seconds)* It feels good. It's what I want. (T: Mm-hm.) I deserve it, um . . .

T: What happens as you say that, "I deserve love"? *(promote awareness and symbolization)*

C: I deserve love, uh, well, I love myself, and I want to feel loved too.

T: What's happening inside right now? *(promote awareness and symbolization)*

C: (Cough) I feel peaceful, and it feels good to have said that.

T: Mm-hm, mm-hm, – – so sort of more calm? *(understanding reflection)*

C: Oh, yeah, and acceptance, um, because that's all he can do.

T: Tell him that – "If that's all you can do, then . . ." *(expression)*

C: If that's all you can do, then, um, just to me it isn't enough. That's not good enough for me – it's not what I want, um, I want more than that.

T: Tell him what you want, what would be – what you want, what's acceptable. *(promoting assertion and need)*

C: Um, your support at home with the children, and – – to not make me feel uncomfortable with you – or to not make me feel afraid of you, or, to not laugh at me – to treat me like G.

T: Uh-huh, so the treatment – the laughing at you – – you resent – What happens, when he laughs at you? *(promote awareness and symbolization)*

C: Well, when he laughs at me, he's, like, laughing at a child. (T: Uh-huh.) Um, it's ha ha ha, yeah, say what you want, but, you know, I don't go along with it, I don't believe you, or, um, you shouldn't have that – – you don't deserve it.

T: So, that message is – just, you don't really matter . . . *(promote awareness and symbolization of negative message)*

C: You're worthless, yeah, you don't matter. *(here we see the shame, which needs to be transformed)*

T: Okay, come over here. I'm not sure if this is you that says that or if it's J., but – but, somehow or other, you get this message from him, that your feelings don't matter. *(enact negative voice to promote specification and to ultimately amplify feeling in the self)*

C: Right, right.

T: So, tell her, "How do you do that, somehow you make her feel really small, it sounds like." *(amplify the negative)*

C: Um, well, I – okay, I'm V. again.

T: Yeah, well, okay be J. and sort of like, rather than describing it just enact it – like be him, telling "How do you make her feel bad; how do you make her feel like a child?" *(promote expression and specification)*

C: By laughing – just straight – not taking her seriously.

T: What's this, like pushing her back? (C: Yeah.) Do it some more. (C: Um.) Like even, like, do it with your hands. *(promote action engagement)*

C: (Action of pushing aside with her hands) Um, forget it, you don't need this, and – move out of my way so I can try to get dressed and go out. (laugh) (T: Mm-hm.) You're not important and you're just there for, because the kids are there, not because, um . . . (sigh, crying) *(pause for 8 seconds)*

T: What's happening? *(awareness and symbolization in words)*

C: (Crying) I'm me. Again.

T: OK. Come here, what are you feeling? *(awareness and symbolization in words)*

C: (Crying) As I was saying, that – that he just doesn't love me.

T: So, he sweeps you aside and you feel unloved. *(reflection of feeling)*

C: (Sniff) Yeah.

T: Tell him about that feeling. *(expression)*

C: Um – – – it's like, I try so hard but you continue stepping on me, um, I feel like I'm there just for his slave, just, but not as your wife.

T: Uh-huh, what's it like to feel like a slave? *(experiential question)*

C: Just, to do everything for – for you and the kids or everybody that, you know. But not to do things together. It's like not having me there, you don't want me there.

T: Tell him what it's like to feel unwanted and unloved. *(expression)*

C: It's – it's very resentful, I resent you when – (T: Uh-huh.) when you push away, I resent you, I resent you.

T: "I resent you," tell him. *(promotes expression of resentment)*

C: No, I'm not important, um . . .

T: Tell him what it's like to feel unimportant. (C: Um.) What's your experience with feeling unloved – I mean I would imagine it's . . . *(differentiation)*

C: Um, other people come first – your friends, or your sports come first and – that makes me feel very neglected, and, um, I'm tired of not feeling that I'm good enough or that I'm doing – the best I can . . .

T: Tell him that – "I'm tired of feeling neglected." *(expression)*

C: I'm tired of feeling – just shoved aside!

T: What do you want? *(expression of heartfelt need)*

C: Um, what do I want – I want . . .

T: – – "I'm tired of feeling shoved aside. It's like, I want . . ." *(expression of heartfelt need)*

C: You think I want a new life, or, I'm tired of you.

T: Uh-huh, tell him, "I'm tired of you." *(express feeling)*

C: I'm tired of you! I don't want to go on living like this. I want – I want something – I – I know I deserve something else.

T: Uh-huh, is there pain when you say that? "I deserve something else." Tell him. *(awareness and amplifying the need)*

C: Um, I deserve better, I deserve something, I deserve to be happy. I don't want to walk around the rest of my life feeling this way.

T: So, what happens when you say this? *(experiential question to raise awareness)*

C: Um, I see that you're never going to change because I – I don't see that you love me.

T: Uh-huh, so you feel really unloved by your husband. *(empathic understanding)*

C: Yes.

T: Tell him what it feels like to be so unloved and alone. *(express the core painful feelings)*

C: Yeah, it's very lonely, and – – I just have to soothe myself.

A few minutes later, the dialogue continues.

C: I've given up! I've had enough! That's it, I can't take any more. (crying)

T: And what happens inside when you say that? *(experiential question)*

C: (Sniff) I'm being laughed at.

T: Uh-huh, he's laughing at you. *(empathic reflection)*

C: Uh-huh.

T: Okay, come over here. What did you say, who's laughing.

C: J. – J. is laughing at me.

T: What does he say, what's the message in his laugh? *(specify)*

C: It's like – – yeah, yeah, um – – you can't go anywhere – you've got – you can't do it on your own, you, um . . .

T: So, scare her, tell her what you see, as J. again. *(amplifies the negative)*

C: Yeah, yeah.

T: Um, what he – he's laughing at you, saying you're not going to be able to do it on your own (cough) – so you're scaring her a bit right? Do it. *(clarifying and expression)*

C: Yeah, you don't have enough courage to – (T: Mm-hm.) to do, what you did the first time – you know, you're the one that came back to me, or – – honey, you're stuck with me and – and that's just the way it's going to be, like it or not. (T: Uh-huh.) That's what I see. Him telling me that that's just the way it's going to be.

T: Like you don't have, kind of the gumption or the wherewithal to stick it out, is that what you mean? *(clarifying question)*

C: Um, well I've done that and – – I get lonely.

She then goes into her sadness. Her husband is again represented as nonresponsive, saying he will not change, to which she replies she doesn't wish to live like that and wants to enjoy life and to blossom. At this point, it is becoming clear that she is caught in a cycle of feeling hopeless and sad, then angry at seeing her husband as unresponsive, and then sad again. In response to his refusal to change she says, "I want to blossom, and I deserve this," but she then collapses into the sadness of helplessness and hopelessness, arguing—in a very meek and helpless manner—that she is worthwhile. It is apparent she is experiencing terrible conflict between feeling resentful about having to be the good, supportive wife and being too afraid of disapproval, rejection, and loneliness to voice her resentment.

The processing problem lies in her automatic, dynamic self-organizing process. She enters more assertive states supported by resentment but then automatically shifts to a weaker sad state, fueled by the sadness of helplessness and sometimes hopelessness and even to submissive acceptance. One of the issues is the discrepancy, at one level, between her narrative and her actual experience or, at a more fundamental level, her self-organizational shifts from strength to weakness in her experiential process. Part of her says she is deserving and feels strong, but it is hard for her to sustain that feeling, and she moves rapidly to feeling weak. There is a difference between knowing what she deserves and feeling deserving of it. Her awareness of what she feels and a narrative of self-assertion are developing, but she still lacks the backing of any congruent experience of anger entitlement, worth, and adaptive anger at unfairness and violation that would help her set firm boundaries. At this point in the session, her sadness was more a secondary hopeless sadness, and her words, when they expressed anger, were not congruent with her experience, which was more a sad helplessness.

After one round of this cycle, she is asserting herself behaviorally, saying she knows she deserves more but also that she loves him:

T: And yet, you're saying, "I want you to take me seriously and treat me like a woman." *(supports assertive organization)*

C: Yes, yeah, um, I want you to believe that what I say – I'm going to stand up for it. You're not going to change my mind. (T: Uh-huh.) You're not going to manipulate me to believe what you believe or what you want.

T: So, I'm not going to budge from this position. *(supports assertive organization)*

C: No, no, I'm going to just – I know I deserve to be treated well. (T: Yeah, yeah.) I know I deserve to be treated well and, and I deserve a good life but . . .

T: So, what happens as you say that and you look at him – what is that look? *(awareness)*

C: Um, he is saying "Do what you want."

T: You feel that towards him? *(awareness)*

C: No, he's telling me.

T: He's telling you, okay, just come over here.

C: Do what you want to do.

T: Do what you want, what does that mean? *(awareness of critical voice)*

C: Um, *(pause for 9 seconds)* I accept, I accept you, um – – it's okay, you've – – you've (crying) tried the best you can – you've tried (crying) best you can and it's not your fault. (sniff) *(She enacts him as essentially excusing her for failing to help him.)*

T: Yet you feel sad as you say that. (C: Yeah.) It's not your fault. *(empathic exploration)*

Throughout, she describes a mixture of undifferentiated sadness, disappointment, tiredness, helplessness, and hopelessness. She feels like a victim of her emotions, which she experiences as somewhat overwhelming. Her emotions are highly aroused with almost no restriction, and her speech patterns are quite disrupted.

It is worth noting that her sense of primary sadness of loneliness could be productive if she were able to stay with the emotion and process it as an agent, "I feel sad and lonely . . ." rather than as a victim, "It, or he, makes me sad," but she finds this difficult to do. The session ends with her feeling more like an agent, accepting that she has tried her best, that it's not her fault that he gambles, and that if they divorce it's not her fault. There is a quality of letting go of some of the pain of how her husband has treated her and some grieving that something has been lost and that it won't be changed. During this expression of sadness at loss she is not overwhelmed and remains composed. However, she is clearly still in an emotional tangle, with a mixture of sadness, anger, shame, guilt, and love. Therapy needs to help her develop a new way of organizing emotionally that helps her feel more integrated, stronger, and at peace.

SESSION 5

At the beginning of this session, the client says she should be strong and support her husband. She says that when her husband tells her she is selfish for not supporting him, she believes it at the time. Although she is now learning to stand up for herself and her own needs, she says she feels that she is still abandoning him and is pushing him to engage in more gambling behavior. She says her fear of getting hurt by her husband leads her to avoid expressing her feelings. In the session, this leads into her sense of lonely abandonment and her core primary maladaptive pain of not feeling loved. She is able to process these emotions without collapsing into her secondary helplessness or hopelessness.

A few minutes later, the therapist introduces a two-chair dialogue highlighting the conflict between Gisella's demanding self-critical part that says she should be there for him and a part that cannot take anymore and needs to distance herself from him. The setup of the self-critical split is shown in the following dialogue.

T: One part of you saying – – be there for him. *(identifying this part)*

C: Yeah – yeah, you're treating him really bad and – (T: And.) – – you shouldn't be treating him like this, you should – comfort him, let him know that it's – – it's painful and (T: Mm-hm, mm-hm.) yeah, all that . . .

T: So, did you want to try a – a, um, I know this is a conflict, right? *(getting agreement on task)* (C: Mm-hm.) In – in a sense, there's really two parts of you . . .

C: Yeah (clears throat) – yeah, that's the way it feels.

T: – So, if we were to do a dialogue which involves another chair but it's a bit different than – what we've been doing – um – but it's like putting the two sides of yourself – in two different chairs and having a dialogue between them (C: OK – yeah.) just sort of try to – work through – the conflict. *(structuring the experiment)*

C: OK, yeah, that – makes sense, 'cause that's the way it feels.

T: Yes, because you're – you choose, different – different – different parts, right – – so what – which side are you more in touch with right now? *(structuring the experiment)*

C: Um – – – supporting him.

T: Yeah – – OK. Actually, if you want to get ready, come on over here – – OK, so these are two different parts to you; they're both Gisella. Right? – – Put Gisella here and – and tell her – how – what she should do. – This is the part of you that says you should support him. *(structuring the experiment, and express)*

C: Um – – – to – to understand what's happening to him – and . . .

Speaking from the critical, coercive part of herself, the client expresses contempt at her inability to support her husband. She condemns herself. In response to this negative self-treatment, she at first agrees with the negative voice but then shifts into her often-experienced state of secondary sadness and hopelessness. The client then expresses some anger to the critic when her needs are not acknowledged and self-reorganizes into a stronger sense of self. She expresses her need to be taken seriously and to not be laughed at. The client then loses her power and becomes predominantly sad and weak and, later, childlike in relation to her husband's dominance in the empty chair. Ultimately, she becomes angry and strong again. This oscillation between different dynamic self-organizing states becomes the main process that changes over the therapy. Over the session she moves progressively forward in a nonlinear process, two steps forward and one step backward (A. Pascual-Leone, 2009), becoming reactively angry and then either collapsing into hopeless sadness or entering into her core painful feelings of lonely sadness and fear and ultimately to adaptive anger and strength.

Toward the end of the session, she begins to construct a narrative. She says to her husband in the empty chair, "You're making the whole family suffer, not – not just me but – your own children." She tells him she wants him to listen, to let someone in to help him, and she says, "It's not good enough – um – I don't feel loved – this way." After this declaration the therapist asks a key question and the dialogue continues:

T: What are you feeling right now? *(awareness)*

C: I feel strong – (T: Mm-hm.) You know – – support within myself – peace – um – – – I'm going to stick it out.

T: Yeah, mm-hm. You feel like a little bit stronger, maybe? (C: Yeah.) That emotion is more of . . . *(validation)*

C: It's stronger than – than it was before, you know, so it was easy to find. When I came in it was hopeless and, um – it was my fault again – and I should be doing more (T: Mm-hm. Mm-hm.) and now it's like – – you know, I've done enough – um, what I can . . .

T: "The best I could do." (C: Mm-hm.) Yeah, more accepting of yourself in a way. *(empathic validation)*

C: – Yes, yeah, I accept myself, the way I am – – – and what I need.

Having alternated between collapsing into sad hopelessness and anxious helplessness, she ends by expressing adaptive anger, which facilitates therapeutic change by allowing her to set a boundary between herself and her husband. This therapeutic change leads to her feeling that she deserves to have her needs met and that she can accept herself.

SESSION 6

This session takes place 3 weeks later because holidays interrupted their regular schedule. Gisella says her husband has been gambling more and that "it's scary living and coping with him." She says that previously she had let it slide and just avoided it. Now that she was facing it, she felt sad, scared, and weak, but at other times, she felt strong.

The client once again enters into a self-critical process that leads to her feeling sad. She expresses that she feels a sense of shame when leaving the house while fighting with her husband, although she then expresses a need to look after herself. She also expresses sadness when she speaks about her children and the effect the fighting has on them. The client states that she is beginning to realize how alone her husband makes her feel when he fights with her and rejects her views.

As the session progresses, the client begins to access the loneliness regarding her situation. Her loneliness is an important part of her primary maladaptive emotional organization, as it is connected to a lifelong sense of yearning for closeness and validation. In this session, she is able to stay with this feeling. She does not become overwhelmed by it and can reflect on it to create meaning. Also, at times in the session, she experiences and expresses some compassion toward herself.

The main process in the session is a two-chair dialogue between a part that says "keep trying" and another that says "it's too painful to keep trying." At some point in this dialogue, the therapist guides Gisella into the pain with the understanding that by experiencing the pain, her self-organizing process will work toward meeting needs that promote survival and well-being and find a way to emotionally reorganize. As herself, and at times as her husband from the other chair, she basically admonishes herself for not being a good wife, to which she responds by saying, "Leave me alone," in pain rather than in anger.

By going into the depth of her pain and fear, Gisella accesses some healthy resources, feels stronger, and sees possibilities. Later in the session when she returns to her shame-based organization, the therapist asks her to shame herself, which she does by saying she's not a good wife. The dialogue continues, and she, as the shamer, says she's trying to protect her by telling her to toe the line. The client then responds, saying that she wants to be accepted. The session ends with the client asserting her needs for acceptance. This session shows both sides in this internal conflict beginning to shift, with the critic becoming a bit more compassionate and the self feeling stronger and more deserving.

SESSION 7

Gisella begins this session by saying she values the sessions and feels safe when she comes to therapy, and that's why her sad feelings come back in the sessions. She says that she now has more understanding of her situation and is accepting it but during the week she gets very anxious. She just gets up and cleans the house because the anxiety is so high, and she guesses that's how she just blocks out her pain. Early in the session, they again enter into a dialogue with her husband.

In this dialogue, she gets to a point at which she says their fighting affects the children, and she doesn't want that because she had that when she was young, and it was very painful and left her feeling very neglected. The client comments that she sees that the relationship between her husband is similar to that between her and her father. Her father was also a gambler, and his fights with her mother led to his absence from the house. As a child, she would feel shame believing that it was her fault when her parents fought. The therapist shifts the dialogue to her father; the client says he is the parent she needs to speak to about this.[2]

Enacting her father in the other chair, he protectively stifles her, saying such things as "Just stay where you are, uh, don't leave home, uh, don't get married, it's – it's not trusting you, can't trust yourself." The therapist guides her to unpack more of the message sent by the father, and they get to a core message of "stay where you are and don't learn anything else." As the client says this, the therapist notices how the client, in the father's chair, uses her hands to suppress herself and inquires into this action. She says that he is suppressing her and not allowing her to speak.

When the client moves to the self chair, in response to the therapist saying, "Tell him what you needed," she says she needed comfort and to be seen and accepted. Her father responds by feeling sad and saying that he loves her. She responds with her own sadness, saying she never heard that enough. The client now grieves the loss of the love she never had and says she forgives him and loves him.

C: Um, I missed out on that, of having a good relationship with you. (sniff)

T: Just stay with this sense of loss, right, what you missed out on. *(encourages tolerance of the emotion)*

C: Yeah, it is a loss. He did . . . (sniff)

T: Tell him what you lost out on. *(encourages elaboration of the emotion)*

After grieving, she goes on to express her core underlying feelings of being unloved and neglected. The session ends with her saying she missed

---

[2]This therapy contains a large number of dialogues, almost one every session, which is more than the average. In a therapy of 16 to 20 sessions, dialogues occur on average in half of the sessions, and for about half of those sessions.

him being there, she wanted him to love her and just have a good relationship with her. She expresses the sadness of grief over the loss of relationship, and this sadness has a letting-go quality. She says she feels stronger and at peace.

As the therapy progresses, a new sense of self is emerging from all the emotional processing, from accessing her core sadness of loneliness and her sense of shame in conjunction with her empowering anger, along with a new narrative of not being responsible for her husband's problems. Gisella is also developing a much more differentiated sense of herself as separate and not "glued to him." She now has her own voice, one that differs from what her significant others have said she should be. She is also clearly aware of links between her current functioning and the way she was raised. Chair work has aided her in becoming aware of parts of herself that have been in conflict and has allowed her to explore its impact on her. She is more able to disembed from her situation and adopt an observer's perspective to help her reflect on what was occurring, which helps her create new meanings. Gisella saw that while she was still in conflict, she felt clear she was not responsible for her husband's behavior, even though what he did still hurt, and she knew it would be hard not to monitor him.

SESSION 8

Gisella starts this session saying she definitely feels stronger and during the week she walks around trying to be happy and keep it all together, but then the loneliness still comes in. She feels hopeful, but the loneliness comes back if she's alone in the house. She says she likes having the security of her husband being there: "It's like I can't do without him, but then, all the bad feelings come so it's mixed feelings." She says she feels a lot more at peace with herself, accepting herself. The therapist reflects, "it sounds as though some of the heaviness has gone away, like that burden of 'he's gambling because of me' has lightened," and the client says, "Yeah, that's gone, but then I still feel as – I still feel lonely."

About 10 minutes into the session, she outlines how emotionally torn she feels:

T: Yeah, so there is still a lot of feelings there, that's what you're saying. *(focus on internal)*

C: Yeah, there are *(pause for 7 seconds)* um, feelings, um, of sadness. (crying) (T: Mm-hm.) Um, of still, I guess, resentment.

T: Mm-hm. Resentment towards him? *(focus on interrupted anger)*

C: Mm-hm, um – – – – and that's, that's where I'm at right now.

T: You're feeling resentful? *(focus on internal)*

C: As much as I don't want to and, you know, we're all supposed to forgive. I feel cheated . . . (laugh)

T: Cheated. *(empathic reflection on internal)*

C: Cheated, um, by doing all the work, you know, and just . . .

T: Do you want to tell him some of these things here because there's a lot of stuff that you're feeling in relation to him, right? *(proposing a dialogue)* (C: Okay.) Just put him in the chair and just – it might help to kind of separate some of these things out. (C: Okay.) – So, what do you – do you see him over there? (C: Um, yeah.) And you said the last thing you said was you felt cheated. *(awareness and expression)*

Gisella oscillates between strength and then doubt, resentment and guilt, and hopeless sadness. This is the dynamic self-organizing system in play, automatically synthesizing different states moment by moment, leading to shifts from one feeling to another. The process of therapy is to help the client have new experience that lays down new pathways to help the client begin to self-organize and construct themselves more resiliently. She moves on to express some sadness of grief in relation to having to block out her feelings with her children because of the problems with her husband. Her sadness has a sense of acceptance and a quality of letting go.

In the self-critical dialogue in this session, Gisella expresses primary adaptive anger in relation to not getting her needs met, but she still finds it difficult to stay with her expressions of anger. She expresses a fear of expressing anger, associating it with not being a "good girl" and a "good wife." However, she identifies a pattern in how she has reacted to her husband, originating from how she observed her mother's response to her father. She says she now wants to focus on her children's feelings and not allow them to witness the same thing. Her anger helps her overcome her fear. Toward the end of the session, the client becomes more assertive and says she feels comfort and calmness and feels stronger coping with her problems. She restates her dilemma, saying, "I know that it will just carry on, but I'm afraid and even ashamed of not being a good wife." Gisella seems much more differentiated from her husband and family of origin and more aware of her own emotional functioning. Experiencing her core fear allows more access to her anger to help overcome her fear.

SESSION 9

At the beginning of this session, the client expresses shame at not being able to assert herself in life in general. She talks about her fear of disapproval and her feelings of loneliness in relation to what she is going through. The client narrates a difficult situation with a lodger in her house, in which she couldn't say no even though she wanted to. She believes she has the right to feel angry and assert her needs, but instead she fears asserting herself and setting boundaries with the lodger. When these feelings are explored, a fear of criticism and rejection emerges and acts as a self-interruptive process that prevents her from standing up for herself. The therapist again introduces a two-chair enactment for self-interruption to explore how she holds herself back. She resolves this interruption by standing up to her interrupter, asserting her right to set boundaries with her lodger, and having a dialogue with the imagined lodger. She says no to her lodger's request, and the session ends with her feeling good about herself.

SESSION 10

This session occurs a couple of weeks after the last session. Gisella says she feels clearer on her own feelings and her responsibilities. She has a clearer idea of what her needs are and realizes that she can't change her husband. She reports more acceptance of herself and her feelings. She states that she is going to keep progressing even if her husband is adamant he's not going to change. Gisella engages in a dialogue with him and demands that he take responsibility for himself. She asserts herself and says she no longer feels little, but big, alive, and optimistic and she expects honesty from him and for him to carry through on what he says. She ends by saying she's going to let him fall and is no longer going to protect him. These feelings are then further explored and expressed in an empty-chair dialogue with him. A large part of the session is spent on holding him responsible, expressing resentment, and making demands.

The client makes many statements indicating a sense of empowerment and agency. As she enacts her imagined husband and he asks her to accept him the way he is because he is not going to change his behavior, she begins to feel her hurt, which points toward her core emotional pain of not feeling loved. The client moves to expressing sadness at seeing her husband still suffer and being powerless to do anything about it. She also expresses the sadness of her own loneliness at her sense of abandonment. She later moves to expressing sadness of grief at the sense of loss she feels at having so long suppressed herself and for her own woundedness, without any blame or self-pity. This grieving facilitates more healthy adaptive responses to her husband's behavior. She believes she can relate to his feelings of loneliness (which he experienced as a child) but realizes she can't stop him from engaging in behavior that ultimately is hurting him.

SESSIONS 11 AND 12

In these sessions, the client reports continued progress in different aspects of her life, particularly in being able to express her feelings instead of holding them in. This makes her feel more empowered. She considers herself "over the obstacle" of expressing feelings, and she can now express her disapproval if needed. She continues to have a new perspective on her husband, no longer trying to change him or make him see he has a problem. She now lets him know how she feels, but this is not an attempt to make him feel bad. She describes it as a relief to express herself to him and thus enables her to feel stronger and more like an individual.

Throughout Session 11, Gisella seems pretty secure in her capacity to be aware of herself and to differentiate herself from others. She held other members of the family accountable for the family problems and expressed anger to them for not addressing her needs. In Session 12, Gisella reports being more assertive toward her husband but still feeling some self-criticism and guilt for standing up for herself. Toward the end of the session, she is able to respond to her critic with assertive anger.

SESSION 13

At the beginning of the session, which occurred 3 weeks later because of scheduling issues, Gisella says her depression is gone and she is feeling hopeful for the future. She considers herself stronger now and more able to assert herself. She states that she feels better about herself, as her feelings are not blocked anymore. She considers that she has grieved for some of her past, in terms of missing out on getting her needs met by not expressing her feelings. She questions herself as to why she held back her true feelings for so long and allowed others to manipulate her. As the therapist explores this tendency, the client identifies the message she received from her parents as a child, which contributed to her suppression of emotions. Her parents always told her they knew what was right for her. She did not believe she was given the opportunity to make choices about issues growing up. Furthermore, both her mother and father regularly suppressed their emotions regarding difficulties the family had. The client believes this behavior led her to deny her own feelings and rely on others to know how to feel. The client states that she doesn't have any resentment toward her parents for this.

Gisella believes her husband has treated her in a similar way. She then describes how he continues to "put her down." When she tries to stand up for herself, something stops her. She feels intimidated, views herself as "small," and then puts herself down instead. She says she has a clearer picture of her problem and what to do and then begins to grieve the time wasted.

By Session 13, she has developed a new narrative, understanding that the way she had been raised led her to not know any better. She shows compassion to herself, has developed an understanding of how to manage things differently, and has learned that she can extricate herself from the cycle she was stuck in by allowing and listening to what she feels. Gisella now feels separate from her parents and her husband and has synthesized her two feelings, not wanting to feel resentment toward them but also wanting to stand firm and take care of herself and her needs, into a form of acceptance.

SESSION 14

Gisella enters the 14th session talking about having peace with herself. She has overcome the feelings that she had, has put it all together, and is feeling comfortable with herself. She says therapy has really done wonders for her. She and the therapist talk about ending, which brings up sadness for her and feelings of insecurity. She says she knows the struggle will still be there with her husband, but she feels so much stronger in herself and has a much better understanding of her feelings.

In this session she has a final dialogue between two sides of herself: one painful side who resents him and the other who says to accept him and not let it weigh her down. As she responds from the self chair, she again cycles through fear of being alone and sadness, but this cycle is much quicker. She spends less time in the painful states and arrives more quickly at her need for acceptance, support, and understanding. She addresses these needs to her husband in the empty chair and says she wants him to accept responsibility for his problems and do something about them. The dialogue ends with her feeling strong and strongly asserting what she wants while simultaneously feeling that he probably won't change.

SESSION 15: TERMINATION

At the beginning of this session, the client cancels her next (final) session because of her employment timetable. She says she doesn't see her husband as so powerful now and it's more like seeing him as weak. She says that before she felt she was glued to him but now she feels she is a separate individual and therapy has planted a seed no one can take away from her. The therapist tells her that's a great metaphor and it's nice to hear that therapy has been helpful.

Gisella states she is continuing to assert a boundary between herself and her husband and articulates a plan for the future. The therapist validates the change the client has perceived in herself and the strengths that the client has displayed in therapy. Toward the end of the session, the client expresses some grieving as to the sadness that remains as she chooses to stay in the marriage. She ends the session saying,

C: Coming here and what I've accomplished, I think it – it's a lot, you know, in a short time, it's not like years and years. (laugh) (T: No, it's not.) It – it takes, I think it's, um, a part of it is, um, if you really want it. (T: Mm-hm.)

DISCUSSION

Throughout the therapy, the client and therapist worked on Gisella's internal and interpersonal conflicts, and by the end she was able to differentiate out from the voices of her husband and her parents. The therapist followed the client's affect with empathic understanding, empathic exploration, and evocative reflections and guided the process with empathic conjectures, refocusing, and process observation and guidance, all of which proved to be useful and were used productively by the client.

The therapist offered a lot of chair work to promote awareness and expression, which provided Gisella the opportunity to deepen her experience of her internal and interpersonal conflicts. This process allowed Gisella to experience affirming herself and finding her own voice. Her interrupted anger changed into assertive anger, which allowed her to feel entitled to having her needs met and to reclaim her painful feelings. She further had important new experiences of adaptive anger, grief, and compassion that helped transform her shame and led to the development of a sense of worth and a new narrative of no longer being glued to her husband and of forgiving her parents.

These sessions illustrate the quintessential aspects of the emotional change process. It involves repeatedly intensifying the forces that make her feel small and hopeless to evoke the painful core maladaptive feelings of sad loneliness and core fear of rejection, and doing this for a number of rounds. It has been shown that emotional processing in successful therapies occurs in this type of two-steps-forward, one-step-back fashion (A. Pascual-Leone, 2009; A. Pascual-Leone & Greenberg, 2007). It is a fluid, dynamic process in which maladaptive emotional states are transformed over time by experiencing a greater degree of adaptive emotional states more often and for longer amounts of time. In this view, an individual may still experience their core emotional pain, but the emotional pain occurs less often, is processed more rapidly, and continues to develop over time.

Note also that therapy for Gisella involved a process of both changing to be where she is and not trying to be where she is not. Gisella had to truly arrive at where she was before she could leave. Then, out of the depth of her painful maladaptive emotions of sadness, shame, and fear came the organismic will to survive based on the need to be accepted, supported, loved, and valued. It is also important to note that experiential change involves having a new experience, not only a new understanding, and that psychodramatic enactments engage the client in a form of doing, not of knowing. Feeling the anger and asserting it is a form of doing and thus is important in laying down new neural pathways.

Over the therapy, the client moved away from having secondary, undifferentiated emotions of global distress as her predominant emotion and gradually experienced a larger range of feelings, the most important of which was assertive anger. She was able to stand up to, and let go of, self-critical beliefs that she was responsible and had to support her husband; she accepted that she was not responsible for his behavior. Gisella also was able to tolerate and process her underlying primary maladaptive emotions of sadness of loneliness, fear of rejection, feeling unloved, and shame. She showed greater differentiation of emotional states over the course of therapy and an overall greater degree of in-session resolution of the client's core emotional pain. Reaching assertive anger led to a strengthened sense of self, and the client's reflection on these emotional states allowed her to create new meaning.

There were two main change processes. One was accessing her anger that had been interrupted, leading to an assertion of needs. This example highlights how accessing interrupted anger is an important process that undid years of suppression—this is the process of arriving at and accepting her previously disowned adaptive anger and the needs implicit in it. The second process was one of changing emotion with emotion (Greenberg, 2021). Her newly experienced assertive anger, sadness of grief, and compassion helped her undo her core maladaptive sadness, fear, and shame. Reclaiming her unmet needs led to adaptive protective/assertive anger and compassion for herself. She also grieved for the pain of having never had that need met, and this sadness was expressed from a position of sad reflection rather than hopelessness. She ended in a state of acceptance.

13 ANGER AND SHAME, FOR BETTER OR FOR WORSE

A man who has not passed through the inferno of his passions has never overcome them.

—Carl Jung

Shame and anger both are highly painful emotions and are the source of much distress. Often, therapists and clients alike find these emotions difficult to face in therapy, shame because it seems so consuming and self-destroying and anger because it is so frightening because of its potential destructiveness. These emotions underlie many disorders, and working on changing these emotions offers specific mechanisms of change for some of the underlying determinants of the disorders. For example, working on the underlying shame and anger that substance abuse is being used to regulate gives one direct access to the cause of the problem rather than just managing the problematic behavior. Similarly, with disorders such as anxiety and depression, it is far better to treat the underlying unexpressed anger and the underlying shame than only to provide coping skills.

---

https://doi.org/10.1037/0000393-013
Shame and Anger in Psychotherapy, by L. S. Greenberg
Copyright © 2024 by the American Psychological Association. All rights reserved.

These two major emotions are difficult to deal with in therapy because they are connected and need to be worked on in conjunction with each other. Therefore, a good understanding of each emotion, and how each helps or hinders the other, is needed. Because shame and anger have adaptive as well as maladaptive forms, effective intervention depends on the type of shame and/or anger being experienced and the sequence in which they occur. The therapist needs to make process diagnoses of what each emotion is conveying on each occasion of its in-session occurrence and how each emotion is related to the other.

Another aspect therapists need to keep in mind in working with these two highly socially relevant emotions is the way culture, race, and gender affects their experience and expression. The empathic process at the base of the emotion-focused approach in which clients are treated as experts on their own experience, avoids imposing a singular cultural interpretation on clients' emotional experience. In addition, it is always important to be informed about each person's views on shame and anger from their cultural and subcultural perspectives.

Importantly, this book is about the therapeutic value of activating shame and anger *in therapy,* not on how to manage emotion *in the world* and not that it is good to increase the expression of these emotions in everyday life. The unbridled expression of anger in interpersonal situations is not being proposed, nor is the venting of anger in public. Rather, the experience and expression of previously unacknowledged or disowned anger from past injuries is therapeutic. The purpose of activating shame in therapy is not to make clients feel worse about themselves but to make the shame amenable to transformation. The therapist's goal is to provide a way of transforming the shame by acknowledging and experiencing it viscerally, in the safety of the therapeutic situation, to make it amenable to transformation, based on the principle that one needs to arrive at a place before one can leave it. It is generally expected that outside of therapy, and because of therapy, clients will feel less maladaptive shame and less secondary reactive anger.

At a societal level, Flanagan (2022) proposed that North Americans should embrace shame as a uniquely socializing emotion, one that can promote moral progress where undisciplined anger does not. He made a case, based on recent political events mainly but not exclusively in the United States, for the need to turn down anger and turn up shame. He described how anger based on revenge or payback, which has become so prevalent in North America, is a highly destructive form of social action because it passes hurt on to others. He called for an increase in certain forms of social shame, the kind that protects positive values including humility, kindness, and honesty. He suggested that we should embrace (primary adaptive) shame as a uniquely socializing emotion, one that can promote moral progress, and eschew undisciplined (secondary reactive) anger, which promotes moral deterioration. Society suffers from too much explosive anger and too little modesty and embarrassment about personal behavior and desires, and so what is needed at the societal level is greater valuing of shame and a greater rejection of rage. But again, the increase in anger and in maladaptive shame that is proposed in this book refers to change processes in therapy, not to behavior in the world.

The main objective of this book is to show that anger and shame have both adaptive and maladaptive forms and that therapy often involves working with both of them because they are intimately related. Knowing when to regulate and when to activate shame and anger is also important. Generally, the primary emotion needs to be activated, and secondary emotions need to be regulated. Emotion-focused therapy offers ways of working directly with underlying emotions by providing a safe empathic relationship in which these emotions can be accessed, faced head-on, regulated when necessary, and ultimately transformed so that clients no longer have to struggle to manage them. Transformation means that the anger and shame are not merely managed once activated; rather, they are no longer activated.

Throughout the book, I have emphasized that although coping skills are useful, transformation should be the ultimate goal of effective therapy. Deliberate behavioral and cognitive forms of regulation—more left-hemispheric processes—are useful for people when they feel out of control. When shame or anger are overwhelming, calming and soothing the self and having a safe place to go in imagination can help to counteract these feelings. Another strategy for change proposed by methods inspired by cognitive behavior therapy is reappraisal (J. S. Beck, 2011). However, these strategies are temporary coping skills that don't penetrate to amygdala-based emotional reactivity. Rather, for enduring change, people need to build implicit or automatic capacities for affect transformation and regulation that help to prevent automatic amygdala-based processes from being activated. Direct experience with aroused emotion transformed by synthesis—by changing emotion with emotion—is what is needed.

The two major change processes I have discussed in this book are (a) accessing core maladaptive shame and transforming it with adaptive anger and (b) accessing blocked anger by overcoming its interruption, often caused by shame. Other processes, such as regulating both shame and anger when they are too overwhelming and exploring maladaptive anger to get to its origins, are also important but not as central as transforming maladaptive shame and accessing interrupted anger. I have described how clients often can experience and express intense anger and rage when their self-esteem is threatened, and this anger protects them against feeling the excruciating underlying feelings of shame. In these situations, the secondary anger needs to be explored or bypassed in therapy to get to the underlying shame so that the painful shame can be processed therapeutically. On the other hand, newly re-owned assertive primary anger can be a healthy antidote to primary shame. Healthy assertive anger often needs to be accessed in therapy as an antidote to the shame of worthlessness because it can help to transform shame's tendency to withdraw into self-assertion and confidence. In summary, anger can be an unhelpful secondary reactive emotion to underlying shame, or it can help people change submissive shame into confidence and self-worth.

The importance of accessing previously unacknowledged, interrupted anger is the other key change process. Clients block their assertive anger, often with shame, and then react by withdrawing reactions because they feel that assertive anger would violate or has violated a norm. This secondary shame suppresses or makes people feel bad about being angry. Therapists, therefore, need to help clients access their interrupted anger. Finally, and possibly surprisingly, shame can be a healthy antidote to unwarranted anger and can help transform blaming or defensive anger into apologetic forgiveness seeking. In this situation, shame provides submissive approach tendencies that can be conciliatory and relationally reparative.

With the current move in the field away from a disorder-based differential treatment approach and toward a process-oriented view of treatment based on knowledge of mechanisms of change (Greenberg, 1986; S. C. Hayes & Hofmann, 2018; S. C. Hayes et al., 2020; Rice & Greenberg, 1984), knowing how to work to transform shame and anger as processes, independent of disorder, will be most useful. A process-based approach leads therapists to ask what the dysfunctional processes at the base of the client's problem are and then to intervene to change these processes. Therapists thus develop a case formulation for this person and intervene based on knowledge of mechanisms of change. Therapy involves the transdiagnostic application of change processes in all types of people, regardless of presenting problems or disorders. Shame and anger, and their interrelationship, underlie many types of client problems regardless of diagnostic classification, and often the disavowal of these two emotions is at the root of much dysfunction.

I hope the offerings in these chapters have helped highlight the crucial role shame and anger and their interaction play in therapeutic change. Further, and importantly, the methods presented will help therapists work more effectively with shame and anger and their interaction.

References

Abbass, A. (2015). *Reaching through resistance: Advanced psychotherapy techniques*. Seven Leaves Press.

Akhavan, S. (2001). Comorbidity of hopelessness depression with borderline and dependent personality disorders: Inferential, coping, and anger expression styles as vulnerability factors. *Dissertation Abstracts International: B. The Sciences and Engineering, 61*(12-B), 6694.

Alexander, F., & French, T. M. (1946). *Psychoanalytic therapy: Principles and application*. Ronald Press.

Angus, L. E., & Greenberg, L. S. (2011). *Working with narrative in emotion-focused therapy: Changing stories, healing lives*. American Psychological Association. https://doi.org/10.1037/12325-000

Archer, J. (2004). Sex differences in aggression in real-world settings: A meta-analytic review. *Review of General Psychology, 8*(4), 291–322. https://psycnet.apa.org/doi/10.1037/1089-2680.8.4.291

Aristotle. (1926). *The "art" of rhetoric* (J. H. Freese, Trans.). Heinemann. (Original work published ca. 350 B.C.E.)

Aristotle. (2009). *The Nicomachean ethics* (D. Ross, Trans.; L. Brown, Ed.). Oxford University Press. (Original work published ca. 350 B.C.E.)

Auszra, L., Greenberg, L., & Herrmann, I. (2013). Client emotional productivity—Optimal client in-session emotional processing in experiential therapy. *Psychotherapy Research, 23*(6), 732–746.

Averill, J. R. (1983). Studies on anger and aggression: Implications for theories of emotion. *American Psychologist, 38*(11), 1145–1160. https://doi.org/10.1037/0003-066X.38.11.1145

Barlow, D. H. (1988). *Anxiety and its disorders: The nature and treatment of anxiety and panic*. Guilford Press.

Beauboeuf-Lafontant, T. (2007). "You have to show strength": An exploration of gender, race, and depression. *Gender & Society, 21*(1), 28–51. https://doi.org/10.1177/0891243206294108

Beck, A. T., Ward, C. H., Mendelson, M., Mock, J., & Erbauch, J. (1961). *Beck Depression Inventory (BDI)* [Database record]. APA PsycTests. https://doi.org/10.1037/t00741-000

Beck, J. S. (2011). *Cognitive behavior therapy: Basics and beyond* (2nd ed.). Guilford Press.

Bedford, O. (2004). The individual experience of guilt and shame in Chinese culture. *Culture and Psychology, 10*(1), 29–52. https://doi.org/10.1177/1354067X04040929

Berkowitz, L. (1990). On the formation and regulation of anger and aggression. A cognitive-neoassociationistic analysis. *American Psychologist, 45*(4), 494–503. https://doi.org/10.1037/0003-066X.45.4.494

Beutler, L. E., Daldrup, R., Engle, D., Guest, P., Corbishley, A., & Meredith, K. E. (1988). Family dynamics and emotional expression among patients with chronic pain and depression. *Pain, 32*(1), 65–72. https://doi.org/10.1016/0304-3959(88)90024-3

Beutler, L. E., Engle, D., Mohr, D., Daldrup, R. J., Bergan, J., Meredith, K., & Merry, W. (1991). Predictors of differential response to cognitive, experiential, and self-directed psychotherapeutic procedures. *Journal of Consulting and Clinical Psychology, 59*(2), 333–340. https://doi.org/10.1037/0022-006X.59.2.333

Bishop, S. R., Lau, M., Shapiro, S., Carlson, L., Anderson, N. D., Carmody, J., Segal, Z. V., Abbey, S., Speca, M., Velting, D., & Devins, G. (2004). Mindfulness: A proposed operational definition. *Clinical Psychology: Science and Practice, 11*(3), 230–241. https://doi.org/10.1093/clipsy.bph077

Bohart, A. C. (1980). Toward a cognitive theory of catharsis. *Psychotherapy: Theory, Research, & Practice, 17*(2), 192–201. https://doi.org/10.1037/h0085911

Bohart, A. C., & Greenberg, L. S. (1997). *Empathy reconsidered: New directions in theory research & practice*. American Psychological Association.

Bowlby, J. (1982). Attachment and loss: Retrospect and prospect. *American Journal of Orthopsychiatry, 52*(4), 664–678. https://doi.org/10.1111/j.1939-0025.1982.tb01456.x

Bowlby, J. (1988). *A secure base: Parent–child attachment and healthy human development*. Basic Books.

Bradshaw, J. (1988). *Healing the shame that binds you*. Health Communications Inc.

Brewin, C. R. (2001). Memory processes in post-traumatic stress disorder. *International Review of Psychiatry, 13*(3), 159–163. https://doi.org/10.1080/09540260120074019

Bridewell, W. B., & Chang, E. C. (1997). Distinguishing between anxiety, depression, and hostility: Relations to anger-in, anger-out, and anger control. *Personality and Individual Differences, 22*(4), 587–590. https://doi.org/10.1016/S0191-8869(96)00224-3

Bridges, M. R. (2006). Activating the corrective emotional experience. *Journal of Clinical Psychology, 62*(5), 551–568. https://doi.org/10.1002/jclp.20248

Brody, C. L., Haaga, D. A. F., Kirk, L., & Solomon, A. (1999). Experiences of anger in people who have recovered from depression and never-depressed people. *Journal of Nervous and Mental Disease, 187*(7), 400–405. https://doi.org/10.1097/00005053-199907000-00002

Brown, B. (2012). *Daring greatly: How the courage to be vulnerable transforms the way we live, love, parent, and lead.* Gotham.

Budiarto, Y., & Helmi, A. F. (2021). Shame and self-esteem: A meta-analysis. *Europe's Journal of Psychology, 17*(2), 131–145. https://doi.org/10.5964/ejop.2115

Bushman, B. (2002). Does venting anger feed or extinguish the flame? Catharsis, rumination, distraction, anger, and aggressive responding. *Personality and Social Psychology Bulletin, 28,* 724–731.

Buss, A. H., & Durkee, A. (1957). An inventory for assessing different kinds of hostility. *Journal of Consulting Psychology, 21*(4), 343–349. https://doi.org/10.1037/h0046900

Carter, R. T., & Forsyth, J. (2010). Reactions to racial discrimination: Emotional stress and help-seeking behaviors. *Psychological Trauma: Theory, Research, Practice, and Policy, 2*(3), 183–191. https://doi.org/10.1037/a0020102

Castonguay, L., & Hill, C. (Eds.). (2012). *Transformation in psychotherapy: Corrective experiences across cognitive behavioral, humanistic, and psychodynamic approaches.* American Psychological Association. https://doi.org/10.1037/13747-000

Chemaly, S. (2018). *Rage becomes her: The power of women's anger.* Simon & Schuster.

Chou, T., Asnaani, A., & Hofmann, S. G. (2012). Perception of racial discrimination and psychopathology across three U.S. ethnic minority groups. *Cultural Diversity & Ethnic Minority Psychology, 18*(1), 74–81. https://doi.org/10.1037/a0025432

Compas, B. E., Jaser, S. S., Bettis, A. H., Watson, K. H., Gruhn, M. A., Dunbar, J. P., Williams, E., & Thigpen, J. C. (2017). Coping, emotion regulation, and psychopathology in childhood and adolescence: A meta-analysis and narrative review. *Psychological Bulletin, 143*(9), 939–991. https://doi.org/10.1037/bul0000110

Consedine, N. S., Magai, C., & Bonanno, G. A. (2002). Moderators of the emotion inhibition–health relationship: A review and research agenda. *Review of General Psychology, 6*(2), 204–228. https://doi.org/10.1037/1089-2680.6.2.204

Cooley, C. H. (1902). *Human nature and the social order.* Scribner.

Cox, D. L., Stabb, S. D., & Bruckner, K. H. (1999). *Women's anger: Clinical and developmental perspectives.* Brunner-Mazel.

Cozolino, L. J. (2002). *The neuroscience of psychotherapy: Building and rebuilding the human brain.* W. W. Norton & Co.

Craske, M. G., Treanor, M., Conway, C. C., Zbozinek, T., & Vervliet, B. (2014). Maximizing exposure therapy: An inhibitory learning approach. *Behaviour Research and Therapy, 58,* 10–23. https://doi.org/10.1016/j.brat.2014.04.006

Dalai Lama. (1995). *The power of compassion: A collection of lectures by His Holiness the XIV Dalai Lama* (T. Jinpa, Trans.). Thorsons.

Dalgleish, T., Yiend, J., Schweizer, S., & Dunn, B. D. (2009). Ironic effects of emotion suppression when recounting distressing memories. *Emotion, 9*(5), 744–749. https://doi.org/10.1037/a0017290

Damasio, A. R. (1999). *The feeling of what happens: Body and emotion in the making of consciousness*. Harcourt Brace.

Darwin, C. (1872). *The expression of emotion in man and animals*. John Murray. https://doi.org/10.1037/10001-000

Davidson, R. (2000). Affective style, mood, and anxiety disorders: An affective neuroscience approach. In R. Davidson (Ed.), *Anxiety, depression, and emotion* (pp. 88–108). Oxford University Press. https://doi.org/10.1093/acprof:oso/9780195133585.003.0005

Dearing, R. L., & Tangney, J. P. (Eds.). (2011). *Shame in the therapy hour*. American Psychological Association. https://doi.org/10.1037/12326-000

Deffenbacher, J. L. (2011). Cognitive-behavioral conceptualization and treatment of anger. *Cognitive and Behavioral Practice, 18*(2), 212–221.

De la Fuente, V., Freudenthal, R., & Romano, A. (2011). Reconsolidation or extinction: Transcription factor switch in the determination of memory course after retrieval. *The Journal of Neuroscience, 31*(15), 5562–5573.

DeYoung, C. G. (2015). Cybernetic Big Five Theory. *Journal of Research in Personality, 56*, 33–58. https://doi.org/10.1016/j.jrp.2014.07.004

DeYoung, P. (2022). *Understanding and treating chronic shame: Healing right brain relational trauma*. Routledge.

Dickerson, S. S., & Kemeny, M. E. (2004). Acute stressors and cortisol responses: A theoretical integration and synthesis of laboratory research. *Psychological Bulletin, 130*(3), 355–391. https://doi.org/10.1037/0033-2909.130.3.355

Ekman, P. (2003). *Emotions revealed*. Holt Paperbacks. https://doi.org/10.1080/02699939208411068

Elliott, R., Watson, J. C., Goldman, R. N., & Greenberg, L. S. (2004). *Learning emotion-focused therapy: The process-experiential approach to change*. American Psychological Association. https://doi.org/10.1037/10725-000

Fava, M., Anderson, K., & Rosenbaum, J. F. (1990). "Anger attacks": Possible variants of panic and major depressive disorders. *The American Journal of Psychiatry, 147*(7), 867–870. https://doi.org/10.1176/ajp.147.7.867

Fernandez, E. (2010). Toward an integrative psychotherapy for maladaptive anger. In M. Potegal, G. Stemmler, & C. Spielberger (Eds.), *The international handbook of anger: Constituent and concomitant biological, psychological, and social processes* (pp. 499–513). Springer. https://doi.org/10.1007/978-0-387-89676-2_28

Fernandez, E. (Ed.). (2013). *Treatments for anger in specific populations: Theory, application, and outcome*. Oxford University Press. https://doi.org/10.1093/med:psych/9780199914661.001.0001

Fernandez, E., & Johnson, S. L. (2016). Anger in psychological disorders: Prevalence, presentation, etiology and prognostic implications. *Clinical Psychology Review, 46*, 124–135. https://doi.org/10.1016/j.cpr.2016.04.012

Fernandez, E., & Malley-Morrison, K. (2013). Gender-inclusive and gender-informed treatment of anger. In E. Fernandez (Ed.), *Treatments for anger in specific populations: Theory, application, and outcome* (pp. 213–235). Oxford University Press. https://doi.org/10.1093/med:psych/9780199914661.003.0012

Fernandez, E., & Scott, S. (2009). Anger treatment in chemically-dependent inpatients: Evaluation of phase effects and gender. *Behavioural and Cognitive Psychotherapy, 37*(4), 431–447. https://doi.org/10.1017/S1352465809990075

Fernandez, E., Vargas, R., & Garza, C. (2010, May). *Five parameters for mapping the angry person: Results from a community sample* [Paper presentation]. Association for Psychological Science 22nd Annual Convention, Boston, MA, United States.

Flanagan, O. (2022). *How to do things with emotions: The morality of anger and shame across cultures.* Princeton University Press.

Fonagy, P., Gergely, G., Jurist, E. L., & Target, M. (2002). *Affect regulation, mentalization, and the development of the self.* Other Press.

Fonagy, P., & Target, M. (2005). Mentalization and the Changing Aims of Child Psychoanalysis (1998). In L. Aron & A. Harris (Eds.), *Relational psychoanalysis: Innovation and expansion* (Vol. 2, pp. 253–278). Analytic Press.

Forgas, J. P. (1995). Mood and judgment: The affect infusion model (AIM). *Psychological Bulletin, 117*(1), 39–66. https://doi.org/10.1037/0033-2909.117.1.39

Forgas, J. P., & Bower, G. H. (1987). Mood effects on person-perception judgments. *Journal of Personality and Social Psychology, 53*(1), 53–60. https://doi.org/10.1037/0022-3514.53.1.53

Forgas, J. P., & Locke, J. (2005). Affective influences on causal inferences: The effects of mood on attributions for positive and negative interpersonal episodes. *Cognition and Emotion, 19*(7), 1071–1081. https://doi.org/10.1080/02699930541000093

Fosha, D. (2000). *The transforming power of affect: A model for accelerated change.* Basic Book.

Fredrickson, B. L., Mancuso, R. A., Branigan, C., & Tugade, M. M. (2000). The undoing effect of positive emotions. *Motivation and Emotion, 24*(4), 237–258. https://doi.org/10.1023/A:1010796329158

Freud, S. (1923). *The ego and the id.* W. W. Norton & Co.

Frijda, N. H. (1986). *The emotions.* Cambridge University Press.

Frijda, N. H. (1988). The laws of emotion. *American Psychologist, 43*(5), 349–358. https://doi.org/10.1037/0003-066X.43.5.349

Geller, S. M., & Greenberg, L. S. (2002). Therapeutic presence: Therapists' experience of presence in the psychotherapy encounter in psychotherapy. *Person-Centered and Experiential Psychotherapies, 1*, 71–86. https://doi.org/10.1080/14779757.2002.9688279

Geller, S. M., & Greenberg, L. S. (2012). *Therapeutic presence: A mindful approach to effective therapy.* American Psychological Association. https://doi.org/10.1037/13485-000

Geller, S. M., & Greenberg, L. S. (2023). *Therapeutic presence: A mindful approach to effective therapy* (2nd ed.). American Psychological Association. https://doi.org/10.1037/0000315-000

Geller, S. M., Greenberg, L. S., & Watson, J. C. (2010). Therapist and client perceptions of therapeutic presence: The development of a measure. *Psychotherapy Research*, *20*(5), 599–610. https://doi.org/10.1080/10503307.2010.495957

Gendlin, E. T. (1981). *Focusing*. Bantam.

Germer, C. K., & Neff, K. D. (2013). Self-compassion in clinical practice. *Journal of Clinical Psychology*, *69*(8), 856–867. https://doi.org/10.1002/jclp.22021

Gilbert, P. (2006). A biopsychosocial and evolutionary approach to formulation with a special focus on shame. In N. Tarrier (Ed.), *Case formulation in cognitive behaviour therapy: The treatment of challenging and complex cases* (pp. 81–112). Routledge/Taylor & Francis Group.

Gilbert, P., & Andrews, B. (Eds.). (1998). *Shame: Interpersonal behavior, psychopathology, and culture*. Oxford University Press.

Gilbert, P., & Gilbert, J. (2003). Entrapment and arrested fight and flight in depression: An exploration using focus groups. *Psychology and Psychotherapy: Theory, Research and Practice*, *76*(2), 173–188. https://doi.org/10.1348/147608303765951203

Goldin, P. R., Jazaieri, H., & Gross, J. J. (2014). Emotion regulation in social anxiety disorder. In S. G. Hofmann & P. M. DiBartolo (Eds.), *Social anxiety: Clinical, developmental, and social perspectives* (3rd ed., pp. 511–529). Elsevier.

Goldman, R. N., & Fox-Zurawic, A. (2012, July). *Self-soothing in emotion-focused therapy: Findings from a task analysis* [Paper presentation]. Tenth annual conference of the World Association for Person Centered and Experiential Psychotherapy & Counseling, Antwerp.

Goldman, R. N., & Greenberg, L. S. (2015). *Case formulation in emotion-focused therapy: Co-creating clinical maps for change*. American Psychological Association. https://doi.org/10.1037/14523-000

Goss, K., & Allan, S. (2009). Shame, pride and eating disorders. *Clinical Psychology & Psychotherapy*, *16*(4), 303–316. https://doi.org/10.1002/cpp.627

Greenberg, L. S. (1979). Resolving splits: Use of the two chair technique. *Psychotherapy: Theory, Research, & Practice*, *16*(3), 316–324. https://doi.org/10.1037/h0085895

Greenberg, L. S. (1984). A task analysis of intrapersonal conflict resolution. In L. N. Rice & L. S. Greenberg (Eds.), *Patterns of change: Intensive analysis of psychotherapy process* (pp. 67–123). Guilford Press.

Greenberg, L. S. (1986). Change process research. *Journal of Consulting and Clinical Psychology*, *54*(1), 4–9. https://doi.org/10.1037/0022-006X.54.1.4

Greenberg, L. S. (2002). *Emotion-focused therapy: Coaching clients to work through their feelings*. American Psychological Association. https://doi.org/10.1037/10447-000

Greenberg, L. S. (2007). A guide to conducting a task analysis of psychotherapeutic change. *Psychotherapy Research*, *17*(1), 15–30. https://doi.org/10.1080/10503300600720390

Greenberg, L. S. (2011). *Emotion-focused therapy*. American Psychological Association.

Greenberg, L. S. (2012). Emotions, the great captains of our lives: Their role in the process of change in psychotherapy. *American Psychologist, 67*(8), 697–707. https://doi.org/10.1037/a0029858

Greenberg, L. S. (2015). *Emotion-focused therapy: Coaching clients to work through their feelings* (2nd ed.). American Psychological Association. https://psycnet.apa.org/doi/10.1037/14692-000

Greenberg, L. S. (2021). *Changing emotion with emotion: A practitioner's guide*. American Psychological Association. https://doi.org/10.1037/0000248-000

Greenberg, L. S., & Angus, L. E. (2004). The contributions of emotion processes to narrative change in psychotherapy: A dialectical constructivist approach. In L. E. Angus & J. McLeod (Eds.), *The handbook of narrative psychotherapy* (pp. 331–349). Sage Publications. https://doi.org/10.4135/9781412973496.d25

Greenberg, L. S., & Bolger, E. (2001). An emotion-focused approach to the over-regulation of emotion and emotional pain. *Journal of Clinical Psychology, 57*(2), 197–211. https://doi.org/10.1002/1097-4679(200102)57:2<197::AID-JCLP6>3.0.CO;2-O

Greenberg, L. S., & Foerster, F. S. (1996). Task analysis exemplified: The process of resolving unfinished business. *Journal of Consulting and Clinical Psychology, 64*(3), 439–446. https://doi.org/10.1037/0022-006X.64.3.439

Greenberg, L. S., Ford, C. L., Alden, L. S., & Johnson, S. M. (1993). In-session change in emotionally focused therapy. *Journal of Consulting and Clinical Psychology, 61*(1), 78–84. https://doi.org/10.1037/0022-006X.61.1.78

Greenberg, L. S., & Goldman, R. N. (2008). *Emotion-focused couples therapy: The dynamics of emotion, love, and power*. American Psychological Association. https://doi.org/10.1037/11750-000

Greenberg, L. S., & Iwakabe, S. (2011). Emotion-focused therapy and shame. In R. L. Dearing & J. P. Tangney (Eds.), *Shame in the therapy hour* (pp. 69–90). American Psychological Association. https://doi.org/10.1037/12326-003

Greenberg, L. S., & Malcolm, W. (2002). Resolving unfinished business: Relating process to outcome. *Journal of Consulting and Clinical Psychology, 70*(2), 406–416. https://doi.org/10.1037/0022-006X.70.2.406

Greenberg, L. S., & Paivio, S. C. (1997). *Working with emotions in psychotherapy*. Guilford Press.

Greenberg, L. S., & Pascual-Leone, J. (1995). A dialectical constructivist approach to experiential change. In R. A. Neimeyer & M. J. Mahoney (Eds.), *Constructivism in psychotherapy* (pp. 169–191). American Psychological Association.

Greenberg, L. S., & Pascual-Leone, J. (1997). Emotion in the creation of personal meaning. In M. J. Power & C. R. Brewin (Eds.), *Transformation of meaning in psychological therapies: Integrating theory and practice* (pp. 157–173). Wiley.

Greenberg, L. S., Rice, L. N., & Elliott, R. K. (1993). *Facilitating emotional change: The moment-by-moment process*. Guilford Press.

Greenberg, L. S., & Safran, J. D. (1987). *Emotion in psychotherapy: Affect, cognition, and the process of change.* Guilford Press.

Greenberg, L. S., & Safran, J. D. (1989). Emotion in psychotherapy. *American Psychologist, 44*(1), 19–29. https://doi.org/10.1037/0003-066X.44.1.19

Greenberg, L. S., & Watson, J. C. (1998). Experiential therapy of depression: Differential effects of client-centered relationship conditions and process experiential interventions. *Psychotherapy Research, 8*(2), 210–224.

Greenberg, L. S., & Watson, J. C. (2006). *Emotion-focused therapy for depression.* American Psychological Association. https://doi.org/10.1037/11286-000

Greenberg, L. S., & Webster, M. C. (1982). Resolving decisional conflict by Gestalt two-chair dialogue: Relating process to outcome. *Journal of Counseling Psychology, 29*(5), 468–477. https://doi.org/10.1037/0022-0167.29.5.468

Greenberg, L. S., & Woldarsky Meneses, C. (2019). *Forgiveness and letting go in emotion-focused therapy.* American Psychological Association.

Gross, J. J. (2001). Emotion regulation in adulthood: Timing is everything. *Current Directions in Psychological Science, 10*(6), 214–219. https://doi.org/10.1111/1467-8721.00152

Gross, J. J. (2013). Emotion regulation: Taking stock and moving forward. *Emotion, 13*(3), 359–365. https://doi.org/10.1037/a0032135

Gross, J. J., & John, O. P. (2003). Individual differences in two emotion regulation processes: Implications for affect, relationships, and well-being. *Journal of Personality and Social Psychology, 85*(2), 348–362. https://doi.org/10.1037/0022-3514.85.2.348

Gross, J. J., & Levenson, R. W. (1997). Hiding feelings: The acute effects of inhibiting negative and positive emotion. *Journal of Abnormal Psychology, 106*(1), 95–103. https://doi.org/10.1037/0021-843X.106.1.95

Ha, F. I. (1995). Shame in Asian and Western cultures. *American Behavioral Scientist, 38*(8), 1114–1131. https://doi.org/10.1177/0002764295038008007

Hariri, A. R., Bookheimer, S. Y., & Mazziotta, J. C. (2000). Modulating emotional responses: Effects of a neocortical network on the limbic system. *Neuroreport, 11*(1), 43–48. https://doi.org/10.1097/00001756-200001170-00009

Harmon-Jones, E., Abramson, L. Y., Sigelman, J., Bohlig, A., Hogan, M. E., & Harmon-Jones, C. (2002). Proneness to hypomania/mania symptoms or depression symptoms and asymmetrical frontal cortical responses to an anger-evoking event. *Journal of Personality and Social Psychology, 82*(4), 610–618.

Harmon-Jones, E., Lueck, L., Fearn, M., & Harmon-Jones, C. (2006). The effect of personal relevance and approach-related action expectation on relative left frontal cortical activity. *Psychological Science, 17*(5), 434–440. https://doi.org/10.1111/j.1467-9280.2006.01724.x

Harmon-Jones, E., Peterson, C., Gable, P. A., & Harmon-Jones, C. (2008). Anger and approach-avoidance motivation. In A. J. Elliot (Ed.), *Handbook of approach and avoidance motivation* (pp. 399–413). Psychology Press.

Harper, F. W. K., & Arias, I. (2004). The role of shame in predicting adult anger and depressive symptoms among victims of child psychological maltreatment.

Journal of Family Violence, 19(6), 359–367. https://doi.org/10.1007/s10896-004-0681-x

Hatch, H., & Forgays, D. K. (2001). A comparison of older adolescent and adult females' responses to anger-provoking situations. *Adolescence, 36*(143), 557–570.

Hayes, J. A., & Vinca, M. (2017). Therapist presence, absence, and extraordinary presence. In L. G. Castonguay & C. E. Hill (Eds.), *How and why are some therapists better than others?: Understanding therapist effects* (pp. 85–99). American Psychological Association. https://doi.org/10.1037/0000034-006

Hayes, S. C., & Hofmann, S. G. (Eds.). (2018). *Process-based CBT: The science and core clinical competencies of cognitive behavioral therapy*. New Harbinger Publications, Inc.

Hayes, S. C., Hofmann, S. G., & Ciarrochi, J. (2020). A process-based approach to psychological diagnosis and treatment: The conceptual and treatment utility of an extended evolutionary meta model. *Clinical Psychology Review, 82*, Article 101908. https://doi.org/10.1016/j.cpr.2020.101908

Hebb, D. (1949). *The organization of behavior*. Wiley.

Herrmann, I. R., Greenberg, L. S., & Auszra, L. (2016). Emotion categories and patterns of change in experiential therapy for depression. *Psychotherapy Research, 26*(2), 178–195. https://doi.org/10.1080/10503307.2014.958597

Högberg, G., Nardo, D., Hällström, T., & Pagani, M. (2011). Affective psychotherapy in post-traumatic reactions guided by affective neuroscience: Memory reconsolidation and play. *Psychology Research and Behavior Management, 4*, 87–96. https://doi.org/10.2147/PRBM.S10380

Hoglund, C. L., & Nicholas, K. B. (1995). Shame, guilt, and anger in college students exposed to abusive family environments. *Journal of Family Violence, 10*(2), 141–157. https://doi.org/10.1007/BF02110597

Holowaty, K. A. M., & Paivio, S. C. (2012). Characteristics of client-identified helpful events in emotion-focused therapy for child abuse trauma. *Psychotherapy Research, 22*(1), 56–66. https://doi.org/10.1080/10503307.2011.622727

Hume, D. (1882). *A treatise on human nature* (T. H. Green & T. H. Grose, Eds.). Longmans, Green & Co.

Inda, M. C., Muravieva, E. V., & Alberini, C. M. (2011). Memory retrieval and the passage of time: From reconsolidation and strengthening to extinction. *The Journal of Neuroscience, 31*(5), 1635–1643. https://doi.org/10.1523/JNEUROSCI.4736-10.2011

Izard, C. E. (1971). *The face of emotion*. Appleton-Century-Crofts.

Izard, C. E. (1977). *Human emotions*. Plenum.

Izard, C. E. (1990). Facial expressions and the regulation of emotions. *Journal of Personality and Social Psychology, 58*(3), 487–498. https://doi.org/10.1037/0022-3514.58.3.487

Izard, C. E. (1993). Four systems for emotion activation: Cognitive and noncognitive processes. *Psychological Review, 100*(1), 68–90. https://doi.org/10.1037/0033-295X.100.1.68

Jack, D. C. (1991). *Silencing the self: Women and depression*. Harvard University Press.

James, W. (1890). *The principles of psychology* (Vol. 1). Henry Holt and Co.

Julle-Danière, E., Whitehouse, J., Mielke, A., Vrij, A., Gustafsson, E., Micheletta, J., & Waller, B. M. (2020). Are there non-verbal signals of guilt? *PLOS One*, *15*(4), Article e0231756. https://doi.org/10.1371/journal.pone.0231756

Jurist, E. (2018). *Minding emotions: Cultivating mentalization in psychotherapy*. Guilford Press.

Kannan, D., Henretty, J., Piazza-Bonin, E., Levitt, H., Coleman, R., Bickerest-Townsend, M., & Mathews, S. (2011). The resolution of anger in psychotherapy: A task analysis. *The Humanistic Psychologist*, *39*(2), 169–181. https://doi.org/10.1080/08873267.2011.563724

Kassinove, H., & Tafrate, R. C. (2002). *Anger management: The complete treatment guide for practitioners*. Impact.

Kaufman, G. (1996). *The psychology of shame: Theory and treatment of shame-based syndromes* (2nd ed.). Springer Publishing Co.

Kelly, A. C., Carter, J. C., Zuroff, D. C., & Borairi, S. (2013). Self-compassion and fear of self-compassion interact to predict response to eating disorders treatment: A preliminary investigation. *Psychotherapy Research*, *23*(3), 252–264. https://doi.org/10.1080/10503307.2012.717310

Kiecolt-Glaser, J. K., McGuire, L., Robles, T. F., & Glaser, R. (2002). Emotions, morbidity, and mortality: New perspectives from psychoneuroimmunology. *Annual Review of Psychology*, *53*(1), 83–107. https://doi.org/10.1146/annurev.psych.53.100901.135217

Kim, S., Thibodeau, R., & Jorgensen, R. S. (2011). Shame, guilt, and depressive symptoms: A meta-analytic review. *Psychological Bulletin*, *137*(1), 68–96. https://doi.org/10.1037/a0021466

Kircanski, K., Lieberman, M. D., & Craske, M. G. (2012). Feelings into words: Contributions of language to exposure therapy. *Psychological Science*, *23*(10), 1086–1091. https://doi.org/10.1177/0956797612443830

Kitayama, S., Markus, H. R., & Matsumoto, H. (1995). Culture, self, and emotion: A cultural perspective on "self-conscious" emotions. In J. P. Tangney & K. W. Fischer (Eds.), *Self-conscious emotions: The psychology of shame, guilt, embarrassment, and pride* (pp. 439–464). Guilford Press.

Klein, M. H., Mathieu, P., Gendlin, E., & Kiesler, D. J. (1986). *The Experiencing Scale: A research and training manual* (Vol. 1). Madison, University of Wisconsin Extension Bureau of Audiovisual Instruction, 1969.

Kohut, H. (1977). *The restoration of the self*. University of Chicago Press.

Kolts, R., Bell, T., Bennett-Levy, J., & Irons, C. (2018). *Experiencing compassion-focused therapy from the inside out: A self-practice/self-reflection workbook for therapists*. Guilford Press.

Kramer, U., Pascual-Leone, A., Berthoud, L., de Roten, Y., Marquet, P., Kolly, S., Despland, J. N., & Page, D. (2016). Assertive anger mediates effects of dialectical behaviour-informed skills training for borderline personality disorder:

A randomized controlled trial. *Clinical Psychology & Psychotherapy, 23*(3), 189–202. https://doi.org/10.1002/cpp.1956

Kramer, U., Pascual-Leone, A., Rohde, K. B., & Sachse, R. (2018). The role of shame and self-compassion in psychotherapy for narcissistic personality disorder: An exploratory study. *Clinical Psychology & Psychotherapy, 25*(2), 272–282. https://doi.org/10.1002/cpp.2160

Kring, A. M. (2000). Gender and anger. In A. H. Fischer (Ed.), *Gender and emotion: Social psychological perspectives* (pp. 211–231). Cambridge University Press. https://doi.org/10.1017/CBO9780511628191.011

Kuhn, T. S. (1962). *The structure of scientific revolutions*. University of Chicago Press.

Lane, R. D., Ryan, L., Nadel, L., & Greenberg, L. (2015). Memory reconsolidation, emotional arousal, and the process of change in psychotherapy: New insights from brain science. *Behavioral and Brain Sciences, 38*, Article e1. https://doi.org/10.1017/S0140525X14000041

Lawrence, P., & Rozmus, C. (2001). Culturally sensitive care of the Muslim patient. *Journal of Transcultural Nursing, 12*, 228–233.

Leach, C. W., & Cidam, A. (2015). When is shame linked to constructive approach orientation? A meta-analysis. *Journal of Personality and Social Psychology, 109*(6), 983–1002. https://doi.org/10.1037/pspa0000037

LeDoux, J. (1996). *The emotional brain: The mysterious underpinnings of emotional life*. Simon & Schuster.

LeDoux, J. (2003). The emotional brain, fear, and the amygdala. *Cellular and Molecular Neurobiology, 23*, 727–738. https://doi.org/10.1023/A:1025048802629

Leventhal, H. (1979). A perceptual-motor processing model of emotion. In P. Pliner, K. Blankenstein, & I. M. Spigel (Eds.), *Perception of emotion in self and others* (Vol. 5, pp. 1–36). Plenum. https://doi.org/10.1007/978-1-4684-3548-1_1

Levinas, E. (1969). *Totality and infinity*. Duquesne University Press.

Lewis, H. B. (1971a). *Shame and guilt in neurosis*. International Universities Press.

Lewis, H. B. (1971b). Shame and guilt in neurosis. *Psychoanalytic Review, 58*(3), 419–438.

Lewis, H. B. (1987). The role of shame in depression over the life span. In H. B. Lewis (Ed.), *The role of shame in symptom formation* (pp. 29–50). Lawrence Erlbaum Associates, Inc.

Lewis, M. (2008). Self-conscious emotions: Embarrassment, pride, shame, and guilt. In M. Lewis, J. M. Haviland-Jones, & L. F. Barrett (Eds.), *Handbook of emotions* (pp. 742–756). Guilford Press.

Lieberman, M. D., Eisenberger, N. I., Crockett, M. J., Tom, S. M., Pfeifer, J. H., & Way, B. M. (2007). Putting feelings into words: Affect labeling disrupts amygdala activity in response to affective stimuli. *Psychological Science, 18*(5), 421–428. https://doi.org/10.1111/j.1467-9280.2007.01916.x

Lindsay-Hartz, J., de Rivera, J., & Mascolo, M. F. (1995). Differentiating guilt and shame and their effects on motivation. In J. P. Tangney & K. W. Fischer (Eds.), *Self-conscious emotions: The psychology of shame, guilt, embarrassment, and pride* (pp. 274–300). Guilford Press.

Linehan, M. M. (1993). *Cognitive-behavioral treatment of borderline personality disorder.* Guilford Press.

Linehan, M. M., Bohus, M., & Lynch, T. R. (2007). Dialectical behavior therapy for pervasive emotion dysregulation: Theoretical and practical underpinnings. In J. J. Gross (Ed.), *Handbook of emotion regulation* (pp. 581–605). Guilford Press.

Loader, P. (1998). Such a shame—A consideration of shame and shaming mechanisms in families. *Child Abuse Review, 7*(1), 44–57. https://doi.org/10.1002/(SICI)1099-0852(199801/02)7:1<44::AID-CAR334>3.0.CO;2-7

Mackay, H. C., Barkham, M., Stiles, W. B., & Goldfried, M. R. (2002). Patterns of client emotion in helpful sessions of cognitive-behavioral and psychodynamic-interpersonal therapy. *Journal of Counseling Psychology, 49*(3), 376–380. https://doi.org/10.1037/0022-0167.49.3.376

Mallinckrodt, B. (2010). The psychotherapy relationship as attachment: Evidence and implications. *Journal of Social and Personal Relationships, 27*(2), 262–270. https://doi.org/10.1177/0265407509360905

Maren, S. (2011). Seeking a spotless mind: Extinction, deconsolidation, and erasure of fear memory. *Neuron, 70*(5), 830–845. https://doi.org/10.1016/j.neuron.2011.04.023

Markus, H., & Kitayama, S. (1991). Culture and the self: Implications for cognition, emotion, and motivation. *Psychological Review, 98*(2), 224–253. https://doi.org/10.1037/0033-295X.98.2.224

Martens, W. H. J. (2005). Shame and narcissism: Conflicting dimensions of pride, self-esteem and pathological vulnerability. *Annals of the American Psychotherapy Association, 8*(2), 10–17.

Masters, R. A. (1999). *Until the fire is but light: An interdisciplinary psychospiritual investigation of anger* (UMI No.9934606) [Doctoral dissertation, Saybrook University]. Dissertation Abstracts International 60(5-B).

Matsumoto, D., Hee Yoo, S., & Chung, J. (2010). The expression of anger across culture. In M. Potegal, G. Stemmler, & C. Spielberger (Eds.), *International handbook of anger: Constituent and concomitant biological, psychological, and social problems* (pp. 125–137). Springer.

Mauss, I. B., Butler, E. A., Roberts, N. A., & Chu, A. (2010). Emotion control values and responding to an anger provocation in Asian-American and European-American individuals. *Cognition and Emotion, 24*(6), 1026–1043. https://doi.org/10.1080/02699930903122273

Mayne, T. J. (1999). Negative affect and health: The importance of being earnest. *Cognition and Emotion, 13*(5), 601–635. https://doi.org/10.1080/026999399379203

McGilchrist, I. (2009). *The master and his emissary: The divided brain and the making of the western world.* Yale University Press.

Miller, R. S. (1997). Inattentive and contented: Relationship commitment and attention to alternatives. *Journal of Personality and Social Psychology, 73*(4), 758–766. https://doi.org/10.1037/0022-3514.73.4.758

Miller, S. (2021). *Changing emotion with emotion: A change process in depressed clients with shame* [Unpublished doctoral dissertation]. York University.

Mohr, D. C., Shoham-Salomon, V., Engle, D., & Beutler, L. E. (1991). The expression of anger in psychotherapy for depression: Its role and measurement. *Psychotherapy Research, 1*(2), 124–134. https://doi.org/10.1080/10503309 112331335551

Morrison, A. P. (1989). *Shame: The underside of narcissism*. Analytic Press.

Moscovitch, M. (2009). Consciousness and memory in amnesia. In W. P. Banks (Ed.), *Encyclopedia of consciousness* (pp. 183–192). Academic Press.

Moscovitch, M., & Nadel, L. (1999). Multiple-trace theory and semantic dementia: Response to K. S. Graham (1999). *Trends in Cognitive Sciences, 3*(3), 87–89. https://doi.org/10.1016/S1364-6613(99)01290-5

Nadel, L., & Bohbot, V. (2001). Consolidation of memory. *Hippocampus, 11*(1), 56–60. https://doi.org/10.1002/1098-1063(2001)11:1<56::AID-HIPO1020>3.0.CO;2-O

Nader, K., Schafe, G. E., & Le Doux, J. E. (2000). Fear memories require protein synthesis in the amygdala for reconsolidation after retrieval. *Nature, 406*(6797), 722–726. https://doi.org/10.1038/35021052

Nagel, E., Bromberger, S., & Grunbaum, A. (1973). *Observation and theory in science*. Johns Hopkins University Press.

Nathanson, D. L. (1994). *Shame and pride: Affect, Sex, and the Birth of the Self*. W. W. Norton & Co.

Neff, K. (2011). *Self-compassion: The proven power of being kind to yourself*. William Morrow.

Neimeyer, R. A., & Mahoney, M. J. (Eds.). (1995). *Constructivism in psychotherapy*. American Psychological Association. https://doi.org/10.1037/10170-000

Novaco, R. W. (1975). *Anger control: The development and evaluation of an experimental treatment*. Lexington.

Oatley, K. (1992). *Best laid schemes: The psychology of the emotions*. Cambridge University Press.

Ochsner, K. N., Bunge, S. A., Gross, J. J., & Gabrieli, J. D. (2002). Rethinking feelings: An FMRI study of the cognitive regulation of emotion. *Journal of Cognitive Neuroscience, 14*(8), 1215–1229. https://doi.org/10.1162/089892902760807212

Olatunji, B. O., Lohr, J. M., & Bushman, B. J. (2007). The pseudopsychology of venting in the treatment of anger: Implications and alternatives for mental health practice. In T. A. Cavell & K. T. Malcolm (Eds.), *Anger, aggression, and interventions for interpersonal violence* (pp. 119–141). Lawrence Erlbaum Associates.

Paivio, S. C. (1999). Experiential conceptualization and treatment of anger. *Journal of Clinical Psychology, 55*(3), 311–324. https://doi.org/10.1002/(SICI)1097-4679(199903)55:3<311::AID-JCLP4>3.0.CO;2-Y

Paivio, S. C. (2013). Essential processes in emotion-focused therapy. *Psychotherapy, 50*(3), 341–345. https://doi.org/10.1037/a0032810

Paivio, S. C., & Greenberg, L. S. (1995). Resolving "unfinished business": Efficacy of experiential therapy using empty-chair dialogue. *Journal of Consulting and Clinical Psychology, 63*(3), 419–425. https://doi.org/10.1037/0022-006X.63.3.419

Paivio, S. C., Hall, I. E., Holowaty, K. A. M., Jellis, J. B., & Tran, N. (2001). Imaginal confrontation for resolving child abuse issues. *Psychotherapy Research, 11*(4), 433–453. https://doi.org/10.1093/ptr/11.4.433

Paivio, S. C., & Pascual-Leone, A. (2010). *Emotion-focused therapy for complex trauma: An integrative approach.* American Psychological Association. https://doi.org/10.1037/12077-000

Panksepp, J. (2008). The affective brain and core consciousness: How does neural activity generate emotional feelings? In M. Lewis, J. M. Haviland-Jones, & L. F. Barrett (Eds.), *Handbook of emotions* (pp. 47–67). Guilford Press.

Pascual-Leone, A. (2009). Dynamic emotional processing in experiential therapy: Two steps forward, one step back. *Journal of Consulting and Clinical Psychology, 77*(1), 113–126. https://doi.org/10.1037/a0014488

Pascual-Leone, A., Gilles, P., Singh, T., & Andreescu, C. A. (2013). Problem anger in psychotherapy: An emotion-focused perspective on hate, rage, and rejecting anger. *Journal of Contemporary Psychotherapy, 43*(2), 83–92. https://doi.org/10.1007/s10879-012-9214-8

Pascual-Leone, A., & Greenberg, L. S. (2007). Emotional processing in experiential therapy: Why "the only way out is through." *Journal of Consulting and Clinical Psychology, 75*(6), 875–887. https://doi.org/10.1037/0022-006X.75.6.875

Pascual-Leone, A., & Paivio, S. C. (2013). Emotion-focused therapy for anger in complex trauma. In E. Fernandez (Ed.), *Treatments for anger in specific populations: Theory, application, and outcome* (pp. 33–51). Oxford University Press.

Pascual-Leone, J. (1990). An essay on wisdom: Toward organismic processes that make it possible. In R. J. Sternberg (Ed.), *Wisdom: Its nature, origins, and development* (pp. 244–278). Cambridge University Press. https://doi.org/10.1017/CBO9781139173704.013

Pascual-Leone, J., & Johnson, J. M. (2021). *The working mind: Meaning and mental attention in human development.* The MIT Press. https://doi.org/10.7551/mitpress/13474.001.0001

Pennebaker, J. W. (Ed.). (1995). *Emotion, disclosure, and health.* American Psychological Association. https://doi.org/10.1037/10182-000

Pennebaker, J. W. (1997). Writing about emotional experiences as a therapeutic process. *Psychological Science, 8*(3), 162–166. https://doi.org/10.1111/j.1467-9280.1997.tb00403.x

Pennebaker, J. W., & Francis, M. E. (1996). Cognitive, emotional, and language processes in disclosure. *Cognition and Emotion, 10*(6), 601–626. https://doi.org/10.1080/026999396380079

Perls, F. S., Hefferline, R. F., & Goodman, P. (1951). *Gestalt therapy.* Julian Press.

Phelps, E. A., & LeDoux, J. E. (2005). Contributions of the amygdala to emotion processing: From animal models to human behavior. *Neuron, 48*(2), 175–187. https://doi.org/10.1016/j.neuron.2005.09.025

Pittman, C. T. (2011). Getting mad but ending up sad: The mental health consequences for African Americans using anger to cope with racism. *Journal of Black Studies, 42*(7), 1106–1124. https://doi.org/10.1177/0021934711401737

Plaks, J. E., Robinson, J. S., & Forbes, R. (2022). Anger and sadness as moral signals. *Social Psychological & Personality Science, 13*(2), 362–371. https://doi.org/10.1177/19485506211025909

Plutchik, R. (1962). *The emotions: Facts, theories and a new model.* Crown Publishing Group/Random House.

Plutchik, R. (2000). *Emotions in the practice of psychotherapy: Clinical implications of affect theories.* American Psychological Association. https://doi.org/10.1037/10366-000

Porges, S. W. (2007). The polyvagal perspective. *Biological Psychology, 74*(2), 116–143. https://doi.org/10.1016/j.biopsycho.2006.06.009

Porges, S. W. (Ed.). (2011). *The polyvagal theory: Neurophysiological foundations of emotions, attachment, communication, and self-regulation.* W. W. Norton & Co.

Pos, A., Geller, S., & Oghene, J. (2011, June 29–July 2). *Therapist presence, empathy, and the working alliance in experiential treatment for depression* [Paper presentation]. Meeting of the Society for Psychotherapy Research, Bern, Switzerland.

Potter-Efron, R. (2011). *Healing the angry brain: How understanding the way your brain works can help you control anger and aggression.* New Harbinger Publications.

Pulakos, J. (1996). Family environment and shame: Is there a relationship? *Journal of Clinical Psychology, 52*(6), 617–623. https://doi.org/10.1002/(SICI)1097-4679(199611)52:6<617::AID-JCLP3>3.0.CO;2-H

Ralston, M. B. (2006). *Imaginal confrontation versus evocative empathy in emotion-focused trauma therapy* [Unpublished doctoral dissertation]. University of Windsor.

Ramirez, J. M., Santisteban, C., Fujihara, T., & Van Goozen, S. (2002). Differences between experience of anger and readiness to angry action: A study of Japanese and Spanish students. *Aggressive Behavior, 28*, 429–438. https://doi.org/10.1002/ab.80014

Retzinger, S. M. (1995). Identifying shame and anger in discourse. *American Behavioral Scientist, 38*(8), 1104–1113. https://doi.org/10.1177/0002764295038008006

Rice, L. N., & Greenberg, L. S. (Eds.). (1984). *Patterns of change: Intensive analysis of psychotherapy process.* Guilford Press.

Ritter, K., Vater, A., Rüsch, N., Schröder-Abé, M., Schütz, A., Fydrich, T., Lammers, C. H., & Roepke, S. (2014). Shame in patients with narcissistic personality disorder. *Psychiatry Research, 215*(2), 429–437. https://doi.org/10.1016/j.psychres.2013.11.019

Rizvi, S. L., & Linehan, M. M. (2005). The treatment of maladaptive shame in borderline personality disorder: A pilot study of "opposite action." *Cognitive and Behavioral Practice, 12*(4), 437–447. https://doi.org/10.1016/S1077-7229(05)80071-9

Rogers, C. R. (1959). A theory of therapy, personality and interpersonal relationships, as developed in the client-centered framework. In S. Koch (Ed.), *Psychology: A study of a science* (Vol. 3, pp. 184–256). McGraw Hill.

Ross, C. E., & Van Willigen, M. (1996). Gender, parenthood, and anger. *Journal of Marriage and Family, 58*(3), 572–584. https://doi.org/10.2307/353718

Rubin, Z. (1970). Measurement of romantic love. *Journal of Personality and Social Psychology, 16*(2), 265–273. https://doi.org/10.1037/h0029841

Scheff, T. J., & Retzinger, S. M. (1991). *Emotions and violence: Shame and rage in destructive conflicts*. Lexington Books/D. C. Heath and Com.

Schopenhauer, A. (1969). *The world as will and representation*. Dover Pub.

Schore, A. N. (2003). *Affect dysregulation & disorders of the self*. W. W. Norton & Co.

Shahar, B., Doron, G., & Szepsenwol, O. (2015). Childhood maltreatment, shame-proneness and self-criticism in social anxiety disorder: A sequential mediational model. *Clinical Psychology & Psychotherapy, 22*(6), 570–579. https://doi.org/10.1002/cpp.1918

Sharkin, B. S. (1993). Anger and gender: Theory, research, and implications. *Journal of Counseling and Development, 71*(4), 386–389. https://doi.org/10.1002/j.1556-6676.1993.tb02653.x

Shore, A. N. (2003). *Affect regulation and the repair of the self*. W. W. Norton & Co.

Short, D. (2001). Mandatory counseling: Helping those who do not want to be helped. In B. B. Geary & J. K. Zeig (Eds.), *The handbook of Ericksonian psychotherapy* (pp. 333–351). The Milton H. Erickson Foundation Press.

Sicoli, L. A. (2005). *Development and verification of a model of resolving hopelessness in process-experiential therapy of depression* [Unpublished doctoral dissertation]. York University.

Siegman, A. W., & Snow, S. C. (1997). The outward expression of anger, the inward experience of anger and CVR: The role of vocal expression. *Journal of Behavioral Medicine, 20*(1), 29–45. https://doi.org/10.1023/A:1025535129121

Smart Richman, L., & Leary, M. R. (2009). Reactions to discrimination, stigmatization, ostracism, and other forms of interpersonal rejection: A multimotive model. *Psychological Review, 116*(2), 365–383. https://doi.org/10.1037/a0015250

Snell, W. E., Gum, S., Shuck, R. L., Mosley, J. A., & Kite, T. L. (1995). The Clinical Anger Scale: Preliminary reliability and validity. *Journal of Clinical Psychology, 51*(2), 215–226. https://doi.org/10.1002/1097-4679(199503)51:2<215::AID-JCLP2270510211>3.0.CO;2-Z

Spielberger, C. D., Reheiser, E. C., & Sydeman, S. J. (1995). Measuring the experience, expression, and control of anger. *Issues in Comprehensive Pediatric Nursing, 18*(3), 207–232. https://doi.org/10.3109/01460869509087271

Spinoza, B. (1967). *Ethics (Part IV)*. Hafner Publishing Company. (Original work published 1677)

Stern, D. N. (1985). *The interpersonal world of the infant: A view from psychoanalysis and developmental psychology*. Basic Books.

Tangney, J. P., & Dearing, R. L. (2002). *Shame and guilt*. Guilford Press. https://doi.org/10.4135/9781412950664.n388

Tangney, J. P., Miller, R. S., Flicker, L., & Barlow, D. H. (1996). Are shame, guilt, and embarrassment distinct emotions? *Journal of Personality and Social Psychology, 70*(6), 1256–1269. https://doi.org/10.1037/0022-3514.70.6.1256

Tangney, J. P., Wagner, P. E., Hill-Barlow, D., Marschall, D. E., & Gramzow, R. (1996). Relation of shame and guilt to constructive versus destructive responses to anger across the lifespan. *Journal of Personality and Social Psychology, 70*(4), 797–809. https://doi.org/10.1037/0022-3514.70.4.797

Tarba, L. R. (2015). *Relating a model of resolution of arrested anger to outcome in emotion-focused therapy of depression* [Unpublished doctoral dissertation]. York University.

Tarba, L. R. (2007). *A task analysis of the expression of arrested anger in the resolution of depression in emotion-focused therapy* [Unpublished master's thesis]. York University.

Tausch, N., & Becker, J. C. (2013). Emotional reactions to success and failure of collective action as predictors of future action intentions: A longitudinal investigation in the context of student protests in Germany. *British Journal of Social Psychology, 52*(3), 525–542. https://doi.org/10.1111/j.2044-8309.2012.02109.x

Terrizzi, J. A., Jr., & Shook, N. J. (2020). On the origin of shame: Does shame emerge from an evolved disease-avoidance architecture? *Frontiers in Behavioral Neuroscience, 14*, Article 19. https://doi.org/10.3389/fnbeh.2020.00019

The Canadian Oxford Dictionary. (1998). *The Canadian Oxford dictionary*. Oxford University Press.

Thomas, S. A., & González-Prendes, A. A. (2009). Powerlessness, anger, and stress in African American women: Implications for physical and emotional health. *Health Care for Women International, 30*(1–2), 93–113. https://doi.org/10.1080/07399330802523709

Thomas, S. P. (1989). Gender differences in anger expression: Health implications. *Research in Nursing & Health, 12*(6), 389–398. https://doi.org/10.1002/nur.4770120609

Thompkins, T. (2004). *The real lives of strong Black women: Transcending myths, reclaiming joy*. Agate Publishing.

Tignor, S. M., & Colvin, C. R. (2017). The interpersonal adaptiveness of dispositional guilt and shame: A meta-analytic investigation. *Journal of Personality, 85*(3), 341–363. https://doi.org/10.1111/jopy.12244

Timulak, L., & Keogh, D. (2022). *Transdiagnostic emotion-focused therapy: A clinical guide for transforming emotional pain*. American Psychological Association. https://doi.org/10.1037/0000253-000

Tompkins, S. S. (1963). *Affect, imagery, consciousness: II. The negative affects*. Springer.

Tompkins, S. S. (1987). Shame. In D. L. Nathanson (Ed.), *The many faces of shame* (pp. 133–161). Guilford Press.

Toohey, M. J. (2021). Cognitive behavioral therapy for anger management. In A. Wenzel (Ed.), *Handbook of cognitive behavioral therapy: Applications* (pp. 331–359). American Psychological Association. https://doi.org/10.1037/0000219-010

Traister, R. (2019). *Good and mad: The revolutionary power of women's anger.* Simon & Schuster.

Tregoubov, V. I. (2006). *Resolving clinical depression by accessing arrested anger* [Unpublished thesis]. York University.

Troop, N. A., Allan, S., Serpell, L., & Treasure, J. L. (2008). Shame in women with a history of eating disorders. *European Eating Disorders Review, 16*(6), 480–488. https://doi.org/10.1002/erv.858

Tugade, M. M., & Fredrickson, B. L. (2004). Resilient individuals use positive emotions to bounce back from negative emotional experiences. *Journal of Personality and Social Psychology, 86*(2), 320–333. https://doi.org/10.1037/0022-3514.86.2.320

Van Velsor, P., & Cox, D. L. (2001). Anger as a vehicle in the treatment of women who are sexual abuse survivors: Reattributing responsibility and accessing personal power. *Professional Psychology, Research and Practice, 32*(6), 618–625. https://doi.org/10.1037/0735-7028.32.6.618

Velotti, P., Elison, J., & Garofalo, C. (2014). Shame and aggression: Different trajectories and implications. *Aggression and Violent Behavior, 19*(4), 454–461.

Vrij, A. (2018). Nonverbal detection of deception. In H. Otgaar & M. L. Howe (Eds.), *Finding the truth in the courtroom: Dealing with deception, lies, and memories* (pp. 163–185). Oxford University Press.

Watson, J. C. (2021). Responsiveness in emotion-focused therapy. In J. C. Watson & H. Wiseman (Eds.), *The responsive psychotherapist: Attuning to clients in the moment* (pp. 171–194). American Psychological Association. https://doi.org/10.1037/0000240-009

Watson, J. C., & Greenberg, L. S. (2017). *Emotion-focused therapy for generalized anxiety.* American Psychological Association.

Webb, M., Heisler, D., Call, S., Chickering, S. A., & Colburn, T. A. (2007). Shame, guilt, symptoms of depression, and reported history of psychological maltreatment. *Child Abuse & Neglect, 31*(11–12), 1143–1153. https://doi.org/10.1016/j.chiabu.2007.09.003

Weiss, J., Sampson, H., & the Mt Zion Psychotherapy Research Group. (1986). *The psychoanalytic process: Theory, clinical observations, and empirical research.* Guilford Press.

Whelton, W. J., & Greenberg, L. S. (2005). Emotion in self-criticism. *Personality and Individual Differences, 38*(7), 1583–1595. https://doi.org/10.1016/j.paid.2004.09.024

Wille, R. (2014). The shame of existing: An extreme form of shame. *The International Journal of Psycho-Analysis, 95*(4), 695–717. https://doi.org/10.1111/1745-8315.12208

Wingfield, A. H. (2010). Are some emotions marked "Whites only"? Racialized feeling rules in professional workplaces. *Social Problems, 57*(2), 251–268. https://doi.org/10.1525/sp.2010.57.2.251

Woldarsky Meneses, C., & Greenberg, L. S. (2011). The construction of a model of the process of couples' forgiveness in emotion-focused therapy for couples. *Journal of Marital and Family Therapy, 37*(4), 491–502. https://doi.org/10.1111/j.1752-0606.2011.00234.x

Woldarsky Meneses, C., & Greenberg, L. S. (2014). Interpersonal forgiveness in emotion-focused couples' therapy: Relating process to outcome. *Journal of Marital and Family Therapy, 40*(1), 49–67. https://doi.org/10.1111/j.1752-0606.2012.00330.x

Wolfgang, L. E. (1998). *Relationship between childhood sexual abuse in women, internalized shame, and attachments to peers, mother, and father* [Unpublished doctoral dissertation]. New Mexico State University.

Index

A

Abandonment, 172, 195, 213–214
Abuse, 43, 113, 124, 195, 234
Abused clients, 46–47
Abuse memories, 108–111, 118, 123–124, 128–130
Acceptance, 59, 72, 90, 110, 197
Achievement, 18, 36
Acting out, 85, 196
Action tendencies, 25–27, 35, 37, 48
Adaptive anger, 104–105, 107, 117, 173, 188
Adaptive emotions, 24, 26, 103
Adaptive guilt, 35
Adaptive needs, 109–111
Adaptive shame, 35–37
Adjustment disorder, 168
Affect, 21
Affective-cognitive networks. *See* Emotion schemes
Affective schemes, 19
Affect regulation, 82–83
Affect theory, 18
Affirmation, 55, 58, 64
Agency, client's awareness of, 121
Aggression, 39, 44, 85
Alcohol use, 85, 89
Alternative perspectives, 205–206, 211–212
Amygdalas, 17, 22, 69, 158, 231, 233, 285
Angelou, Maya, 183
Anger. *See also specific headings, e.g.:* Assertive anger
  activation of, 188
  appropriate target of, 189
  awareness of, 169–170, 239
  control of, 159, 237
  and culture, 177–180
  destructive vs. empowering, 160
  downregulation of, 228–230
  emotional experience of, 102
  expressions of, 54, 169–170, 184
  externalization of, 159
  fusions of sadness and, 208, 223
  and gender, 176–177
  gradual expression of, 193
  healthy, 162, 171, 173
  healthy expression of, 169, 173–175, 188–190
  hot vs. cold, 160
  inhibition of, 158
  intensity of, 169, 177, 190
  internalization of, 159
  markers of, 235–236
  markers of resolution of, 204–205
  overview of, 8–9, 160–163
  problems with, 168–169
  rational control of, 190–191
  recognition of interruption of, 190–191
  in relationships, 169
  research on, 172–176
  resolution of, 198–201, 204–205, 235
  suppression of, 9, 159, 172–173
  types of, 163–168
  unacknowledged, 184
  uncontrolled, 89
  unresolved, 171–172

307

"Anger in, anger out, and anger control," 159
Anger management, 39, 171–172
Animals, 36
Annoyance, 160
Anticipation, errors of, 21
Antisocial personality disorder, 44
Anxiety, 38, 48, 110, 159, 209, 245–281, 283
  shame-, 38, 47, 49, 110, 115, 120, 123, 184
  social, 11, 44
Anxiety disorders, 44
Apple, Fiona, 81
Archer, J., 177
Aristotle, 83, 163
Arousal
  emotional, 25
  organismic, 21
Arrested anger, 158–159
Arriving at shame, 57–80
  case examples, 75–80
  facilitating acknowledgment of shame, 67–68
  facilitating approaching and revealing shame, 68–75
  provision of a corrective emotional experience, 64–67
  provision of a safe relationship, 58–64
  relational validation, 58
Ashamed-shaming interaction patterns, 74
Asian Americans, 180
Assertive anger, 103, 113, 162, 210, 252, 286
Assertive expression, of interpersonal needs, 195
Assertiveness, 158, 205, 223
Assessment, emotion, 167
Attachment bonds, 41
Attachment injuries, 213
Attachment motives, 18
Attachment relationships, 89
Attachment ruptures, 197
Attachment shame, 67–68
Attentional regulation, 84
Attunement, empathic, 60–61, 72, 90, 114, 185–186, 250
Automatic internal processes, 90, 191
Averill, J. R., 177
Avoidance, 48, 74, 85, 218–219, 221

B

Balance, emotional, 83
Beck Depression Inventory (BDI), 111
Behavioral analysis, 229
Behavioral experiences, 94
Behavioral extinction, 26
Behavioral regulation, 84
Beliefs, 17, 219–220
Bereavement, 113
Betrayal of spouse/partner, 12, 45–46, 161
Beutler, L. E., 175
Binge drinking, 89
Binge eating, 89
Bipolar disorders, 168
Bitterness, 204
Black Americans, 11–12, 178–180
Blake, William, 157
Blame, 123, 174, 191, 204, 234. *See also* Self-blame
Blaming anger, 208–210, 223
Blaming the victim, 39
Blocking anger, 184
Blocking shame, 48–49
Blood pressure, 159
Bodily expressions, 87
Bodily sensations, 87
Body language, 33, 38, 124
Body shame, 51
Body tension, 191
Borderline personality disorder, 44
"Bottle-up-blow-up syndrome," 173
Boundaries, 157, 159, 164, 172, 190, 195, 196, 276
Brain
  amygdalas, 17, 22, 69, 158, 231, 233, 285
  emotional, 23, 104
  left hemisphere of, 83, 99, 230, 285
  limbic system, 69
  midbrain, 85
  neural pathways, 22, 24, 125, 242
  prefrontal cortex, 85
  processes of, 125, 242
  right hemisphere of, 83, 89, 90
Breathing, 83–85, 88, 231–232, 239
Bridewell, W. B., 159
Brody, C. L., 174
Brown, B., 56, 57
Buddha, 92, 203

C

Calming, 86
Carter, R. T., 178
CBT. *See* Cognitive behavioral therapy
CEMS (Coding System for Emotional Processing of Maladaptive Shame), 111
Chair dialogues, 93, 103, 118, 175, 197, 218–219
  empty-chair, 120, 123–125, 195–196, 278
  two-chair, 120–123, 191–193, 269, 272–273
Chang, E. C., 159
Changing the topic, 190
Chemaly, S., 158
Child, universal, 98
Child abuse, 174. *See also* Abuse memories
Childhood, lost, 197, 251
Childhood experiences, 174
Child self, 95–96, 98
Choice, 86
Circulatory disease, 179
Clarifying the threat and owning emotions (stage in change of anger), 236
Class, 47
Clemens, Samuel, 227
Client-centered therapy, 90, 185
Client fragility, 71, 73, 89, 91, 193
Coding narrative processes, 246
Coding System for Emotional Processing of Maladaptive Shame (CEMS), 111
Cognition, 16, 90, 125, 192
Cognitive behavioral therapy (CBT), 230, 232, 235–237, 285
Cognitive change, 105
Cognitive experiences, 94
Cognitive regulation, 84
Collectivist cultures, 53–54
Common humanity, 92
Community, 53
Compassion, 90, 103, 125, 197
Complaint, 115, 123, 191, 204, 208
Compulsive sex, 85
Conceptual-level information, 19
Confidence, 51, 286
Conflict resolution, 174
Confrontation, avoidance of, 218–219
Connecting guilt, 68
Connecting with others, 65, 72, 88

Conscious thought, 16
Consequences, 229
Contempt, 33, 85, 161
Contentment, 54
Control precedence, 231
Cooley, C. H., 36
Coping, 84, 89
Coping, failure to, 38, 45
Coping self-soothing, 93
Coping skills, 283, 285
Core anger, 164
Core emotion schemes, 66
Core maladaptive shame, 42, 50, 111, 123
Core primary maladaptive shame self-organizations, 42
Core shame, 41, 47–48, 64, 105
Corrective emotional experiences, 24, 64–68, 186
Cox, D. L., 174
Criticism, 38, 204, 209
Cues, 19–21
Culture, 177–180, 284

D

Dalai Lama, 92
Damasio, A. R., 16
Darwin, C. R., 27, 36–37
DBT (dialectical behavior therapy), 174, 229
Defensiveness, 222
Depression, 43–44, 48, 111–112, 158–159, 172–173, 176, 178, 191, 204, 209, 283
Depression (case example), 142–155, 245–281
Deservingness, 23, 26, 104, 105, 110, 184, 194, 252. *See also* Entitlement
Dialectical behavior therapy (DBT), 174, 229
Dialectical constructivism, 22
Diaphragmatic breathing, 84, 239
Dickens, Charles, 101
Disgust, 33, 37, 161
Disintegration, 89
Dismissal (case example), 135–139
Dissatisfaction, 208
Distaste, 33
Distraction, 84, 88, 232
Distress, 110
Distress tolerance, 84

Divorce, 113, 172
Domestic violence, 166
Dorsal vagal shutdown, 85
Doubt, 222
Downregulation of anger, 228–230
Dysregulated anger. *See* Nonadaptive anger
Dysregulation, emotional, 84

E

Eating disorders, 44, 51
Effecting component, of emotion schemes, 20
EFT. *See* Emotion-focused therapy
Embarrassment, 31, 33–34, 83
Emotion(s). *See also specific headings, e.g.:* Guilt
  coactivation of, 27
  cognition vs., 16
  core maladaptive, 29
  instrumental, 7–8
  intensity of, 165, 172, 194, 228–229
  and motivation, 18
  negative, 172–173
  positive, 84
  primary adaptive, 6–7, 29, 109–112, 184
  primary maladaptive, 6–7
  regulation of, 82–88, 188, 228–232
  secondary, 6–7
  secondary reactive, 29
  types of, 5–6
Emotion, nature and function of, 15–30
  changing emotion with emotion, 22–28
  cognition vs., 16
  emotion schemes, 18–21
  and language, 17–18
  and motivation, 18
  routes to emotional change, 28–29
  self-organizations, 21–22
Emotional arousal, 25
Emotional balance, 83
Emotional brain, 23, 104
Emotional dysregulation, 84
Emotional experiences, new. *See* New emotional experiences
Emotional memories, 26
Emotional neglect, 204
Emotional states, transition of, 66
Emotion assessment, 167
Emotion-focused theory, 19

Emotion-focused therapy (EFT), 21–23, 25, 36, 56, 103, 107–108, 122, 163, 166, 174, 185, 233, 235–237, 285
Emotion-Focused Therapy (Greenberg), 198
Emotion generation, 82
Emotion-schematic memories, 19, 42
Emotion schemes, 18–21, 24
Emotion system, 22
Empathic attunement, 60–61, 72, 90, 114, 185–186, 250
Empathic conjecture, 69–70
Empathic exploration, 194
Empathic understanding, 61, 106, 216–218
Empathy, 56, 65, 90, 187
Empowered anger, 23, 25, 184
Empowerment, 170, 204, 276
Entitlement, 107, 170, 204–205, 209, 268. *See also* Deservingness
Evasion of responsibility, 39
Evolution, 31
Exhalations, 85
Expectancies, 21
Experiences, emotional, 94
Experiencing scale, 90
Experiential focusing, 194
Experiential homework, 196
Experiential therapies, 185
Explicit regulation of emotion/affect, 83
Exploration of the anger marker (stage in change of anger), 236
Exploring options (stage in change of anger), 237
Expression of Black anger (case example), 11–12
Expressive methods, 104
External mode, of narrative coding, 246
External shame, 44
Extinction, 25, 26
Eye contact, 61, 125

F

Facial expressions, 63, 87, 191
Facilitative needs, 110, 111
Failure to cope, 38, 45
Family conflict, 43
Fear, 37, 58, 123, 192, 193, 219–220
Feminism, 56, 158, 235
Fight or flight response, 158
Flanagan, O., 284
Focusing therapy, 90

Fonagy, P., 90
Forgiveness, 46, 216–218
Forsyth, J., 178
Fragile clients, 71, 73, 89, 91, 193
Franklin, Benjamin, 3
Frustration, 161
Fury, 160

G

Gadsby, Hannah, 3
Gambling (case example), 245–281
Gender, 47, 176–177, 284
Gestalt therapy, 185
Gilbert, J., 158
Gilbert, P., 158
Global distress, 115
Goals for future, 205
Going blank, 190
Greenberg, L. S., 198
Grief, 197, 213. *See also* Sadness, of grief
Guilt, 31, 34–35, 47, 68, 117

H

Habituation, 25, 26
Hair-trigger temper, 164–165
Hatred, 160, 161
Headaches, 159
Healing memories, 174
Heartfelt compassion, 96
Heartfelt needs, 104, 110–112, 116, 122, 205, 210, 262–263, 266
Heart rate, 83, 84, 160
Hebb, D., 27
Helplessness, 110, 114, 115, 173, 191
Hiding, 87–88
Historical context, client's, 65
Holowaty, K. A. M., 174
Homework, 196
Honor cultures, 165
Hopelessness, 110, 115, 159, 173, 191, 204, 218–219, 221–222
Hope optimism, 205
Hostile aggression, 39
Hume, D., 16
Humiliation, 34, 41, 50, 54, 62, 107, 172

I

Identity-based achievements, 18
Identity invalidation, 213

Identity shame, 67–68
Identity violations, 197
Imagery, 87, 194
Imaginal confrontations, 106, 117, 123–124
Imaginal re-entry, into shaming scenes, 103
Immigrant clients, 53
Implicit affect regulation, 89–92
Implicit anger, 208
Implicit regulation of emotion/affect, 83
Inadequacy, 25
Indigenous people, 180
Indignation, 160
Infants, 18
Inhibitory learning, 25
Instrumental anger, 167, 188
Instrumental emotions, 7–8
Instrumental shame, 40
Integrating change (stage in change of anger), 237
Intellectualizing, 118, 190
Interdependent cultures, 53–54
Interest, 105
Intermittent explosive disorder, 168
Internalization of humiliation, 42
Internalized criticism, 47
Internalized maladaptive core shame, 46
Internalized shame, 42–44
Internal mode, of narrative coding, 246
Internal safe place, 71, 87, 95–96, 242–243, 285
Internal self-evaluative component of shame, 37
Interrupted anger, 158, 170, 172. *See also* Interrupted anger, model of resolution of
accessing, 184, 186
case example, 198–201
criteria for healthy anger expression, 188–190
expression of, 193–195
markers of, 204
process diagnosis of, 187–188
relational context of, 185–187
steps in treating, 185, 190–198
Interrupted anger, model of resolution of, 203–225
consideration of alternative ways of seeing reality, 212–213
empathic understanding of the other and forgiveness, 215–216

expressing assertive anger and standing up, 207–208
need expression, 210–211
nonessential components and hindrances, 218–220
nonresolution components, 220–222
sadness and grief, 213–215
undifferentiated anger and sadness with complaint, 207–208
validation by the other, 215–216
Interruption, protective function of, 192
Interruptive processes, 219–220
Invalidation, 195, 209, 213. *See also* Validation
Irritation, 160, 161
Isolation, 43

J

Jack, D. C., 173
James, Alison, 245
Jefferson, Thomas, 171
Joy, 105
Judgment, fears of, 58
Jung, C. G., 31, 283

K

Kaufman, G., 32, 42
Keogh, D., 162
Kring, A. M., 176

L

Labeling, 88, 239
Labels, 17–18
Language, 17–18, 21, 24, 63, 121–122, 160–161, 216, 221–222
Latinos, 180
Leaving stage, of therapy, 102
LeDoux, J., 231
Left hemisphere, of brain, 83, 99, 230, 285
Letting go, 216
Levinas, E., 61
Lewis, H. B., 31
Limbic system, 69
Linehan, M. M., 25
Lived experiences, 54
Loathing, 161
Loneliness, 250, 253, 261, 269, 276
The Looking Glass Self (Cooley), 36

M

Maladaptive anger, 27–28, 186, 188
Maladaptive emotions, 24
Maladaptive rage, 107
Maladaptive shame, 27–28, 35–37, 50, 64, 102, 107
Maltreatment, 195
Manipulation, 167
Marital difficulties, 113, 245–281
Markers of interrupted anger, 204
Markers of resolution of anger, 235
Matsumoto, D., 177
Mauss, I. B., 180
Meaning, 17, 22, 195–196, 198, 208
Medication, 84
Meditation, 85
Memory(-ies)
 of abuse, 108–111, 118, 123–124, 128–130
 activation of, 23, 26
 emotional, 26
 emotion-schematic, 19, 42
 evocation strategies, 234
 generic, 208
 healing, 174
 primary maladaptive schematic, 42
 reconsolidation of, 23, 26, 241–243
Men, 179. *See also* Gender
Mentalization, 24, 89
Midbrain, 85
Miller, S., 108
Mindful breathing, 84
Mindfulness, 85, 92, 240
Minimizing, 190
Minoritized groups, 52–56, 158
Mistreatment, 204
Model of self-compassion dialogue, 97
Modesty, 83
Mohr, D. C., 174
Montaigne, Michel de, 127
Mortification, 41
Motivation, 18
Motivational/behavioral component of shame, 37
Multicultural therapy, 177
Muscular tension, 160
Muslim clients, 178

N

Narcissism, 44–45, 107
Narrative coding, 246

Narratives, 16–17, 22, 24, 62, 102, 125, 191, 198
Need(s), 104, 109–111, 195, 210. *See also* Heartfelt needs; Unmet needs
Neff, K., 92
Neglect, 43, 124, 204
Neural pathways, 22, 24, 125, 242
Neuroception of safety, 61
Neurons, 27
New emotional experiences, 23–26, 28, 29, 65–66, 103, 105
Nicomachean Ethics (Aristotle), 163
Nietzsche, Friedrich, 15
Nonadaptive anger, 227–243
　acceptance of, 238–241
　different forms of regulation, 230–232
　downregulation of anger, 228–230
　emotion-focused approach to, 232–235
　memory reconsolidation, 241–243
　two ways of working with, 235–238
Non-resolution clients, 220–222
Nonverbal communication, 38, 61–62, 90, 124, 167, 191–192, 194, 204. *See also* Eye contact; Facial expressions
Numbness, 82, 190

O

Opposite action, 229–230
Organismic arousal, 21
Other, validation by the, 215–216
Outcomes, of therapy, 112–113, 117, 125–126, 175, 203, 224
Overexposure, 31
Ownership, of experience, 189
Oxytocin, 61

P

Pain, 38, 70, 110–111, 115–116
Paivio, S. C., 31, 174
Parasympathetic nervous system, 83
Parental humiliation, 172
Parental unprotectiveness, 172
Parents, 43, 172, 204, 245–281
Partners, 204. *See also* Spouses
Pascal, Blaise, 31
Passions, 17
People of color, 55, 178–180
Perceived criticism, 38
Perfectionism, 113, 114
Personal experiences, of therapist, 194

Personality disorders, 89, 168
Personal meaning, 22
Physical abuse, 43
Physical health, 172–173, 178
Physiological component of shame, 37
Physiological symptoms, 159–160
Pittman, C. T., 178
Polyvagal theory, 61
Positive emotions, 84
Possibilities, lost, 197, 213
Posttraumatic stress disorder (PTSD), 44, 165, 168
Potter-Efron, R., 38
Poverty, 179
Powerlessness, 41, 114
Prefrontal cortex, 85
Prelinguistic beings, 16
Presence, therapist, 65, 185
Pride, 28, 35–36, 54, 103, 105, 113, 117, 234
Pride/anger, 117
Primary adaptive anger, 106–108, 163–164
Primary adaptive emotions, 29, 109–112, 184
Primary adaptive guilt, 117
Primary adaptive shame, 39–41, 45–46, 284
Primary anger, 188, 209
Primary emotions, adaptive vs. maladaptive, 6–7
Primary maladaptive anger, 164–166, 234
Primary maladaptive core shame, 46–49, 109–110
Primary maladaptive schematic memories, 42
Primary maladaptive shame, 10, 39, 41–45, 111, 112, 114–115
Primary shame, 286
Problem behavior, 229
Prompting event, 229
Protective function of interruption, 192
Protest, 123
Psychoeducation, 74, 84, 87, 196, 230
Psychological abuse, 43
Psychological maltreatment, 43
Psychopathy, 41
Psychotic disorders, 168
PTSD. *See* Posttraumatic stress disorder

R

Race and racism, 47, 55, 178–180, 284
Rage, 107, 158, 160, 164, 178, 231

Rational control of anger, 190–191
Rational/empirical model of resolution of interrupted anger, 203–225
Rational/empirical model of resolution of shame, 108–111
Reappraisal, 285
Recognition, by therapist, 187
Reconciliation, refusal of, 222
Reflection of client's meaning, therapist's, 208
Reflexive mode, of narrative coding, 246
Refocusing intervention, 71
Refractory period, 231
Reframing the problem (stage in change of anger), 236–237
Refusal to reconcile, 222
Regulation of emotion, 82–88, 188, 228–232
Regulation of shame, 81–99
  deliberate regulation of emotion, 84–88
  downregulation, 88–89
  implicit affect regulation, 89–92
  with self-compassion, 92
  self-soothing, 93–99
Rejecting anger, 115
Rejection, 43, 47, 58, 222, 234
Relational connections, 18
Relational processes, 90
Relational safety, 91, 185
Relational soothing, 91
Relational threats, 237
Relational validation, 58
Relationships, 197, 213
  anger in, 169
  attachment, 89
  safe, 58–64, 101
  shame-anger, 4–5, 10
  and suppressed anger, 159
  therapeutic, 63, 186
Relaxation, 84, 232
Releasing component, of emotion schemes, 20
Reluctance to talk, client's, 72
Resentment, 160, 161, 172
Resignation, 159, 191, 204
Resolution states, 111
Resonance, reciprocal affective, 61
Respiratory rhythm, 191
Responsibility, 39, 212, 223
Right hemisphere, of brain, 83, 89, 90
Ruptures, in therapeutic relationship, 63

S

Sadness
  fusions of anger and, 208, 223
  of grief, 105, 117, 125, 128, 197, 213, 274–276
Safe place, internal, 71, 87, 95–96, 242–243, 285
Safe relationships, 58–64, 101
Schizophrenia, 168
Schopenhauer, A., 16
Secondary anger, 10–11, 162, 166, 186, 188, 232–233, 285
Secondary emotions, 6–7, 195
Secondary shame, 39, 49–52
Self-acceptance, 28, 184
Self-affirmation, 105, 170
Self-assertion, 106, 246, 286
Self-assertive anger, 172, 196
Self-blame, 46, 106, 239
Self-coherence, 32, 33
Self-compassion, 92, 93, 97, 113, 117, 125, 238–240
Self-concept, 36, 38, 52–53
Self-confidence, 51, 205
Self-contempt, 47–48, 108–110, 112, 114–115, 121–122, 130–135, 139–142
Self-critical shame, 49–50
Self-criticism, 62, 108–111, 113, 118, 120–122, 124, 175, 257
Self-efficacy, 51, 174
Self-empathy, 91
Self-empowerment, 195
Self-esteem, 36, 71, 166
Self-evaluation, negative, 47–48
Self-expression, 105, 106
Self-harm, 48, 85, 89, 91
Self-interruption, 191, 219–220
Self-kindness, 92
Self-medication, 89
Self-organization, 21–22, 42, 102–104, 109–111, 184, 268, 275
Self-pity, 222
Self-preservation, 102
Self-reflection, 89
Self-regulation, 85–86
Self-soothing, 84, 86, 87, 90, 92–99, 252
Self-worth, 28, 36, 51, 73
Sense of self, 125, 274
Sensorimotor stimuli, 19
Sensory experiences, 94
Sensory regulation, 84
Sex, compulsive, 85

Sexual abuse, 43, 73, 174
Sexual identity, 55
Sexual orientation, 47
Shame, 31–56, 83. *See also specific headings, e.g.:* Adaptive shame
  acceptance of, 86
  activated experience of, 110
  adaptive vs. maladaptive, 36–37
  anticipation of, 41
  aversion to, 68
  of being, 42, 48, 64
  bodily experience of, 69
  components of, 37–39
  covering behaviors, 69
  deficiency statements of, 38
  differentiating, from other emotions, 101, 122–123
  emotional component of, 37
  experiencing, 101
  externalization of, 67
  facilitation of experience of, 70
  forms of, 45–52
  intensity of, 63, 67, 72, 88, 120, 160
  markers of, 113–114
  in minoritized groups, 52–56
  naming, 69
  for non-resolution clients, 221–222
  normalization of experience of, 59
  overview, 8
  and related emotions, 33–36
  sexual, 49
  showing, 41
  symbolization of, 89–90, 101, 110, 125–126
  as term, 52
  therapist's experiences of, 74
  tolerance of, 84, 88
  triggers of, 38, 74
  untreated, 101
  varieties of, 39–45
  vocabulary for, 63
  working distance from, 85
Shame-anger relationships, 4–5, 10
Shame-anxiety, 38, 47, 49, 110, 115, 120, 123, 184
Shame-based emotion schemes, 102
Shame cues, 62–63
Shame-humiliation, 31
Shameless (term), 41
Shame narrative, 66
Shame-rage dynamic, 45, 166
Sharkin, B. S., 177
Shutting off processes, 219–220

Shyness, 41
Sicoli, L. A., 175
Significant others, 172, 195. *See also* Partners
Silences, 204
"Silencing the self," 173
Situation regulation, 84
Sleep, 84
Social anxiety, 11, 44
Social component, of shame, 37
Social diminishment, 38
Social media, excessive use of, 85
Societal shame, 50–51
Somatization, 158
Soothing, 83–84
Spinoza, B., 17, 27
Spousal betrayal, 172
Spouses, 204
Stereotype threats, 51–52
Stigma, 51–52
Stress management, 84
Stretching, 85
Subconscious processes, 16
Submissive behavior, 158
Substance use and abuse, 85, 89, 168, 178
Suffering, 72
Suicidality, 89, 178
Suppressed anger, 159
Symbolization of internal experience, 232
Sympathetic nervous system, 81–82, 84
Symptom stabilization, 74
Synthesis, of primary adaptive and maladaptive emotion, 25

T

Tai Chi, 85
Tangents, 118
Target, M., 90
Task-analytic method, 108
Temper, hair-trigger, 164–165
Therapeutic engagement, 61
Therapeutic presence, 60–61, 65, 185
Therapeutic relationship, 63, 186
Therapist
  interventions by, 117–125
  personal experiences of, 194
  recognition by, 187
  reflection of client's meaning by, 208
  shame experienced by, 74
  validation by, 71, 90
Time, lost, 197, 213
Time outs, 232

Timulak, L., 162
Toddlers, 36
Tompkins, S. S., 18, 32–33
Traister, R., 158
Transformation of shame, 102–126
  with primary adaptive anger, 106–108
  process of, 113–117
  by synthesis, 22, 24–25
  task-analytic study of, 108–113
  therapeutic intervention, 117–125
  and validation, 125–126
Trauma, 124, 165, 174
Tregoubov, V. I., 205
Triggers, 84
Twain, Mark, 227
Tying anger to the past (stage in change of anger), 236

U

Unacknowledged anger, 184
Underlying feelings, 196
Understanding
  empathic, 61, 106, 216–218
  of one's own behavior, 212–213
Unemployment, 113
Unfairness, 125, 159, 161
Universal child, 98
University of Massachusetts, 235
Unmet needs. *See also* Assertive expression of interpersonal needs
  expression of, 193–195
  and grief, 96, 117
  and instrumental shame, 40
  and interrupted anger, 193–195, 197
  mobilizing, 195
  validation of, 73, 104, 184
Unresolved anger, 171–172
Unworthiness, 43

V

Validation
  of adaptive emotions, 103
  of anger, 187–188, 195, 234
  of models, 204, 224
  and narrative change, 125
  by the other, 215–216
  statements of, 59
  by therapist, 71, 90
  of unmet needs, 73, 104, 184
Van Velsor, P., 174
Verbal indicators, of pain, 38
Verbal narrative, 62
Victim stance, 207–208, 223
Violation, 123, 159, 161, 197
Violence, 89, 166, 196
Violent behavior, 44, 174
Virtual reality, 98
Visceral experience, of anger, 189
Visualizations, 85
Vocal qualities, 62, 124, 167
Volatility, 178
Vulnerability, 211, 229, 232

W

Walking, 85
Webb, M., 43
Weeping, 85
White men, 158
Withdrawal, 31, 85, 87–88, 103, 218–219
Women, 56, 158, 173, 178, 180. *See also* Gender
Worthiness, 113
Worthlessness, 49, 106, 124, 126, 221–222, 286

Y

Yoga, 85
York University Psychotherapy Research Lab, 108, 203

Z

Zone of proximal development, 93, 95
Zone of tolerance, 72, 88, 101, 231

About the Author

Leslie S. Greenberg, PhD, is Distinguished Research Professor of Psychology at York University in Toronto, Ontario, Canada. He is a leading authority on working with emotion in psychotherapy and the developer of an evidence-based approach, emotion-focused therapy. He has authored the major texts on emotion-focused approaches to treatment for individuals and couples. His most recent book is *Changing Emotion With Emotion* (2021). Dr. Greenberg has published extensively on research on the process of change. He has received the Distinguished Research Career award of the International Society for Psychotherapy Research as well as the Carl Rogers award of the American Psychological Association. He also has received the Canadian Council of Professional Psychology Program Award for Excellence in Professional Training and the Canadian Psychological Association Professional Award for distinguished contributions to psychology as a profession. He is on the editorial board of many psychotherapy journals. Dr. Greenberg is a founding member of the Society of the Exploration of Psychotherapy Integration (SEPI) and a past President of the Society for Psychotherapy Research (SPR). He is an honorary member of the board of the International Society for Emotion Focused Therapy (ISEFT) and is currently retired but still working. He trains and supervises people internationally in emotion-focused approaches. When he is not working, he loves spending time with his wife Shelley, his two children and their partners, and importantly, his two grandchildren.